Medjugorje and the Supernatural

Medjugorje and the Supernatural

Science, Mysticism, and Extraordinary Religious Experience

DANIEL MARIA KLIMEK

OXFORD
UNIVERSITY PRESS

OXFORD
UNIVERSITY PRESS

Oxford University Press is a department of the University of Oxford. It furthers
the University's objective of excellence in research, scholarship, and education
by publishing worldwide. Oxford is a registered trade mark of Oxford University
Press in the UK and certain other countries.

Published in the United States of America by Oxford University Press
198 Madison Avenue, New York, NY 10016, United States of America.

CIP data is on file at the Library of Congress
ISBN 978–0–19–067920–0

Everything beautiful has a mark of eternity

—SIMONE WEIL

Contents

Acknowledgments

I AM INCREDIBLY grateful to Cynthia Read at Oxford University Press for supporting this book and for all the hard work that she and her staff put into its production. A much earlier draft of the book began as my doctoral dissertation. I would like to thank the Rev. Dr. Raymond Studzinski, O.S.B., my dissertation director, for guiding the original work with patience, earnestness, and great insight. Thank you also to Dr. William Dinges, the Rev. Msgr. Stephen Rossetti, the Rev. Dr. John P. Beal, and Dr. Kurt Martens for their interest in my work and for their helpful advice. Thank you to my religious community, the Franciscan Friars of the Third Order Regular of the Province of the Most Sacred Heart of Jesus, for all the friars who have supported and encouraged me in this work. I would particularly like to thank Br. Gabriel Mary Amato, T.O.R., who provided the time, support (and coffee!) that I needed to finish the very first draft during my postulant year with the friars. Thank you to the Rev. Thomas Acklin, O.S.B., Ph.D., for wisdom and life-transforming guidance in both my spiritual and academic life. I am grateful to Br. Marius Strom, T.O.R., for assistance in helping me with technical matters. I wish to acknowledge gratitude for my family, especially for my mother Janina, my father Szymon, and my brother Konrad, for loving support.

Researching and writing about Medjugorje one enters a world of authors, journalists, bloggers, filmmakers, pilgrimage and conference organizers, all dedicated to the topic. To all the friends, colleagues, and interlocutors with whom I have had the pleasure, these past years, of discussing the topic of Medjugorje, with great gratitude and love, I thank you.

To the memories of Fr. Sean Sullivan, T.O.R., and Fr. Michael Scanlan, T.O.R., I dedicate this book.

Medjugorje and the Supernatural

Introduction

THE SILENCE OF THE BIRDS

IT SOUNDS LIKE something out of C. S. Lewis or J. R. R. Tolkien, master storytelling at the grandest level. And yet it is not a fairy tale. It is not Narnia, nor Middle-earth, but an actual place: a mysterious, Slavic village hidden in between the mountains of Central Europe where miraculous and supernatural things are said to happen. A village where children experience the supernatural on a daily basis, not through their imaginations but—they claim—through direct divine intervention; a village where a heavenly visitor brings messages from another realm—messages from above, messages that answer some of life's greatest questions: What is the meaning of life? What happens when a person dies? Does God exist? Is there an afterlife? What happens to people of different religions? Is salvation open to all?

It is a village of visionaries, apparitions, weeping statues, dancing suns, rosaries mysteriously turned gold; a village, in a time when secularism permeates much of the Western world, where religious and priestly vocations flourish; a village where lives are transformed, where healings and miracles are said to happen, where millions of pilgrims have traveled from all corners of the earth, hoping to encounter a touch of the divine in a place where, it is said, heaven meets earth.

The village is called Medjugorje, located in Bosnia-Herzegovina, in the former Yugoslavia. The greatest claim connected to Medjugorje, one that is at the center of the events there and from which everything else stems, is that the Virgin Mary began visiting Medjugorje in 1981 and has, through her chosen visionaries, returned every day since for over thirty-five years now, communicating important messages to the world. It is a bold and monumental claim. It began with six Croatian youngsters—five teenagers and a ten-year-old child—all reporting to experience daily visitations from the Virgin Mary. Three of the six seers claim to continue to experience daily apparitions of the Mother of Jesus over thirty years later, as adults.

The reputation of Medjugorje has transcended popular piety or geographical boundaries and has reached the West, even touching popular and elite culture. *National Geographic* dedicated the cover story of its December 2015 issue, titled "Mary: The Most Powerful Woman in the World," to the topic of Marian apparitions and devotion, featuring Medjugorje prominently. The late U.S. Supreme Court justice Antonin Scalia once mentioned Medjugorje in a speech he gave to the Catholic legal society, the St. Thomas More Society, while being honored with the Man for All Seasons Award. The popular late-night comedian Stephen Colbert mentioned Medjugorje while discussing his Catholic faith, and specifically the topic of Marian apparitions, with the actress Patricia Heaton, a fellow Catholic, on the *Late Show*. Hollywood actor Martin Sheen, known for many important film roles and for playing the president of the United States on the television series *The West Wing*, has not only traveled to Medjugorje but has also played the role of Father Jozo Zovko, the Croatian Franciscan priest who was pastor of the parish at Medjugorje when supernatural events in the village were reported to begin in 1981. Similarly, Jim Caviezel, chosen by Mel Gibson to play the role of Jesus Christ in the 2004 epic film *The Passion of the Christ*, has made pilgrimages to Medjugorje and has claimed that without the significance of Medjugorje in his life he would never have been able to portray Jesus. Loretta Young, the glamorous starlet of both television and film in the 1950s and '60s, traveled to Medjugorje as a pilgrim in the '80s and explained, in an authorized biography, that Medjugorje gave her life meaning.[1]

What is it about this village that is so special, that has attracted so much attention? And, can the supernatural events associated with Medjugorje be taken seriously? Pope John Paul II, himself a believer in the apparitions of Medjugorje, once articulated what he believed to be at the center of its appeal, explaining: "Today's world has lost its sense of the supernatural, but many are searching for it—and find it in Medjugorje, through prayer, penance, and fasting."[2] As the events in Medjugorje unfolded, other mysterious happenings, alleging a supernatural origin, became associated with the site.

In 1994, Don Pablo Martin, a Spanish priest, was the parish priest of Saint Agostino's Church in the Pantano district of Civitavecchia in Italy.

Don Pablo, making a pilgrimage to Medjugorje in September of that year, bought a sixteen-inch, white plaster statue of the Virgin Mary as a souvenir from the village. The statue would one day gain international attention and be recognized under the name *La Madonnina*, meaning "Little Madonna." In his spiritual life, Don Pablo had a strong devotion to the renowned Capuchin friar and priest Padre Pio (1887–1968), the Italian mystic who was famous for the stigmata, purportedly supernatural wounds corresponding to the crucifixion marks of Jesus's body. In Padre Pio's case, the stigmata wounds appeared on his hands, feet, and side. Pope John Paul II would canonize the Italian stigmatic in 2002 as a saint. This devotion is noteworthy because Don Pablo credits Padre Pio's intercession with helping him select that statue from Medjugorje. It was Padre Pio who assured him, according to Don Pablo, that "the most beautiful event of his life" would result for selecting that statue.[3] How exactly Padre Pio did this Don Pablo did not specify, though it can be assumed that Don Pablo was referring to spiritual discernment through prayer, as Padre Pio had been dead since 1968; and as it is the practice of many Catholics to pray for the intercession and guidance of the saints. It merits attention that even when Padre Pio walked the earth and greeted pilgrims in his friary, in San Giovanni Rotondo, he made what is believed to be a prophecy about the coming of the apparitions in Medjugorje. Mary Craig reports that a few years before the apparitions began, Padre Pio had told a group of pilgrims from the diocese of Mostar, "The Blessed Virgin Mary will soon be visiting your homeland."[4] The parish of Medjugorje exists within the Mostar diocese.

Don Pablo decided to give the statue of the Madonna as a gift to a particularly devout parishioner in his church, Fabio Gregori. Gregori was a family man who was an electrician by trade. It was on the evening of February 2, 1995, the Feast of the Purification of the Virgin Mary, that Gregori— planning to attend the rosary service at Saint Agostino's Parish—was told by his alarmed, six-year-old daughter that the statue of the Madonna was crying in their home. Coming up to the statue to see for himself, Gregori saw red streaks on the Madonna's cheeks, and he reached out to touch the flowing substance with the tip of his finger. He described in that moment "a great blast of fire" surging through his body as he touched the red substance.[5]

Many more people would also witness seeing this phenomenon— the weeping statue—in the following weeks, including then bishop of Civitavecchia, Gerolmo Grillo, who initially declared his skepticism about the claims. The bishop remained skeptical until the statue of the Madonna cried a tear of blood in front of him, his sister, her husband, and two religious sisters visiting from Romania. Bishop Grillo appeared on a national newscast in prime time on April 5, 1995, testifying to this occurrence, which had transpired three weeks before, on March 15. Before that moment, not only was he skeptical about the whole situation but he was also hostile, initially requesting Don Pablo to destroy the statue. The priest refused to do so. The bishop also reached out to the police to investigate the Gregori family and sent his own physician to take a sample of the alleged blood from the statue to test it. The doctor reported back that the tears did, indeed, constitute blood. Bishop Grillo then took the statue to Rome for it to be tested by two more, separate teams of physicians. They also confirmed that the substance from the weeping statue was blood.[6] Laboratory tests showed the DNA from the blood to be that of a male in his mid-thirties, which eventually led Bishop Grillo and much of the faithful to the conviction that this statue from Medjugorje was shedding the blood of Jesus Christ.[7]

Skeptics took a different perspective on the matter, alleging that the blood must belong to Fabio Gregori and that this must be nothing more than an elaborate hoax. Many conspiracy theories began to arise. Giovanni Panunzio, the head of an Italian group in Sardinia known for exposing religious frauds, argued that the most likely explanation was a "blood-filled syringe, encased in the plaster and attached to a small battery that could be activated by remote control," or perhaps, "the culprits had employed special contact lenses that would expand and release liquid when exposed to heat."[8] These theories were disproven when separate CAT scans run on the statue—at the behest of Italy's largest consumer protection agency (Codacons), the public prosecutor's office, and the Catholic Church— showed that the weeping Madonna did not contain any hidden devices, none being found in the statue.[9]

The case of the inexplicable weeping statue from Medjugorje acquired so much attention in the Italian press that, in addition to the Church, state officials and public agencies also got involved in investigating the matter. The public prosecutor's office charged a criminal complaint of pious fraud against Fabio Gregori, the state attorney's office even seizing and sealing up the statue during their investigations. The outcry against these actions was loud in Italy as protests ensued, people taking to the streets against the state's intervention. At the suppression of the statue, the Vatican made a very public gesture of support for Gregori and the cause of the weeping statue. This came, journalist Randall Sullivan explains, when John Paul II "dispatched his close friend and fellow countryman Cardinal Andrej Maria Deskur to Civitavecchia to address Gregori's congregation at an Easter Mass, where the cardinal presented Fabio a blessed copy of *La Madonnina*, and compared what was taking place to events in Poland during 1967, when communist authorities had sequestered the revered Madonna of Czestochowa in Krakow."[10] The allusion to the Polish icon refers to the most famous image of the Virgin Mary in Polish Catholicism, which was a national symbol and, for a while, was confiscated by communist officials as a politically motivated act of suppression.

Though taking many years to be resolved in the courts, on March 20, 2001, Judge Carmine Castalado, who was hearing the pious fraud case brought against Gregori by the public prosecutor's office, announced his ruling on the matter, concluding that there was "no trickery" found by Gregori or anyone else connected to the statue of the weeping Madonna.[11] Indeed, no natural explanation, or one implying fraud, was ever found in the case of the weeping statue, despite years of investigations performed by state officials, by a Church commission, and by private and public groups that hoped to expose the matter as a hoax—groups who have had a history of successfully exposing frauds.[12] The February 6, 1997, issue of the Italian newspaper *Il Messaggero* explained that the opposite of fraud had been deemed as an explanation for the phenomenon by a panel of theologians, stating: "A statue of Our Lady of Medjugorje that cried tears of blood on 14 occasions in early 1995 after being brought from the Marian Sanctuary of Medjugorje to the Italian port city of Civitavecchia was judged 'supernatural' by a panel of Italian theological experts, who had spent nearly two years studying the controversy."[13] There have, however, been mixed reactions from Church authorities on the status surrounding the statue, another theological commission expressing the opinion that supernatural origins could not be confirmed—which was not a denial of supernatural origins but was a recognition that it could not be determined.[14] Bishop Grillo's belief in the supernatural origins of the weeping statue was announced on April 6, 1995, in the Italian news daily *La Stampa*, which reported: "Bishop Grillo has disclosed to the press without any further reservation that the Blessed Virgin Mary's weeping is a miracle!"[15]

What was not widely known is that Pope John Paul II, during these years of controversy surrounding the weeping statue, venerated the Virgin of Civitavecchia and requested that the statue be brought to the Vatican. In a recent book on the entire matter titled *La Madonnina de Civitavecchia*,

Bishop Grillo revealed these facts, even including as evidence in his book a letter signed and dated by John Paul II speaking to a meeting between the two men. It was on June 9, 1995, that John Paul II's personal secretary and longtime confidant, Monsignor Stanislaw Dziwisz, asked Bishop Grillo to bring the statue of the weeping Madonna to the Vatican.

When the statue was brought to the Vatican, John Paul II venerated the Madonna, praying before the statue and, after his prayer, placing a crown on the head of the Virgin—a crown that the pope himself brought for the occasion.[16] Pope Benedict XVI acknowledged his predecessor's devotion to the weeping Virgin Mary. In 2005, Benedict addressed the Italian Bishops' Conference on the matter, sharing with them that John Paul II had venerated the weeping statue of Mary.[17] At the end of this meeting, Benedict greeted Bishop Grillo with enthusiastic words, declaring that the Madonna of Civitavecchia will accomplish great things.[18]

Bishop Grillo was no stranger to the things that were already being accomplished. The Madonna's tears did not come in vain, for the phenomenon began to be associated with fruits of faith, ranging from conversions to reported miracles. In February 2005, Bishop Grillo declared that the shrine in Civitavecchia which was dedicated to the weeping Madonna had become a center of evangelization. He was especially impressed with the remarkable transformation that the city of Civitavecchia underwent owing to the influence of the weeping statute. Before the miracle of the statue came to the city, Bishop Grillo noted, Civitavecchia "was considered 'the Stalingrad of Latium'—60% communist, an anti-clerical and anarchic city."[19] Today, Civitavecchia is a place of pilgrimage and prayer, becoming a sacred site venerated by millions—to the point that Italian tourist brochures began referring to the city as "the doorway to Rome."[20] In October 2006, one year after Benedict XVI announced to the Italian Bishops' Conference that his predecessor venerated the statue of the weeping Madonna, a very curious occurrence took place, something that had not happened in years: the statue from Medjugorje began to shed tears again.[21]

The supernatural is a mysterious realm, one that many believe in and one whose existence many others doubt. It is a topic, furthermore, that makes many uncomfortable.

There are those who even feel the need to attempt to disprove any claims of the supernatural when they are made. Such was the case with Dr. Marco Margnelli, an Italian neurophysiologist and an ardent atheist who traveled to numerous locations trying to disprove claims of mystical phenomena—he traveled, for example, to San Giovanni Rotondo in 1987, years after the death of the famous friar, to try to disprove the stigmata of Padre Pio.

A year later, in the summer of 1988, Dr. Margnelli traveled to Medjugorje, hoping, he admitted, to find "any evidence that would contradict it or expose it as a fake."[22] He would be in a perfect position to examine the ecstasies of the visionaries during their claimed Marian apparitions, having authored a work on altered states of consciousness, an area of expertise for Dr. Margnelli.[23] Dr. Margnelli conducted an array of medical tests on the visionaries and gradually came to the conclusion that, during their apparitions, the visionaries do in fact enter into a "genuine state of ecstasy."[24] While acknowledging that as a scientist he could not judge whether the apparitions are authentic or not, he did admit that "we were certainly in the presence of an extraordinary phenomenon."[25]

Dr. Margnelli was a witness in Medjugorje to a number of events that baffled his beliefs, one of which included the seemingly miraculous healing of a woman from leukemia. What moved him most personally, however, was the behavior of the birds before and during the apparitions.

Before the apparitions of the visionaries would begin in the church rectory, where they met in those days to experience their daily apparitions, there were hundreds of birds outside in the trees, chirping and cooing, being incredibly—at times, deafeningly—loud. Until the exact moment that the apparitions began, that is: the second the visionaries dropped to their knees and went into ecstasy, the moment that it is believed they encounter the Virgin Mary, every bird outside would go completely silent.

This was something that stayed with Dr. Margnelli for a long time. But that absolute silence of the birds not only remained with him, it also haunted him, he admitted. It was a few months after returning to Milan from Medjugorje that Dr. Margnelli became a practicing Catholic.

EXPERIENCES LIKE THE weeping statue from Medjugorje and the silence of the birds, the latter an occurrence that many pilgrims have reported, can be identified as "concurring phenomena," as they are events related to the primary phenomenon, the alleged Marian apparitions. Such events can have strong influences on many lives, often inspiring faith and devotion. As John Paul II reflected, such events represent something deeper for people that the modern world cannot offer: an encounter with a higher reality, a touch of the supernatural. Questions, however, arise. Can the supernatural be real? Can such occurrences be investigated or authenticated? Can claims of supernatural experiences be empirically tested by science?

Like Dr. Margnelli, countless of doctors and scientists from various countries have traveled to Medjugorje to investigate and study the apparitions of the visionaries. Throughout the past three decades, the Medjugorje visionaries have been subjected to an extensive amount of medical, psychological, and scientific examination, even *while* experiencing their apparitions. Neuroscience has been used prominently, as electroencephalograms (EEG) have been applied on the visionaries to study their ecstasies, the altered state of consciousness they enter during their apparitions, by observing what is happening inside their brains as they undergo their mystical experiences. Scientists and journalists have noted that this is the first time in history that visionary experiences have been subjected to such meticulous and in-depth study through modern scientific technology. The results of these studies do not only shine light on the experiences of the Medjugorje visionaries but can also make a contribution to understanding popular theories about past religious experiences and to debates surrounding their authenticity.

An academic debate about extraordinary religious experiences has emerged in recent decades. Two main groups of scholars have been at the center of this debate. One of these groups, recognized as "constructivists," are scholars who have emphasized the role of language, tradition, and culture in constructing mystical experiences, pointing first and foremost to human construction in the religious experience.[26] This constructivist hermeneutic challenges the classic interpretation of religious experiences, known as the "perennialist" perspective. The perennial philosophy has argued that mystical experiences cannot be reduced to human construction but, at their core, they share certain characteristics that transcend culture, language, or time period, pointing to a shared spiritual experience among devotees that indicates an encounter with something higher: with the transcendent.

In the 1990s, a new group of scholars, led by Robert K. C. Forman, renewed the perennialist perspective with a "new perennialism" that presented a hermeneutical challenge to constructivist scholars. This "new perennialism" centers on presenting a "pure consciousness" experience, a documented experience of mystical union that people have reported whose fundamental tenets question the epistemological assumptions of a constructivist interpretation.[27]

Eventually, after twenty years of debate between the two sides, Forman and co-author Jensine Andresen published an article calling for scholars of religion to put down their swords in the "methodological war that has been waging between constructivists and perennialists in the study of religion."[28] Instead, they recommended that scholars explore new disciplines of study, particularly research on consciousness, in order to make methodological progress on this subject. Forman and Andresen recommended exploration into fields like cognitive neuroscience and neuropsychology. They explained:

> The study of religion will benefit greatly from a more interdisciplinary consideration of how consciousness and subjective experiences, including religious ones, may actively influence, and be influenced by, human physiology. To undergo a vision of any divine form, or even to believe that we are having such a vision, will no doubt effect our heart rate, our blood chemistry and pressure, our serotonin levels, etc. It is high time that we studied how, and how much.
>
> It is time for scholars of religion to leap with both feet into the discussion of consciousness, spirituality, and the role of direct experience as important and creative elements of human religions. . . . We must explore the nature of spiritual experiences in more detail by drawing more guidance from consciousness studies. We must learn how physiology connects with spiritual experiences by increasing research on the biology of religious experience. We must examine the implications of research on the biology of religious experience for views on the "validity" of those experiences.[29]

As a response to Forman's and Andresen's challenge, an exploration of the various neuroscientific, psychological, and medical studies associated with the Marian apparitions of the Medjugorje visionaries will be pursued here. Combining these studies with debates on mysticism can exponentially increase our understanding of extraordinary religious experiences, making a significant contribution.

The first part of this book will examine a brief history of the apparitions in Medjugorje, concentrating on the earliest days when the visionaries first claimed a supernatural encounter with the Virgin Mary. Chapter 1 will also explore the messages of Medjugorje that the visionaries report the Madonna has given them—many of these messages are meant specifically, they explain, to be transmitted to the world. We will also explore visions of the afterlife that the visionaries have said to receive as part of their experiences, testifying to realms that purportedly exist in the hereafter where every human being ends up after death. We will consider whether such claims can be empirically examined, especially through the emerging science of studying near-death experiences.

Chapter 2 will examine the theology that the Catholic Church has developed in understanding and articulating the differences between forms of revelation. The chapter will further observe how the Church investigates a claim of supernatural phenomena such as apparitions or revelations, noting the various dynamics that are involved. A very brief examination of Medjugorje's current status within the Church will also be considered, given the unique case that Medjugorje presents to the Church as an ongoing apparition site.

Chapter 3 will move into examining the history of interpretation regarding religious and mystical experiences throughout the twentieth century, beginning with the influence of William James and continuing to James's contemporary Evelyn Underhill. James and Underhill constitute two of the most influential thinkers of the twentieth century who wrote about mysticism; James was probably the most significant person in prompting the academic exploration of mysticism among scholars, while Underhill is the most significant person in introducing mysticism to a popular audience, particularly to the English-speaking world, with her work. We will see how both James and Underhill used discourses on mysticism. Underhill has studied visionary experiences and other such extraordinary religious phenomena (including locutions, or auditory phenomena) under the umbrella of "mysticism," as she acknowledges that mystics throughout history have recorded experiencing visions, apparitions, and voices or locutions. Underhill's study will be essential to our discourse of visionary experiences, as Underhill outlines in impressive detail the variations and intricacies of visionary experiences, providing an explanation of the multidimensional manner in which such phenomena are encountered.

A topic that needs to be addressed is the relationship (often an intertwining one) between extraordinary religious experiences, mysticism, and visionary experiences. Frequently it is impossible to study one of these subjects without giving due attention to the other, as each is intrinsically connected and at times terminology overlaps. Mystical experiences are recognized as a type of religious experience. Visionary experiences can be traced back to some of the earliest writings on mysticism, specifically mystical theology that, in the Greek and Christian traditions, has for centuries recognized three types of visionary experiences: imaginative, intellectual, and corporal visions.[30] Marian apparitions qualify in the third category as *corporal visions*, the definition of which we will explore in depth in the third chapter. Therefore, having their roots in mystical theology, discourses on visionary experiences such as Marian apparitions cannot avoid the essential subject of mysticism.

Chapter 4 will continue the hermeneutical history with a closer examination of the perennialist–constructivist debate. The underlying issues that are at stake in the discourse will be considered, as will the various implications behind the methodological approaches applied by scholars from each side. This hermeneutical history will also dialogue with the work of modern scholars who reduce extraordinary religious experiences to natural or pathological explanations.

Chapter 5 will examine in detail the major scientific studies conducted on the Medjugorje visionaries and their apparitions. The various scientific data will be examined by presenting the procedures and results of studies that have been carried out by four major teams of doctors and scientists. Chapter 6 will consider the importance of the Medjugorje studies in relation to reductionistic theories on religious experiences that attempt to explain such experiences through a natural or pathological interpretation. Chapter 7 will explore what contributions the Medjugorje studies can make to epistemological and hermeneutical debates about studying religious experiences.

Medjugorje constitutes a unique phenomenon in being a modern case of alleged Marian apparitions, thus of visionary experiences, that have been empirically investigated with advanced medical, psychological, and neuroscientific studies *while transpiring*. This will be the first time that the scientific studies in Medjugorje will be placed into conversation with prominent thinkers who have written about extraordinary religious experiences. The results of such a unique case study can make an important contribution to the philosophical, methodological, and hermeneutical understanding of extraordinary religious experiences, and can have significant consequences on ways to move forward in the study of religion and related disciplines. In short, the case of Medjugorje affords a rare opportunity to understand a deeper dimension of extraordinary religious phenomena like visionary experiences through empirical examination.

_____

The Young Woman on the Hill

Everything great is done in the storm.

—PLATO

THE EVENING SKIES were pierced with lightning, the aggressive weather continuing into the night. The thunder was deafening. In half a century, nothing like it was seen in the village: a storm as severe as the one that struck on June 23, 1981, the very day before the famous apparitions would begin. Lightning strikes caused fires throughout the village, even burning down to the ground a local dance hall and half of the village post office before firefighters were able to save the other half.[1] The main telephone switchboard was struck as well, and the phone lines would be down for days. The gravity of the storm constituted a rare and curious event, as if prefiguring the real storm that would soon be breaking out in the quiet village. In biblical and apocalyptic literature the word *storm*, literally meaning "earthquake," often denoted a shaking up of an old world in the light of God bringing in his kingdom, a new reality. In that sense, for the village of Medjugorje the storm was just beginning.

The events that would forever change the village and touch millions of people around the world began the very next day, on June 24th. On the Roman Catholic calendar, the date signified the Feast Day of Saint John the Baptist, the prophet chosen by God, according to the New Testament, to announce the coming of his divine son, Jesus Christ, to the world. On that day in the sleepy little village located in the mountains of central Yugoslavia, a group of Croatian teenagers reported that the mother of Jesus, the Virgin Mary, appeared to them. The following day two more Croatian youths, this time a teenage girl and a ten-year-old boy, would also report to experience the same phenomenon, claiming—with the others—to see an apparition of the Virgin Mary.[2]

In Medjugorje, the etymology of the village's name speaks well to its rural and isolated location in the midst of the mountains of Bosnia-Herzegovina, since in Croatian *Medju* means "in between" and *gorje* "the mountains." It was not, however, on one of the surrounding mountains but on a local hillside that Ivanka Ivanković and Mirjana Dragičević first reported a supernatural encounter, alleging to witness an apparition. The teenage girls admitted later that they were planning to sneak cigarettes that afternoon. The fifteen-year-old Ivanka and the sixteen-year-old Mirjana walked along together from the hamlet of Bijakovici, neighboring Medjugorje, talking about last night's terrible thunderstorm and discussing "everyday things— what we had done in school, new friends we had made, the latest fashions, and other things teenaged girls usually talk about."[3] They passed a small hill called Crnica—a hill which would be renamed Podbrdo, coming to be known as "The Hill of Apparitions," or "Apparition Hill," after that day.

It was around 6:30 in the evening, author Wayne Weible writes, when "Ivanka casually glanced to her right and was startled to see a brilliant flash of light half-way up the rocky, thistle-covered hill that overlooked their village. In the center of the strange light was the unmistakable silhouette of a young woman, holding an infant."[4] At the very first sight of the vision, Ivanka was convinced that it was the Virgin Mary.

"Look, Mirjana, the Madonna!" she exclaimed in shock, her face turning pale white with fear.[5] Ivanka would later recall: "To this day, I don't know how I knew, but somehow I just did."[6]

Mirjana, refusing to look toward the spot where Ivanka was pointing, dismissed the audacious claim with a wave of the hand. "Yeah, sure it's Our Lady!" she remarked sarcastically. "She came to see what the two of us are up to because she has nothing better to do."[7] Ivanka continued to describe what she was seeing, but Mirjana still refused to look that way. She later recollected: "But as Ivanka continued to tell me what she saw, I got upset at her. Our parents had taught us to respect faith and never take God's name in vain, so when I thought Ivanka was joking about the Blessed Mother, I felt uncomfortable and afraid."[8]

Mirjana began to head home, declaring to Ivanka, "I'm leaving." However, as she reached the village something began to draw her back, later testifying that "a powerful sensation seized my heart. *Something* was calling me back—a feeling so strong that it forced me to stop and turn around." When Mirjana returned to the spot where she left her friend, she "found Ivanka in the same place, gazing at the hill and jumping up and down. I had never seen her so excited, and chills went through my body when she turned to look at me. Her normally-tanned skin looked as pale as milk, and her eyes were radiant."[9]

"Look now, *please!*" Ivanka pleaded.

Mirjana recalled the experience poignantly: "I slowly turned and looked up at the hill. When I saw the figure, my heart whirled with fear and wonder but my brain struggled to process it. No one ever climbed that hill, but what I saw was unmistakable—there, among the rocks and brambles, was a young woman."[10]

The two girls would be joined by other children who also would report to see the apparition on the hill; among them there was a younger friend, Milka Pavlović, who was on her way to round up her family's small flock of sheep. The girls experienced an admixture of emotions as they looked at the apparition. "We didn't know what to do, where to put ourselves," Ivanka explained. "We felt a mixture of joy and fear. So much joy, yet so much fear, it's impossible to describe."[11]

In the distance, upon the hill, the apparition appeared in the light as a beautiful young woman in a bluish-gray dress, wearing a white veil, the girls reported. The visionaries would later describe her as having blue eyes, long dark hair, rosy cheeks, and radiating a mystical beauty that words could not capture. Mirjana gave the most detailed description of the apparition in a written account, describing the mysterious woman on the hill thus:

Her skin was imbued with an olive-hued radiance, and her eyes reminded me of the translucent blue of the Adriatic. A white veil concealed most of her long, black hair, except for a curl visible near her forehead and locks hanging down below the veil. She wore a long dress that fell past her feet. Everything I saw seemed supernatural, from the unearthly blue-gray glow of her dress to the breathtaking intensity of her gaze. Her very presence brought with it a feeling of peace and maternal love, but I also felt intense fear because I did not understand what was happening.[12]

The visionaries would be asked countless times after that day to describe the beauty of the Virgin as they saw her. They have testified numerous times that no words can be adequate to describe that reality. Mirjana has tried to elaborate:

I wanted to describe what made her so beautiful, but I couldn't pinpoint anything specific. When people speak of physical beauty, they often highlight someone's eyes, hair, or other distinguishing feature. But Our Lady's beauty was different. Every feature was beautiful, and everything was harmonized. A white veil framed her oval face. The color of the skin was similar to the sun-glazed complexion of most Mediterranean people, and, paired with her black hair, she resembled a person from the Middle East. Her diminutive nose was perfectly aligned with her almond-shaped eyes, and the slight rosiness on her cheeks was similar to the color of her lips, which were small, fill, and tender-looking.[13]

Mirjana would emphasize, however, that there was a deeper depth to the beauty that the visionaries were encountering in the Virgin which transcended physical appearance, explaining: "But her 'appearance' was also a feeling, one best described by the word *maternal*. Her expression conveyed the qualities of motherhood—care, compassion, patience, tenderness. Her eyes held such love that I felt like she embraced me every time she looked at me."[14]

As the three girls remained looking at the apparition, Vicka Ivanković, who was at seventeen a highly passionate, extraverted friend of the girls, started walking up along the path and saw her friends who were staring at the mysterious figure before them. At first Vicka could not see what they were looking at. She called out to them.

Mirjana turned toward Vicka and, seeing her, called out words that, from that day, would change the course of Vicka's life.

"Hurry, Vicka, we see Our Lady!"

At Mirjana's words Vicka stopped in terror, as Mirjana continued to point with excitement to the side of the hill, to the spot where the girls were staring in fascination. Shocked at Mirjana's bold proclamation, Vicka turned right around and ran back down toward the village in the opposite direction.

Running back along the road, Vicka encountered two boys who were picking apples, Ivan Dragičević and Ivan Ivanković.* She told them what just happened nearby on the hill and asked the two to come back with her to Podbrdo. Vicka was confused and scared. She wasn't sure whether her friends meant to frighten her with a bad joke or whether they were truly

---

* Many of the Croatian names in Medjugorje are identical, although without signifying relation. The visionaries Mirjana Dragičević and Ivan Dragičević, for instance, are not related. Neither are Ivanka Ivanković and Ivan Ivanković.

seeing something, something that deserved her attention. The boys agreed to go with Vicka.

As the three made their way toward the hill, joining the other girls, they also—immediately—saw the apparition of the mysterious young woman. Vicka described the moment thus:

> But then, all of a sudden, I looked up and saw her standing there. . . . She wore a grey dress with a white veil, a crown of stars, blue eyes, dark hair and rosy cheeks. And she was floating about this high in the air on a grey cloud, not touching the ground. She had something in her left hand that she kept covering and uncovering – but you couldn't see what it was. She called us to go nearer, but none of us dared to.[15]

When Vicka turned to say something to Ivan Dragičević, who at sixteen was the younger of the two boys, she saw that he was no longer standing by her side but running off into the distance. Ivan, who was a very shy and introverted teenager, would later testify that he ran straight home that evening and locked himself in his room out of fear.

The other Ivan stayed. He and Vicka knelt down and, with the other girls, started praying in front of the apparition of the woman. The five youngsters felt a great peace overcome them, some continuing to pray while others cried quietly, tears gently streaming down their cheeks in a state of overwhelmed joy. Although Vicka testified that the Madonna was cradling something in her left hand, covering and uncovering it, it was Ivanka who first distinguished and identified that something as the baby Jesus. With her other hand, the Madonna beckoned the children to come forward—to come up to her.

"Then she called us to come closer," Vicka recalled in an interview, "but who was going to get any closer? We were saying to each other: 'She is calling us, but who is going to go?' "[16]

Though overjoyed by the encounter, the children were still too frightened on that first day to come up and speak to the woman on the hill. One by one, as darkness started descending and the evening twilight was slowly hinting at night's coming, they began reluctantly to leave the hill and head back to their homes. They were curious to tell family members about the experience, but as to be expected, were quickly rebuked with suspicion and disbelief, some even facing ridicule, and were told to stay silent about the matter. Fear was especially a prevalent reaction among family members since persecution from the local communist police and ridicule from neighbors would possibly result, were word to get out about what the children claimed to have seen that evening.

Nevertheless, word did get out, and on day two of the apparitions of Our Lady of Medjugorje, the children were joined by others at the hill, those who, out of curiosity, came to see whether the mysterious apparition would return to them. On day two of the events not all the youngsters came back to the hill.

Ivan Ivanković decided that he would not be returning with the others. Ivan Dragičević, however, who ran away during the first encounter, decided to face his fear and was propelled to return to the site. The young Milka Pavlović did not come back; not because she did not desire to but because her mother needed her to do some work in the fields that evening, being occupied with family chores. Milka's older sister, however, Marija, who was absent during the first day, decided that she would like to come along if the Madonna were to reappear.

Marija, a sixteen-year-old girl with a shy smile and a deeply serene presence, would become one of the central visionaries of Medjugorje. She would later be granted the mission of receiving a heavenly message that was to be transmitted to the entire world on the 25th of each month. It was a sincere request that Marija asked of Vicka on the second day of the apparitions that would lead to her role as a visionary. Marija asked Vicka to come and get her, were the Virgin to appear to them again, hoping to be in the Madonna's presence. "If you see the Madonna today, call me," she pleaded. "I don't mind if I don't see her, but I'd love just to be there."[17] One journalist has noted the peace that many pilgrims would experience through Marija's presence. "Marija's whole life bears witness to her conviction that there is a loving God. Her calm and clear-eyed serenity have become almost legendary."[18]

A small group of people followed the youngsters who returned to the hill that evening, gathering behind them. It was around 6:00. Ivanka was leading the way and, once again, she was the first one to spot the apparition. "Look, Our Lady!" she cried.

The other visionaries looked up and, with amazement, saw the mysterious woman again. This time they saw her with greater clarity than the day before. Vicka recollected that it was still light that evening and that she could see the Madonna's face and eyes clearly. Despite the profundity of the moment, Vicka recalled her promise to Marija and quickly rushed from the hill to find her friend who also wanted to be present. Calling Marija, she found her at home with the ten-year-old Jakov Colo, a boy who was a first cousin to Marija and Milka. Hearing that the Virgin had returned, Marija and Jakov rushed out of the house together toward the hill, hurrying behind Vicka. From that day, these two, Marija Pavlović and Jakov Colo, would—with Ivanka, Mirjana, Vicka, and Ivan—become two of the six visionaries of Medjugorje. With the others, their lives would be transformed forever.

They saw her that evening, the visionaries claimed, the second day of the apparitions. She signaled again for the youngsters to come up to her, summoning them. Then something astonishing happened. As if moved by an invisible force, the children advanced up the tall, rocky hill together, at a super-human speed, a speed that transcended their normal capacities. Through brambles and sharp stones, they seemed to fly up the hill toward the apparition. Vicka said that it "was not like walking on the ground" but felt "as if something had pulled us through the air. I was afraid. I was also barefoot, but no thorns had scratched me."[19] Mirjana commented: "The onlookers below were baffled as they watched us scale the steep slope at an impossible speed, seemingly coasting over boulders and thorn bushes. Some people tried to run after us, but they could not keep pace. I was a city girl and not particularly athletic, but it felt effortless. It was as if I simply glided—or like something carried me—to the place where the woman was standing."[20]

Among the villagers who tried to run up with them was Jozo Ostojić. While only twelve years old, Jozo was well known in the village for setting a regional record for the hundred-meter dash, and it was believed that one day he would be on the Olympic team. When Jozo saw the children flying up the hill, it was little Jakov who surprised him most. He would testify with amazement to what transpired that evening:

> Jakov was two years younger than me, and not really athletic; nor-
> mally I can outrun him by a huge distance. But on this day, I can't
> come close to keeping up with him. He and the others seemed to be
> flying up that hill. There is no path, just rocks and thornbushes, but
> all six of them are moving at an incredible speed, bounding from
> rock to rock, taking enormous strides. I am running as fast as I can,
> but falling further and further behind, and so are the grown men
> running with me. We are gasping for breath, almost in tears, unable
> to believe what is happening.[21]

Mary Craig, who authored one of the earliest books on Medjugorje and was a BBC journalist while covering the apparitions, explains that Mirjana's uncle was present that evening at the hill and he later reflected: "It takes at least twelve minutes to get up there. Yet they did it in two. It scared me to death."[22]

The Messages of Medjugorje

When the children reached the top, only a few feet before the apparition, they stopped and felt as if a force had thrown them to their knees. They kneeled before the vision of the mysterious woman. Yet nothing hurt or even scratched them—an extremely peculiar occurrence, given the rough surface of the hill. Perhaps most interesting, as the children kneeled before the apparition, was the case of little Jakov, who was kneeling right in the middle of a thorn bush. Despite being thrown into that position, he came out of it without a scratch on his body.[23]

The villagers who gathered around the children at the bottom of the hill were deeply surprised, even troubled, by the speed with which the youngsters flew up the rocky hill. While the villagers could not see the apparition as could the youngsters, it was clear that something unusual was happening. Many of them tried to follow the visionaries up to the top but were unable, only reaching them many minutes later after making arduous efforts to climb up the difficult and thorny path. By the time they reached the children—who by then were so close to the vision in front of them—they found them kneeling on the rocks and praying. The children were reciting three prayers: the Our Father, the Hail Mary, and the Glory Be—three prayers that they knew. It took them some time in prayer before one of them acquired the courage to address the luminous woman who drew them. It was Ivanka, the one who first saw her, who was to be the first one to speak to her.

Only a few weeks earlier Ivanka had suffered the tragedy of losing her mother Jagoda, who died alone in the hospital. Stricken by great grief, Ivanka asked the apparition about her mother. The Madonna reassured Ivanka that her mother was well and happy. Ivanka still wanted to know whether her mother wanted to say anything special to her children. "Just that you should obey your grandmother, and take special care of her now that she's old and unable to work."[24] They were on the hill about fifteen minutes that evening before the luminous woman left them with the words, "Go in the peace of God."[25]

This second day of the apparitions, June 25th, would henceforth be celebrated in Medjugorje as the anniversary of the apparitions of Our Lady of Medjugorje, since it was on this day (and not the first one) that the visionaries spoke to the apparition for the first time, and it was on this day that all of them—that is, the six who would become the visionaries of Medjugorje—came to the hill. The other two youngsters who came on the first day but did not return—Milka and the other Ivan—would never experience an apparition again.

The next evening the visionaries reported that the apparition identified herself. Nearly the entire village was present on the hillside this evening as the visionaries claimed to see the mysterious woman for the third time. More than five thousand people saw the visionaries bathed in a strange but beautiful abundance of light, and they became believers of their claimed mystical experiences. It was Vicka who courageously tested the spirit behind the apparition that day. Urged by her grandmother, she sprinkled holy water at the apparition while making the sign of the cross, and proclaimed, "If you are the Madonna, stay with us. If you are not, be gone!"[26] The mysterious woman smiled with an expression of love, the visionaries reported, and replied: "Do not be afraid, dear angels. I am the Mother of God. I am the Queen of Peace. I am the mother of all people."[27] Two years later, in a message dated June 16, 1983, another message from the Madonna of Medjugorje, according to the seers, would expound on the meaning of her appearances, explaining:

> I have come to tell the world: God is Truth. He exists. In Him is true happiness and abundance of life. I present myself here as Queen of Peace to tell the world that peace is necessary for the salvation of the world. In God is found true joy from which peace flows.[28]

The "Queen of Peace,"[29] a traditional title for the Virgin Mary in Catholic devotion, is the title by which the Madonna of Medjugorje would come to be known by devotees, indicative of the reported message. The messages to the visionaries stressed that God exists and emphasized the need for people to return to God in order to find peace and meaning in their lives. The messages further stressed the practice of a specific spirituality. Mirjana explained, "During these daily encounters, Our Lady emphasized things like prayer, fasting, confession, reading the Bible and going to Mass."[30] These five spiritual practices would come to be understood as the core spirituality of Medjugorje, being identified as the "five stones," a reference to the biblical story of David and Goliath. Prayer, fasting, confession, the Bible, and the Mass were identified as the five stones with which to defeat one's Goliath—a spirituality which would bring one closer to God and lead to personal transformation by living out these practices. "She was not asking us to pray or fast just for the sake of it," Mirjana said. "The fruit of living our faith, she said, was love. As she said in one of her messages, *"I come to you as a mother, who, above all, loves her children. My children, I want to teach you to love."*[31] Mirjana would reemphasize the importance of this message, "Our Lady spoke of the importance of prayer and fasting, and she invited us to conversion—to abandon sin and put God first in our lives. Only then would we know real love, she said."[32]

In Medjugorje, the villagers, and eventually many pilgrims and devotees worldwide, would adopt a spirituality of fasting on bread and water, first on Fridays and eventually also on Wednesdays, following the messages. One of the messages specifically reported that the best form of fasting is on bread and water. This spirituality traces its roots to an ancient Christian tradition, as both early and medieval Christians practiced fasting on Wednesdays and Fridays—medieval Christians even including Saturdays in honor of the Virgin, as Saturday was recognized as a Marian day. These traditional fasting days were recognized as penitential days because Wednesday is identified, in Christian tradition, as the day that Jesus was betrayed, while Friday was the day he was crucified and killed.

The emphasis on prayer in the messages often stresses "prayer of the heart," meaning developing an intimate prayer life that rises above mere lip service. In his dissertation on Medjugorje, the Mariologist Mark Miravalle explained, "The messages have emphatically called for prayer, both in greater quantity and intensity, establishing prayer as the principal means of attaining the peace of Christ."[33] One such message reported from the Madonna asked for prayer at least three hours a day, and stressed a depth of intimacy that should be sought in prayer: "When I say, 'Pray, pray, pray,' I do not mean only to increase the hours of prayer, but increase the desire to pray and to be in contact with God; to be in a continuous prayerful state of mind."[34] The message of prayer has also been connected with renewing a love for Scriptures, for the Bible. As with the emphasis on prayer—not to keep it at the surface level but to delve deeper into a contemplative interiority of the heart—the message on Scriptures has also asked for a greater depth, not to simply read the text of the Bible but to internalize and live the meaning contained therein. One message explained:

> I will tell you a spiritual secret: if you wish to be stronger than evil, make an active conscience for yourself. That is, pray a reasonable amount in the morning, read a text of Holy Scripture, and plant the

divine word in your heart, and try to live it during the day, especially in moments of trial. So you will be stronger than evil.[35]

Evil in the messages of Medjugorje is not an abstract concept but, rather, one that pertains to the presence of an actual spiritual entity: to God's ancient nemesis, Satan (or the devil). Not only is the existence of the devil recognized in many of the messages, as a nefarious force acting in the world and in the lives of people, but so is the power of prayer and fasting as spiritual weapons against this enemy. One message reported from the Virgin reads: "Satan is working even more violently to take away the joy from each one of you. Through prayer, you can totally disarm him and ensure happiness."[36] Another message explained: "Satan is enraged because of those who fast and are converted."[37] The messages have emphasized the reality of spiritual warfare, an active battle between the divine and the demonic for the human soul that is at the center of human existence. Mirjana has said that the Virgin "told me that Jesus struggles for each of us, but the devil tries to interfere. The devil, she warned, prowls around us and sets traps. He tries to divide and confuse us so that we will detest ourselves and abandon ourselves to him. An invisible spiritual war rages all around us, but Our Lady is here to help us."[38]

Mirjana has testified that once, during her earlier apparitions, while expecting to experience the Madonna, she encountered instead the devil appearing to her. "Although I rarely speak about the devil, I can tell you with certainty that he exists. I saw him once. . . . In that moment, I learned that nothing in this world compares to his ugliness and his hatred for God—but unlike God's power, his is limited."[39] The ominous apparition disappeared, according to Mirjana, by being driven away by the Madonna's presence, who then said to the visionary: "That was a trial, but it will not happen to you again."[40] Mirjana has commented on how the devil works in the world, explaining that "unlike in the movies, he doesn't come as some grotesque creature lurking in the shadows—he attacks through people who have allowed him to reign in their hearts. People unknowingly accept his influence through their choices in life."[41] When she gave an early interview on the topic in 1983, the visionary said: "Today, as we see all around us, everyone is dissatisfied; they cannot abide each other. Examples are the number of divorces and abortions. All this, the Madonna said, is the work of the devil."[42] The power of prayer, however, has been highlighted as a remedy: "Most do not realize how easy it is to get under his control, and that's one reason Our Lady always stresses the importance of prayer. If God reigns in your heart, then there is no room for anything bad."[43]

The messages go further, stressing not only the existence of the devil but also that of his domain, the realm of hell. Hell is recognized in the Medjugorje messages as a realm of the afterlife where many souls end up after death amid torturous and eternal suffering. In fact, the Medjugorje visionaries have claimed to have been shown three realms of the afterlife. Miravalle explains: "The reality of Heaven, Purgatory, Hell, and the active efforts of Satan in the world has been downplayed in contemporary society, but not in the content of the messages reported by the visionaries."[44] Let us turn to the content of the afterlife and consider it in detail.

Visions of the Afterlife

What exactly do the messages of Medjugorje say about the afterlife, about what happens after death? Can the alleged apparitions provide answers to some of the perennial mysteries that have haunted the human race? What happens to us after we die? Is there a soul? Is there life hereafter, or is this material reality the end of our existence? Throughout life, no matter what religious (or nonreligious) background one comes from, we all ask ourselves these big questions. We all ponder the answers, especially when we lose loved ones. Will we ever be reunited? Is there life after death? Is there a soul that continues to live on after the body stops? Or is there nothing else afterward? Is this the end?

Deep questions about death and the afterlife, eternal questions, have also occupied much cultural fascination in recent years. The 2010 book *Heaven Is for Real*, documenting the near-death experience of a young boy, Colton Burpo, who claimed to experience heaven and encounter Jesus Christ, as well as deceased family members of whom Burpo as a child was not aware, became a national bestseller, eventually being made into a major motion picture.[45] The book and film also featured the story of Akiane Kramarik, a child prodigy and artist who, coming from an atheist family, reported experiencing visions from God, some of which included depictions of Jesus and heaven, eventually turning her visionary experiences into art. Kramarik's most famous painting, *Prince of Peace*, a portrait of the face of Jesus based on her visions, was completed when she was eight years old. After seeing an image of Kramarik's painting on CNN years later, Colton Burpo recognized the depiction as the only one corresponding to the image of Christ that he encountered in his near-death experience. *Heaven Is for Real* was not the only work that showed a growing cultural fascination with the afterlife. The same year that the book was published, the Academy Award–winning filmmaker and actor Clint Eastwood released a movie on the afterlife called *Hereafter*, starring Matt Damon as a man with psychic abilities who may provide some answers about the hereafter. Two years later, in 2012, the neurosurgeon Eben Alexander, who has taught at the medical schools of both Duke and Harvard Universities, and was a skeptic on near-death experiences until he underwent one, published the bestselling book *Proof of Heaven: A Neurosurgeon's Journey into the Afterlife*.[46]

The topic of the afterlife has fascinated people for centuries—hints of near-death experiences are even present in Plato—and it is a topic that continues to fascinate in numerous ways in our own time. What contribution, therefore, does Medjugorje make to our understanding of this subject?

The message that the visionaries report to have received from the Virgin about the afterlife recognizes three possible realms that exist after death: heaven, hell, and purgatory. The visionaries have experienced these realities in different ways; a couple of the visionaries have even reported being physically taken to these realms by the Virgin.[47] For the seer Mirjana, these realities were conveyed as visionary experiences that reflected something "similar to a movie projection"[48] or "like a scene from a film"[49] that was shown before her. For Vicka and Jakov, the form of communication was a more immediate and intense experience. On All Souls' Day in November 1981, Vicka and Jakov reported leaving the world. They explained that the Virgin appeared to them unexpectedly, as the two were together, and told them that she would take them to heaven. Presuming that this meant death, the ten-year-old Jakov panicked and pleaded with the Virgin: "Don't take me! Take Vicka! She has seven brothers and sisters, and I'm my mother's only child!"[50] That very day the two visionaries were in the house of Vicka's friend Jakisa. Vicka and Jakov claimed that they "returned to earth" feeling, journalist Randall Sullivan writes, "as if they had been physically absent, a belief that was confirmed when Jakisa's mother asked where they had been hiding, then said she had spent the past twenty minutes looking for them."[51]

The three realms of the afterlife that the visionaries have claimed to encounter have been described thus: heaven, according to the seers, is a huge place of great lights, beauty, and immense joy. Nature is featured prominently as meadows, mountains, hills, and beautiful countrysides are all present; people possess an inner light, a serene joy radiates from their presence. "The people there were youthful, joyful, and dressed in pastel robes, but they looked different from people on Earth, radiating light from within," Mirjana reported. "They dwelt in an endless space surrounded by the most beautiful trees and meadows, all of which emanated the same light. There was something like a sky overhead which seemed to be *made* of that light, and the light itself was imbued with joy—the kind of joy that makes you want to sing or cry."[52] Vicka also reported seeing in heaven a "huge endless tunnel filled with an unearthly kind of light." She further described seeing many people: "all as if filled with some indescribable joy. Your heart stands still when you look at it."[53]

Purgatory is a very sad and chilling place. One visionary described it as a misty area with gray fog through which people could be heard weeping, trembling, moaning, and where an extreme loneliness permeates the sadness of the atmosphere, comparing it to the feeling of entering a foggy cemetery on a winter day. Mirjana reported being given "a brief glimpse of Purgatory" in which "I saw a vast, gloomy mist in which obscure human forms shivered and writhed."[54] Vicka heard "moanings and lamentations, and the sound of countless fingers knocking, as though they want to get out."[55] Marija said that when she had her experience of purgatory, "I did not see any people in purgatory, but I could hear them crying and asking us to pray for them."[56] Mirjana reported that the Virgin explained to her that there are different levels to purgatory, "levels closer to Hell and levels closer to Heaven. Every soul there is already saved, which is why I envision Purgatory to be more like an outer rim of Heaven instead of a separate place altogether. Even the word 'place' is inadequate to describe something that exists beyond the temporal world."[57] The vision of purgatory that she received, Mirjana explained, "lasted a few seconds and it troubled me deeply, but Our Lady assured me that Purgatory was more of a mercy than a penalty."[58] According to Vicka, the Madonna emphasized that purgatory is "the place where souls are purified, and that much prayer is needed for the people there."[59] Explaining why such a place like purgatory was necessary, the Virgin apparently told Mirjana: "Since nothing can live in the sight of God but pure love, God's justice cleanses."[60]

The theology and necessary spiritualty associated with purgatory was explained to the visionaries. The souls who are in purgatory no longer possess free will, unlike the living, and therefore they cannot atone for their sins—meaning, their prayers cannot help them. The souls in purgatory depend completely on the prayers of the living for their atonement: to be cleansed and to have their suffering ended in order to enter heaven. Being shown the suffering souls, the visionaries reported that the Madonna said to them: "Those people are waiting for your prayers and sacrifices."[61] From the visionaries it is Marija who has given one of the most detailed accounts about the spirituality and theology surrounding purgatory. "Our Lady said that the suffering of these people [in purgatory] was because they wanted to go to heaven, but could not unless they had our prayers to assist them. She said that when we prayed for them, we helped them towards heaven."[62] Marija spoke about the inner dynamics of the sadness that permeates this realm. "I felt great sadness in purgatory, because I was allowed to understand that these people know that God exists, that heaven exists. They want to be with God, but it is not possible for them to be with Him, because their sins are still on their souls."[63] She explained that the pain that these souls experience is not physical, that it has a deeper component. "Their cries are not because they are in physical pain, I understood, but because they are in spiritual pain, wishing to be with God. Every day they spend in purgatory they understand more the situation they are in and the result of their own sins. And they learn the way to love God."[64] Like the other visionaries Marija also emphasized the importance of praying for the souls in purgatory; however, she also mentioned how that prayer leads to a reciprocal spiritual relationship between the souls of that realm and the ones on earth praying for them. "Our Lady said that we should pray for the souls in purgatory, that our prayers will help them to reach heaven. And she said that we should tell others to pray for them. She said that when we pray for these souls, they become our friends and they pray for us in return. And now I pray for all the souls in purgatory, not just those I know, but all souls."[65] The visionaries further stated that there is an annual date as to when the most souls are released from purgatory and enter into heaven, conveying that the largest number of souls leave purgatory on Christmas Day.[66]

Hell, as may be expected, is the most disturbing of the three realms that the visionaries have reported to encounter. The visionaries have described it as a vast place with many people and a great sea of fire in the center. According to the visionaries, the souls in hell are enraged, cursing, ugly, occupied with unending anger. They enter the torturous fires naked and come out horrific, no longer in human shape; in vastly darkened, blackened skin. Vicka had watched the damned approach the fires. They threw themselves into the flames naked. "Before they went into the fire, they looked like normal people. The more they are against God's will, the deeper they enter into the fire, and the deeper they go, the more they rage against Him," she said.[67] When emerging from the flames these souls are no longer recognizable. "They don't have human shapes anymore," Vicka said; "they are more like grotesque animals, but unlike anything on earth."[68] Marija described her experience of hell thus:

> There was a big fire burning and Our Lady allowed us to see this young girl, a very beautiful young girl. When she went into the fire, she became like a beast. It was very frightening. But Our Lady said that it was important for us to know while we are still on this earth, that another life exists and the decisions we make in this life decided where we spend eternity.[69]

When asked as a youngster about hell, Jakov replied, "I do not want to speak about Hell. Hell exists; I have seen it. Perhaps before, I had some doubts, but now I know it really exists."[70] Mirjana, who saw heaven and purgatory but refused to see hell, asking to be spared the experience, has said that even today Jakov does not like to talk about hell.[71]

Regarding the question of how many people today experience which afterlife after their deaths, Mirjana reported that, according to the Madonna, today "most people go to Purgatory, the next greatest number go to Hell, and only a few go directly to Heaven."[72] The fact that most go to purgatory means that eventually, after a period of purification, these souls will be in heaven. "Our Lady told me that our prayers on Earth can help the souls there [in purgatory]. Occasionally a person will ask me to pray for a loved one who they believe is in Purgatory, but only God knows where our deceased ones are. The most beautiful thing we can do is pray and fast for our deceased, and participate in Masses while keeping them in our hearts and minds."[73] Mirjana, however, was shaken by the idea that people can go to hell for all eternity and undergo unending suffering, claiming to ask the Virgin for clarity on the matter. "For example, I asked her how God can be so unmerciful as to throw people into Hell, to suffer forever. I thought: If a person commits a crime and goes to jail, he stays there for a while and then is forgiven—but to Hell, forever?"[74] The response that the visionary received stressed the importance and power of free will, the fact that so many have *chosen* hell. "*Souls who go to Hell have ceased thinking favorably of God,*" the Madonna reportedly told Mirjana. Mirjana expounded: "In life they cursed Him, she explained [to me], and in death they will continue to do the same. In essence, they've already become part of Hell. God does not send people to Hell. They choose to be there."[75] Mirjana continued to plead for clarity, however, asking whether people in hell can pray for their salvation. She thought, why could God not deliver them from their ordeal by responding with mercy to their prayers?[†] "Then the Madonna explained it to me. People in Hell do not pray at all; instead, they blame God for everything. In effect, they become one with Hell and they get used to it. They rage against God, and they suffer, but they always refuse to pray to God."[76] In this realm the tormented souls evidently experience a profound hatred. "In Hell, they hate God even more than they hated Him on Earth."[77]

Marija's explanation about the realm of hell also stressed the power of free will in determining a soul's eternal destiny. Marija said that according to the Madonna it is not God who sends people to hell but that it is a decision that people reach by themselves in how they live their lives. "God gave us freedom, the ability to understand good and evil, so it is we who decide where our eternal lives will be spent. Those people who go to hell are those who choose to go there."[78] Given the stark realities of two of the realms of the afterlife that were revealed to Marija, author Heather Parsons asked the visionary whether she was afraid of death. "No," Marija replied. "Death is not a tragedy for any person who really believes in God. It's a joy to meet God. Who could be afraid of spending eternity with the person who loves us more than anybody has ever loved us?"[79]

Near-Death Experiences: A Comparative Study

A question must be asked. Is it possible to provide any type of empirical study of the claims about the afterlife that the Medjugorje visionaries have reported, particularly on a subject as (literally) otherworldly as this? The sociologist Craig R. Lundahl has made one of the most interesting attempts in this regard, empirically examining the claims of the visionaries through a comparative study. Lundahl, who has written a number of works on near-death experiences, authored an article in the *Journal of Near-Death*

[†] It is noteworthy that in her questioning here, Mirjana was not abiding by a Catholic theology of hell, which understands this realm as one where all hope is lost, where there is complete separation from God, and where prayer would no longer have any efficacy for the salvation of the souls therein (salvation no longer being a possibility). Mirjana's questioning may be based more on a lack of knowledge of the Catholic teaching for the then-teenager, as opposed to a deliberate denial of the teaching. However, her line of reasoning is noteworthy because it shows that the visionary is not imposing the teachings of her own faith tradition onto the experience. This challenges a constructivist interpretation of the mystical experience, which presupposes that every such experience is culturally constructed and informed by the visionary's or mystic's preexistent religious and cultural ideas and concepts.

Studies in 2000 titled "A Comparison of Other World Perceptions by Near-Death Experiences and by the Marian Visionaries of Medjugorje."[80] Lundahl's article, as the title suggests, compared the visions of the afterlife that the Medjugorje seers reported with encounters of the afterlife that people who have undergone near-death experiences (NDE) have reported. Before delving into his findings, let us first offer some brief commentary on the unique, but constantly growing, field of research into near-death experiences.

The near-death experience is believed by many to be an otherworldly encounter, wherein a person has an out-of-body experience and enters another reality, a spiritual realm beyond this one, often reporting to see unusually bright light, deceased persons, angelic or heavenly figures, or heavenly cities, or experiencing a vivid revival of memories (sometimes an entire life flashing before the person) and great peace, bliss, and weightlessness; other near-death experiences, although less frequently reported, describe negative and even horrific encounters with a more ominous afterlife. While near-death experiences are believed by many to be true experiences with a spiritual dimension, there are many others who believe that such phenomena and all their characteristics are nothing more than a construction of the human brain. There is a small number of academic institutes that systematically and scientifically study such experiences across the world. Among them there is the Division of Perceptual Studies, a research unit of the Department of Psychiatry and Neurobehavioral Sciences at the University of Virginia. Similarly, in Scotland, there is the Koestler Parapsychology Unit at the University of Edinburgh.

The Division of Perceptual Studies at Virginia has probably done the most significant research on near-death studies in the United States. The division was founded in 1967 by Dr. Ian Stevenson, who resigned from his position as chair of the Psychiatry Department in order to become the director of the research unit. It was also at the University of Virginia that Raymond Moody, who coined the expression "near-death experience," completed his Ph.D. in philosophy only two years later, in 1969. In addition to his work in philosophy, Moody pursued the path of psychiatry, and while doing his medical residency at Virginia, Moody's seminal book, *Life After Life,* was published in 1975.[81] Documenting case studies of near-death experiences, the book brought to public awareness an experience that many people have encountered but few knew how common it was and how to talk about it, introducing discussion of the phenomena of NDEs into the mainstream. The book's foreword was written by the prominent Swiss-American psychiatrist Elisabeth Kübler-Ross, most famous for her theory on the five stages of grief as articulated in her 1969 book *On Death and Dying*.[82] Kübler-Ross also wrote extensively on death experiences and, with Moody, became a pioneering voice in the study of near-death experiences.

It is important to note, however, that because institutes like the Division of Perceptual Studies at Virginia and the Koestler Parapsychology Unit at Edinburgh study unique phenomena like near-death experiences, that does not imply that the scholars who work at these centers have a monolithic or unified view of such subjects. Much debate exists. Professor Caroline Watt, the Koestler Chair of Parapsychology at Edinburgh, co-authored an article with neuroscientist Dean Mobbs that has taken a very critical view of near-death experiences, believing that they can be explained as stemming from psychological and neurophysiological factors influencing the brain.[83] This work by Mobbs and Watt has been challenged by a number of scholars, among them Bruce Greyson, professor emeritus of psychiatry and neurobehavioral sciences at Virginia.

Greyson and co-authors Janice Miner Holden and Pim van Lommel suggest that to reach their conclusions Mobbs and Watt had to ignore important aspects that they could not explain about near-death experiences and ignore "a substantial body of empirical research on NDEs" that would challenge their results.[84] What Mobbs and Watt did was look at five principal features often associated with the near-death experience—an awareness of being dead, having an out-of-body experience, seeing a tunnel of light, meeting deceased people, and feeling positive emotions—and attempt to explain how all these features can be actualized from natural, neurobiological processes.[85] The problem, according to Greyson and his co-authors, is that in order to advance their claims, Mobbs and Watt had to make selective arguments that ignore essential aspects about the neurophysiology of near-death experiences—essential aspects that would not be able to support their results.

Mobbs and Watt attributed out-of-body experiences during NDEs to two factors: REM-intrusion and the activation of the temporal brain lobe. REM refers to rapid eye movement experienced during a sleep state, which is associated with vivid dreaming and thoughts. Greyson et al. point out, however, that it is fallacious to associate REM-intrusion as one natural explanation for the out-of-body experience during NDEs because NDEs often "occur under conditions that in fact inhibit REM," and the authors notice that when NDE patients do experience REM it is no more than the general population.[86] Furthermore, the electrical stimulation of the "temporal lobe typically elicits frightening, distorted experiences quite unlike NDEs."[87] Therefore, neither is REM-intrusion nor temporal lobe activation a convincing argument for explaining NDEs, according to Greyson and his colleagues.

Hallucinations that transpire in neurological disorders is another theory that Mobbs and Watt apply to explain why NDE patients often report seeing deceased people. There are phenomenological differences, however, between hallucinations stemming from neurological conditions and encounters with the deceased that transpire during NDEs. Greyson et al. explain that "hallucinations in these neurological conditions involve only vision and are usually accompanied by fear and confusion, quite unlike realistic, interactive visions of deceased persons in NDEs, which are usually welcoming and often seen, heard, smelled, and touched."[88] Thus both the usual emotions and the diversity (in NDE cases) versus the singularity (in hallucinating visions) of the human senses are distinct. Further, Greyson et al. make a significant point that Mobbs and Watt ignore: NDE patients often report accurate information that was acquired during their near-death experiences about deceased persons—sometimes of deceased persons they never met, and other times of persons they did not know were deceased. This highly documented phenomenon substantially challenges the interpretation of these encounters as hallucinations.[89]

The famous case of Colton Burpo, the boy who encountered a near-death experience leading to the book and film of the same title that depicted his journey, *Heaven Is for Real*, constituted one such case wherein the NDE patient reported encountering deceased relatives he never knew of and gained information about them—information that was later verified. There is a technical term for such a near-death experience. This is known as a *veridical NDE*. A veridical NDE is the occurrence during a near-death experience when the individual undergoing the NDE acquires verifiable information that could not have been attained through the ordinary senses, meaning through natural ways. This can include encountering a deceased relative whom the NDE patient did not know and who conveys information not previously known by the patient but that can be verified. This can also include perception during the near-death experience by the patient of happenings that are transpiring at a distant location, as in other rooms in the hospital or even in another city. All these phenomena count as veridical NDEs.[90]

Greyson and his co-authors emphasize that, in the past four decades, work on near-death literature has moved beyond collecting anecdotes of experiences into a rigorous scientific examination of such cases, often studying the neurophysiological correlates of near-death experiences. In this regard, they challenge scholars to look at all the relevant data pertaining to NDEs instead of assuming, without complete empirical evidence, that such cases can all be reduced to neurophysiological explanations. Such explanations remain speculative and frequently cannot account for the totality of most near-death experiences.[91] In a separate article, Greyson articulates the matter thus: "A number of reductionistic hypotheses have been proposed to explain NDEs, attributing them to psychopathology, personality traits, altered blood gases, neurotoxic metabolic reactions, or neuroanatomical malfunctions, although such speculations generally lack any empirical support and address only selected aspects of the phenomenon."[92] Mobbs has written a short reply to the claims made against his and Watt's article, a reply that curiously does little to engage the arguments that Greyson and his co-authors put forward but, instead, briefly concentrates on questioning the authority of their sources.[93]

Critics of near-death experiences see the phenomenon as nothing more than a construction of the brain with possible neurophysiological explanations. A key assumption of this perspective is the idea that the brain is the basis for consciousness and, therefore, the mind cannot live on once the brain stops functioning at brain death. A critical response to this claim is that many who have reported near-death experiences have been pronounced clinically dead, with brain functions halted and flat EEGs recorded, and yet still reported out-of-body experiences of consciousness carrying over in the light of these clinical realities—thus, their minds and perception continued functioning, often in more enhanced and vivid ways, while the brain was inactive or impaired, indicating that consciousness may survive bodily death.[94] Michael Grosso comments on Dr. Eben Alexander's experience in this regard, how the neurosurgeon's skepticism about this reality disappeared after Alexander personally encountered a near-death experience:

What struck Alexander was that just when the normal adaptive functions of the brain were knocked out of commission, the "impossible" happened; not only did he continue to be conscious, but the quality of his consciousness was exceptional—to use Dr. Alexander's words, "hyper-real." He found himself forced to let go of his "addiction to simplistic, primitive reductive materialism."[95]

However, the veracity of near-death experiences remains a highly debated topic. A central reason for that debate includes the fact that deeper metaphysical implications, about the nature of reality itself, are at stake when it comes to accepting or denying the claims of many near-death experiences.[96] Such experiences have the capacity to touch on questions of whether the mind can function outside the brain or physical body, and on whether human beings survive after physical death, speaking to the potentiality of a soul.[97] Such possibilities, while supported by much data on scientific examination into near-death experiences, challenge cherished beliefs—especially of a materialist worldview—and, therefore, lead to much debate.[98]

Craig Lundahl's findings concerning the Medjugorje visions and near-death experiences of the afterlife do, therefore, lead to further interesting studies into these matters, as two separate areas of research, the science of near-death experiences and the theological/visionary content of Marian apparitions, are combined to construct a more holistic and interdisciplinary approach toward studying the afterlife through a comparative analysis. According to Lundahl, individuals who have undergone near-death experiences "describe life after death as consisting of two major divisions with a possibility of a third division."[99] The first division that Lundahl analyzed is the "Cities of Light," a division that is very similar to what the Medjugorje visionaries describe as heaven. Numerous people who have reported near-death encounters have described seeing these Cities of Light. Lundahl explains how patients have described this realm:

> This division contains countrysides with beautiful landscapes of mountains, hills, valleys, fields of golden grass and flowers, meadows, paths, trails, lanes, roads, great forests, brooks, streams, rivers, ponds, and lakes. The plant life includes grass, flowers, trees of all kinds, shrubs, and vegetable and flower gardens. There is a variety of animal life and insects such as butterflies and bees. Buildings such as houses and some larger buildings are also found in the countrysides.[100]

Lundahl further explains that the "beautiful gardens, flowers, shrubs, and trees in the Cities of Light perfectly complement their physical structures, which include walls, gates, streets, houses, and various buildings with magnificent interiors and furniture. . . . The cities in this first division emanate light."[101]

There are both comparisons and contrasts to consider in relation to the Medjugorje accounts of heaven. Considering the comparison to the accounts of the visionaries, there are important parallels to note. Not only were the Medjugorje descriptions similar, and at times identical, to the near-death experiences in speaking of beautiful countrysides, mountains, hills, and meadows—thus the various expressions of nature they reported to see in heaven—but there is also similarity in the radiating light that the seers reported experiencing in the celestial realm. Lundahl describes this radiating light in further detail, taking the following description from a report by NDE patients:

> It was a city of light. It was similar to cities on earth in that there were buildings and paths, but the buildings and paths appeared to be built of materials which we consider precious on earth. They looked like marble, and gold, and silver, and other bright materials, only they were different. The buildings and streets seemed to have a sheen and to glow. The entire scene was one of indescribable beauty. . . .There was a feeling of love and peace. After soaring for a while, she (the angel) sat me down on a street in a fabulous city of buildings made of glittering gold and silver and beautiful trees.[102]

The account continues to describe a "beautiful light [that] was everywhere—glowing but not bright enough to make me squint my eyes."

> and then I saw, infinitely far off, far too distant to be visible with any kind of sight I knew of . . . a city. A glowing, seemingly endless city, bright enough to be seen over all the unimaginable distance between. This brightness seemed to shine from the very walls and streets of this place, and from the beings which I could now discern moving about within it. In fact, the city and everything in it seemed to be made of light. . . . The beauty of the countryside was incredible but even it could not compare with the splendor of the city because of the glow.[103]

The Medjugorje visionaries describe the inhabitants of heaven as people from whom a light radiates while, likewise, in Lundahl's article there are reports of a brightness that "seemed to shine from the very walls and streets of this place, and from the beings which I could now discern moving about within it." Before considering the contrasts, let us first examine the other realms.

The second realm that Lundahl describes is referred to, in near-death studies, as the "Realm of Bewildered Spirits." Lundahl describes "this division as a dark, gloomy, and hostile environment where millions of unhappy and wicked people who are gray, bewildered, confused, miserable, anguished, dreary, angry, and do not seem to communicate much are confined until they can solve whatever problem they have that appears to be keeping them there."[104] In this realm we again see many similarities to what the Medjugorje visionaries have described as purgatory: a dark, gloomy, and gray environment occupied by misery, by unhappy and confused souls. It is noteworthy also how Lundahl describes this realm as a place where souls are confined until they can resolve whatever problem is keeping them there. Thus, there is a notion of "unfinished business," a restlessness of sorts for the souls in this realm. The acknowledged temporality of this realm, as a place where souls remain until they resolve what is keeping them there, also corresponds to a theology of purgatory, which is understood in the Catholic tradition as a temporary realm of purification where a soul remains until it is cleansed and ready to enter heaven. Thus, unlike hell, this is not an *eternal* state of suffering.

Lundahl also wonders whether what near-death researchers deem as the "Realm of Bewildered Spirits" could constitute another division, one that is hell; for he acknowledges that many who enter the Realm of Bewildered Spirits describe it as a hellish experience—for some more brutal than others. While near-death researchers have not officially separated the Realm of Bewildered Spirits into two divisions, Lundahl suggests that such a separation may be necessary. The various patients who have encountered a dark and disturbing realm in the afterlife may be, in fact, encountering two different realities, one worse than the other, Lundahl argues. Known cases in near-death studies like the account of Don Brubaker, who experienced a hellish near-death experience, or the more famous case of Howard Storm, whose own hellish near-death encounter is recollected in his book *My Descent into Death*, point to the possibility that a third realm exists, even darker and more ominous than the one resembling purgatory.[105] "The [Medjugorje] visionaries' observations in the other world suggest the possibility of a third division or realm, of which near-death researchers are not yet cognizant," Lundahl explains. "These observations lend support for further study of frightening NDEs to determine whether or not those NDErs who travel to a less than heavenly realm may be going to two separate places instead of one. Various frightening NDE cases suggest this might be a possibility."[106]

To make a coherent comparison between what the Medjugorje visionaries reported and what near-death patients reported about the afterlife, Lundahl used "basic features" that he and fellow researcher H. A. Widdison recorded in their 1997 book that documents accounts of near-death experiences, *The Eternal Journey: How Near-Death Experiences Illuminate Our Earthly Lives*.[107] Basic features that they recorded of the Cities of Light included "the world of light and preternatural beauty, vegetation, and physical structures, inhabited by content and happy people who emanate light."[108] In this case, Lundahl sees a clear correspondence between the realm of the Cities of Light as reported by near-death accounts and the realm of heaven as reported by the Medjugorje visionaries. Both cases describe a world of light and preternatural beauty, vegetation, and happy people who emanate light.[109] Where Lundahl sees a discrepancy is in the basic feature of physical structures, which near-death patients have described in identifying magnificent buildings, walls, gates, streets, and houses in the Cities of Light while the Medjugorje visionaries did not describe such structures. Here, it is important to note that Lundahl is not claiming that the visionaries reported something different but simply that, in their descriptions, the visionaries did not specify physical structures (even if they did see them).

Regarding the Realm of Bewildered Spirits, Lundahl identifies the basic features as containing a "world of darkness and fog, the damp, musty, and lonely environment, and earthen structures and walls, inhabited by bewildered, confused, miserable, anguished, dreary, angry, and unhappy people who have a gray or dark appearances."[110] On all counts, Lundahl found a clear correspondence with what the Medjugorje visionaries described as purgatory. Where Lundahl noted a qualification, however, is in the basic feature of "bewildered, anguished, unhappy, gray/dark people."[111] Whereas the visionaries have described *hearing* such people, in their anguish and confusion, they have not described *seeing* such people in a gray or darkened appearance. Nevertheless, while the description of appearance has a qualification, "both the NDErs and the Visionaries appear to agree that people are unhappy in this division of the other world."[112]

The realm of hell is one where Lundahl was not able to establish clear connections, explaining that this constitutes "a realm that to date has not been well delineated in near-death studies" while highlighting the basic features that the Medjugorje visionaries have attributed to this realm: a world of fire, raging flames, structures, and enraged, grotesque, blackened people that no longer appear human.[113] Lundahl is open, however, to the possibility that near-death experiences that report on a "less than heavenly realm" may be describing two separate realms, beyond the singularly established Realm of Bewildered Spirits. "Various frightening NDE cases suggest this might be a possibility."[114] He qualifies, however, that in most such cases the individual undergoing the near-death experience feels to be in "hell" because of the foreboding nature of the experience when, in fact, it is possible that the realm that is being experienced can be what the Medjugorje visionaries have described as purgatory. Lundahl suggests further study of frightening near-death cases to see whether specific characteristics can be distinguished and separate realms denoted. Lundahl's conclusion was that if "the observations of the Marian visionaries do nothing else, at least they provide some corroboration for the City of Light and Realm of Bewildered Spirits elements of the NDE from a source other than NDEs."[115]

Other researchers, such as Nancy Evan Bush and Bruce Greyson, have identified three types of distressing near-death experiences, describing one of the types as "hellish."[116] While distressing NDEs are less reported, the authors suggest that one reason for the lack of data may be not so much that such experiences happen infrequently but that they are seldom related, in comparison to pleasant NDEs, because distressing NDEs bring a lot of trauma to the individuals who undergo them and there is less desire to share such experiences. They explain that there is a "notorious reluctance to report a distressing NDE," which "may lead to long lasting trauma for individuals as well as limiting the data on occurrence." The authors admit, however, that a "literature review covering thirty years of research concludes that as many as one in five NDEs may be predominantly distressing."[117] What is important to distinguish, however, is that the authors do not categorize every "distressing NDE" as a hellish experience: one of the types of NDEs that they document under the "distressing" category they identify as an "inverse NDE." By *inverse* they mean that the experience has the same characteristics as a pleasant NDE—such as an out-of-body experience, a sense of traveling toward a bright light, encountering deceased friends or relatives—however, the experience has an inverse effect on the person undergoing the NDE, who finds it distressing, especially since the person may be under the impression that he or she has died without being ready to face this reality.[118]

In the hellish NDEs that Bush and Greyson relate there is a greater degree of correspondence with what the Medjugorje visionaries described as hell, compared to Lundahl's earlier study. As one example, Bush and Greyson note that such terrifying experiences often provoke a response of conversion from the person who has undergone the NDE, the experience being "interpreted as a warning about unwise or wrong behaviors, and to turn one's life around."[119] This corresponds to how Marija described hell as a horrifying place to witness but one that was necessary because, according to the visionary, "Our Lady said that it was important for us to know while we are still on this earth, that another life exists and the decisions we make in this life decided where we spend eternity."[120] Furthermore, compared to the descriptions that the visionaries gave of witnessing grotesque beings in hell, Bush and Greyson have documented NDEs with similar content. They note the account of a woman who attempted suicide and felt herself sliding down toward a dark, cold, and watery environment that resembled the entrance to a cave. She explained, "I heard cries, wails, moans, and the gnashing of teeth. I saw these beings that resembled humans, with the shape of a head and body, but they were ugly and grotesque. . . . They were frightening and sounded like they were tormented, in agony."[121] Granted, it would still be difficult from such a description to discern, as Lundahl has noted, whether the experience corresponds closer to what the visionaries have described as hell or purgatory.

Other descriptions, however, leave less to the imagination, describing horrific beings in an afterlife and a complete separation from God that is more in line with what the visionaries described as hell. Bush and Greyson relate the account of a woman who experienced hemorrhaging from a ruptured fallopian tube (also known as the uterine tube) and underwent a near-death experience in which she encountered "horrific beings with gray gelatinous appendages grasping and clawing at me. The sounds of their guttural moaning and the indescribable stench still remain 41 years later. There was no benign Being of Light, no life video, nothing beautiful or pleasant."[122]

More Questions on the Afterlife: Deceased Persons and Reincarnation

There are a couple other noteworthy elements to information about the afterlife that the Medjugorje visionaries claim to have received. First, the matter of deceased persons; and second, the subject of reincarnation.

The visionary Ivanka Ivanković has testified that she has no doubt about the reality of life after death, explaining that she was given the opportunity—through her apparition of the Virgin—to encounter her deceased mother, Jagoda. Ivanka's last daily apparition ended on May 7, 1985, when she claimed to have seen her deceased mother. Ivanka would report, "All of us ask ourselves, is there life after life? I am standing here before all of you as a living witness, and I can tell you there is life after life because on that day in May I was able to see my late mother. I was able to hug her and my mother told me—My daughter, I am proud of you."[123]

Not only have the visionaries claimed that the afterlife is real and have explained that the deceased are part of that afterlife, as Ivanka highlighted with her experience, but they have also reported to receive a message about the topic of reincarnation. The visionaries said that they were invited to ask any question to the Virgin. On the topic of the afterlife, they once asked about reincarnation. The reply to the question, as one journalist noted, "had been unusually lengthy and detailed," as many of the messages reported from Medjugorje were known for their brevity and frequently general scope.[124] The given response, however, delved deeper:

> We go to Heaven in full conscience; that which we have now. At the moment of death, we are conscious of the separation of body and soul. It is false to teach people that we are reborn many times and that we pass to different bodies. One is born only once. The body, drawn from the earth, decomposes after death. It never comes back to life again. Man receives a transfigured body. Whoever has done very much evil during his life can go straight to Heaven if he confesses, is sorry for what he has done, and receives communion at the end of his life.[125]

The Question of Other Religions

Whereas the aforementioned message on reincarnation constitutes an obvious critique of a belief that is prominently present in Eastern religious traditions, while at the same time highlighting the spiritual prowess of Roman Catholic sacraments like reconciliation and the Eucharist, it is noteworthy that there still is a very ecumenical, even pluralistic, component to the Medjugorje messages. Ivanka said in an early interview that it is important "not [to] be snobbish toward other religions, but respect them insofar as they praise God."[126] She further commented on the topic: "The

Madonna said that religions are separated in the earth, but the people of all religions are accepted by her Son."[127] Asked whether this means that all people can go to heaven, Ivanka replied that that is based on what each person deserves and that Jesus Christ understands that not all people have heard of him, indicating a theology of salvation—a Christological soteriology—that judges each individual on the basis of how much responsibility the person has been given.

"The religious unity of Christians, of all peoples who worship the one God, and a sincere respect for other religions also presents itself in the content of the messages," Miravalle explains.[128] Such an ecumenism and pluralism has led to numerous critiques of the Medjugorje message by very traditional Catholic commentators, who see in these messages attributed to the Virgin an "indifferent ecumenism."[129] Mariologists like Mark Miravalle and the French scholar René Laurentin have responded to such critiques. Miravalle has emphasized that the "message reported by the visionaries which attests to the lack of religious division in the eyes of God, is careful to point out that while man has created religious division not intended by God, the one mediator to the Father remains Jesus Christ; and that one's particular religion is not a matter of indifference because the Holy Spirit is not equally present in every Church."[130] The specific message that Miravalle is referencing, attributed to the Virgin at Medjugorje, articulated:

> In God's eyes, there are no divisions and there are no religions. You in the world have made the divisions. The one mediator is Jesus Christ. Which religion you belong to cannot be a matter of indifference. The presence of the Holy Spirit is not the same in every Church.[131]

A similar message attributed to the Madonna explained:

> It is not equally efficacious to belong to or pray in any church or community, because the Holy Spirit grants his power differently among the churches and ministers. All believers do *not* pray the same way. It is intentional that all apparitions are under the auspices of the Catholic Church.[132]

A balance has been present in the messages of Medjugorje that, on the one hand, elevates the theology of the Christian tradition with a proclivity toward Catholicism and, on the other hand, speaks about the importance of respecting people of other religions and their faiths. There is a constant critique present throughout the messages, as well, of the separation of religions. The visionary Mirjana commented on the Madonna's displeasure over this lack of religious unity:

> She also emphasized the failings of religious people, especially in small villages—for example, here in Medjugorje, where there is a separation from Serbians and Moslems. This separation is not good. The Madonna always stresses that there is but one God, and that people have enforced unnatural separation. One cannot truly believe, be a true Christian, if he does not respect other religions as well.[133]

Even such messages were not received without controversy. A number of theologians critical of Medjugorje argued that the Virgin's alleged insistence that Christians must respect other religions, particularly Islam, undermined Catholic orthodoxy and the primacy of the Catholic Church. Laurentin has countered such critiques by emphasizing that the messages of Medjugorje ask the Christian faithful to respect Muslim peoples and not necessarily Muslim doctrines, isolating an essential distinction.[134]

Secrets of Medjugorje

As happened in Fátima, Portugal, in 1917, when three shepherd children reported experiencing apparitions of the Virgin Mary and claimed to be given three secrets, in Medjugorje the visionaries have also claimed to have been given a set of secrets by the Virgin. Each visionary is supposed to receive ten secrets, which allegedly pertain to the Church and to monumental events that will affect the world; these include a number of chastisements for the sins of the world. As of today, three of the visionaries—Ivanka, Mirjana, and Jakov—claim to have received all ten secrets and (consequently) no longer experience daily apparitions. The other three visionaries—Vicka, Ivan, and Marija—claim to have received nine of ten secrets and reportedly continue to experience daily apparitions. It is believed that the *daily* apparitions of the visionaries will conclude once all receive their tenth secret, which is purported to happen when the events described in the secrets begin to unfold.[135] The visionaries have said that the Virgin has allowed them to reveal one of the secrets, the third secret.

The third secret states that at the conclusion of the apparitions a permanent, supernatural, and indestructible sign will appear on Podbrdo Hill, the site of the first apparition. This sign, "permanent, indestructible, and beautiful,"[136] as one visionary described it, will prove to the world that God exists and that the apparitions were real. The sign would appear after the first two secrets happen. When the first secret transpires, according to an interview Mirjana gave, it would convince a majority of people that it was an act of God—divine intervention. The time period between the second and third secrets would be a time of grace, when many conversions will come. However, a large number of people, particularly in the West, would insist that the events of the first two secrets must have "a natural explanation," Mirjana reported.[137] No one on earth would be able, however, to doubt the third secret, the promised sign, as constituting an act of God; its supernatural character would be undeniable. In her book *Encountering Mary: From La Salette to Medjugorje*, Sandra L. Zimdars-Swartz explains that the "function of the sign here would be twofold: it would stand as a witness to the authenticity of the apparitions, and it would be a call to conversion."[138]

There is an apparent similarity here to the apparitions at Fátima. A supernatural sign was promised by the three visionaries to appear from heaven during the last apparition of Our Lady of Fátima: this was the famous miracle of the dancing sun, which was witnessed by an estimated 70,000 people in the Cova da Iria fields in Fátima on October 13, 1917. Many devotees have seen a connection and continuity between the apparitions of Fátima and Medjugorje. The visionaries themselves have said that the Virgin has told them, "What I started in Fátima, I will complete in Međugorje. My heart will triumph."‡ [139]

In addition to commonalities and possible connections between the two apparition sites, there are a number of significant contrasts between what the Medjugorje visionaries have said about the promised sign and what happened with events in Fátima. In Fátima, the reported supernatural sign was temporary. In Medjugorje, the supernatural sign is supposed to be permanent, lasting forever. In Fátima, the supernatural sign was witnessed by an estimated 70,000 people in Portugal. In Medjugorje, the supernatural sign could be witnessed by millions, if not billions, of people

---

‡ Note that the spelling of "Medjugorje" is different here, as Mirjana uses the Croatian spelling, which is "Međugorje," dropping the first *j*, in contrast to the English spelling, and adding an accent over the *d*.

throughout the world. The visionaries have not given a number but have implied the possibility of international awareness. This is a reality of living in the digital age of smartphones and the Internet, where anything can be recorded and uploaded for the world to see within seconds. Mirjana has said that she has been allowed by the Virgin to reveal a few details about the sign, noting that it will be a phenomenon that can be photographed and filmed when it transpires. In a written account she has stated:

> I can say this much—after the events contained in the first two secrets come to pass, Our Lady will leave a permanent sign on Apparition Hill where she first appeared. Everyone will be able to see that human hands could not have made it. People will be able to photograph and film the sign, but in order to truly compre-hend it—to experience it with the heart—they will need to come to Medjugorje. Seeing it live, with the eyes, will be far more beautiful.[140]

She continued:

> I cannot speak about the details of the other secrets before the time comes to reveal them to the world, except to say that they will be announced before they occur. After the events take place as pre-dicted, it will be difficult for even the staunchest skeptics to doubt the existence of God and the authenticity of the apparitions.[141]

Most of the events contained within the secrets were revealed to Mirjana, the visionary explained, through words from the Madonna, but some of the events were also conveyed to her "like scenes from a film."[142] Mirjana has said that each secret will happen exactly as it was relayed to her with the exception of one. When the seventh secret was entrusted to the visionary, the contents of the secret troubled her greatly. Asking the Virgin whether it would be possible to lessen the gravity of the secret, Mirjana was told sim-ply, "Pray." Mirjana took the exhortation very seriously. "I rallied friends, family members, nuns and priests to pray and fast for the intention of changing the seventh secret, and we did so with intensity and conviction. We often met in Sarajevo as a group to pray about it." After eight months of praying for the intention, Mirjana says she experienced an apparition during which the following message was delivered by the Virgin about the seventh secret: "By the grace of God, it has been softened. But you must never ask such things again, because God's will must be done."[143] When

Mirjana was entrusted with the final secrets, however, she realized they were even worse than the seventh.

There is some question regarding the number of secrets. While the visionaries have claimed that each is supposed to receive ten secrets, there remains ambiguity as to whether all the secrets are the same for each visionary or whether they are receiving distinct secrets that, therefore, add up to much more than ten, or whether certain secrets are the same while others are distinct. Zimdars-Swartz notes the ambiguity, explaining that reports "about these secrets often convey the idea that the ten secrets are identical for all the seers and that there is variation only in the rate at which they are revealed to each seer" while noting that the visionaries' "responses to close questioning, however, suggests that this might not be the case and that each set of secrets might be distinctive."[144] An early interview with Mirjana conducted in 1983 has hinted at the latter possibility of distinctive secrets. A Franciscan priest asking Mirjana about the secrets found out that none of her ten secrets pertains to her personal life while noting that another visionary, Ivan Dragičević, did receive secrets that pertained to him personally.[145] Mirjana clarified that the "six of us visionaries do not speak to each other about the secrets. The only part of the secrets that we know we share in common is the permanent sign."[146]

The promise of a supernatural sign from God that will be permanent, beautiful, and indestructible, proving to the world that God exists and that the reported apparitions of the Virgin Mary have been authentic, is an exponentially bold and monumental claim to make. To a great extent, so much relating to Medjugorje will depend on the sign, a phenomenon that can make or break the credibility of the apparitions and the devotions there. The promised sign's failure to appear would constitute one of the biggest hoaxes in human history, as Medjugorje is a place revered and visited by millions of people—believers in the messages that the visionaries report to receive from heaven. Conversely, were the sign to appear, as promised, it would constitute one of the most monumental occurrences in human history, essentially changing the world and influencing all of humanity. This is exactly the bold promise that the visionaries are making, with its seismic implications. Mirjana has said, "I cannot divulge much more about the secrets, but I can say this—Our Lady is planning to change the world."[147]

2

Public Revelation and Private Revelation

HOW THE CATHOLIC CHURCH
DISCERNS THE SUPERNATURAL

Beloved, do not trust every spirit but test the spirits to see whether they belong to God, because many false prophets have gone out into the world.

—1 JOHN 4:1

Revelation terminated with Jesus Christ. He himself is the Revelation. But we certainly cannot prevent God from speaking to our time through simple persons and also through extraordinary signs that point to the insufficiency of the cultures stamped by rationalism and positivism that dominate us. The apparitions that the Church has officially approved— especially Lourdes and Fatima—have their precise place in the development of the life of the Church in the last century. They show, among other things, that Revelation—still unique, concluded and therefore unsurpassable—is not yet a dead thing but something alive and vital.

—JOSEPH CARDINAL RATZINGER, *The Ratzinger Report*

IN ITS THEOLOGY of revelation, the Catholic Church makes a significant distinction between public revelation and private revelations. It is under the second category, as private revelations, that visionary experiences like Marian apparitions are classified. Public revelation, on the other hand, pre-dates private revelation and refers to the divine revelation of God that has been transmitted through Scripture and the Apostolic Tradition, given to the prophets and apostles, and comprises the deposit of faith within the

Catholic Church that is understood to be complete and that constitutes the fullness, or totality, of what is necessary for human salvation. The two pillars of authority within the Catholic Church are Scripture and Tradition, but they are also intrinsically connected to the Magisterium, which includes the pope and the bishops, as a teaching body whose authority is exercised in the name of Jesus Christ to safeguard and give an authentic interpretation of this deposit of faith.[1] Private revelation, on the other hand, pertains to subsequent, post-Scriptural revelations given to Christians throughout Church history after the death of the last Apostle. These types of revelations can include various forms of spiritual communications, such as visionary experiences, apparitions, locutions, or prophecies that Christians have experienced after the Apostolic Period. While Christians have reported experiencing private revelations throughout the Church's history, it is only in the eighteenth century that a systematic treatment of the topic was undertaken by Pope Benedict XIV (1740–1758) with his five-volume work *De Servorum Dei Beatificatione et de Beatorum Canonizatione*. Benedict wrote this definitive study of private revelation before assuming the papacy, while he was still known as Cardinal Prospero Lambertini.[2] It is from this work that much of the Church's theological teaching about private revelations owes its depth.

While having their own purpose in strengthening and renewing Christian faith, believing in private revelations is not required for salvation—meaning that the Catholic faithful are not bound to believe in them even if they are authentic. Benedict articulated an important distinction about the levels of assent that the Catholic faithful need to give to revelations. He explained that a private revelation should be given the assent of human faith (*fides humana*) whereas public revelation needs be given the assent of catholic faith (*fides catholica*). In Catholic ecclesiology, the first level of assent, that of human faith, means that Catholics are *not required* to believe in these revelations, even if they are supernaturally authentic and thus approved by the Church as worthy of belief—as all that is necessary for one's salvation (and, therefore, necessary for personal belief) is already contained within public revelation. However, Catholics do have the option to believe in private revelations because Church-approved revelations are recognized as piously believable and therefore as probable in their divine origin. Benedict explains that even revelations that have received Church approval—identifying the revelations of Saint Catherine of Siena, Saint Bridget, and Hildegard of Bingen— "cannot receive from us any assent of Catholic, but only of human faith, which the aforesaid revelations are probable, and piously to be believed."[3]

The other level of assent, the assent of catholic faith, means that Catholics *are required to believe* in this revelation (public revelation), as it constitutes the origins of the faith and the totality (in its doctrines and teachings) of what is necessary to gain salvation. Benedict, in contrasting the authority of public and private revelations, underscores that the former come from divine testimony while the latter from human testimony.[4] This does not mean that private revelations lack authority, but it does distinguish degrees of authority and the corresponding assent that should be offered to that authority. Private revelations, as offered to so many saints, are *probable*, Benedict makes clear, and thus believable; however, they do not possess the same degree of moral certainty and foundational stature that commands the assent of catholic faith as public revelation does.[5]

What is implicit here is the reality that private revelations, although having their purpose in renewing faith and inspiring a deeper Gospel life, do not add anything new to the Church's doctrines. However, it would be an error—although, granted that a number of interpreters have made this mistake—of painting too dichotomous a picture between public revelation and private revelations. To say that one (public) does not need the other (private) is to ignore the multilayered dynamic of the relationship between these forms of divine revelation.

Pope John XXIII, in an address delivered in February 1959 at the close of the celebration marking the hundredth anniversary of the Marian apparitions of Lourdes, urged the faithful to "listen with simplicity of heart and sincerity of mind to the salutary warnings of the Mother of God"; and, he noted, that if popes "are instituted the guardians and interpreters of divine Revelation, contained in Holy Scripture and Tradition, they also take it as their duty to recommend to the attention of the faithful—when, after responsible examination, they judge it for the common good—the supernatural lights [i.e., private revelations] which it has pleased God to dispense freely to certain privileged souls, not for proposing new doctrines, but to guide us in our conduct."[6] While it is objectively true, in accordance with Roman Catholic orthodoxy, that the teachings of public revelation are enough to guarantee salvation, it is also true that private revelations have their purpose in inspiring and guiding souls toward living more fully the Gospel truths as constituted in public revelation, in the deposit of faith of the Church. Often this is seen in how the message of a private revelation may convey and accentuate a Gospel truth that has always been present but whose emphasis has been lost or overshadowed during a certain period in Church history; thus, the private revelation can help strengthen and revive that truth. A great example of this reality transpired in the early twentieth century in Poland.

Sister Faustina Kowalska[7] (1905–1938) was a Polish nun and mystic living in a convent in Warsaw before the outbreak of World War II. It was in the 1930s that she reported experiencing private revelations: locutions and visions of Jesus Christ, claiming to hear his voice and on a number occasions to see him. She recorded her experiences in writing by keeping a spiritual diary. Historian Steven Fanning explains how diverse Sister Faustina's private revelations were: "Faustina's diary reveals her almost constant contact and communication with the world of the divine." As examples of this mystical life, Fanning elaborates: "Normally she heard the voice of Jesus speaking to her but she also frequently discerned the presence of the three persons in the Trinity within her. The Virgin Mary came to her often both as a voice and in visions, as did other saints and angels, especially St. Michael."[8] According to her visions, Christ was calling Faustina to become the "Apostle of Mercy" by, as George Weigel explains, renewing "Catholic devotion to God's mercy, which in turn would lead to a general renewal of Catholic spiritual life."[9] The message of mercy is prominent in the Gospel teachings of Jesus; however, it is also a message whose vitality, in certain historical stages, has been downplayed or lost in favor of an emphasis on judgment. Thus, the mission of Faustina, as conveyed by her private revelations, was intended to renew an essential message contained within public revelation.

Private Revelations and the Development of Doctrine

Another element of private revelations that is important to understand is that, while such revelations cannot add or change doctrine, they can contribute to the Church's *development of doctrine*. Faustina's revelations especially have had such an influence. Throughout her diary, Faustina recorded Jesus telling her that he wanted the Sunday after Easter to be declared "Divine Mercy Sunday," meaning to be recognized as a new liturgical feast day that celebrated God's infinite mercy and allowed special indulgences to be granted to the faithful who would partake in the spiritual practices associated with the feast. Furthermore, Faustina reported that Jesus taught her a new prayer, known as the Divine Mercy Chaplet, which was to be recited on rosary beads each day at three o'clock. The hour is recognized as the hour when Jesus died on the cross, and thus in the

Divine Mercy devotion it is known as the "Hour of Mercy." God, according to Faustina, promised great graces when the chaplet would be prayed faithfully. In her diary, Faustina reports that God the Father himself spoke to her about the chaplet:

> When I entered my solitude, I heard these words: "At the hour of their death, I defend as My own glory every soul that will say this chaplet; or when others say it for a dying person, the pardon is the same. When this chaplet is said by the bedside of a dying person, God's anger is placated, unfathomable mercy envelops the soul, and the very depths of My tender mercy are moved for the sake of the sorrowful Passion of My Son."[10]

Faustina was further given a very visual and symbolic apparition during one of her special visionary experiences that asked her to have the image, which she is being shown, painted and promulgated as a devotional symbol. It was on the evening of February 22, 1931, that she received the mission to become the Apostle of Mercy. On that evening in her cell she reported to see Jesus "clothed in a white garment":

> One hand (was) raised in the gesture of blessing, the other was touching the garment at the breast. From beneath the garment, slightly drawn aside at the breast, there were emanating two large rays, one red, the other pale. In silence I kept my gaze fixed on the Lord; my soul was struck with awe, but also with great joy. After a while, Jesus said to me: "Paint an image according to the pattern you see, with the signature: Jesus, I trust in You. I desire that this image be venerated, first in your chapel and (then) throughout the world."[11]

Jesus would speak to Faustina during this visionary experience, explaining that the soul who venerates this image would have the promise of victory over enemies on earth and especially at the hour of death, telling Faustina, "I Myself will defend it as My own glory."[12] Faustina's description of this vision has been painted into a popular artistic portrayal of Jesus known as the "Divine Mercy Image," an image that is venerated today throughout the world.

Pope John Paul II, who as a fellow Polish countryman was aware of Sister Faustina's revelations long before they gained international recognition in the Church, was greatly influenced by the spirituality of the Divine Mercy revelations. As pope, he made sure that the spiritual and liturgical requests that Faustina claimed God was asking of her would come to be, honoring the devotions with his pontifical activities. "John Paul has pushed no devotion further or faster," Vatican journalist John Allen Jr. explained, than the devotions stemming from Faustina's revelations:

> His second encyclical, 1980's *Dives in Misericordia*, was inspired by Faustina. He beatified her in 1993, and canonized her in April 2000 as the first saint of the third Christian millennium. He approved a special Divine Mercy Mass for the Sunday after Easter in 1994, and celebrated it himself in St. Peter's Square before a crowd of 200,000 in April 2001. He assigned the Church of the Holy Spirit in Sassia in Rome as a headquarters for the Divine Mercy movement in 1994, and just this month approved a special indulgence for taking part in Divine Mercy Sunday.[13]

Here we have a perfect illustration of how a visionary's private revelations can influence the development of doctrine, to the point of affecting the Church's liturgical life. Another significant account of such an influence stems from France.

In the nineteenth century, a French sister would report to experience a set of Marian apparitions that would inspire one of the most popular devotions in worldwide Catholicism, as well as the papal definition of an eminent Marian dogma. On November 27, 1830, Sister Catherine Labouré (1802–1876), who belonged to the Daughters of Charity, the congregation founded by Saint Vincent de Paul, reported experiencing a special Marian apparition in the sanctuary of the chapel of her convent at Rue du Bac. She reported seeing the Virgin Mary in front of her, standing on a globe, and beneath Mary's feet, the apparition was crushing a serpent. The Madonna's hands were outstretched with rays of light streaming forth from each hand, in symbolism of the graces that come from Christ through Mary's intercession. Around this vision of Mary, Catherine saw a written prayer: "O Mary, conceived without sin, pray for us who have recourse to thee." This image and prayer, which eventually were placed on the front side of the Miraculous Medal, would play an influential role in inspiring Church doctrine.[14]

Similar to Faustina's encounter with Jesus, the apparition of Mary asked Catherine to take the details of the vision she was shown and turn them into a devotional item, this time into a medal. In 1832, the Archbishop of Paris, Monsignor de Quelen, granted permission for the promulgation of the first medals based on Catherine's visionary experiences.[15] Four years later, a Church-led investigation of Catherine's apparitions resulted in a positive conclusion acknowledging the authenticity of her experiences. Only a few years later, in 1842, the Holy See granted official approval for the Miraculous Medal devotion. The devotion became very popular, spreading throughout Europe. The Miraculous Medal has been worn by millions of Christians. The widespread devotion to the medal is believed to have been an inspiration for the declaration of the dogma of the Immaculate Conception, the teaching that Mary was born without original sin. Pope Pius IX would solemnly declare the Immaculate Conception a dogma in 1854 in his papal bull *Ineffabilis Deus*.

Before the pope made it official for Catholics, the theological truth of the Immaculate Conception was stated by Catherine Labouré's apparitional experience decades earlier, as found in the prayer that the French visionary was shown in November 1830: "O Mary, *conceived without sin*, pray for us who have recourse to thee" (emphasis added). This same prayer was placed on the Miraculous Medal devotions, resulting in popular piety to the Immaculate Conception for Catholics throughout the continent. Thus the content of a private revelation was instrumental in influencing the official proclamation of a dogma, understood as the highest form of doctrine in the Catholic Church, as a universal truth that is binding for all believers.

It is important to note that the theological concept of the Immaculate Conception was an idea believed by many Christians throughout the centuries, even before Catherine's time, and even existed as a topic of debate, most famously between the late medieval Dominicans and Franciscans. The Franciscan philosopher and theologian John Duns Scotus (1266–1308) developed the most sophisticated theological defense of the Immaculate Conception against the critiques of the Dominicans, who at the time did not believe in the teaching. This means that when the dogma was officially declared in 1854 it was not a "new idea" that was being recognized; but the papal declaration constituted the official approval, given in its highest form, to an already existing, but still debated, Mariological concept of Christian theology. This is why it is appropriate to acknowledge such a declaration as not a change to Church teaching but as part of the Church's *development of doctrine*, highlighting a continuity in the recognition of a centuries-old belief.

In addition to Catherine Labouré's Marian apparitions inspiring the dogma of the Immaculate Conception, and Faustina's revelations of Jesus leading to the liturgical feast of Divine Mercy Sunday and the popular devotion of the Divine Mercy Chaplet, other private revelations have had significant effects on the Church's liturgical life. The Marian apparitions of Lourdes, experienced by the French peasant girl Bernadette Soubirous (1844–1879), have led to the liturgical memorial of Our Lady of Lourdes to be celebrated by Roman Catholics on February 11th each year. Furthermore, the apparitions of Jesus that the French nun Margaret Mary Alacoque (1647–1690) received and the revelations of Jesus that the German nun Mary of the Divine Heart (1863–1899), countess of Droste zu Vischering, received both led to the spreading of the popular devotion to the Sacred Heart of Jesus within Catholicism. There are various examples of private revelations that, although not changing Church doctrine or teachings, have been responsible for the development of doctrine in Catholicism, the emergence of popular devotions, and the renewal of forms of spirituality central to the Gospel life. This speaks to a vibrant dynamic that is present between private revelations and their relation to public revelation in ecclesial life.[16]

Official Norms for Evaluating Apparitions or Revelations

In November 1974, under the papacy of Pope Paul VI, the Congregation for the Doctrine of the Faith (CDF) held an annual plenary session during which members discussed the matter of alleged apparitions and the revelations (or messages) often associated with them. The CDF was pursuing this work in order to issue official Church guidelines and principles that could assist the proper authorities in evaluating claims of private revelations. It was under Francis Cardinal Šeper, then the prefect of the Congregation, that on February 24, 1978, the CDF issued the "Norms Regarding the Manner of Proceeding in the Discernment of Presumed Apparitions or Revelations."[17]

Initially known as *Normae S. Congregationis*, this was a unique Church document in the sense that, unlike most Church documents and decrees, it was not published in the *Acta Apostolicae Sedis*, the Holy See's official archival journal. In an interview, Cardinal Angelo Amato, the prefect of the Congregation for the Causes of Saints, explained that *Normae S. Congregationis* "is a document that was sent to all diocesan bishops

and religious superiors. But it is true that it has never been officially published, or in *Acta Apostolicae Sedis*."[18] Though Cardinal Amato did not
elaborate why this was the case, from the document itself, which stresses
that the local bishop is the first authority to judge a report of private revelation, the answer can be deduced: it is a private document intended, first
and foremost, for bishops partaking in ecclesial investigation of reported
mystical phenomena. It was thirty-three years later, under Pope Benedict
XVI, that on December 14, 2011, the Vatican made the Norms publicly
available, beyond treating it as an "in-house" document solely for the eyes
of bishops.

Mark Miravalle who, in addition to working academically as a
Mariologist, has assisted the Catholic Church in investigating reports of
private revelations, particularly Marian apparitions, explains how the process of investigation works. Miravalle notes that when a local bishop deals
with a report of private revelation and, based on preliminary indications
that point to potential authenticity, thinks that the revelation is worthy of
further investigation, the bishop would contact the CDF. At that point,
the congregation would "typically sent the norms for evaluation, and the
Vatican confirmation that he [the bishop] is to be the first ecclesiastical
judge of authenticity and any potential approval of devotion stemming
from the revelation"[19] Thus before the Norms were made publicly available the Vatican would produce the document specifically when a bishop—
therefore, the proper authority—made the request in light of a private
revelation claim in his diocese that was worthy of further examination.
What happened afterward?

After receiving the CDF Norms, the bishop usually proceeds toward
forming an investigative commission. "This commission will normally
study theological, spiritual, historical, psychological, medical, and scientific elements of the reported revelation."[20] Consequently, such a commission brings together the work of theologians, experienced spiritual
directors, psychologists, and doctors to establish a systematic and professional investigation of the claimed supernatural phenomenon.[21] After the
commission performs all its investigations in examining the purported
visionaries and their revelations, a final report and recommendation is
given to the bishop, but the report is only advisory in nature—since, as the
Norms explain, the bishop is ultimately the exclusive judge of discerning
the phenomenon on the local (diocese) level. If the bishop decides to make
a public declaration on the reported revelation, he will articulate his judgment using one of three categories:

1. *Constat de supernaturalitate*—a declaration affirming the supernatural origins of the revelation.
2. *Non constat de supernaturalitate*—a declaration stating that the revelation has not been established as supernatural, nor has it been determined to be false.
3. *Constat de non supernaturalitate*—a declaration stating that the *reported* revelation has been declared not to be of a supernatural origin.[22]

The first declaration affirms the authenticity of the reported phenomenon and is, therefore, seen as an ecclesial seal of approval for Catholic devotions at the site of the private revelation. The second declaration allows for further examinations to continue since the investigation has not reached a conclusive decision. The third declaration is often accompanied by prohibitions from Church authorities concerning any further promulgation of the messages or devotions connected to the condemned revelation.

Let us now examine the content of the CDF Norms and consider what the exact criteria are that Church authorities look for in discerning the authenticity, or lack thereof, of a claim reporting supernatural experiences.

First Criterion of Discernment: The Visionary

The first criterion of discernment is primarily oriented around the behavior and activities, spiritual, moral, and psychological, of the alleged visionary who reports a supernatural experience—"in particular mental balance, honesty and rectitude of moral life, habitual sincerity and docility towards ecclesiastical authority, ability to return to the normal manner of a life of faith, etc."[23] Thus what is stressed here, in addition to the spiritual, moral, and psychological dimensions, is also respectful compliance toward Church authority. The Church is trying to evaluate whether the reported revelation has had a positive influence on the visionary's life and whether the purported visionary is not simply someone looking for attention or trying to deceive with his or her claims. Thus, as negative criteria, the CDF Norms list any evidence "of a search for profit or gain" that is strictly connected to the reported revelation as casting doubt on the claim. "Gravely immoral acts" are also emphasized as a negative criterion to watch out for, whether committed by the purported visionary or "his or her followers" when the claimed revelation was said to occur or in connection to it.[24] The visionary also needs to be properly evaluated for any psychological disorder "or psychopathic tendencies," which if present would cast doubt on the supernatural character of the reported claim. In this regard, the Norms list psychosis, collective hysteria, "or other things of this kind" as pathological possibilities.[25] Therefore, in evaluating negative criteria, psychological and pathological explanations must be considered as possible alternative explanations for the reported revelation.

In short, what is evaluated in regard to the alleged visionary is the individual's faith and moral life, the presence of sincerity and docility toward Church authorities, and the mental health and psychological stability of the alleged visionary. All of these criteria are meant to discern two aspects: (1) whether the reported private revelation is having a good influence on the visionary's life; and (2) whether there are any signs in the visionary's personality or behavior indicating fraud or pathology that could undermine the authenticity of the reported revelation. In considering the first aspect, which speaks to the moral and faith life of the visionary, it is necessary to note an important distinction: an authentic visionary is not judged negatively on the basis of whether he or she had a sinful or immoral life *before* experiencing the private revelation; again, what the Church looks at is the effect that the revelation has had on the visionary's life; therefore, it's the matter of what becomes of the visionary's moral and spiritual life *after* experiencing the revelation.

Second Criterion of Discernment: The Theological Content of the Revelation

The second positive criterion that the CDF Norms list is specifically concerned with the revelation communicated by the apparition or locution— that is, the content of the message. Regarding the content of the revelation, Church authorities look for "true theological and spiritual doctrine" that is "immune from error."[26] The Norms name what kinds of errors Church authorities should watch for when investigating a private revelation claim while acknowledging, at the same time, the nuance that even a genuine supernatural revelation can have errors associated with it because of human error in understanding or in communicating the message. Therefore, investigators should look for:

> Doctrinal errors attributed to God himself, or to the Blessed Virgin Mary, or to some saint in their manifestations, taking into account however the possibility that the subject might have added, even unconsciously, purely human elements or some error of the natural

order to an authentic supernatural revelation (cf. Saint Ignatius, *Exercises*, no. 336).[27]

The first part of this passage, referring to alleged visionaries attributing erroneous teachings to God and other sacred figures, is self-explanatory as to why that would be an issue to look for in discerning problems with reported revelations. This speaks, again, to the reciprocal relationship between public and private revelation. In this case, for the Church it is important to examine whether the messages of private revelations are in line with the truths of the teachings of public revelation, with the Church's deposit of faith. The second part of this passage, which takes as its source the principles of spiritual discernment that the sixteenth-century Spanish saint, and founder of the Jesuits, Ignatius of Loyola articulated in his classic work *The Spiritual Exercises*, deserves further comment and explanation.

The section from Ignatius's work that the Norms cite comes from his chapter on "Rules for the Discernment of Spirits." This chapter pertains to guided principles in understanding the inner workings of the spiritual life in regard to the spiritual consolations and desolations that the soul receives, and comments on the importance of distinguishing the sources of such movements of the soul within the second week of the Ignatian retreat; that is, Ignatius's *Spiritual Exercises* were used as a retreat manual to guide persons making, traditionally, a four-week spiritual retreat—a method used for centuries, and continuing to the present-day, by Jesuits. In the section that the Norms reference, paragraph 336, Ignatius writes about the possibility of a person wrongly attributing plans and resolutions that the human mind, or even an evil spirit, has constructed to a divine source. This can happen, Ignatius explains, because of previously experienced consolations that did come from God and whose aftereffects, especially the fervor and positive feelings associated with those aftereffects, are mistaken as God's continued consolation, which has in fact passed. Therefore, the human mind, as well as the presence of the demonic, can also influence thoughts that a person *believes* to be from God.[28] Ignatius thus speaks to the subtleties and nuances that need to be distinguished and discerned so as to make proper spiritual judgments.

Such subtleties and nuances have been developed in important twentieth-century scholarship on the topic, particularly through the work of the French Jesuit Augustin Poulain, S.J., and the American Franciscan Benedict Groeschel, C.F.R. Poulain authored a classic treatise on mystical theology titled *The Graces of Interior Prayer*, originally published in French in 1901 and translated into English in 1910.[29] This large volume deals with a wide range of subjects associated with mystical phenomena, including discerning how an authentic revelation can still be linked to mistakes. Groeschel authored the much smaller, but deeply informative study that has in its own right become a classic on private revelations, titled *A Still, Small Voice: A Practical Guide on Reported Revelations*, published in 1993.[30] These works are connected, as Groeschel relies heavily on Poulain's work to form his approach.

Groeschel lists the various factors that can lead even authentic revelations to contain errors. In this list he is relying on Poulain's criteria. These include:

1. Faulty interpretation on the part of the recipient or others;
2. A tendency to use a revelation to write history rather than use it symbolically;
3. The tendency of the visionary to mix subjective expectations and preconceived ideas with the action of divine grace;
4. A subsequent altering or amplification of the testimony after the revelation;
5. Errors made in good faith by those who record the testimony.[31]

Let us consider the nuances of this list in detail, starting with the first criterion.

1. *Faulty Interpretation by Recipient or Others.* All of these criteria make clear that when errors happen in an authentic revelation, it is *not* because of the apparition or the content of the revelation—which is genuine but can become distorted—but through mistakes in reception, transmission, and interpretation of the message by the visionary or by those to whom the visionary has communicated the message. Thus it is human weakness that is involved in terms of distorting, most often without any ill intent, the message that is conveyed. This is especially the case when the visionary experience is a corporal or imaginative vision, two types of visionary experiences that we will discuss in detail later in the following chapter, wherein the human senses are highly involved in receiving and filtering the message of the revelation that can lead to error in interpretation and understanding. This is what the first criterion by Poulain and Groeschel indicates in highlighting the possibility of a faulty interpretation by the

recipient or by others to whom the content of the message has been conveyed.

2. *Using a Revelation to Write History and Ignoring Symbolic Interpretation.* The second criterion that they list, the tendency to use a revelation to write history rather than understanding it symbolically, pertains especially to the revelations of certain mystics who have said that the historical life of Jesus—and often Mary too, as existing in first-century Palestine—has been revealed to them in a series of visions and dictations. Such revelations have been transcribed into multivolume works, prominent examples in this genre including the revelations of the Spanish mystic Maria of Agreda (1602–1665), the German nun and stigmatic Anne Catherine Emmerich (1774–1824), and the Italian mystic Maria Valtorta (1897–1961). Some of these revelations have been impressive especially for the knowledge that they contain—for example, scholars who have studied Valtorta's multivolume work depicting the life of Jesus note how she accurately identifies and describes Palestinian locations that were obscure or unknown during her years of writing, in the mid-twentieth century, but authenticated decades later, after Valtorta's death, by subsequent discoveries as in fact existing in first-century Palestine.[32]

However, a problem lies in the fact that revelations that have been reported by such mystics have contained inconsistencies between their individual accounts, meaning that there are important discrepancies between the historical accounts that Maria of Agreda, Anne Catherine Emmerich, and Maria Valtorta have claimed to receive from their visionary experiences. Groeschel suggests that Emmerich "perhaps summed it all up very well in her critique of Maria of Agreda when she said that this Spanish visionary had taken her visions too literally and should have understood them allegorically and spiritually."[33] Hence this is what is meant by the second criterion for discerning mistakes—certain mystics misinterpreting their revelations as historical accounts rather than comprehending a symbolic meaning that is being conveyed.

3. *Expectations and Preconceptions Mixed with Workings of Grace.* The third criterion, the tendency of a visionary to mix his or her subjective expectations and preconceived ideas with the workings of divine grace, can be easily seen in something that transpired in Medjugorje during the early weeks of the apparitions. The visionaries initially believed that their apparitions, instead of continuing for decades to come, would end on July 3, 1981. They held this preconceived expectation because,

in order to understand their experiences, the children read a book on the Marian apparitions in Lourdes and presumed that they would experience the same number of daily apparitions as had Bernadette Soubirous in 1858. Therefore, the crowds of people who gathered for the "last" apparition on July 3 in Medjugorje were under the impression that the Madonna had conveyed to the visionaries that this would be her last appearance, as the seers were so convinced of the fact. The following evening, on July 4, the visionaries no longer met in church in front of a crowd with the expectation of receiving another apparition but, rather, went their separate ways, believing that their life-changing experiences had come to an end. Although each of the seers went his and her separate way, without expecting it each one of them experienced an individual apparition that evening. This was the first time that their apparitions transpired outside the context of the group. Sullivan relates the details:

Vicka was picking flowers with some friends at 6:25 P.M. when she complained that her fingers had gone suddenly numb, then fell to her knees a moment later and began to stare fixedly at a spot just above her head. The Madonna had appeared to her, she told her companions a few minutes later, sounding, they said, at once frightened and joyous. Each of the others made a similar report. Ivan said that he had seen the Virgin while washing up after a day spent helping his family with the tobacco harvest; Marija's apparition had taken place in her bedroom at home in Bijakovici. Mirjana was the most emotional, phoning from Sarajevo to say that the Madonna had come to her during a grueling police interrogation that had lasted from early that morning until well into the night.[34]

It was after this experience, Marija recalled, that, "We realized then that this was not like Lourdes."[35]

4. *The Visionary Altering or Amplifying the Testimony.* The fourth criterion, the altering or amplifying of the testimony after the revelation, refers to mistakes that can come from attempts to remember and record the content of the revelation after it transpired. Groeschel explains that the "recipient of a revelation can forget things, have difficulty putting it all into words, and even select the wrong words to describe what has happened."[36] Two important factors that are involved here include (1) the visionary's experience, most often, is processed through his or

her senses and the memory can, through mistakes in recollection and recording, convey distorted information without any ill intention on the part of the visionary; and (2) the visionary is often reporting on a profoundly sublime experience whose depths are not easy to translate and communicate into human language.

5. *Errors by Those Recording the Testimony.* The fifth criterion, errors made in good faith by those recording the testimony, refers to a dynamic that is present between the visionary and another individual, usually a secretary who may be transcribing the content of the mystical experiences of the seer or recording the content afterward through the testimony of the seer. Poulain explains that such secretaries "may easily alter the text without any wrong intention. For their own personality intervenes in the choice of expressions. They sometimes, with a certain amount of good faith, think that they can add whole sentences under pretext of making the thought clear."[37] In addition to such motives, Groeschel notes that what can also alter the testimony is the possibility of "open falsification done for pious motives."[38] Poulain provides examples of such instances. There is the example of the first German edition of Anne Catherine Emmerich's revelations, which included a sentence that states that Saint James the Greater was present at the Virgin Mary's death. The chronology of this detail, however, contradicts the testimony of the Acts of the Apostles, as present in the New Testament. Thus it is an example wherein content within a private revelation is contradicting the knowledge of public revelation, posing a problem. Because of this problematic fact, Poulain points out that in at least one later edition of Emmerich's revelations, "the erroneous phrase has simply been effaced."[39] Poulain is highly critical of such redaction by the editors, calling the approach "deplorable, for it robs the serious reader of a means of forming his opinions." He explains that the issue could have been easily remedied regarding the problematic sentence. "The sentence should have been retained, adding a note saying: the Sister was mistaken here."[40]

ALL FIVE CONDITIONS, explaining the possibilities of how an authentic revelation can be associated with error, make clear how multilayered and nuanced the process of discernment can be under the second major criterion of the CDF Norms in evaluating the theological content of the revelation.

Third Criterion of Discernment: Spiritual Fruit and Healthy Devotion

The final major criterion that the CDF Norms list in investigating a private revelation is the cultivation of healthy devotion at the site of the phenomenon and constant spiritual fruit that results from the event. The foundations of the teaching on spiritual fruit comes directly from the Gospel message of Jesus, which articulates that a tree is known by its fruit:

> Beware of false prophets, who come to you in sheep's clothing, but inwardly they are ravenous wolves. You will know them by their fruits. Do men gather grapes from thornbushes or figs from thistles? Even so, every good tree bears good fruit, but a bad tree bears bad fruit. A good tree cannot bear bad fruit, nor can a bad tree bear good fruit. Every tree that does not bear good fruit is cut down and thrown into the fire. Therefore by their fruits you will know them. (Matt. 7:15–20, NKJV)

The Norms list a spirit of prayer, conversion, and "testimonies of charity" as examples of spiritual fruit to look for. Also important to note is the wording here: the fact that reference is made in the document to *constant* spiritual fruit. Constancy is key, as even a case of a false revelation can inspire a call to such things like prayer and conversion *temporarily*, but if the reported revelation does not have divine origins, then those fruit will not last. Miravalle lists some of the fundamentals that the Church looks for: "Significant increases in prayer, conversion, sacramental confession, Christian charity, and the return to the overall prayer and sacramental life of the Church should be evidenced and should perdure in abundance when the reported apparitions are of supernatural origin."[41] Unlike the previous criteria that looked at what effect the revelation is having on the visionary, the focus here is more extensive, concentrating on the masses who are affected by the occurrence, both people in the surrounding area and pilgrims who may come from all corners of the world, especially if the apparition site attains a high level of popularity. This is why the CDF Norms emphasize testimonies, as often it is the testimonies of pilgrims that can speak volumes for discerning the possibility of divine origins at a reported apparition site.

Miravalle also names another common component of private revelations to look for: concurring phenomena. Concurring phenomena can include miraculous healings transpiring at the site of the apparition or even such unique phenomena like solar miracles, such as the famous miracle of the dancing sun in Fátima, Portugal, where an estimated 70,000 people reported witnessing extraordinary solar activity at the conclusion of the final apparition on October 13, 1917.[42] However, concurring phenomena like miracles and healings—although able to add to the testimony of God's presence (cf. Heb. 2:4) at the site—are not required as evidence of the divine origin of the revelation, as foremost the Church looks for spiritual fruit such as conversion, prayer, reconciliation, and charity.

Testing the Religious Ecstasy

Although it is not specified in the CDF Norms, another common way that Church investigators examine the authenticity of apparition claims is by testing the ecstasy that the seers enter during their visionary experiences. This is the area where scientific technologies, such as EEG brain tests or EKG heart examinations, both of which have been applied onto the Medjugorje visionaries, can be used to measure ecstatic states during apparitions. "It is generally agreed that at least some form of ecstasy, whereby the subject is partially suspended from their own time-space reality or from full external sense operation, is a normative characteristic when receiving external or sensible apparitions."[43] Today there are empirical ways to measure the interior dimensions of such unique states.

Intervention of Competent Church Authorities

The final sections of the CDF Norms, sections II–IV, all deal with the intervention of the proper Church authorities in investigating private revelation claims. It is explained, in section II, that the "competent Ecclesiastical Authority" can, if the five criteria have been met, promote some form of devotion at the apparition site. Interestingly, the document insists that the faithful be careful not to interpret such an action as approval of the supernatural origins of the apparition on behalf of the Church. Thus here an important pastoral point is being made: devotions at an apparition site can exist even if the Church has not reached a final decision on the supernatural character of the phenomenon reported at the site. Conversely, this section also states that the "competent Authority" can intervene in grave circumstances "to correct or prevent abuses in the exercise of cult and devotion, to condemn erroneous doctrine, to avoid the dangers of a false or unseemly mysticism, etc."[44]

The following section outlines the order of jurisdiction in terms of which Church authorities can intervene in an investigation. First and foremost, responsibility for an investigation is given to "the Ordinary of the place," meaning the bishop in whose diocese the private revelation is reported to be occurring. However, a regional or national Conference of Bishops can intervene in an investigation if circumstances call for such an intervention. Two circumstances that are listed for such intervention include (1) the bishop, having done his part in the investigation, turns to the Conference of Bishops "to judge the matter with greater certainty"; and (2) the matter may concern the regional or national level, alluding to the popularity that an apparition site can attain. At the same time, it is qualified that for such an intervention of a Conference of Bishops to take place, the prior consent of the local bishop is necessary, speaking to a level of collegiality. Finally, the Apostolic See, meaning the Vatican, can as the highest body of authority intervene in investigating an apparition claim. This may be done at the request of the bishop, or "by a qualified group of the faithful," or even more directly by the universal jurisdiction of the pope himself.[45] The document does not explain what is meant by a "qualified group of the faithful," but it is clear that in order for the Vatican to intervene, the permission of the bishop is no longer necessary, as such a qualified group can request the intervention or the pope himself can authorize it.

The final section of the Norms speak about the intervention of the Congregation for the Doctrine of the Faith (CDF), again specifying that a qualified group of the faithful or the bishop have the right to request such intervention while also allowing for the Congregation to intervene by its own authority. The Congregation is also given the authority to judge the investigations of a bishop and, if necessary, initiate new examinations independent of the bishop to be carried out either by the Congregation or by a special commission. This is exactly what has happened in the case of Medjugorje. Let us turn to this example by considering a brief examination of Medjugorje's current status within the Church.

Medjugorje and the Church

The story of six Croatian children who began receiving apparitions of the Virgin Mary in 1981 has gripped many people. Medjugorje has become a global phenomenon, a site visited by millions of pilgrims worldwide. Author Elizabeth Ficocelli explains that it "is estimated that since the events were first reported in 1981, more than 20 million people from around the world have traveled to this obscure village," even during the bloody wars of the former Yugoslavia in the early 1990s.[46] The global attention that Medjugorje has received by the faithful has led the Catholic Church to examine and investigate the credibility of the apparitions. In this regard, there has been much controversy surrounding Medjugorje, as the apparition site has gained both influential supporters and detractors within the Church. Some of the most influential supporters of the apparitions include the late pope John Paul II, Mother Teresa of Calcutta, the Archbishop of Vienna Christoph Cardinal Schönborn, who has hosted Medjugorje visionaries at his cathedral St. Stephen's to share their testimonies and apparitions, and even giants of the Catholic scholarly world, such as the Swiss theologian Hans Urs von Balthasar and the French Mariologist René Laurentin, among other Church leaders. Some of the most significant and influential critics of the apparitions included Bishop Pavao Žanić, the late bishop of Mostar, the diocese within which Medjugorje is located, and his successor, Bishop Ratko Perić.

The historian Robert A. Orsi notes that "Our Lady of Medjugorje attracted a vast international following that included many members of the Catholic hierarchy, among them Pope John Paul II."[47] After his death in 2005, John Paul II's lifelong friends Marek and Zofia Skwarnicki made available letters that he wrote to them in Polish, which positively mentioned Medjugorje.[48] In one letter, John Paul II directly referenced the presence of the Virgin Mary in Medjugorje, alleviating ambiguity about his personal conviction on the topic.[49] Moreover, Monsignor Slawomir Oder, the Judicial Vicar of the Appellate Tribunal of the Vicariate of Rome, as well as the postulator for the beatification and canonization of John Paul II, dedicated a section in his book *Why He Is a Saint* to examining John Paul II's devotion to the apparitions in Medjugorje, as well as mentioning the details of a personal meeting that the pope held with visionary Mirjana Dragičević-Soldo.[50]

It was in July of 1987 that Mirjana met with John Paul II. Addressing a group of pilgrims, Mirjana shared the details of her encounter with the late pope, which began as a general audience at St. Peter's Basilica in Rome. However, after John Paul II found out who, among the pilgrims in the audience, Mirjana was, as one of the Medjugorje visionaries, he extended an invitation for a private meeting at the pope's residence at Castel Gandolfo. Mirjana recalled:

> However, in the afternoon we received an invitation tomorrow morning to come to Castel Gandolfo, close to Rome in order to talk to [the] Holy Father. I don't have to tell you that I couldn't sleep all night. Tomorrow when I reached the place, he saw that I was so excited. We were alone and then he started talking to me in Polish. He thought I would understand because both [Polish and Croatian] are Slavic languages. He wanted to make me feel comfortable but I didn't understand a word because it's not even close to our language. However, I was crying and I couldn't catch a breath to say a word. So when I finally succeeded to say a word, I said "Holy Father, can we try in Italian?" Then we talked and among other things he said to me, "If I were not Pope, I would be in Medjugorje a long time ago. I know everything, I have been following everything. Ask pilgrims to pray for my intentions. And take good care of Medjugorje because Medjugorje is the hope for the entire world."[51]

Fr. Jozo Zovko, O.F.M., the pastor of St. James Church at Medjugorje when the apparitions began, first met with John Paul II during a visit to Rome that the priest made on June 17, 1992, in the midst of the wars in the former Yugoslavia. During their encounter, John Paul II's words to Fr. Jozo were blunt. "I give you my blessing," the pope said. "Take courage, I am with you. Tell Medjugorje I am with you. Protect Medjugorje. Protect Our Lady's messages!"[52] Journalist Randall Sullivan noted that in the Holy See it was common knowledge that the Polish pope loved Medjugorje, explaining that in Vatican circles John Paul II even acquired the nickname "Protector of Medjugorje."[53]

The protection that John Paul II offered Medjugorje included halting a negative judgment on the apparitions from the bishop of Mostar, Pavao Žanić, whose diocese was responsible for Medjugorje and who formed a commission to investigate the apparitions. Bishop Žanić's history with Medjugorje has been controversial. Beginning as a supporter of the apparitions, Žanić retracted his position and became the most vocal opponent of the phenomenon, often making incendiary and unsubstantiated remarks against the visionaries, the Franciscans of Medjugorje, and eminent Churchmen who supported the apparitions, like the Archbishop of Split Frane Franić and the French Mariologist Fr. René Laurentin.[54] On February

18, 1985, Archbishop Franić sent a letter to Cardinal Joseph Ratzinger in Rome, the future Pope Benedict XVI, who then was the Prefect of the Congregation for the Doctrine of the Faith. He voiced his concerns about how Žanić was handling the situation in Medjugorje and asked for an international commission to be appointed by the Holy See to take over the investigation of the apparitions.[55]

It was in April 1986 that Bishop Žanić went to Rome to submit his commission's findings on Medjugorje. During this trip Žanić received a great shock. Cardinal Ratzinger summoned him to a personal meeting and reportedly chastised the bishop, telling him that he disapproved of his methods of investigation.[56] Furthermore, the Prefect of the CDF ordered Žanić to suspend his negative judgment, dissolve his commission, and place the entire matter of the investigation into the hands of the Holy See. "Before Žanić returned to Mostar, the Congregation for the Doctrine of the Faith announced that it 'freed' the bishop and his commission from further investigative duties and was ordering the Yugoslav Bishops' Conference to appoint a new commission under its direction."[57] In addition to these monumental shifts, not only was Žanić instructed by the Vatican to no longer involve himself in any future investigations of the apparitions but, furthermore, he was instructed to maintain silence about Medjugorje as the Yugoslav Bishops, to whom the responsibility for investigating the apparitions was handed, pursued their newly assigned work.[58]

Owing to the outbreak of the catastrophic wars in the former Yugoslavia in the early 1990s, the Episcopal Conference assigned by the Yugoslav Bishops to investigate Medjugorje was never able to finish its work. The Yugoslav Bishops did, however, issue an early declaration (known as "the Zadar Declaration") on the subject in April 1991, which stated:

On the basis of the investigations so far, it cannot be affirmed that one is dealing with supernatural apparitions and revelations.

However, the numerous gatherings of the great numbers of the faithful from different parts of the world, who are coming to Medjugorje prompted by motives of belief and various other motives, do require attention and pastoral care—in the first place by the Bishop of the diocese and with him also of the other Bishops, so that both in Medjugorje and in everything connected with it a healthy devotion to the Blessed Virgin Mary may be promoted in accordance with the teaching of the Church.

For this purpose the Bishops will issue specially suitable liturgical-pastoral directives. Likewise, through their Commissions they will continue to keep up with and investigate the entire event in Medjugorje.[59]

It is the first line of this declaration that for years had caused the most controversy about what the official Church status is regarding Medjugorje. The greatest controversy has been attached specifically to the words, "On the basis of the investigations so far, it cannot be affirmed that one is dealing with supernatural apparitions and revelations." Medjugorje's critics have interpreted these words as meaning that the reported apparitions are not supernatural. For example, Bishop Žanić's successor in Mostar, Bishop Ratko Perić, who has upheld his predecessor's negative position toward the apparitions, gave a homily in the parish of Medjugorje on June 6, 1993, wherein he invoked the Yugoslavian Bishops' findings to articulate that the apparitions are not supernatural. He explained that the "Commission has declared a **'non constat de supernaturalitate'** [it is established that there is nothing supernatural]."[60] However, Franc Perko, the Archbishop of Belgrade, has challenged this interpretation by Perić, who (according to Perko) is misrepresenting the conclusion of the Yugoslav Bishops' declaration. The archbishop explained:

It is not true that from the document summarized by the bishops at the end of November it expressly follows nothing supernatural is happening in Medjugorje. The bishops wrote: "non constat de supernaturalitate" (supernaturality is not established) and not: "constat de non supernaturalitate" (it is established that there is nothing supernatural). This is an enormous difference. The first formulation does not permit itself to be interpreted in a definitive way; it is open to further developments.[61]

According to this interpretation, *non constat de supernaturalitate*, the statement of the Yugoslav Bishops announced that it was not possible to declare *yet*, within that phase of their investigation, the supernatural character of the apparitions, but that such a possibility does remain open for future consideration and is not excluded. This interpretation was verified as, indeed, the Church's official position in 1998, when Archbishop Tarcisio Bertone, the secretary to the CDF under Cardinal Joseph Ratzinger, issued these words of clarification in a letter:

What Bishop Peric said in his letter to the Secretary General of "Famille Chretienne," declaring: "My conviction and my position is not only 'non constat de supernaturalitate,' but likewise, 'constat de non supernaturalitate' of the apparitions or revelations in Medjugorje," should be considered the expression of the personal conviction of the Bishop of Mostar which he has the right to express as Ordinary of the place, but which **is and remains his personal opinion.**

Finally, as regards pilgrimages to Medjugorje, which are conducted privately, this Congregation points out that they are permitted on condition that they are not regarded as an authentication of events still taking place and which still call for an examination by the Church.[62]

In addition to Archbishop Bertone's clarification, recent events further confirm the fact that Archbishop Perko was correct in interpreting the Zadar declaration as saying *non constat de supernaturalitate* and, therefore, leaving the case open to future examination instead of conclusively deciding against supernaturality. This is reflected in what transpired on March 17, 2010, when under Benedict XVI's authority the Vatican made an unprecedented announcement about Medjugorje. An international Vatican Commission was formed under the direction of the Congregation for the Doctrine of the Faith to examine the apparitions in Medjugorje. This was a historic commission, as this was the first time in the Church's two-thousand-year history that the judgment of an apparition site was taken away from the diocesan and national levels and would be decided at the highest level by the Vatican itself.[63]

It was announced that the international commission would be led by Cardinal Camillo Ruini, who for many years was a close associate of John Paul II. Under John Paul II's papacy, Cardinal Ruini served as the Vicar General of the Diocese of Rome and the secretary-general of the Italian Bishops' Conference. Alongside Cardinal Ruini, the international commission employed a number of bishops, cardinals, and academic experts to study the events in Medjugorje; these included experts in spirituality, Mariology, theology, psychology, psychiatry, and psychoanalysis.

There is evidence that suggests the decision for an international commission to examine Medjugorje came from the highest level of power— from Pope Benedict XVI himself. Archbishop Allessandro D'Errico, Apostolic Nuncio to Bosnia and Herzegovina, has testified to this reality, releasing a statement on March 18, 2010, the day after the new commission was announced, in which he expounded on the reasons why Benedict decided to form the new commission:

> Whenever I would meet the Holy Father, he was always very much interested in Medjugorje. He was involved in everything, starting with the time when he was Head of the Congregation for the Doctrine of the Faith. He is aware that this is the issue of special importance, and he, as supreme authority of the Church, needs to give his precise statement about that matter. The Holy Father is very much familiar with [the] Medjugorje phenomenon; he even mentioned that to me personally. He is aware of a huge amount of positive and good influence of local priests, religious, Franciscans, lay people, and therefore, it is very difficult for him to perceive that there can be so many opposing information about the same matter. That is why he wanted to establish this Commission that is on really high level.[64]

Papal opinions have differed greatly regarding Medjugorje. While Pope John Paul II was an enthusiastic supporter of the events in Medjugorje, and while his successor Pope Benedict XVI did much to give Medjugorje a fair hearing, Pope Francis has expressed skepticism toward the apparitions. In an interview he gave to journalists while flying back from Fátima, Portugal, in May 2017, where he canonized two of the Marian visionaries of Fátima, Pope Francis spoke negatively, even sarcastically, about the apparitions in Medjugorje. "I prefer the Virgin Mary as a mother, our mother, not as head of a post office that sends a message every day at a specific time, this is not the mother of Jesus. And these alleged appearances do not have much value. This I say as personal opinion." Francis did, however, acknowledge that great spiritual fruits have come from Medjugorje, explaining in the same interview that there "are people who go there and convert, people that find God, whose lives change. And this is not thanks to a magic wand, this is a spiritual and pastoral fact that cannot be denied."[65] For that very reason, just a couple months earlier, on February 11, Francis appointed the Polish archbishop Henryk Hoser, the Bishop of Warszawa-Praga, as a special envoy of the Holy See to Medjugorje. The point of Archbishop Hoser's work, it was announced, was not to pass judgment on the apparitions but to study the pastoral situation in Medjugorje, evaluating how to best care for the millions of pilgrims coming to Medjugorje.

Seven years after Pope Benedict formed the international Vatican Commission to investigate the apparitions, and a day after Pope Francis's negative opinion was reported, the Vatican officially announced the findings of the international commission, on May 16, 2017. The Vatican Commission voted 13 to 1 that the Virgin Mary appeared in Medjugorje in 1981. Specifically, thirteen members voted in favor of recognizing the supernatural nature of the first seven apparitions, which took place between June 24 and July 3, 1981. The commission members expressed more ambiguity regarding the current, ongoing apparitions, noting that the apparitions continue to the present day whereas as youngsters the visionaries believed they would end in 1981. The commission also took note of realities such as conflicts between the Franciscans of Medjugorje and the local bishop, the seemingly apocalyptic nature of the secrets associated with Medjugorje, and the spiritual fruit coming from the apparition site. Taking into consideration these various elements, the commission made a distinction between the early apparitions (which were viewed favorably) and the current apparitions (which are viewed with more ambiguity and mixed opinions).[66]

The commission also made pastoral endorsements, recommending that Medjugorje receive the status of a "pontifical shrine" and that the ban on public pilgrimages to Medjugorje be lifted. Previously, as Archbishop Bertone's 1998 letter on behalf of the CDF clarified, only private pilgrimages to Medjugorje were allowed on the condition that they were not perceived as authentication of the events in Medjugorje, since the Church needed to continue its investigations. With the conclusion of the Vatican Commission's investigation, the supernatural nature of the early apparitions has, for the first time, been recognized, opening the door to the possibility of making Medjugorje an official shrine and of lifting the ban on public pilgrimages—were the pastoral recommendations of the Vatican Commission to be implemented.

3

Mysticism in the Twentieth Century

*I did not know where I was: I did not know whether I was
Alphonse or another. I only felt myself changed and believed
myself another me; I looked for myself in myself and did
not find myself. In the bottom of my soul I felt an explosion
of the most ardent joy; I could not speak; I had no wish to
reveal what had happened. But I felt something solemn
and sacred within me which made me ask for a priest. . . .
All that I can say is that in an instant the bandage had
fallen from my eyes; and not one bandage only, but the
whole manifold of bandages in which I had been brought
up. One after another they disappeared. . . . I came out
as from a sepulcher, from an abyss of darkness; and I was
living, perfectly living. But I wept, for at the bottom of that
gulf I saw the extreme of misery from which I had been
saved by an infinite mercy; and I shuddered at the sight of
my iniquities, stupefied, melted, overwhelmed with wonder
and with gratitude.*

—ALPHONSE RATISBONNE

THE WORD MYSTICAL, from which we derive the vocabulary for concepts like "mysticism," "mystical experiences," "mystical theology," and as a subcategory, "visionary experiences," is a broad, complex, and often ambiguous term whose understanding and definition have been altered, modified, and developed throughout religious history, often dependent on the historical context of its usage. We will explore popular meanings of the word. Let us begin by considering a significant understanding of "mysticism" that was fashioned by one of the most influential thinkers of the twentieth century on the subject.

William James and the Study of Mysticism

It is universally acknowledged by scholars of religious experience, even those who disagree with his hermeneutical approach, that no one had a greater impact on the study of mysticism in the twentieth century than the Harvard psychologist and philosopher William James (1842–1910). James's classic work on the subject is *The Varieties of Religious Experience: A Study in Human Nature.* The book was published in 1902 and was based on his famous Gifford Lectures delivered at the University of Edinburgh.[1] Harvey Egan notes that James's groundbreaking book "has, in fact, influenced to some extent almost every noteworthy contemporary study of mysticism."[2] G. William Barnard explains that James is considered "one of the founding fathers of the academic study of mysticism,"[3] noting that almost "every contemporary scholarly text on mysticism acknowledges James' importance to the field. . . ."[4] The editors of a recent study on Christian mysticism further corroborate the fact, noting: "Without doubt, the father of the modern study of mysticism is William James."[5] The Jesuit scholar William Harmless emphasizes what an eclectic influence James's study has had, explaining that it "helped put mysticism on the academic map, sparking a spate of scholarly studies in psychology and physiology, sociology and history, literature and philosophy. Not all agreed with James's analysis of this or that question, but his study set a clear trajectory in the modern study of mysticism."[6]

James's study of religion was unique for many reasons, perhaps most prominently for the methodological decision that James made to refocus attention away from theology, dogma, doctrine, or any form of institutional religion, and concentrate, instead, on direct experientialism. James did this by concentrating in his lectures not on theological or doctrinal abstractions but on the human person as a "document" of study. The *documents humains,* James called the approach.[7] Concentrating on accounts of extraordinary religious experiences of individual persons, thus the mystical elements of faith, James believed that he was reframing the emphasis onto the truest and most important aspect of religion, essentially the founding principle of all religions: the experience of the transcendent. Ann Taves highlights the widespread influence that resulted from James's methodological emphasis on extraordinary experiences:

> In privileging sudden, discrete authenticating moments of individual experience (such as revelations, visions, and dramatic conversion experiences) over ordinary, everyday experience or the

experience of groups, he introduced a bias toward sudden, individual experience that not only shaped the contemporary Western idea of religious experience but also related concepts such as mysticism and spirituality as well.[8]

Taves's point is important on a few levels. One is her emphasis that James had a significant epistemological influence on the very understanding of the concept "mysticism," as connected directly to individual experience. The word *mysticism* is often interpreted in modern discourse as a term denoting experience, particularly immediate and extraordinary religious experience. This is much different from the various ways that *mysticism* has been interpreted and understood by Christians from early centuries. While the late medieval form of mysticism was closely in line with James's experientialist bent, earlier interpretations of Christian mysticism had more of a liturgical, apophatic, and even exegetical understanding: Origen was the first to use the word—*mystical*—in a Christian context, doing so exegetically in identifying a "mystical sense" of Scriptural interpretation.[9] James's emphasis on unmediated experience played no small role in advancing a modern understanding of the concept.

Expounding on a definition of mysticism, James designated four marks that states of mystical consciousness possess: ineffability, noetic quality, transiency, and passivity.[10] By using the terminology of "mystical consciousness" James was framing the mystical experience as an encounter that includes a state of altered consciousness. In formulating his definition, James acknowledged that the concepts "mysticism" and "mystical" have an ambiguous history, often being used in their contemporary context in a pejorative way; thus, he was aiming for a purer, more useful and constructive definition.

> The words "mysticism" and "mystical" are often used as terms of mere reproach, to throw at any opinion which we regard as vague and vast and sentimental, and without a base in either facts or logic. For some writers a "mystic" is any person who believes in thought-transference, or spirit return. Employed in this way the word has little value: there are too many less ambiguous synonyms. So, to keep it useful by restricting it, I will do what I did in the case of the word "religion," and simply propose to you four marks which, when an experience has them, may justify us in calling it mystical for the present lectures.[11]

Let us consider James' four marks of mysticism with some detail.

James's Four Marks of the Mystical State

Ineffability

"The handiest of the marks by which I classify a state of mind as mystical is negative," James writes.[12] By "negative" James means that the state has an *apophatic* quality. In other words, it defies expression. The mystical experience is so powerful and sublime that it transcends the capacity to be expressed or communicated by language, concepts, logic, or any human faculty. Here, with mysticism, we are not dealing with a subject that is encapsulated by the limitations of reason but encompasses the transcendent elements of revelation. In connection to this James stresses the importance of *understanding*, as being regulated only to the one who has a direct experience. "It follows from this that its [mysticism's] quality must be directly experienced; it cannot be imparted or transferred to others."[13]

James emphasizes that no one "can make clear to another who has never had a certain feeling, in what the quality or worth of it consists."[14] To push this point with poetic quality, James compares it to the state of being in love, or to the person who has a musical ear and can, therefore, truly appreciate a beautiful symphony for what it is. He emphasizes how inadequate the understanding of such things is to those with experiential deficiency. "Lacking the heart or ear, we cannot interpret the musician or the lover justly, and are even likely to consider him weak-minded or absurd. The mystic finds that most of us accord to his experiences an equally incompetent treatment."[15]

Noetic Quality

The second mark—"noetic quality"—means that the mystical state is also one with infused knowledge, bringing with it "illuminations, revelations, full of significance and importance, all inarticulate though they remain."[16] James notices that this revealed knowledge carries a "curious sense of authority" afterward for the person who experiences the mystical state, as it is something perceived to come from above, from a higher source and thus from a greater authority. Once again, as with the mark of ineffability, James emphasizes how this state transcends the limitations of reason, of the intellectual faculties; for the wisdom revealed through mystical states originates from a deeper dimension. "They are states of insight into depths of truth unplumbed by the discursive intellect."[17]

Transiency

James articulates in his third mark that mystical states cannot be sustained for long. He stresses that there may be rare exceptions but that, most of the time, half an hour or (at most) an hour or two seem to be the duration of such states.[18]

Passivity

With the fourth mark, James emphasizes that the person who experiences a state of mystical consciousness usually feels a suspension of the will, as if an external force has taken over, "sometimes as if he were grasped and held by a superior power."[19] Hence, what transpires is a *gift*, a grace that comes from Another Source. Explaining this mark, James makes an interesting distinction with other phenomena. He considers that the peculiarity of having one's will suspended during a mystical state "connects mystical states with certain definite phenomena of secondary or alternative personality, such as prophetic speech, automatic writing, or the mediumistic trance."[20] However, James sees an important distinction of discernment between such phenomena and the mystic state. Something like a mediumistic trance or automatic writing can be simply "interruptive," the person experiencing it having no recollection of the phenomenon afterward, "and it may have no significance for the subject's usual inner life. . . ."[21] By contrast, mystical states are "never merely interruptive. Some memory of their content always remains, and a profound sense of their importance. They modify the inner life of the subject between the times of their reoccurrence."[22] James ends the explanation, however, by warning that there is a lot of gray area between such phenomena and that admixtures of qualities do exist, making sharp divisions difficult to always discern.

A Pragmatist's Approach: Discerning the Fruits of Experience

By emphasizing that mystical states modify the inner lives of persons who experience them, James was articulating the major basis for his process of discerning authentic inspiration from false. How does one discern a true mystical experience from a false one? James applied the centuries-old method, first articulated by Jesus in the Gospels, that a tree is known by its fruit.[23] Thus, the authenticity of a mystical encounter can be discerned by the fruits that it produces, particularly in the life of the person who undergoes the experience.

James noticed, throughout the numerous cases of extraordinary experiences that he studied, that those persons who encountered a genuine mystical state of consciousness were significantly transformed by the experience. The fruits of such transformation can include greater courage, charity, inner peace, invulnerability, and a deep desire for a pure and holy life. James was so convinced by the fruits of genuine mysticism in having the power to transform a life toward deeper holiness, sacrifice, and purity that he dedicated five of his Gifford lectures to the topic of saintliness.[24]

In studying the fruits of such experiences, James also challenged a popular preconception that has, perhaps too often, plagued the reputation of mystics and the value of mysticism. James confronted the issue of whether such intense focus on the interior life takes away from the exterior life.

Destroying the stereotype, James highlighted the example of the great Spanish mystics: Ignatius of Loyola, Teresa of Avila, and John of the Cross. These three sixteenth-century saints, masters in spirituality and mysticism, all of whom reported personally encountering extraordinary mystical experiences, also led incredibly active lives which, in many ways, have worked to renew the Church and transform much of the world. Ignatius was the founder of the Society of Jesus, the Jesuits. One of the most influential religious orders in the history of Christianity, the Jesuits have produced priests and religious who have also been scientists, explorers, missionaries, scholars, educators, writers, inventors, and innovators. The Jesuit missions, spreading Christianity and culture to the ends of the earth, have become legendary, as has the Society of Jesus for its spiritual and intellectual prowess. Teresa and John, furthermore, the great reformers of the Carmelite order and founders of numerous monasteries, were also instrumental in leading the renaissance of the Catholic Counter-Reformation in modern Europe when Protestantism was spreading throughout the continent. The two are likewise known as contributing to the golden age of Spanish literature, with their writings on the spiritual life. All three mystics led very active lives that were instrumental in affecting the Church and the world. The most important point here, which James stresses, is that the energy, activism, and ingenuity of these mystics cannot be separated from their mysticism; it is, in fact, a product of it, the fruit of their spiritual lives. Thus, it is the intimate, mystical encounter and associated spirituality of a life dedicated to God that provides the energy, capability, and desire to influence and transform the exterior world.

"The extremely dynamic, useful, practical, creative lives of so many of the great mystics impressed the father of American pragmatism," Harvey

Egan highlights. "The fruits of the mystics' lives, the great benefits to society which flowed from the great active mystics, proved for James the great value of the mystical life."[25] In James's writings this is evident, and obviously this appeals to James's philosophical disposition as a pragmatist; for him, true mysticism inspired a vibrant pragmatism.

"Saint Ignatius was a mystic," writes James, "but his mysticism made him assuredly one of the most powerfully practical human engines that ever lived."[26] James underscores that the Spanish mystics were souls who underwent some of the deepest, most ecstatic, extraordinary religious experiences ever recorded, and that it is these experiences that allowed them to be such influential catalysts of inspiration and transformation. "The great Spanish mystics, who carried the habit of ecstasy as far as it has often been carried, appear for the most part to have shown indomitable spirit and energy, and all the more so for the trances in which they indulged."[27]

James's observations about the Spanish mystics are important for a couple of reasons: (1) they reiterate James's hermeneutic of discernment that true mysticism is known by its fruits; and (2) they challenge the pervasively present, but often contradicted, belief that mystics remove themselves from the world, as if mysticism constitutes a form of escapism from reality. On the contrary, James points out that authentic mysticism has often shown the opposite to be true: it can lead to enhanced participation in the active life. Here, Mary and Martha, as the Gospel example goes, are not at odds but, rather, become a model of unity, enforcing a mutual life of contemplation and action. James was not alone in this assessment.

Evelyn Underhill, whose pioneering work on mysticism we will observe in greater detail in the following section, wrote:

> All records of mysticism in the West, then, are also the records of supreme human activity. Not only of "wrestlers in the spirit" but also of great organizers, such as St. Teresa and St. John of the Cross; of missionaries preaching life to the spiritually dead, such as St. Francis of Assisi, St. Ignatius Loyola, Eckhart, Suso Tauler, Fox; of philanthropists such as St. Catherine of Genoa or St. Vincent de Paul; poets and prophets, such as Mechthild of Magdeburg, Jacopone da Todi and Blake; finally, of some immensely virile souls whose participation in the Absolute Life has seemed to force on them a national identity. Of this St. Bernard, St. Catherine of Siena, and Saint Joan of Arc are the supreme examples. "The soul

enamoured of My Truth," said God's voice to St. Catherine of Siena, "never ceases to serve the whole world in general."[28]

Similarly, emphasizing that the mystics' experiences do not lead to an inward form of escapism but instead provide the inspiration for great pragmatic achievements, William Harmless writes about the late medieval German mystic and visionary Hildegard of Bingen: "Hildegard's experiences, which she routinely described as 'mystical,' as offering 'mystical knowledge' or 'mystical secrets,' led her more outward than inward. They prompted her to create a vast body of work: theological texts, illuminations, music, drama, and much else."[29]

Respecting the "More" of Religious Experiences

Union is another major component of James's understanding of mysticism. Here, we can even see a reason as to why James's study was unique. Unlike many intellectuals of his time, James did not dismiss the integrity of mystical experiences, or succumb to reductionism, but he emphasized that such experiences constitute an encounter—a *union*—with something "more," something that psychology or any natural science cannot fully explain. Egan notes how unique James's work as a psychologist studying mystical experiences was compared to predominant psychological studies on mysticism that hoped to denigrate the subject into pathological or (at best) natural categories of interpretation:

> Past psychological studies of mystical phenomena have frequently reflected an unusually strong hostility toward religion. These studies, moreover, often attempted to explain mysticism away by reducing it to deviant behavior, repressed eroticism, madness, mental illness, regression to infantile states, or an escape from the problems of daily life. The older psychology tended to label the great mystics of the Eastern and Western traditions as misfits, deviants, lunatics, and the victims of self-hypnosis and auto-suggestion.[30]

By contrast to such pejorative treatments, James took religious experiences seriously as a psychologist, using a methodological approach that considered the mystery and integrity of such experiences while applying psychological categories and concepts to evaluate and study the phenomena, reaching an impressive balance. Ann Taves notes, "Indeed, his aim as a psychologist was to explain religious experience in psychological terms, while at the same time leaving the possibility that it pointed to something more."[31] Egan emphasizes the impact that this approach had in contrast to dismissive psychological takes on mysticism by noting that perhaps no book in the twentieth century "has done more to render psychology benevolent to mysticism and religion than William James' classic on psychology of religion, *The Varieties of Religious Experience.*"[32]

Challenging the Limitations of Rationalism

James was critical of a rationalistic skepticism that presupposes to be the basis of all truth while eliminating other possibilities—in this case, eliminating other states of consciousness. The mystical consciousness challenges the limitations of rationalism, James argued, showing that rationalism only constitutes one order of consciousness.[33] Thus, James was challenging an Enlightenment-influenced mentality which articulates that what is factual or true is only that which is empirically observable through the senses. Here, James was grappling with an epistemological issue that predated psychology and was based in philosophy, particularly philosophies of knowledge and religion.

"In part, James was reacting to rationalist theories of religion; particularly that of Immanuel Kant (1724–1804)."[34] This is important to consider, and Kant's influence will be observed in greater detail later, as Kant's theories on religious experience have had a large impact on many contemporary scholars, crafting much of the modern debate about mysticism and its interpretations. G. William Barnard points out that "so many of the contemporary understandings of the dynamics of mystical experience are, on the face of it at least, indebted to Kant."[35] The emphasis of this Kantian epistemology was, again, based on a highly rationalistic conception of knowledge that restricted human understanding to that which is empirically observable by the senses:

> According to Kant, only the accuracy of knowledge claims that rely on the evidence of the senses can be analyzed properly. Religious beliefs and experiences, by contrast, have no distinct sensory content. They refer only to supernatural objects, and, as such, Kant regarded such beliefs as having practical consequences only. This means, strictly speaking, that we cannot *know* that God exists. This is because claims to know God are not based on sensory experience.

However, we can act out morally commendable lives *as if* there were a God.[36]

Against such an epistemological framework, restricting knowledge to sensory perception, James "postulates of a faculty in human beings that is deeper than the senses—which allows an intuitive grasp of reality beyond that which the evidence of our senses can provide."[37] It is this faculty that James refers to as the mystical consciousness.[38]

James's identification of a human faculty that is deeper than the senses has a strong *etymological* connection to the word *ecstasy*, so prominent in discourses on mystical and religious experiences. *Ecstasy*, in the original Greek, is a word that denotes a coming "out of the self," or outside of the senses.[39] James's mystical consciousness is a state that transcends the human senses, pointing to a deeper faculty of perception (therefore, signifying "an alienation of the senses"), and it is a state that denotes experience with something "more"—a common phrase for James throughout his *Varieties* lectures.

For James, the mystics experienced a union with something "more," a union that produced deep feelings of inner peace, joy, invulnerability, energy, expansion, and freedom (great fruits).[40] This experience constituted an altered state of consciousness, one that transcends the rational faculties and delves into the depths of a deeper dimension. However, James did not specify the theological content behind the "more" that the mystics encounter, thus allowing the experience to be open to a pluralistic and ecumenical interpretation. "The mystic's experience of union is mysticism's salient feature, according to James. Union with the Absolute and awareness of this union 'is the everlasting and triumphant mystical tradition hardly altered by differences of clime or creed.' . . . The mystic considers what he experiences to be somehow ultimate."[41]

Thus, James did not claim that mystical experiences prove any one creed, religion, or theology, but emphasized that persons from all the major religions have recorded similar experiences, of ecstasy and union with an ultimate or Absolute, even providing examples from various religious traditions in his lectures. James writes:

> This overcoming of all the usual barriers between the individual and the Absolute is the great mystic achievement. In mystic states we both become one with the Absolute and we become aware of our oneness. This is the everlasting and triumphant mystical tradition,

hardly altered by differences of clime or creed. In Hinduism, in Neoplatonism, in Sufism, in Christian mysticism, in Whitmanism, we find the same recurring note, so that there is about mystical utterances an eternal unanimity which ought to make a critic stop and think, and which brings it about that the mystical classics have, as has been said, neither birthday nor native land. Perpetually telling of the unity of man with God, their speech antedates languages, and they do not grow old.[42]

Here, we see the formulations of a perennialist philosophy. Perennialism, so influential in the early twentieth-century study of mysticism and religious experiences, articulates that genuine extraordinary experiences share similar, underlying themes across countries, cultures, religions, and languages, transcending constructed boundaries through a unifying, mutually encountered, spiritual experience.[43] The opposite of perennialism, its hermeneutical rival, or its inversion, is *constructivism*, so influential in the latter half of the twentieth century. Constructivism articulates that there is no such thing as a direct, unmediated mystical experience but that each experience is mediated and constructed through the individual's preexistent cultural, religious, or linguistic knowledge and beliefs.[44] Thus, rather than seeing it as a pure, immediate spiritual experience, as perennialists do, constructivists view such experiences as mediated and constructed by the human mind. It should be noted, however, that notwithstanding the general principles of these hermeneutical frameworks, there are different degrees of both perennialism and constructivism, a reality that we will delve into in the next chapter by observing the nuances behind these interpretative paradigms.[45]

While James, as a perennialist, sees a unifying quality in the mystical experiences that practitioners from the various religious traditions receive, he is sensitive enough to consider theological differences between the traditions in understanding such key concepts as *mystical union*. Egan explains it thus: because "the mystic in some traditions claims to become the Absolute, James stresses the pantheistic, monistic, optimistic, and conversion traits of mystical consciousness. Since Christians speak of unity, not merging, with a personal God, however, James distinguishes Christian mysticism from a 'naturalistic pantheism.'"[46] James noticeably does not use mystical experiences to verify the teachings or dogmas of any one religion, but he acknowledges their universal presence within all the major faiths while stressing the obvious existence of theological differences.

The Authority of Mystical Experiences

In James's understanding of mysticism, an issue that deserves attention is the question of authority. What authority did William James attribute to such extraordinary experiences? This matter constitutes an essential feature of James's hermeneutic on religious experiences. Let us, therefore, consider his answer.

James divided his answer into three parts. The first explained that mystical states, "when well developed," have the right to be "absolutely authoritative" over the person who experiences them.[47] The second part, however, enunciated that no authority comes out of such states which should make them binding to outsiders—those who have not experienced them. Only the one who experiences the phenomenon has the right to call it authoritative. No one else, according to James, has a duty or obligation to abide by the revelations given by these states. The third part articulated that which we have already touched on: the epistemological issue that mystic states "break down the authority of the non-mystical or rationalistic consciousness."[48] Therefore, mystic states challenge the epistemological rationalism that reduces knowledge to nothing but sense perception. Mystic states show such modes of perception to be only one kind of consciousness and, therefore, open the possibility to "other orders of truth."[49] Thus, our everyday state of wakeful consciousness constitutes only one state of consciousness, and we should not narrowly reduce all knowledge to this single perception, James argued, challenging the rationalistic, Kantian paradigm.[50]

While James's work on mysticism is considered to be one of the most, if not *the most*, influential interpretations of the subject, it is not without its critics. In fact, it is important to note that some of the major criticisms against James's interpretation have come from fellow perennialist thinkers. A number of writers, especially (but not exclusively) in the early twentieth century, have maintained a perennialist approach toward interpreting mysticism while, at the same time, critiquing aspects of James's account of it. Let us now turn to one of the most influential thinkers in this group and consider her work.

Evelyn Underhill and Mysticism

If William James is considered the godfather of the modern study of mysticism, then it is Evelyn Underhill (1875–1941) who deserves to be acknowledged as the godmother. This remarkable woman, whose eclectic learning included a grasp of spiritual classics, liturgy, Greek philosophy, medievalism, theology, symbolism, languages, and psychology, authored one of the most consequential books on the topic of mysticism ever written.[51] One can make the argument, although it is open to debate, that Underhill's influence transcends even James's for the simple reason that her breakthrough book surpassed academic interests and reached a popular audience. Steven Fanning explains that while Underhill lacked "the authority of high academic credentials, by dint of her intelligence, determination and spirituality she came to dominate the study of mysticism in England in the first two decades of the twentieth century."[52] Underhill's magnum opus is *Mysticism: A Study in the Nature and Development of Man's Spiritual Consciousness*, first published in 1911. Bernard McGinn notes that "Underhill's long introduction is probably the most read English work on mysticism. Underhill did much to introduce mysticism to the English-speaking audience."[53]

Underhill has had a significant influence on contemporary scholarly understandings of mysticism, particularly regarding the question of definition. Underhill has promulgated a popular, if not generic in its broadness, definition of the word *mysticism* that has gained widespread acceptance by many modern scholars. She describes mysticism as "the direct intuition or experience of God," articulating it even more broadly as "every religious tendency that discovers the way to God direct through inner experience without the mediation of reasoning. The constitutive element in mysticism is immediacy of contact with the deity."[54] The two central components of Underhill's definition, therefore, are *experience* (mysticism is grounded in a personal, unitive, spiritual experience) and *immediacy* (mysticism is grounded in a *direct*—in other words, unmediated—spiritual experience of God). Many scholars have come to accept Underhill's definition and have used it to set the framework for their own academic projects, highlighting immediacy and experience as essential components to understanding mysticism. Some have done this even while substituting their language of God or the Divine with such philosophical parlance as immediate experience with the "absolute" or "ultimate" Reality.

In their work *Mysticism, Holiness East and West*, Denise Lardner Carmody and John Tully Carmody suggest "as a working description of mysticism" the "direct experience of ultimate reality."[55] F. C. Happold, in *Mysticism: A Study and an Anthology*, similarly writes that in "the religious mystic there is a direct experience of the Presence of God."[56] In his book

Mystics of the Christian Tradition, Steven Fanning acknowledges that there is a wide-ranging debate around the definition of the word, but to set a trustworthy framework for his own book, he notes that "the definition of mysticism employed in this present work is that of Evelyn Underhill."[57] In his systematic work *Models of Revelation,* Avery Dulles, S.J., dedicates a chapter to the model of "inner experience," which, he explains, as a model of revelation is directly connected to mysticism. Dulles here identified mystical experiences as being revelatory in character.[58] He describes the form of this model as "of course an immediate interior experience" and, in the process of noting sources, he lists the contribution of Evelyn Underhill, among "several prominent Anglicans," in articulating such a mystical model of revelation.[59]

While Underhill's definition constitutes a useful starting point it is not, by any means, a definition free of flaws or its critics. Perhaps the most pervasive criticism that Underhill's definition has received is one coming from constructivist scholars who do not see mystical experiences as *immediate* experiences but, on the contrary, as experiences that are *mediated* and, therefore, filtered by the mystic's cultural and linguistic preconceptions and ideas (a debate we will tackle in detail in the following chapter). Another issue that needs to be addressed is the question of whether this definition of mysticism would include such extraordinary experiences as Marian apparitions, the primary subject of this work.

On the one hand, it could be argued that Underhill's definition (and other popular definitions) of mysticism would not incorporate the phenomena of Marian apparitions. Underhill's definition stresses immediate experience and, therefore, *union* with the deity (or God). But in Marian apparitions there is an evident *dualism* in the encounter, between the visionary and the Virgin Mary, that does not speak of perfect union: the subject retains his or her identity while encountering the object of experience. The Marian apparition is, therefore, not a self-transcending, unitive encounter with God, as the type that constitutes true mysticism.

On the other hand, it could be argued that the experience of mysticism must not always be free of degrees of dualism in order to be considered a true mystical experience. Ann Taves, for example, writing of the ways that philosophers of religion understand such terms, explains that the word *mystical* is "often used to refer to experiences of unity with or without a sense of multiplicity."[60] Similarly, Jensine Andresen and Robert Forman write of "two distinct kinds of religious experience, non-dualistic and dualistic, roughly apophatic and kataphatic forms of spirituality. We also recognize that some experiences, which we call 'complex experiences,' may include elements of one or both, and thus that there is a continuum of religious experiences."[61] In other words, a mystical experience that is unitive can still have "a sense of multiplicity," a dualism which by itself does not necessarily undermine the unity that is at the core of the encounter. James, in his Gifford Lectures, gave a documented example of such a phenomenon that is both unitive and possesses a dualistic quality, that, perfectly illustrative for our purpose, constituted a vision of the Virgin Mary.

James presented the case of Alphonse Ratisbonne, a "freethinking" French Jewish atheist who had a profound disdain for Catholicism. Yet, he experienced an even more profound conversion to the Catholic faith after encountering an immediate and spontaneous vision of the Virgin Mary in 1842. This vision became for Ratisbonne a unitive experience with the divine. Ratisbonne wrote of the experience in a letter, portions of which James used in his lectures on conversion.[62] Ratisbonne explained how one day in Rome he casually entered a church (the Church of San Andrea delle Fratte), which was "poor, small, empty," explaining that no work of art in the church attracted his attention as Ratisbonne mechanically passed his eyes over the interior of the building.[63] The only other living presence in the church was "an entirely black dog which went trotting and turning before me as I mused." Then, in "an instant the dog had disappeared, the whole church had vanished, I no longer saw anything, . . . or more truly I saw, O my God, one thing alone." He describes seeing the Virgin Mary. "Oh, indeed, it was She! It was indeed She!"[64]

What is especially fascinating is what happened inside of Ratisbonne as he experienced this vision, encountering with it a unitive experience of the soul that led to deep illumination and conversion. He writes of the inner experience:

> I did not know where I was: I did not know whether I was Alphonse or another. I only felt myself changed and believed myself another me; I looked for myself in myself and did not find myself. In the bottom of my soul I felt an explosion of the most ardent joy; I could not speak; I had no wish to reveal what had happened. But I felt something solemn and sacred within me which made me ask for a priest. I was led to one; and there, alone, after he had given me the positive order, I spoke as best I could, kneeling, and with my heart still trembling. I could give no account to myself of the truth of which I had acquired a knowledge and a faith. All that I can say is

that in an instant the bandage had fallen from my eyes; and not one bandage only, but the whole manifold of bandages in which I had been brought up. One after another they disappeared. . . .

I came out as from a sepulcher, from an abyss of darkness; and I was living, perfectly living. But I wept, for at the bottom of that gulf I saw the extreme of misery from which I had been saved by an infinite mercy; and I shuddered at the sight of my iniquities, stupefied, melted, overwhelmed with wonder and with gratitude.[65]

Ratisbonne continued to explain the mysterious illumination of knowledge that this encounter led him to. Not only did his mind become instantly acquainted with the truth of religious doctrines and spiritual realities—constituting a perfect example of an intellectual vision[66]—but he also *felt them*, the prowess behind these truths, in his soul. Again, his soul was experiencing a deeply unitive encounter with something higher, or something "more," as James would say. Ratisbonne explains:

You may ask me how I came to this new insight, for truly I had never opened a book of religion nor even read a single page of the Bible, and the dogma of original sin is either entirely denied or forgotten by the Hebrews of to-day, so that I had thought so little about it that I doubt whether I ever knew its name. But how came I, then, to this perception of it? I can answer nothing save this, that on entering that church I was in darkness altogether, and on coming out of it I saw the fullness of light. I can explain the change no better than by the simile of a profound sleep or the analogy of one born blind who should suddenly open his eyes to the day. He sees, but cannot define the light which bathes him and by means of which he sees the objects which excite his wonder. If we cannot explain physical light, how can we explain the light which is the truth itself? And I think I remain within the limits of veracity when I say that without having any knowledge of the letter of religious doctrine, I now intuitively perceived its sense and spirit. Better than if I saw them, I *felt* those hidden things; I felt them by the inexplicable effects they produced in me. It all happened in my interior mind; and those impressions, more rapid than thought, shook my soul, revolved and turned it, as it were, in another direction, towards other aims, by other paths.[67]

Those other paths for Ratisbonne included not only a conversion to Catholicism but also the pursuit of a vocation of becoming a Jesuit priest.

In the case of Alphonse Ratisbonne we see a powerful example of how a mystical experience can be both dualistic and unitive. The dualism is present, of course, in the fact that Ratisbonne saw a vision of the Virgin Mary, therefore (if authentic) of a spiritual presence separate from him, while the unity is present in the fact that Ratisbonne's mind and soul experienced a profound, unitive encounter during the vision that led to instant conversion and illumination of spiritual mysteries, powerfully touching and transforming his very self. It is fair to deduce, from the description of his experience, that Ratisbonne experienced an altered state of consciousness, being taken at the moment of the vision to another reality of perception, the type that James wrote of when articulating the characteristics of mystical consciousness. It is noteworthy that the four characteristics of ineffability, transiency, passivity, and noetic quality were all present in the experience that Ratisbonne described, making a case that the encounter could very well be what James called an experience of "mystical consciousness."

Underhill's Defining Marks of Mysticism

While "the pioneer work of William James"[68] was acknowledged by Underhill, she argued that "James' celebrated 'four marks' of the mystic state," ineffability, noetic quality, transiency, and passivity, "will fail to satisfy us."[69] As a response, Underhill formed her own definition by applying "four other rules or notes" that she believed could provide a better explanation of what mysticism means.[70] Her points explain that true mysticism: (1) is active and practical, not passive and theoretical; (2) has aims that are purely spiritual and transcendent; (3) pursues as its personal object love for the eternal One; and (4) constitutes an entire orientation of life.

In considering the differences between Underhill's interpretation of mysticism from James's hermeneutic, it is most important to highlight that Underhill does not limit her definition of mysticism to an altered state of consciousness (as James and other authors defined it) but, rather, perceives mysticism in a broader framework as constituting a complete way of life. Thus, for Underhill, the "mystical" is not just a transient, extraordinary experience (whether with or without multiplicity) but also an entire orientation of living—what she calls the "mystic way," which may be grounded in an initial experience of immediacy and union but does not stop there. To better understand Underhill's hermeneutic, let us take a more detailed look at her four points behind what constitutes true mysticism.

"Mysticism is practical, not theoretical."

In explaining that mysticism is practical and not theoretical, Underhill is making the point that one cannot reduce mysticism to abstract theology because at its core it is not intellectual but experiential. "Mysticism, like revelation, is final and personal. It is not merely a beautiful and suggestive diagram but experience in its most intense form."[71] While Underhill is aligning mysticism with spirituality, emphasizing that it is about the personal, inner encounter and not abstract intellectualizing, this does not mean that Underhill is excluding the theological importance of studying mysticism (or "mystical theology"). On the contrary, mysticism "provides the material, the substance, upon which mystical philosophy cogitates; as theologians cogitate upon the revelation which forms the basis of faith."[72]

Underhill makes a distinction between mystical writers (the philosophers and theologians who have written about the mystical experiences of others) and true mystics (those who have had personal experiences with the Absolute), specifying, however, that sometimes the two categories can be personified in a single individual, like Meister Eckhart (who wrote about his own experiences). Though admiring the works of mystical writers, who with the beauty of their prose "are our stepping-stones to higher things,"[73] Underhill does not consider them true mystics because her definition pertains to personal experience, not intellectual speculation on experience.

Mysticism is an entirely "Spiritual Activity."

With her second point, Underhill means that the sole purpose of the mystic is union and love of God, without any ulterior motivations. Reaching union with God, the mystic develops a detachment from all lesser cravings: from personal power, pleasure, money, influence, self-consciousness; even from noble things like a desire for virtue and knowledge. The mystic's sole aim is God, and nothing else. Even considering benevolent goals—like using spiritual power to help others—such are not the aims of the mystic, Underhill argues. The mystic is fully concentrated on the supernatural, not on the natural world. Yet, paradoxically, it is that concentration and development in the supernatural life that will lead the mystic to a deeper benevolence in the natural world, for reaching union with God the mystic becomes "an agent of the Eternal Goodness."[74] Therefore, while the mystic needs nothing but God, and is fully satisfied with this divine union, it is that union that will inspire the mystic's good works; to the point that the mystic "will spend himself unceasingly for other men."[75]

Attainment of this charitable disposition is not the aim of mysticism, which is purely spiritual, but the result of it. Here, we see an obvious parallel to James's focus on the fruits that stem from mysticism, especially the fruits of a holy and saintly life after having an encounter with the "more."

"The business and method of mysticism is love."

Love is the sole purpose of the mystic's path, according to Underhill. Mysticism is not about exploring the knowledge of a higher Reality, but about being in love with that Reality. Egan explains it thus: "The mystic is in love with a Reality which is both living and personal. The God of Love has created a homeward-turning love within every person."[76] In other words, there is a longing and desire within each person that is not satisfied (to use familiar Augustinian logic) until the soul seeks its purpose: an intimate, loving relationship with its Creator. Mysticism, therefore, is about the *relationship* between lovers (the intimacy between the soul who seeks to love God and the God who loves the soul). Again, Underhill emphasizes that this love constitutes an entire orientation of living and being for the mystic (her broader scope of mysticism is in play here), thus this love is not a shallow or superficial emotion—empty affection—but, rather, impacts the mystic's entire life (every tendency, every action and decision) to be focused toward pursuing the great Lover. "Mystic Love is a total dedication of the will; the deep-seated desire and tendency of the soul toward its Source."

Underhill continues to articulate the depths of this love with poignant language: "It is a condition of humble access, a life-movement of the self: more direct in its methods, more valid in its results—even in the hands of the least lettered of its adepts—than the most piercing intellectual vision of the greatest philosophic mind."[77] Here (and in further passages), she reiterates that the essence of this love transcends dialectics and reason, coming from a deeper place of the heart, from the affections of the soul. Underhill also emphasizes the pluralistic reality of this love— mystics across cultures, from all the great religions, she highlights, have been driven by the force of this "Mystic Love" to pursue their Lover, "mystics of every race and creed."[78]

She sums up her examination of this love by explaining that it is, for the mystic: (1) "the active, conative, expression of his will and desire for the Absolute" and (2) "his innate tendency to that Absolute, his spiritual weight. He is only thoroughly natural, thoroughly alive, when he is obeying its voice. For him it is the source of joy, the secret of the universe, the vivifying principle of things."[79] Thus, this love is life-giving for the mystic, the source of all bliss and meaning; the utmost pursuit.

"Mysticism entails a definite psychological decision."

Here, Underhill is reiterating the wholeness that is necessary for true mysticism, as well as giving voice to the path (the stages of the journey) necessary to reach union with the divine; thus psychologically, such a decision and path entails the activity and transformation of every part of the person, conscious and unconscious ("a definite psychological decision"). She is stating, therefore, that the mystic way not only requires a change of attitude, tendency, or will but also "involves the organizing of the whole self . . . a remaking of the whole character on high levels in the interests of the transcendental life."[80]

Underhill is taking the mystic path beyond experience and spiritual desire and emphasizing *action*. She is speaking of the spiritual journey of the mystic, which proceeds to change the psychological makeup of the person, from a lower self to a higher self. She is speaking about the purpose of the journey of conversion, essentially that which bridges the gap between God and the soul: sanctity, thus the moral, virtuous, and spiritual efforts that the mystic makes to reach "transmutation"[81] (Underhill's term)—to be transformed into the One that the mystic seeks (thus to be holy). Underhill articulates that there are several stages, which she later describes in much greater detail, that the mystic's journey entails toward reaching a transformation of the self into a higher self through union with the Real. She cites such classics in this genre as Teresa of Avila and her seven mansions, as stages of ascent that speak to the reality of the mystic path, intended to transform and unite the soul with the Absolute. "The God-experience demands holiness, sanctity, and the remaking of the self on a higher level."[82]

CURIOUSLY, UNDERHILL ADDS a fifth "corollary to these four rules," by reemphasizing a "statement already made" (thus highlighting its importance), enunciating that true mysticism must be understood as never being self-seeking.[83] It is not about spiritual joys, knowledge, the seeking of ecstatic union or any other spiritual, moral, or worldly pleasure or happiness; but, again, mysticism is about love for love's sake. At its center is the purest of intentions, the most sincere act of desire for God: a lover's journey toward the Beloved, leading to an intimate relationship.

Considering that mysticism for Underhill is not a passing, extraordinary experience of an altered state of consciousness but, rather, a complete way of life, paving the way for a spiritual path, or journey, Underhill articulates various stages (or phases) that constitute the "Mystic Way." Adding to the traditional trinity of mystical theology that make up the stages of spiritual ascent—the purgative, the illuminative, and the unitive ways—Underhill writes of various others. Her stages begin with the Awakening of the Self; then the Purification of the Self; the Illumination of the Self; Voices and Visions; Introversion (under which Underhill includes Recollection, Quiet, and Contemplation); Ecstasy and Rapture; the Dark Night of the Soul; and the Unitive Life. Egan explains that no author "thus far has so accurately captured and described the phases and stages of mystical life as Underhill."[84] Giving a detailed account of each stage, and the mystical theology contained therein, would be beyond the scope or purpose of this writing. However, since we are concentrating on extraordinary religious *experiences*, particularly on visionary experiences in subsequent chapters, let us focus on Underhill's treatment of voices and visions (as a stage within the mystic path).

Before entering into an examination of Underhill's treatment of visions, however, let us touch on an important, related topic about Underhill's interpretative approach to mystical phenomena. Underhill refers to the field of extraordinary religious phenomena—her terminology is that of "abnormal psychic phenomena"[85]—as "that eternal battleground."[86] What she means is this: whether the topic pertains to visions, apparitions, voices, the stigmata, or any other extraordinary phenomena, it is subjected to the "battle-ground" of interpretation, of hermeneutics—of the various debates of understanding surrounding such matters. It is the "battle-ground" between believers and skeptics, between perennialists and constructivists, between holists and reductionists, between supernaturalists and rationalists; the "battle-ground" of ideas, beliefs, philosophies and ideologies; and, of course, there are great consequences behind these hermeneutical debates, particularly regarding such issues as the existence of God, faith, the supernatural, the Church, the relationship between spirituality and psychology, and the relationship between belief and doubt.

Underhill articulates the issue thus, noting first what critics of such phenomena have to ask:

The question for their critics must really be this: do these automatisms, which appear so persistently as a part of the contemplative life, represent merely the dreams and fancies, the old digested percepts of the visionary, objectivized and presented to his surface-mind in a concrete form; or, are they ever representations—symbolic, if you like—of some fact, force, or personality, some "triumphing spiritual power," external to himself? Is the vision only a pictured thought, an activity of the dream imagination: or, is it the violent effort of the self to translate something impressed upon its deeper being, some message received from without, which projects this sharp image and places it before the consciousness?[87]

Here, Underhill is conveying the dialogical framework that is present behind major contemporary debates concerning extraordinary religious experiences: Are they constructions of the human mind—"merely the dreams and fancies, digested percepts of the visionary"—that come from within, or on the other hand, are they authentic experiences with a spiritual reality that are not constructed but contain "some message received from without"? Hence, through this dialectic of "within" and "without" we are, essentially, dealing with a debate between constructivism and receptivity; the former postulates that such extraordinary experiences are, at their root, a human construction (and, therefore, either natural or pathological—as the experiences may be hallucinatory—but not supernatural), while the latter postulates that such experiences, when authentic, are received through an external, spiritual agent (and are, therefore, authentic supernatural encounters with a higher power).

Underhill herself takes a middle-ground approach. She argues that such experiences, when authentic, do come from a higher spiritual source (and, therefore, cannot be understood as completely constructed). However, she also claims that such experiences are filtered through the human psyche, which uses its preexistent cultural concepts and ideas—as hermeneutical symbols, we can say—to interpret, understand, and frame the experience (therefore possessing components of constructivism). What Underhill is ultimately getting at, and this is an important characteristic of her hermeneutical framework, is that such extraordinary experiences are usually subjective, not objective. Therefore, there is an admixture in play, an admixture between what the human mind brings and what the spiritual source brings in framing the experience.

While Underhill acknowledges that such experiences are usually not objective, she is not denigrating the authenticity of these experiences. Underhill challenges the prevalent paradigm of thinking on religious experience that has historically influenced discourse by presenting a presupposed complementarity between objectivity and authenticity, on the one hand, and subjectivity and inauthenticity, on the other hand. Underhill, on the contrary, argues that an experience can be both subjective and authentic; the two are not at odds, as has been historically supposed, but constitute complementary components of a fuller, more complex and robust reality. "If we could cease, once for all, to regard visions and voices as objective, and be content to see in them forms of symbolic expression, ways in which the subconscious activity of the spiritual self reaches the surface-mind, many of the disharmonies noticeable in visionary experience, which have teased the devout, and delighted the agnostic, would fade away."[88]

In terms of visionary experiences, a hermeneutic of complete constructivism would argue that the preexistent cultural concepts and symbols of the visionary construct a false experience that is hallucinatory or illusionary in nature. Underhill, on the other hand, would acknowledge the presence and utility of preexistent concepts and symbols in influencing a visionary experience, but—in any authentic experience—she would understand the cultural symbols to operate as a *hermeneutical lens* through which the visionary interprets, understands, and frames the experience. Thus, preexistent knowledge does not act as a source that constructs the experience but, rather, as a lens of interpretation through which the experience is processed and understood. Therefore, the experience can be both authentic and subjective.

It is authentic because the source of the experience is external, spiritual, and transcendent. It is subjective because the human mind filters the experience through the subjectivity of its preexistent concepts and symbols—in other words, through the subjectivity of its preexistent knowledge.[89] As this may sound a bit confusing, let us consider a simple example to illustrate such a reality.

A Christian, a Muslim, and a Buddhist can each have an extraordinary experience in which it is believed that a divine message has been conveyed. A Christian may see (either in the mind or externally) the figure of Jesus conveying the message, while the Muslim may see the figure of Mohammed, while the Buddhist may see the figure of Buddha. The subjectivity of these experiences does not mean that they are simply personal constructions of each individual's religious beliefs and, therefore, false or inauthentic externalizations of the mind. On the contrary, all three, despite the theological distinctions and contradictions that are present therein, can be authentic experiences, Underhill would argue. Here, God can use each visionary's preexistent religious and cultural symbols and beliefs to communicate a message. Underhill articulates it thus: "The transcendental powers take for this purpose such material as they can find amongst the hoarded beliefs and memories of the self."[90] Therefore, to reiterate, the experience can be both subjective and authentic.

Categories of Visions (Visionary Phenomena)

To delve deeper into an understanding of visionary experiences, Underhill considers the classic, threefold categorization that visions, in Christian theology, have been grouped into: the intellectual, the imaginary, and the corporal.[91] Augustine of Hippo was the first major theologian to treat the issue of visions from a theological perspective, hoping to understand the distinctions between, and intricacies of, such concepts in relation to epistemology.[92] It is in two of his works, *Contra Adimantum* (394) and *De Genesi ad litteram* (414), that he tackled the subject.[93]

Augustine was fascinated with the question of epistemology—how human beings acquire knowledge—and in this regard he dealt with the matter of visions.[94] This understanding of a trifold identification of visionary phenomena, however, predates Augustine's influence and derives from Greek philosophy, which the Church Father was using, as before him the philosopher Porphyry separated visions "into the three groups of corporal, imaginary, and intellectual."[95] Niels Christian Hvidt explains: "Even though Augustine's concept of *vision* is very different from how mystical theology treats the visionary category, his thoughts have influenced mystical theology profoundly."[96]

Augustine developed the threefold categorization for identifying and distinguishing visions into the concepts of: (1) corporal visions; (2) spiritual visions; and (3) intellectual visions.[97] The second category here—"spiritual"—has been subsequently rendered by the Christian mystical tradition by the term "imaginative" or "imaginary," mystical writers after Augustine identifying the threefold categorization of corporal, imaginative, and intellectual visions.[98] Gregory the Great, Thomas Aquinas, Bridget of Sweden, and Teresa of Avila are some of the major theologians and mystics who have used this Augustinian framework in their writings on visions, as well as modern theologians like the Dominican neo-scholastic Reginald Garrigou-LaGrange.[99] Augustin Poulain, however, in his classic treatise on mystical theology, identifies the three forms of visions as *exterior*, imaginative, and intellectual. Poulain notes that another term for exterior visions, in addition to "corporal," is "ocular," as such visions are perceived externally by the eyes. He prefers the identification of "exterior," however, as opposed to the more popular usage of "corporal," since taken alone the word *corporal*, according to Poulain, "is ambiguous. It might only mean to signify that the *object* of the vision is corporeal. But it is also intended to point to the exterior *mode* of vision, to the exclusion of the two following modes [imaginative and intellectual]."[100] Notwithstanding the merits of Poulain's distinction, "corporal" has been the term used to identify the category of visionary experience that he prefers to call "exterior" by a majority of mystical writers working in the Christian tradition. Let us consider the three major visionary categories in detail.

Corporal Visions

Corporal visions include the type of phenomena that are very prevalent in modern apparition cases (whether Marian or Christocentric), when a single visionary or a group of visionaries see a presence with their physical eyes that no one else can see. The presence, or object of the vision, is seen as an external, three-dimensional entity such as an apparition. By *external*, this means that the entity appears outside of the individual (it is not an "internal vision") and is perceived by the individual's external senses.[101] Poulain identifies such an exterior vision as one in which a "material being is formed, or seems to be formed outside of us, and we perceive it like anything else that is round about us."[102]

Imaginative Visions

Imaginative visions are visions that are not external, outside of the individual, but internal, perceived by the inner senses. Mark Miravalle describes an imaginative vision as "a vision of a material object without the assistance of the eyes," which is "perceived by the imaginative sense."[103] The understanding is that God uses the faculties of the human imagination through which to infuse such inner visions. Hvidt explains that these "are visions realized through mechanisms of the human psyche that are made up of images that the soul has acquired through contact with the physical reality."[104] Thus, such visions are conveyed through the natural faculties and are made up of the cultural concepts and symbols that the mind already knows and understands, although they are infused by a higher presence and, therefore, are understood to be inspired. Here, what we see in play is an intertwining relationship between the supernatural and the natural, as the infused (thus supernatural) vision is filtered and processed (thus mediated) through the natural, imaginative faculties of the mind.

Intellectual Visions

Intellectual visions are not mediated through any form of sense perception, whether internal or external, but constitute direct, infused knowledge. "The illumination is given to the intellect without any dependence on sense images or external senses."[105] In other words, the mind does not see symbols or concepts (like in an imaginative vision), nor do the eyes see an external entity (like in a corporal vision), but the intellect is filled with new knowledge that is directly communicated. Poulain describes such visions as "visions perceived by the mind alone without any interior image. We may thus see God or the angels, and even material objects, but in the same way as one would see angels intellectually, without any form, that is to say."[106] Teresa of Avila considers it a mystery how the illuminative knowledge of an intellectual vision is conveyed, seeing something deeply ineffable in this visionary experience.[107]

The advantage of this type of visionary communication, Hvidt points out, is that the communication—not being filtered and, therefore, possibly altered by the human senses—retains its purity, its original integrity.[108] It is, therefore, the only type of vision that can be called *objective*, as the human senses—with all their subjectivity—play no role in filtering the vision. The Polish mystic Sister Faustina Kowalska has written: "There is a higher and more perfect union with God; namely, intellectual union. Here, the soul is safer from illusions; its spirituality is purer and more profound. In a life where the senses are involved, there is more danger of illusion."[109]

Passive Imaginary Visions

To this classic, threefold categorization of visions, Underhill adds two subcategories. Specifically, within the category of imaginary visions, Underhill adds these two types: passive imaginary visions[110] and active imaginary visions.[111] Additionally, under one of these subcategories, Underhill adds two more sub-subcategories. Underhill explains passive imaginary visions as being "spontaneous mental pictures at which the self looks, but in the action of which it does not participate," and she expounds that there are two forms of passive imaginary visions: (1) the symbolic and (2) the personal.[112]

Symbolic Passive Imaginary Visions

The *symbolic* refer to passive imaginary visions that are highly allegorical and metaphorical, poetic in their imagery, whose truths are conveyed through symbols. Underhill explains: "Many of the visions of the great prophetic mystics—e.g., St. Hildegarde [of Bingen]—have so elaborate a symbolic character, that much intellectual activity is involved in their interpretation."[113] Perhaps the most stunning example of this kind of vision is the biblical text the Book of Revelation, which (according to its author) is based on a vision and whose extravagant and powerful symbolism is legendary.

Underhill underscores the poetic charge of such visions. Such a vision "is really a visualized poem, inspired by a direct contact with the truth."[114] Furthermore:

> It is an accommodation of the supra-sensible to our human disabilities, a symbolic reconstruction of reality on levels accessible to sense. This symbolic reconstruction is seen as a profoundly significant, vivid, and dramatic dream: and since this dream conveys transcendental truth, and initiates the visionary into the atmosphere of the Eternal, it may well claim precedence over that prosaic and perpetual vision which we call the "real world."[115]

Personal Passive Imaginary Visions

The other type of passive imaginary vision is the *personal.* Underhill describes this vision as vivid and as something that is *concretely* (thus it is distinct from being a *symbolic* vision) related to the devotee's religious beliefs and spiritual passions. To provide a simple example of this type of vision, Underhill references visions of Christ that "so many Catholic ecstatics" have experienced during the moment of consecration at Mass.[116]

Regarding the personalism of the experience, Underhill stresses the interior fruits that such visions produce, emphasizing the "life-enhancing

quality" that include "the feeling states" of certainty and joy, as characteristic fruits of such encounters. If the symbolic vision is like a poem,
Underhill calls the personal vision "a love-letter"—a love letter that is
"received by the ardent soul."[117] Thus, this is a vision of great intimacy,
one that also possesses, in its transcendent beauty, that mystical quality of
ineffability, appearing "under the form of inexpressible beauty" to the soul
that encounters the experience.[118]

Active Imaginary Visions

Alongside passive imaginary visions (both symbolic and personal),
Underhill writes of *active imaginary visions*. Here, the element of a deeper
participation from the soul is present. "In this vision, which always has
a dramatic character, the self seems to itself to act, not merely to look
on."[119] What we see in the description of this visionary category is one
reason why Underhill believed that James's four characteristics of mysticism would fail to satisfy, because in this example "passivity," as a characteristic of mystical consciousness, is undermined with *activity*. Active
imaginary visions can have various characteristics and they always possess
transformative, life-altering fruits for the one who undergoes the experience. They are "active" for, according to Underhill, they are expressions of
the soul's mystical journey, the soul's movement to deeper levels of consciousness, to deeper chambers of one's interior castle (to use Teresa of
Avila's famous imagery).

> Such visions may possess many of the characters of dreams; they
> may be purely symbolic; they may be theologically "realistic." They
> may entail a journey through Hell, Purgatory and Heaven, an excur-
> sion into fairyland, a wrestling with the Angel in the Way. Whatever
> their outward form, they are always connected with inward results.
> They are the automatic expressions of intense subliminal activity;
> not merely the media by which the self's awareness of the Absolute
> is strengthened and enriched, but the outward and visible signs of
> its movement towards new levels of consciousness.[120]

As examples of active imaginary visions, Underhill references the stig-
matization of Francis of Assisi and Catherine of Siena, as well as "the
transverberation of St. Teresa,"[121] referring to Teresa of Avila's famously
erotic mystical encounter with an angel thrusting a golden sphere into her

heart, depicted most vividly in Bernini's baroque masterpiece *St. Teresa in Ecstasy.*[122]

Yet, it is another experience from Catherine of Siena, Underhill argues, that most convincingly portrays the participatory drama of an active imaginary vision. Underhill is referring to Catherine's vision which in Christian art is described as the "Mystic Marriage of Catherine of Siena."[123] It is a vision that Catherine experienced in 1366, vividly depicting her betrothal to Christ, wherein Catherine receives a ring from Christ, is surrounded by heavenly wedding guests—from the Virgin Mary to John the Evangelist, the Apostle Paul, and St. Dominic, founder of Catherine's order—and is formally wed to Christ in a celestial wedding as his bride. Regarding this vision, Underhill makes a fascinating and important observation, one which speaks to the complexity of such visionary experiences, and again tackles the reciprocal relationship between a vision being both subjective and authentic.

Underhill argues that it is not difficult to discern the material, the content, from which Catherine's vision derives, explaining that it is taken from the legend of St. Catherine of Alexandria.[124] Underhill postulates that Catherine of Siena would be familiar with the saint of Alexandria who was her namesake, and therefore suggests that Catherine "showed a characteristic artistic suggestibility and quickness in transforming the stuff of old history into the medium of a profound personal experience."[125] Significantly, while Underhill explains that much of the external material for the vision is culturally constructed, coming from a previous visionary account that Catherine would be familiar with, what is important is not the external material but the interior effects of the vision.

It was the interior effects of the vision that resulted in a permanent change in Catherine that allowed her to enter into a deeper state of mystical consciousness.[126] Therefore, Underhill makes a significant distinction between the external content and the internal prowess of the vision. The former, the external content, may be a subliminal actualization of material that Catherine's psyche was familiar with, thus culturally constructed. But the latter, the internal prowess, taking the visionary into a state of deeper mystical consciousness, is an act of spiritual transformation coming from the transcendent realm. It is an act of grace, something that can only come from outside, from above.[127] Thus, here we see a complex admixture that shows how a vision can have components that are culturally constructed by the visionary's mind, on the one hand, and divinely infused by a higher power (by God), on the other hand.

Benedict Groeschel has pointed out that when dealing with visionary experiences there is a lot of gray area. Most of the time, such encounters are not simply black-and-white manifestations but, rather, more complex and nuanced in their delicate intricacies.[128] Thus, in the case of the "Mystic Marriage of Catherine of Siena," Underhill can conclude:

> Long prepared by that growing disposition of her deeper self which caused her to hear the reiterated promise of her Beloved, the vision when it came was significant, not for its outward circumstances, but for its permanent effect upon her life. In it she passed to a fresh level of consciousness; entering upon that state of spiritual wedlock, of close and loving identification with the interests of Christ, which Richard of St. Victor calls the "Third Stage of Ardent Love."[129]

Active Intellectual Visions

A final note that Underhill wanted to touch on in this visionary category is that "active" visions need not always be recognized as imaginative visions. They can also be intellectual visions, and therefore we enter into another subcategory known as *active intellectual visions*. To illustrate this point, Underhill invokes the example of the medieval Franciscan mystic Angela of Foligno. She cites a lengthy description that Angela gave of one of her mystical encounters, in which Angela described being in the midst of the Trinity and being taken into a higher level of consciousness, so sweet, sublime, and ineffable that she has yet to experience such "great and unspeakable delight."[130] What makes the vision intellectual, and not imaginative, is the fact that it is conveyed through cognitive comprehension, not visible symbols, pictures, or concepts—simply through an infused understanding given to the intellect that one has entered, and is participating in, a higher state of mystical consciousness (in Angela's Christian context, a deeper experience with the holy Trinity).[131]

Categories of Voices/Locutions

As a parallel to the threefold major categorization of intellectual, imaginary, and corporal visions, Underhill discusses the phenomenon of voices (or the phenomenon of mystics hearing voices) through the correspondingly trifold discourse of (1) immediate or inarticulate voices; (2) interior and distinct voices; and (3) exterior words.[132] Augustin Poulain embraced this topic, even before Underhill, by studying the work of Teresa of Avila and John of the Cross in identifying three forms of locutions. Poulain explained that there are "three kinds of supernatural locutions, or words, corresponding in order of superiority to the faculties that come into play: the bodily hearing, the imagination, and the intelligence."[133] Correspondingly it is not difficult to see the complementarity to corporal visions, imaginative visions, and intellectual visions.

With the phenomenon of voices, or "audition," as Underhill titles such graces, the "mystic becomes aware of Something which speaks to him either clearly or implicitly; giving him abrupt and unexpected orders and encouragements."[134] We can think of several prominent examples throughout Christian history that illustrate such phenomena and their influence, from Saul (or St. Paul) hearing the voice of Christ on the road to Damascus, resulting in his great conversion; to Augustine hearing the voices of children singing in the garden in Milan to encourage him to open the Scriptures and read (a pivotal point in his conversion story); to Francis of Assisi hearing the voice of Christ telling him "rebuild my Church" at San Damiano; to Joan of Arc leading the French armies in battle against the English at the encouragement and orders of her Voices. Just considering these four examples, it is by no means a stretch of the imagination to say that this phenomenon has been instrumental, as a catalyst, in influencing some of the most important Christian figures and consequently, by their active lives, movements in Church history.

Intellectual Locutions

The three auditory categories of voices possess the characteristics and nuances of the three main visionary categories, being a reflection. Thus, like the intellectual vision, the first category of audition, intellectual locutions (known also as immediate or inarticulate voices) constitute an "infusion of new knowledge or new life," coming instantly and being a form of divine inspiration.[135] Like the intellectual vision, this category is not filtered by the human senses and, therefore, is the purest form of auditory experience with the greatest authority when compared to the other two. Therefore, since the senses are not in play, the mystic does not technically "hear" a voice in this experience but, rather, receives an infusion of knowledge that directly affects the intellect. Underhill, however, does not make a clear distinction in what would separate and distinguish this type

of locution from an intellectual vision, as both are conveyed through identical terminology in her narrative as conveying an immediate (thus unmediated) infusion of knowledge that comes from a higher source.

Imaginative Locutions

Like the imaginative vision, the second auditory category—imaginative
locutions (known also as interior or distinct voices)—constitutes a combination of the transcendent working with the human senses. Thus here,
the imaginative senses of the mind are in play, as the experience is filtered
through the human psyche. Here, also, the mystic actually "hears within
his mind"[136] distinct interior words. Thus, the mystic's "inner ear," or the
ear of the soul, hears audible, interior words. To accentuate how concrete
this can be, Underhill invokes the example of the medieval Dominican
mystic Henry Suso, who stated that he received a hundred meditations on
the Passion of Jesus Christ in the form of distinct interior words that, he
emphasized, were conveyed to him in German and not in Latin.[137] Suso's
specificity of language illustrates to what degree his senses were involved
in receiving, interpreting, and transmitting the auditory phenomenon, to
the point of identifying the exact language that was used in conveying
the grace.

Exterior Locutions

The third auditory category—exterior locutions (also known as exterior
words)—constitutes a phenomenon, like the corporal vision, wherein the
exterior senses are the lenses of perception. Thus, as in the corporal vision,
by which the mystic sees through outward senses—through the eyes—an
external and three-dimensional presence, in the category of exterior locutions, the mystic hears a voice or a number of voices through his or her
outward ears. Underhill refers to the voices that guided Joan of Arc, and
the voice of Christ which from the San Damiano Crucifix spoke to Francis
of Assisi, as examples of this type of phenomenon.[138]

Mystical Experiences and Visionary
Experiences: Understanding the Nuances

Having covered important nuances of visionary experiences and associated phenomena like locutions, a word of clarification is necessary

regarding interpreting and distinguishing between visionary and mystical experiences. Certain scholars argue that visionary and mystical experiences refer to two very different phenomena that need to be conceptually separated. The Franciscan scholar Michael H. Crosby has, in this regard, criticized my interpretation of the mysticism of Francis of Assisi, arguing that Francis's visionary experiences, particularly his visionary experience of the six-wing seraph on Mount La Verna in 1224, resulting in Francis receiving the stigmata, should not be identified as a *mystical* experience, or even as the core of Francis's mysticism, but understood in a separate category as a visionary experience. Here, Crosby is pointing to the reality that mystical and visionary experiences are two different categories of extraordinary religious experience, stressing—in homage to Evelyn Underhill's definition—that a mystical experience is both experiential and immediate while a visionary experience, on the other hand, does not possess both of these key components.[139] Analyzing Crosby's critiques we can come to a fuller understanding of the multilayered nuances of this topic.

Crosby argues that both William James and Teresa of Avila "move on to discuss the uniqueness of someone's mystical experience that is beyond someone's experience of a vision. The vision is outside of them; the mystical experience is unmediated insofar as it is experiential and immediate."[140] I do not think that James would agree with such a dualistic take on visionary and mystical experiences but would articulate a more holistic and broader understanding that sees the two not as possessing exclusionary elements but as complementary components that point to James's mystical consciousness. There have been different scholarly interpretations of James's work, and here I am in disagreement with Crosby's interpretation. Unfortunately, in his article, Crosby does not specify which sections in James's work he is referring to in formulating the distinction. However, regarding Teresa of Avila, Crosby does specify that it is in her sixth and seventh mansions of the *Interior Castle* wherein Teresa makes the important distinction between visionary and mystical experiences.

My reading of Teresa contains a slight, but important, difference from Crosby's reading. While Crosby notes that Teresa makes a distinction between visionary and mystical experiences, I see a nuance in her text that makes a distinction between *types of visionary experiences*, distinguishing between imaginative and intellectual visions, with an emphasis that the latter constitute an important (epistemological) part of mystical experiences—making it erroneous, in this case, to separate the mystical experience from the visionary experience *when that visionary experience is*

an intellectual vision, a grace that often belongs to higher mystical experiences. In fact, the intellectual vision belongs to such sublime mystical
experiences that Teresa prominently includes it in the experiences of
union with the Trinity she records in her final—seventh—mansion of the
Interior Castle. Teresa explains:

> In this seventh dwelling place the union comes about in a different
> way: our good God now desires to remove the scales from the soul's
> eyes and let it see and understand, although in a strange way, some-
> thing of the favor He grants it. When the soul is brought into that
> dwelling place, the Most Blessed Trinity, all three Persons, through
> an intellectual vision, is revealed to it through a certain representa-
> tion of the truth.[141]

Teresa, therefore, connects the intellectual vision with the mystical union
of the seventh mansion wherein understanding of the Holy Trinity is *expe-
rientially granted* to the soul through the intellectual vision. She expounds
on this:

> First there comes an enkindling in the spirit in the manner of a
> cloud of magnificent splendor; and these Persons [of the Trinity]
> are distinct, and through an admirable knowledge the soul under-
> stands as a most profound that all three Persons are one substance
> and one power and one knowledge and one God alone. It knows
> in such a way that what we hold by faith, it understands, we can
> say, through sight—although the sight is not with the bodily eyes
> nor with the eyes of the soul, because we are not dealing with an
> imaginative vision [but an intellectual]. Here all three Persons com-
> municate themselves to it, speak to it, and explain those words of
> the Lord in the Gospel: that He and the Father and the Holy Spirit
> will come to dwell with the soul that loves Him and keeps His
> commandments.[142]

This sublime encounter with the Trinity *is* a mystical experience and yet it
remains, also, a visionary experience.

Thus, Crosby's interpretation of Teresa's work, in arguing that her sixth
and seventh mansions distinguish between visionary and mystical experiences, is correct in regard to *corporal and imaginative visions*. However,
I see this interpretation as being incorrect in regard to *intellectual visions*.

Teresa does, in fact, make an important distinction between the first two categories of visionary experiences (corporal and imaginative) and mystical experiences. Since the mystical experience is unmediated, neither the corporal vision, which acts through the mediation of external senses, nor the imaginative vision, which acts through the mediation of internal senses, is able to be a part of the mystical experience for Teresa.[143]

But Crosby's argument appears incorrect—at least its implicit proclivity of speaking for all visions—in regard to intellectual visions. Teresa sees intellectual visions as constitutive of mystical experiences, providing their epistemological agency—the means by which the soul comes to understand (beyond any form of mediated sense perception) the content of the experience. Given this reality, it would be erroneous to construct too great a distinction between *all* visionary and mystical experiences, as an essential component of the visionary experience remains in many forms of mystical experiences through the epistemological function that the intellectual vision plays in such phenomena.

At the same time, it is important to acknowledge that not all visionary experiences are mystical experiences. In making a distinction between visionary and mystical experiences, Bernard McGinn argues that there are certain visionary experiences that can be categorized as mystical while, conversely, there are other visionary experiences that are not mystical. "Hence, it is not so much the *fact* that someone makes claims to visionary experience as it is the *kind of vision* presented, the *purpose* for which it is given, and the *effect* it has on the recipient that will determine whether or not any particular vision may be described as mystical."[144] Here, McGinn is connecting the type and function of a visionary experience with his broader definition of Christian mysticism, which McGinn articulates as centering "on a form of immediate encounter with God whose essential purpose is to convey a loving knowledge (even a negative one) that transforms the mystic's mind and whole way of life."[145] With such a definition McGinn is acknowledging the eclectic diversity of the Christian mystical tradition. Christian mysticism cannot be reduced to one category of experiences or phenomena, like visionary experiences, but is more expansive while at the same time remaining inclusive of such experiences. "This view, I believe, can provide categories sufficiently specific and yet flexible enough to include in one broad tradition both the usually nonvisionary and non-autobiographical monastic mysticism dominant prior to 1200 and the mystical aspects of the visionary explosion of the latter Middle Ages."[146]

At least three vital points should be taken away from this discourse. First, visionary experiences are an important part of the Christian mystical tradition—in many examples, visionary phenomena constitute mystical experiences, pointing to a visionary mysticism.[147] Second, there are mystical experiences that are distinct from visionary experiences, as Christian mysticism incorporates other, broader forms of spirituality that remain mystical but are not visionary. And, third, there are visionary experiences that, in general, are not mystical because they do not possess the essential elements that McGinn points to of an immediate encounter with the divine that has a transformative effect on the person undergoing the experience. Here, it is noteworthy to reiterate how both James and Underhill pointed to the transformative fruits of a mystical experience as key criteria for discerning its authenticity.

Critiques of James and Underhill

Although they are both considered to be perennialists within the study of mysticism, there are many differences between Underhill and James when it comes to the interpretation of the subject. One key reality that this speaks to is that there is a plurality to perennialism present among scholars of religion and mysticism; this means that, while various scholars apply a perennialist approach to understanding mystical experiences, there are hermeneutical variations to theories of perennialism. We will tackle this issue in the following chapter, where the perennialist–constructivist debate will be observed in greater detail and where attention will be given to the diverse hermeneutical intricacies behind both perennialism and constructivism. However, for now, let us consider some major areas wherein James and Underhill are vulnerable to critique, as evident shortcomings in their hermeneutical approaches can lead to an exploration of some of the major issues of interpretation, especially present in recent history, that surround the subject of extraordinary religious phenomena.

Critiquing James: Hermeneutical Fallacies

One area where James has received much criticism, and Underhill would agree[148] with the criticism, is in his assertion—something that we have yet to mention—that states of mystical consciousness can be reached not only through spiritual methods or spontaneous occurrences that come from a higher source but also through the usage of self-induced intoxicants such as alcohol, drugs, or anesthetics.[149] Commentators have dismissed this claim of James's as a form of "pseudo-mysticism."[150] Yet, James writes that the "drunken consciousness is one bit of the mystic consciousness, and our total opinion of it must find its place in our opinion of that larger whole."[151] James writes very poetically (though one senses a trace of the comic as well in his description) of the drunken state, explaining:

> The sway of alcohol over mankind is unquestionably due to its power to stimulate the mystical faculties of human nature, usually crushed to earth by the cold facts and dry criticisms of the sober hour. Sobriety diminishes, discriminates, and says no; drunkenness expands, unites, and says yes. It is in fact the greater exciter of the *Yes* function in man. It brings to votary from the chill periphery of things to the radiant core. It makes him for the moment one with truth. Not through mere perversity do men run after it.[152]

Similarly, of other intoxicants James writes:

> Nitrous oxide and ether, especially nitrous oxide, when sufficiently diluted with air, stimulate the mystical consciousness in an extraordinary degree. Depth beyond depth of truth seems revealed to the inhaler. This truth fades out, however, or escapes, at the moment of coming to; and if any words remain over in which it seemed to clothe itself, they prove to be the veriest nonsense. Nevertheless, the sense of a profound meaning having been there persists; and I know more than one person who is persuaded that in the nitrous oxide trance we have a genuine metaphysical revelation.[153]

James's observations here are vulnerable to a lot of easy criticism. The most obvious is that what James tries to convey as a state of mystical consciousness can easily be dismissed as artificial intoxication, hallucinatory in nature and lacking any foundation in the transcendent. Moreover, unwittingly here, James may also be falling into the fallacy of reducing mystical consciousness to a certain "feeling," such as the drunken state induces, while ignoring his own process of discernment that measures the spiritual and practical fruits of the encounter to test its authenticity.

Harvey Egan notes the contradiction of the argument within James's own hermeneutic of discernment in distinguishing between genuine and false mysticism. "If James so highly values strength of personality,

integrity of life, creativity, social concerns, and pragmatic results as stemming from the mystical consciousness, it is difficult to see how he can
accept the drunken consciousness which produces the opposite effects."[154]
In other words, James's own criterion for discerning an authentic mystical
experience, judging the phenomenon by the fruits that it produces in the
life of the one who undergoes the encounter, would forbid the "drunken
state" to qualify as a genuine state of mystical consciousness—thus, failing
the author's own test of discernment.

One may argue that the very topic of intoxicants producing a mystical state is something that deserves little, if any, serious attention, as it is
universally dismissed as a fallacious understanding of genuine mysticism
today. However, it is important to note that there were serious attempts by
eminent scholars in the twentieth century to convey an intoxicated state as
one that belongs to the category of mystical or extraordinary experience,
even leading to debates among academics. Thus, ignoring the issue would
be unfruitful, as it would ignore a hermeneutical framework that, no matter how irrelevant today, was taken seriously in various circles in the past.

Aldous Huxley, who also belongs to the perennialist tradition, wrote
one of the most popular books on mysticism of the twentieth century
with his work *The Perennial Philosophy* (1945). He also wrote *The Doors of
Perception* (1954), in which Huxley made the controversial claim that psychedelic drugs can be used to produce extraordinary religious and mystical
experiences.[155] Hence, we see traces of James's influence in incorporating
intoxicants as mechanisms that can lead to states of mystical consciousness. R. C. Zaehner subsequently wrote the influential, albeit polemical,
book *Mysticism Sacred and Profane* as a reaction and challenge to Huxley's
work. Part of Huxley's theory argued that at the basis of all religions is
the desire to escape from one's daily ego and surroundings, and psychedelic drugs have the power to put this goal into effect. Zaehner rejected
Huxley's theory on religion and mysticism as erroneous, challenging his
provocative claims.[156] Especially disconcerting to Zaehner was how Huxley
was using the example of drug-induced states to support the perennial
idea of a universal mystical experience that is present throughout cultures
and religious traditions. Somewhat sarcastically, albeit sharply, Zaehner
wrote of Huxley's thesis:

> for since he has proved that preternatural experience of the most
> vivid kind can be acquired by the taking of drugs and since the
> state of the drug-taker's consciousness bears at least a superficial

resemblance to that of a religious mystic in that time and space appear to be transcended, must it not follow that this experience is "one and the same" as that of the generally accredited mystics?[157]

Zaehner observed that drugs like mescaline do have the effect of inducing vivid experiences; however, he noted that these *artificial* experiences have more in common with states of psychopathology than with mysticism. He wrote:

> Huxley could, and should, have gone further. Mescaline is clini-cally used to produce artificially a state akin to schizophrenia, more specifically the manic phase of the manic-depressive psychosis. It must therefore follow, if we accept the fatal "platitude," [the per-ennial notion that mysticism is a universal experience throughout traditions] that not only can "mystical" experience be obtained artifi-cially by the taking of drugs, it is also naturally present in the manic. It must then follow that the vision of God of the mystical saint is "one and the same" as the hallucination of the lunatic. There would appear to be no way out, unless the original "platitudinous" premise is unsound.[158]

Ingeniously, Zaehner was challenging Huxley's perennial philosophy by sharply noting the paradox, or contradiction, present therein. Huxley wanted to promulgate his idea of mysticism as universally authentic. Yet to do so, he would have to acknowledge that other, namely pathological, states of consciousness, which have a lot in common with drug-induced states and the effects they produce, are also, by his standard, "mystical." That, of course, would be a self-defeating argument, jeopardizing the integrity of Huxley's thesis.

Even in the late twentieth century, we see with controversial figures like Timothy Leary, the Harvard psychologist who likewise advocated the usage of psychedelic drugs to induce purported mystical and religious experi-ences, traces of James's position in play. Today, however, serious scholars of mysticism, as well as religious institutions who investigate mystical phenomena, reject such notions, purposely perceiving the inclusion of any intoxicants as signs of false or inauthentic experiences that do not come from a transcendent source for they are artificially self-induced.

As we have observed, when the Catholic Church investigates reports of visionary or apparitional experiences (cases of private revelation), one important criterion of discernment is the evaluation of the mental and psychological stability of the purported visionary. Any signs of drug usage in the visionary that could produce hallucinatory or intoxicating effects constitute reasons to doubt the integrity of the experience.

Although, like James, Underhill is someone whose grasp and understanding of mysticism is recognized for its depth, her hermeneutic, like James's, is not beyond reproach, either. In Underhill's case, especially interesting is her treatment of extraordinary phenomena like visions and apparitions. Let us consider this in some detail, as Underhill's hermeneutic on this subject speaks to a deeper question of interpretation, presenting a paradigm that has become prevalent in the study of extraordinary experiences: a hermeneutic of reductionism.

Critiquing Underhill: Hermeneutical Reductionism

When Underhill presents the triune category of visions, she dedicates many pages to intellectual and imaginative visions while giving no attention to corporal visions. Underhill simply dismisses the latter as unimportant to the study of mysticism. The dismissal, as it is not supported by any presented research, appears to convey Underhill's personal biases toward such phenomena, specifically revealing her constructivist approach—a constructivism that, in this case, appears to be complete. This is interesting, for while Underhill is recognized as a perennial thinker, her interpretation of corporal visions constitutes a hermeneutic of complete constructivism, as she reductively perceives such phenomena to be something fully constructed by the human mind.

"As to corporeal vision," Underhill writes, "it has few peculiarities of interest to the student of pure mysticism."[159] She then associates the alleged unimportance of corporal visions with their auditory counterpart in "exterior words," explaining: "Like the 'exterior word' it [a corporal vision] is little else than a more or less uncontrolled externalization of inward memories, thoughts, or intuitions—even of some pious picture which has become imprinted on the mind—which may, in some subjects, attain the dimensions of true sensorial hallucination."[160] That is all that Underhill writes of corporal visions.

Thus, Underhill attaches two characteristics to corporal visions, both of which fall into a hermeneutic of reductionism. The first, as mentioned, is constructivism, as Underhill sees such visions as externalizations of inner memories, thoughts, or intuitions; therefore, they are not phenomena that are *received* from outside, from Another, but are phenomena that are *constructed* from within, from the self. Unlike aspects of imaginative visions, even *active* imaginative visions, like Catherine of Siena's "Mystic Marriage," wherein Underhill articulates a combination between divine inspiration and human construction in forming the content of the vision, here she applies a hermeneutic of *complete constructivism*, the corporal vision being a complete construction of the human psyche.

The second characteristic that Underhill attaches to corporal visions, and here she is probably referring to certain, not all, occurrences, is pathology, as she associates certain corporal visions with reaching the depths of sensorial hallucination. Therefore, a constructivist and (occasionally) a pathological component are in play, according to Underhill's approach toward such experiences.

Underhill is very much aware of the history of reductionism that has been present in interpreting extraordinary phenomena. She writes of this reality eloquently, with sharp knowledge, explaining that a debate between "two great powers" has been at the center of this epistemological battle. With regard to reductionism, Underhill reflects on one side of the debate, the "strangely named rationalists," who, she explains:

> feel that they have settled the matter once for all by calling attention to the obvious parallels which exist between the bodily symptoms of acute spiritual stress and the bodily symptoms of certain forms of disease. These considerations, reinforced by those comfortable words "auto-suggestion," "psychosensorial hallucination" and "association neurosis"—which do but reintroduce mystery in another and less attractive form—enable them to pity rather than blame the peculiarities of the great contemplatives. French psychology, in particular, revels in this sort of thing: and would, if it had its way, fill the wards of the Salpêtrière with patients from the Roman Calendar.[161]

This is a reality that James also wrote about, and challenged with his work, deeming such hermeneutical reductionism as a form of "medical materialism," since by this logic a supposedly spiritual phenomenon is being reduced to a medical condition.[162] Thus, as with Underhill's allusion that the school of thought behind French psychology would place Roman saints into psychiatric wards, James mused very similarly in regard to this kind of reductionism. He wrote:

Medical materialism seems indeed a good appellation for the too simple-minded system of thought which we are considering. Medical materialism finishes up Saint Paul by calling his vision on the road to Damascus a discharging lesion of the occipital cortex, he being an epileptic. It snuffs out Saint Teresa [of Avila] as an [sic] hysteric, Saint Francis of Assisi as an [sic] hereditary degenerate.[163]

As we have noted, one of the trademarks of James's definition of mysticism is that the mystical consciousness transcends a rationalistic worldview, pointing to other, deeper dimensions of reality, and thus pointing beyond the reductive frameworks that both James and Underhill challenged when considering how mystical experiences have been hermeneutically denigrated into pathological categories.

However, as observed, Underhill herself is not free of reductionism in her hermeneutic.

Underhill's discernment in distinguishing true from false experiences is, like James's, based on the life-enhancing fruits that can be produced through such encounters. But, it is noteworthy that in the process of writing of those authentic experiences that lead to powerful conversions and life-changing results, those experiences which must come from a transcendent realm, Underhill reveals her prejudice toward other experiences, such as corporal visions, which she, without presenting evidence behind her case, reductively dismisses as being inauthentic. She writes of authentic, life-transforming visionary experiences—we can assume she is referring to intellectual and imaginative visions, which Underhill favors—although she does so by presenting a dubious contrast to corporal visionary experiences:

> Such visions [life-enhancing ones], it is clear, belong to another and higher plane of experience from the radiant appearances of our Lady, the piteous exhibitions of the sufferings of Christ, which swarm in the lives of the saints, and contain no feature which is not traceable to the subject's religious enthusiasm or previous knowledge. These, in the apt phrase of Godfernaux, are but "images floating on the moving deeps of feeling," not symbolic messages from another plane of consciousness.[164]

Therefore, Underhill continues:

Some test, then, must be applied, some basis of classification discovered, if we are to distinguish the visions and voices which seem to be symptoms of real transcendental activity from those which are only due to imagination raised to the n th power, to intense reverie, or to psychic illness. That test, I think, must be the same as that which we shall find useful for ecstatic states; namely, their life-enhancing quality.[165]

Underhill's reductive approach toward such corporal visions as Marian apparitions—she mentions "radiant appearances of our Lady"—and mystical encounters of the Passion of Christ, both of which she refers to as experiences that contain no feature "which is not traceable to the subject's religious enthusiasm or previous knowledge," constitutes a hermeneutic of complete constructivism. Where Underhill's hermeneutic finds a shortcoming is in her seemingly predetermined conviction, which is two-fold, that such experiences are always traceable to the subject's preexistent knowledge or religious enthusiasm and that such experiences do not produce life-enhancing fruits. Numerous examples of the lives of mystics and visionaries challenge these assumptions. Let us consider a couple of these.

The Case of Maria Valtorta

The Italian Catholic mystic Maria Valtorta, as noted in the previous chapter, was a twentieth-century visionary, one who reported experiencing visions of Jesus, Mary, the saints, and her guardian angel—corporal visions, as she described them as appearing to her externally in a three-dimensional manner. In addition to these corporal manifestations, Jesus apparently revealed to Valtorta his life in first-century Palestine, showing her countless scenes from his life as if they were happening right in front of her.[166] So vivid were these experiences that Valtorta even describes the smells of the scenes she was shown, in addition to the sights and sounds. Jesus apparently asked Valtorta to record all that she was being shown. The result was nearly 15,000 hand-written notebook pages, nearly two-thirds of which have been published in a multivolume work depicting the life of Christ. The original Italian edition was titled *The Gospel as It Was Revealed to Me,* while the English edition was retitled *The Poem of the Man God.*[167]

Many things stand out about Valtorta's multivolume work. One fascinating detail is the fact that scholars who have studied the work have noted that Valtorta correctly identifies in her visionary accounts obscure and *unknown* Palestinian locations. That is, Valtorta identifies and often describes places that were not known during her years of writing (during the 1940s) but have been authenticated decades later (after Valtorta's death) through recent discoveries as, in fact, existing in first-century Palestine.[168] In other words, Valtorta's visionary experiences of Christ and his life in first-century Palestine recorded and conveyed *unknown knowledge*.

The Case of Therese Neumann

Let us also consider the example of the German Catholic mystic Therese Neumann (1898–1962). Neumann was another twentieth-century mystic, a contemporary of Valtorta's, who died only one year after the Italian visionary. Neumann was a simple peasant woman coming from Bavaria. She reported experiencing visions of Christ and her body began manifesting the stigmata. The first recorded stigmatic in history was St. Francis of Assisi, who experienced the phenomenon in 1224. Neumann was also known for the mystical grace of *inedia*, the ability to be sustained for long periods of time by consuming no food other than the Eucharist. It is reported that she lived this way for decades, claiming not to consume any food, or drink any water, other than receiving daily a consecrated host, from 1926 until her death in 1962. In July 1927, a medical doctor and four nurses kept watch over her during a two-week period for 24-hours a day, confirming that Neumann was not consuming anything but one consecrated host a day and astonishingly was not suffering any weight loss, ill effects, or dehydration from this practice.[169]

On Fridays, she would often experience ecstatic visions of Christ's Passion, and her stigmata wounds would have strong manifestations during these experiences, with blood pouring out of the wounds on her hands and feet, as well as from her eyes. During some of these Passion ecstasies, witnesses, including priests and linguists, reported that she would utter phrases that were identifiable as constituting ancient Aramaic, a language that Neumann had no training in, or knowledge of. Yet, this was the language that Jesus spoke during his life in first-century Palestine.[170] As with Maria Valtorta, in Therese Neumann's case we have further evidence of a mystic's visionary experiences conveying *unknown knowledge*.

Underhill's Reductionism

Underhill was particularly critical of mystical experiences that are Christocentric in their imagery, particularly corporal visions that may appear like "piteous exhibitions of the sufferings of Christ" or Marian

apparitions, pointing to Christ's mother. Such experiences, she emphasized, "contain no feature which is not traceable to the subject's" previous
religious knowledge or religious enthusiasm (thus his or her preexistent
beliefs).[171] The experiences of both Maria Valtorta and Therese Neumann
challenge Underhill's point, posing a substantial argument to its validity. Both Valtorta and Neumann, it should be noted, experienced "piteous
exhibitions of the sufferings of Christ" (Valtorta, in fact, vividly depicts
the Passion in over one hundred pages of detail in her visionary writings)
and both women are known for producing knowledge from their visionary
encounters that was not previously known to them or, in Valtorta's case, to
anyone; in other words, knowledge that cannot be traced back to "the subject's religious enthusiasm or previous knowledge" (as Underhill put it).

It is important to note that Underhill's skepticism in her early work in
regard to Christocentric corporal visions may be a reflection of her own
spiritual beliefs at the time, which were at odds with her later spiritual
development. By 1921, Steven Fanning explains, Underhill had a spiritual director in Baron Friedrich von Hügel, himself a prominent English
author of mysticism, whose influence on her spiritual life would be significant. "Underhill had known von Hügel, the foremost Catholic theologian in England, for more than a decade and now, under his direction,
her spiritual life took a decidedly Christocentric turn." This Christocentric
turn would be so great that Underhill would state that von Hügel "com-
pelled me to experience Christ," making various references in her personal notebooks of spiritual experiences of God that were Christ-centered
("and within this glow of God one sees Jesus").[172]

The claim of Underhill's earlier work about such corporal, Christocentric
visions is that they do not come from a higher plane of consciousness, and
therefore are not an example of genuine transcendent activity, that they are
completely constructed by the human imagination. Nonetheless, we see in
evidence from the lives of two modern mystics that such a theory is open
to dispute. Underhill, however, presupposing such visionary experiences
to be fully human in their origin, called for some criteria of discernment
to distinguish them from the true, transcendent experiences. As noted,
she emphasized the life-enhancing quality, thus the fruits of genuine experiences, as essential to discerning true from false mystical encounters.
However, in the process of presupposing most corporal visions to be fully
constructed and calling, therefore, for a measure of discernment to be
found in the life-enhancing quality of an experience, Underhill was implying that most corporal visions do not possess life-enhancing qualities.

Such a presupposition is easily challenged through various examples of major visionary experiences. If we consider Marian apparitions, a study of the apparitions of Our Lady of Lourdes in 1858 will show that they had a strong, life-enhancing impact on the young visionary Bernadette Soubirous, as did the apparitions of Our Lady of Fátima in 1917 on the three shepherd children who were visionaries.[173] Life-enhancing, spiritual fruit have become such a hallmark of genuine apparition cases, of discerning the true from the false, that in its 1978 Norms on discerning such phenomena, as we have observed, the Catholic Church considers as one key criterion the "abundant and constant spiritual fruit" that is produced by authentic apparitions.[174]

Since spiritual fruit have become such a standard of major apparition cases, especially within the widely present phenomena of Marian apparitions, Underhill's claim that such experiences cannot be genuine encounters with a transcendent realm falls short of substance. If we specifically consider this reasoning against Underhill's own criterion of discernment—that an experience can be judged by its fruit—then, as we saw with the case of James and intoxicants, in many examples of apparitions Underhill fails her own test of discernment.

As with Marian apparitions and visions of Christ's Passion in the lives of saints and mystics, Underhill also reveals a reductive skepticism toward alleged encounters with, or manifestations of, the demonic. Hermeneutically speaking, the problem is not that there is a skepticism toward such ominous visionary claims but that, in Underhill's case, there is no evidence offered (whether empirical or philosophical) to justify the skepticism, specifically the denigration of such experiences into pathological categories. Underhill writes:

> When Julian of Norwich in her illness saw the "horrible showing" of the Fiend, red with black freckles, which clutched at her throat with its paws: when St. Teresa was visited by Satan, who left a smell of brimstone behind, or when she saw him sitting on the top of her breviary and dislodged him by the use of holy water: it is surely reasonable to allow that we are in the presence of visions which tend towards the psychopathic type, and which are expressive of little else but an exhaustion and temporary loss of balance on the subject's part, which allowed her intense consciousness of the reality of evil to assume a concrete form.[175]

In a footnote, Underhill writes similarly of Catherine of Siena's alleged experiences with the demonic, enunciating:

> Thus too in the case of St. Catherine of Siena, the intense spiritual strain of that three years' retreat which I have already described (supra, Pt. II, Cap 1.) showed itself towards the end of the period by a change in the character of her visions. These, which had previously been wholly concerned with the intuitions of the good and the beautiful, now took on an evil aspect and greatly distressed her. . . . We are obliged to agree with [James] Pratt that such visions as these are "pathological phenomena quite on a level with other hallucinations."[176]

In all three cases referenced here, that of Julian of Norwich, Teresa of Avila, and Catherine of Siena, Underhill postulates that "exhaustion," a "temporary loss of balance," and "intense spiritual strain" must have been responsible for producing visions of "the psychopathic type"—of "pathological phenomena" that should be considered hallucinatory.[177] The problem is that Underhill produces no evidence, nor gives any arguments, explaining why visionary manifestations of evil have to be considered pathological. She writes of a meaningful transition that Catherine's visions have made, from concentration on the good and the beautiful to evil, and claims that intense spiritual stress must have produced this allegedly pathological transition in Catherine's visionary encounters. Notwithstanding, the issue remains that Underhill provides no reasoning to substantiate or support the claim as to why this visionary transition toward evil has to be deemed "pathological" or hallucinatory.

Why, in other words, could we not consider the possibility that Catherine and the aforementioned mystics have had real visionary manifestations of evil? It may be that Underhill is restricting the spiritual realm to the *good*, to a benevolent, transcendent source and, therefore, perceiving strong manifestations of the demonic as a sign of inauthentic experiences, reductively dismissing them as pathological without providing any explanation for her diagnosis. However, it is interesting how Underhill immediately associates manifestations of concrete evil with pathology, not even considering the question of cultural constructivism, meaning mentally constructed experiences that, stemming from preexistent knowledge, are more a product of culture than of hysteria or hallucination. Here we see another shortcoming of her hermeneutic.

It is ironic, considering that Underhill is very critical of an unhealthy absolutism that is present in the views of both rationalists and supernaturalists, the former denying all mystical phenomena while the latter perceiving objectivity behind all genuine mystical phenomena. However, in the case of corporal visions, whether of the sacred or the profane, Underhill herself appears to fall into an absolutist hermeneutic, the type that she criticizes in rationalists. Her dismissal of Marian or Christocentric corporal visions as culturally constructed phenomena, and her dismissal of Satanic or demonic manifestations as pathological phenomena, without substantiating these reductive claims, reveal a rationalist tendency that seems to be based more on preconceived ideas than on empirical evidence.

A Holistic Approach: The Case of Gemma Galgani

More holistic approaches have been formulated, incorporating theories of the pathological and the demonic alongside the authentic experience. In an introduction to the writings of the modern mystic Gemma Galgani (1878–1903), a young Italian woman and Catholic saint who experienced visions, ecstasies, and the stigmata of Christ on her body, Harvey Egan notes how diverse and multifaceted the experiences of mystics may be. "The mystic experiences genuine, pathological, and diabolical phenomena during the course of her mystical life."[178] Egan recognizes this reality in Galgani's life, emphasizing that God-given, mystical experiences "never occur alone."[179] Therefore, a mystic who has genuine, God-given experiences, such as divine visions, may also receive both demonic and pathological experiences.

Again, there is a lot of gray area and subjectivity when dealing with such experiences; it is not always black and white. Gemma Galgani, Egan notes, "experienced more secondary mystical phenomena than any other mystic in the Christian tradition."[180] By "secondary mystical phenomena" Egan means extraordinary experiences such as "numerous trinitarian, Christ-centered, Marian, and eucharistic illuminations. Raptures, ecstasies, seraphic wounds of love, visions, locutions, the *complete* stigmata, bloody sweat, tears of blood, mystical effluvia (perfumed bodily secretions), satanic attacks, and penetrating discernment of spirits."[181] In considering the various experiences that she encountered, it is noteworthy how Egan lists "satanic attacks" among the secondary phenomena that Galgani underwent: she often claimed to see physical manifestations of the devil and even reported being physically assaulted by these manifestations. [182]

Egan notes how there is a long history of reported spiritual warfare in the lives of the mystics, even starting with Christ himself, with an obvious emphasis on the presence of authentic evil in the form of Satan.[183]

Considering the divine, the demonic, and the pathological in Galgani's life, Egan explains that taken together, "these phenomena manifest God's presence, the devil's presence, and Gemma's own healthy and pathological accommodations and resistances to both the divine and the demonic presence."[184] There are elements of a psychoanalytical diagnosis from Egan, on the one hand, and recognizing genuine fruits of mystical experience, on the other hand, in considering the conditions recorded in Galgani's extraordinary experiences. He enunciates:

> Furthermore, it is not surprising that some of these phenomena may reflect Gemma's infantile dreams, inordinate desires, immature projections, and pathological hallucinations. However, others directly countered Gemma's physically, psychologically, and morally pernicious tendencies. Conversion, renewed energy, strength, courage, authority, and peace accompanied them. They bestowed insight, knowledge, and wisdom upon her and deepened her faith, hope, and love.
>
> The Christian mystics unanimously teach that genuine God-induced extraordinary phenomena leave behind in their wake faith, hope, love, humility, heroic virtue, and peace. The enhancement of life at all levels of the person's being attests to their authenticity. They both produce and flow from holiness.[185]

Thus, here we have a more holistic hermeneutic, wherein a mystic is not reductively categorized into a single label—whether identified as someone who is insane, possessed, or authentic—but where a multifariousness is acknowledged within the realm of experiences belonging to the mystic. Egan suggests that there is no reason, as in the case of Gemma Galgani, as to why a mystic cannot have genuine experiences that come from a transcendent source and also have experiences that are genuinely diabolical or pathological. What is in play here is a recognition of the complexity of the human person, as body, mind, and soul, and the acknowledgment that the various faculties of the person may, at times but not always, be affected by different sources of influence. What is also in play here, from Egan, is an intellectual open-mindedness that does not reduce reality to one worldview, one ontology like naturalism, but humbly and openly considers the

multidimensional potential that may be present in the extraordinary experiences of mystics, including the supernatural and paranormal alongside
the natural. We will discuss in future chapters the necessity of such an
intellectually courageous and open approach toward studying religious
experiences—one that does not reduce perception to a single philosophy
or ideology.

HAVING OBSERVED THE major contributions, as well as limitations, of the
epistemologies of William James and Evelyn Underhill, with an emphasis
on the evolving understanding of mystical and visionary experiences that
developed in the early twentieth century and have influenced the study of
religion since, let us now turn to the major debate between scholars that
originated in the latter half of the twentieth century and has made significant contributions to this topic. Within the examination of this debate we
will enter into an in-depth consideration of the hermeneutics of reductionism that mystical experiences have been subjected to in recent history.

4

The Great Debate

*We now come to that eternal battle-ground, the estab-
lished discussion of those abnormal psychic phenomena
which appear so persistently in the history of the mystics.
That is to say, visions, auditions, automatic script, and
those dramatic dialogues between the Self and some other
factor—the Soul, Love, Reason, of the Voice of God—which
seems sometimes to arise from an exalted and uncontrolled
imaginative power, sometimes to attain the proportions of
auditory hallucination. Here, moderate persons are like to
be hewn in pieces between the two "great powers" who have
long disputed this territory.*

—EVELYN UNDERHILL

THROUGHOUT THE TWENTIETH century, an academic debate between
scholars of mysticism developed concentrating on the best epistemological approach to use in order to understand the essence of extraordinary
religious experiences. The two dominant schools of thought, or theories
of interpretation, to materialize from this hermeneutical debate have been
the *perennial* tradition and the *constructivist* tradition.

The perennial model was the preeminent lens for interpreting religious experiences throughout the first half of the twentieth century, producing works from various scholars in both popular and academic culture.
Prominent perennial thinkers in religious studies have included William
James, Evelyn Underhill, Aldous Huxley, Rudolf Otto, W. T. Stace, Huston
Smith, and the Belgian Jesuit Joseph Maréchal, S.J., to name a few.[1] The
perennial approach to religious experience, however, came under attack
in the latter half of the twentieth century when a group of scholars, in the
1970s and '80s particularly, began challenging perennial interpretations
through the lens of constructivism, as an alternative (and, allegedly, a more
suitable) hermeneutical approach to understanding mystical experiences.

Constructivists include such scholars as R. C. Zaehner, Bruce Garside, Steven T. Katz, Robert Gimello, H. P. Owen, and Hans H. Penner, among others, as well as their precursors, seen in the earlier works of thinkers like William Ralph Inge and Rufus Jones.[2] The debate between perennialists and constructivists has heated up in recent years, entering into the twenty-first century with renewed developments in the perennialist approach advanced by a new generation of scholars, often known as "neo-perennialists." Before examining these developments, let us begin by exploring the main ideas of the traditional perennial philosophy with its earlier roots.

Perennialism

Perennial thinkers have emphasized the cross-cultural and trans-historical unity of mystical experiences. Perennial interpretations, in an ecumenical fashion as the kind portrayed by James, have argued that persons from different religious and cultural backgrounds share immensely similar spiritual experiences. This mutuality, according to perennial logic, has been the case throughout the centuries.[3]

There are remarkable parallels in the language, symbols, and concepts used by persons in cross-cultural settings, reporting similar spiritual phenomena while partaking in diverse religious practices from various faith traditions. For example, perennial logic would argue that in terms of cultivated experiences intense Christian prayer can lead to a similar (if not identical) spiritual experience for a Christian as Buddhist meditation can for a Buddhist. Hence, according to scholar R. L. Franklin, perennialism "presents mysticism as involving a state of consciousness found in virtually all religions, recognizably the same in each, and acknowledged by those who have eyes to see as the highest goal of the religious quest."[4] Thus, the emphasis here is on a universal spiritual experience discernable in every religious tradition through the unifying qualities of a powerful altered state of consciousness—again, what James called the "mystical state of consciousness."

A couple of major criticisms have emerged regarding the perennial perspective. Robert Forman, whose own neo-perennialist approach to extraordinary experiences has much in common with traditional perennial philosophy, does acknowledge that the perennial view has become easy to attack by constructivists, for two reasons. First, the institutional academic paradigm in the humanities has shifted to a constructivist understanding of knowledge, fueling the notion that language and cultural background fully shape human experience—as is apparent in fields like anthropology, sociology, and, often, history—and, therefore, undermining the idea of a pure, unmediated experience. Religious studies, including the study of mysticism and other extraordinary religious experiences, have also been subjected to this intellectual shift.[5] Second, Forman acknowledges that many eminent perennial thinkers have partaken of sloppy and (therefore) irresponsible scholarship, which has not been difficult to refute and discredit—even by neo-perennialists like Forman himself. Forman explains:

> For example, Rudolf Otto's *Mysticism East and West* was an attempt to draw parallels between the mystical writings of Shankara and Meister Eckhart. Otto was rightly criticized for misrepresenting both, however. Shankara's key notions of *maya*, superimposition, the two forms of Brahman, and other technical terms were never given clear exposition by Otto, and thus the distinctiveness of his philosophy was muddled. Similarly, little of the nuance of Eckhart's doctrines of the Birth of the Word, of the boiling up (*ebullition*) of the Godhead, or of the breakthrough (*durchbruch*) were ever clarified; again, what made Eckhart distinctive was lost. Aldous Huxley, in his renowned *Perennial Philosophy*, quoted little bits and pieces out of context from one mystic after another; in his zeal to make them seem identical, he offered little if any exegesis of any of them.[6]

Forman, therefore, concludes that perennialists "like these thus benuded the individual mystics and mystical traditions of their specific teachings. The various traditions seemed to disappear into some bland, characterless anonymity."[7] Of course, this does not mean that all perennial thinkers have been guilty of such impoverished scholarship, or that there is one method that encapsulates every perennialist approach. William Parsons has argued that, within recent surveys of perennialist scholarship, one can "ascertain at least three subtypes" of perennialism.[8] Parsons identifies these specific subtypes as (1) the perennial invariant model; (2) the perennial variant model; and (3) the typological variant model. Let us consider these.

The Perennial Invariant

The first model, according to Parsons, suggests that all mystical experiences are composed of the same core characteristics and are expressed in spiritual texts through presentations that are so similar, from one to the other, as to transcend all cultural, religious, and linguistic influences and boundaries. This is the perennial invariant model.[9]

The Perennial Variant

The second subtype of perennialism, the perennial variant model, argues (like the first) that the underlying characteristics of mystical experiences are the same; however, this model argues that religious and cultural traditions do have an influence on the mode, or form, of expression with which the experiences are conveyed.[10] Thus similar, if not identical, religious and mystical experiences can be conveyed in a diverse manner through spiritual texts, contingent on the traditions influencing the writer of the text. Core characteristics of the experiences are similar, but the subsequent modes of interpretation applied to the experiences, by diverse religious and cultural traditions, give specific expressions of these encounters— expressions that are culturally filtered and can be different in representation. Therefore, there is a *similarity of content* in extraordinary experiences but a *diversity in form* of interpretation and expression.[11]

The Typological Variant

The third subtype of perennialism identified by Parsons is the typological variant model. This model postulates that both the content and the form of expression of mystical experiences have variations that are affected by the religious and cultural influences of the individual. In other words, neither the content of the experience nor its form of expression is pure, but both are mediated through preexistent factors.[12]

THOUGH THE FIRST two subtypes identified by Parsons, the perennial invariant and the perennial variant, are convincing articulations as two interpretative frameworks within the perennialist hermeneutic, the third subtype, the typological variant, is less convincing. The issue is that if this subtype sees both the content and the form of extraordinary religious experiences as being culturally conditioned, then it views experience through a lens that sees more hermeneutical commonality with the constructivist framework rather than that of the perennialist. The key here is the *content* of religious experience, which precedes the *form*—the form being understood as the way in which the content is interpreted. The *form* may be culturally influenced for a hermeneutic to be understood as perennial (as the perennial variant subtype articulates); however, if the *content* of the experience is culturally conditioned, then the hermeneutic that applies this interpretation should be considered *constructivist*, as such an interpretation constitutes a key characteristic of the constructivist thesis in regard to religious experiences.

Robert Forman writes of "the constructivist thesis," explaining what it is by contrasting it to perennialism as a framework for understanding religious experiences. He cites Steven Katz as the foremost proponent of this type of hermeneutic:

> Now, like his fellow constructivists, Katz is making an epistemologically heavy claim. He is not asserting that previously held beliefs and concepts will come into play only in the postexperiential shaping of the descriptions and texts [of mystical experiences], but rather that they will play their role in the shaping of the actual mystical experience(s) themselves.[13]

In other words, it is not only post-experiential interpretations of mystical experiences, thus the form, that are culturally conditioned, according to this view, but, even previously, the actual shaping of the experience and thus the content. This constitutes the core characteristic of a constructivist hermeneutic in understanding religious experience and, therefore, it is not unreasonable to assess that Parsons makes a vulnerable argument in identifying such a hermeneutic within a perennialist category, as the "typological variant" model. Once the content of an experience is understood as being culturally conditioned, then the interpretation's outlook possesses the tenets of constructivism.

Let us now turn to constructivism and explore its tenets with greater depth, as constructivist criticisms of the perennial philosophical approach to religious experience have been influential, highly affecting the contemporary path of religious studies, and as the constructivist approach makes significant contributions to discourses on religious experience.

Constructivism

The hermeneutic of constructivism,[14] in religion as well as in other disciplines of study within the humanities and social sciences, argues that experience is not unmediated but, rather, is based on a number of preexistent circumstances. Thus, if we were to study the cases of mystics, the spiritual experiences that such individuals—whether Jewish, Christian, Muslim, Buddhist, Hindu, or other—report would be highly shaped by the socioreligious, economic, cultural, and linguistic traditions, circumstances, and expectations that form their backgrounds; and owing to such differing backgrounds, there are significant differences in the spiritual experiences that individuals from these traditions report. Therefore, unlike the perennialists, constructivists do not necessarily concentrate on a spiritual unity in mysticism but on a religious pluralism that acknowledges the differences of each mystical tradition on the basis of preexisting cultural contexts influencing their experiences. Forman calls this the "pluralism thesis" and explains that the "pluralism thesis is important to these [constructivist] authors as it is their response to the perennial philosophers' arguments that mysticism is by and large the same across time and tradition."[15]

This constructivist perspective can be understood through Immanuel Kant's epistemology. Kant, as we will shortly see, provides the philosophical foundations for constructivism. Kant argued that no historical object can be observed without a process of mediation, serving as a subjective filtering mechanism between the individual and his or her object of study.[16] In essence, that is what the constructivists are arguing about religion and, particularly, about mystical experiences. A mystical experience cannot be understood properly as an unmediated experience, for it is always mediated and, therefore, highly influenced by an individual's cultural context and by the filtering structures of the mind. Thus the mystical experience of a Christian will be significantly different from that of a Buddhist owing to the different cultural context and religious tradition that each is operating from, and owing to the conditioned processing of the mind that precludes unmediated experiences, Kant would articulate. Steven Katz, as the foremost proponent of the constructivist approach to religious experiences, has, as a result of the epistemologically Kantian connection, developed the reputation of being a neo-Kantian thinker.[17]

The most influential work of the twentieth century to challenge the perennial philosophical approach to mysticism was *Mysticism and Philosophical Analysis*, published in 1978 as a collection of essays by constructivist scholars. The work was edited by Katz, who himself contributed two influential essays to the collection. Katz continued the constructivist crusade with the subsequent publication of *Mysticism and Language*, another edited work bringing constructivist scholars together, this time not simply to challenge the perennial philosophy but, emblematic of the linguistic turn, also to explore further the significant position of language in the study of religious and mystical experiences. In his introductory essay to the work, Katz makes a bold statement on the importance of language and contextualization in understanding mystical experiences:

> It is my view . . . that mystical reports do not merely indicate the postexperiential description of an unreportable experience in the language closest at hand. Rather, the experiences themselves are inescapably shaped by prior linguistic influences such that the lived experience conforms to a preexistent pattern that has been learned, then intended, and then actualized in the experiential reality of the mystic.[18]

Katz's proclamation is bold exactly *because* he emphasizes that mystical experiences are shaped by *prior* linguistic influences. Therefore, Katz is postulating that it is the prior cultural and linguistic context that formulates the experience, not the other way around—a core characteristic of constructivism (seeing conceptual shaping in the content of the experience). Such a claim is bold to many perennial thinkers, as it threatens the authenticity and dignity of the reported experience, denigrating it. However, it is important to point out that, as with perennialism, there are variations of constructivism.

Forman has argued that there are "two or three possible interpretations of the constructivist model."[19] He presents three variations, distinguishing them as "complete constructivism," "incomplete constructivism," and "catalytic constructivism."[20] Let us consider these.

Complete Constructivism

Complete constructivism, according to Forman, constitutes a model of interpretation wherein the mystical experience is "one hundred percent shaped, determined, and provided" by the pre-existent set of beliefs and expectations (thus, the content) of the individual, to the point where it can become a hallucination. A hallucination may be "one such example," Forman explains. He cites the work of the constructivist Robert Gimello in articulating this hermeneutic. Gimello argued that mystical experiences are simply "the psychosomatic enhancement of religious beliefs and values or of the beliefs and values of other kinds which are held 'religiously.' "[21]

Therefore, by "psychosomatic enhancement," Gimello is claiming that such experiences are complete constructions of the human mind without any spiritual foundation to them. This model completely undermines the integrity of mystical experiences, denigrating what is reported as spiritual or supernatural into categories of the natural and, even more severely, into the hallucinatory or the pathological.

Incomplete Constructivism

The second model, incomplete constructivism, is more nuanced in the balance that it maintains, or the admixture that it allows, between the components affecting the shape of a mystical experience. Incomplete constructivism argues, according to Forman, that the shape of an experience is provided by preexistent circumstances, thus it is in large part culturally constructed, but other parts of the experience are provided by "something else."[22] Forman is not clear as to what this "something else" entails, as he simply states, somewhat vaguely (if not dismissively), that this "something else" can include "sensory input or whatever."[23]

In reality, it is not difficult to see the voice of William James here with his mysterious something "more," as an enigmatic dimension of such extraordinary experiences. Forman hints at such an interpretation, that the "something else" of incomplete constructivism is a reference to a deeper (perhaps even transcendent) element of the experience, with his following point. Forman maintains that incomplete constructivism, although seemingly plausible on the surface, "cannot do the work required by the pluralism thesis."[24] The pluralism thesis, which argued that mystical experiences are different throughout cultures, is most easily undermined, according to Forman, through an incomplete constructivist hermeneutic when the role of preexistent beliefs in constructing a mystical experience are minimal; "for if so, then the experiences from different cultures would be distinguishable in only minimal ways."[25] He explains that under such a circumstance the perennialist might say "that mysticism is largely the same but for the 'different flavors' that accrue to those experiences as a result of the constructivist activities of the subject."[26] In other words, "If there are only different flavors to a common experience type, then the perennialists can base their arguments on the underlying parallelism; Katz's plea for the recognition of differences would go unheard. Thus—and this is key— the best way (perhaps the only way) to protect the pluralist hypothesis is through a complete constructivism."[27]

The problem, therefore, is that an incomplete constructivism, in seeing an admixture of mediated and unmediated components in content that shape a mystical experience, does not challenge the fact that the unmediated components, the "something else," can be universally the same at their core throughout cultures. For if they are the same, then the perennialist interpretation of a cross-culturally, universally present, shared mystical experience with mutual characteristics overrides the constructivist notion of a pluralism thesis.

Catalytic Constructivism

A third possible model of constructivism—what Forman calls "catalytic constructivism"—maintains that the original "generating problems"[28] or "starting problems of each doctrinal, theological system,"[29] consciously shape the experience that an individual will encounter (or, more aptly, in this view, *construct*). Katz articulates the idea eloquently, explaining: "The respective 'generating' problems at the heart of each tradition suggest their respective generating answers involving, as they do, differing mental and epistemological constructs, ontological commitments, and metaphysical superstructures which order experience in differing ways."[30] Therefore, to illustrate the point with an example, let us consider Christianity.

Since the "starting problem" of Christianity constitutes Original Sin and humanity's separation from God, the Christian mind will be affected by this conceptual paradigm and generate an experience that solves the problem of this paradigm, being shaped by the same conceptual (thus, theological or doctrinal) framework. This is why, Katz would argue, Christians who experience extraordinary religious experiences generate or construct experiences of *mystical union* (instead of, say, experiences of *nirvana*, as Buddhists do, or *devekuth*, as Jews do): because the "union" of the human and divine in such an experience counters the separation between God and humanity that transpired during the "generating problem" of the Christian tradition, the problem of Original Sin. Therefore, Katz and like-minded thinkers argue that the original problems of faith traditions—conceptual, theological, doctrinal—play a role as catalysts generating specific content experiences. "We are each a unitary consciousness and each of us connects the 'problem' and its answer through forms of connection, synthesis, and objectivity which are integral to our consciousness as conscious agents of the sort we are."[31] Thus, the altered state of consciousness that the Buddhist generates as *nirvana* is different from the Christian's *mystical union* because the former mentally constructs an experience that provides an answer to a specific system of primordial beliefs that differ from the latter's, and vice versa. The Buddhist is not concerned with Original Sin or humanity's separation from God (and, therefore, will not construct an experience of *mystical union*) but is concerned with suffering and impermanence (and will, therefore, generate an experience appropriate to this original dilemma).

What is most important in understanding this final variation of constructivism, catalytic constructivism, is that with this hermeneutic Katz and like-minded constructivists are *not saying* that the Christian encounters a genuine experience of *mystical union* because of the primordial problem of Original Sin and separation from God. On the contrary, what is being articulated is that the Christian *mentally constructs* an experience of *mystical union* because of the primordial problem of Original Sin and separation from God that is present in Christianity's belief system. This is an important distinction to recognize and to distinguish from the perennial views of someone like Evelyn Underhill, for example. As we have seen in the previous chapter, Underhill would argue that God communicates through extraordinary experiences by using the concepts and symbols that the particular culture would understand. Therefore, the divine genuinely communicates through an experience of *mystical union* with the Christian, or through an experience of *nirvana* with the Buddhist, or through an experience of *devekuth* with the Jewish mystic, according to Underhill's perennialism, applying the conceptual framework in the divine communication that each particular tradition would comprehend. In each case, the experience comes from the same source—in Underhill's interpretation—but is flavored with different forms of expression, contingent on cultural and religious understanding.

This is different—an absolute inversion, in fact—from what Katz is articulating. In his view, it is the Christian who constructs the experience of *mystical union*; it is the Buddhist who constructs the experience of *nirvana*; it is the Jew who constructs the experience of *devekuth*. These experiences are not genuine communications of the divine but, rather, subjective constructions of the human mind based on complex processes of indoctrination and epistemological activity within the metaphysical framework of primordial systems of belief. "The mind can be seen to contribute both the problem and the means of overcoming: it defines the origin, the way, and the goal, shaping experience accordingly," Katz concludes.[32] In this view it is the mind, and not something "more" or transcendent, that formulates the origin of the experience.

Developments in the Debate: The Pure Conscious Experience and the New Perennialism

Forman has challenged Katz on this matter, accusing Katz and like-minded constructivists of a cultural reductionism in their analysis of mystical experiences.[33] Like Katz, Forman is an important scholar in the modern perennialist–constructivist debate, having led the counterresponse to the constructivists in recent decades. The most influential work in articulating this response was the publication of *The Problem of Pure Consciousness*, a collection of essays by neo-perennialist scholars responding to the (then-dominant) constructivist paradigm toward understanding extraordinary religious and mystical experiences.[34] The work is edited by Forman who himself has contributed an essay alongside a lengthy introduction.[35]

The Problem of Pure Consciousness attempted to deconstruct the constructivist approach, and a subsequent publication by these neo-perennialists, *The Innate Capacity*, has further attempted to develop a new model by which to examine and understand mysticism.[36] This new model is labeled pure conscious experience (PCE); it is a much more spiritual approach to mysticism than the sociologically laden constructivist version. Proponents of the PCE model argue, similarly to traditional perennialist approaches, that individuals across cultures and time periods tend to report similar religious and mystical experiences notwithstanding the different religious backgrounds they stem from. The neo-perennialists have identified a core, similar experience present across cultures that a constructivist epistemology, according to them, cannot account for. Andrew Newberg describes this experience thus: "In a profound unitary state, there are no boundaries of discrete beings, there is no sense of the passage of time, no sense of the extension of space, and the self-other dichotomy is totally obliterated. In other words, the state consists of an absolute sense of unity without thought, without words, without sensation, and not even being sensed to inhere in a subject."[37] G. William Barnard similarly writes of the PCE as a state of mystical awareness that has been described by neo-perennialists "as simple, contentless awareness itself, a state of consciousness that is free from thoughts and that does not contain a subject/object distinction."[38]

Neo-perennialists have used the PCE to challenge the epistemological assumptions of constructivism, arguing that the central tenets of constructivism, specifically the ideas that *every* mystical experience is mediated and conceptually shaped by preexistent structures of thinking and indoctrination, does not hold up in light of the PCE. The PCE in this regard becomes the exception to the rule, pointing to limitations, in essence to the inapplicability, of constructivist epistemology toward explaining such experiences. Stephen Bernhardt explains the matter eloquently, considering how the characteristics of the PCE, as a contentless, unitive experience of consciousness, transcend the epistemological assumptions of mediation and shaping, as present in constructivist hermeneutics:

> In other words, it is hard to see how one could say that the pure consciousness event is mediated, if by that it is meant that *during the event* the mystic is employing concepts; differentiating his awareness, according to religious patterns and symbols; drawing upon memory, apprehension, expectation, language or the accumulation of prior experience; or discriminating and integrating. Without the encounter with any object, intention, or thing, it just does not seem that there is sufficient complexity during the pure consciousness event to say that any such conceptually constructive elements are involved.[39]

The fact that the PCE has been reported cross-culturally, as a universally present experience in the Jewish, Christian, and Buddhist mystical traditions, further fuels neo-perennialist attacks on constructivist ideas, undermining the pluralism thesis.[40] For, if each religious tradition's contextual structures of belief, thinking, and expectation are supposed to shape and, therefore, produce a different mystical experience, as the pluralism thesis postulates, then how can this explain the presence of identical, contentless, unitive experiences of consciousness as the PCE being present in diverse religious traditions?

Furthermore, neo-perennialists have challenged the methodological reductions of many constructivist scholars. For example, one problem that Forman has with Katz's approach is how the latter reduces the study of mysticism to textual analysis and, specifically, texts of certain mystics. Katz explains that "the only evidence we have . . . is the account given by mystics of their experience. These are the data for study and analysis. No scholar can get behind the autobiographical fragments to the putative 'pure experience'—whatever one holds that to be."[41] As well as claiming that we can *only* study mysticism through the remaining texts left over by mystics, thus providing the only source material, Katz admits that only a few subjects, "the great mystics," deserve our attention.[42] Comparing these constructivists to the perennial thinkers, John Horgan astutely observed: "Unlike [Huston] Smith, Aldous Huxley, and other perennialists, these academic scholars [constructivists] treated mysticism not as a universal human experience but as a literary phenomenon, a collection of 'texts' requiring interpretation in the light of other texts."[43]

Forman's own position argues for a more personal, and contemporary, approach. Forman especially thinks it would be useful to conduct interviews with practitioners of numerous spiritualities to compare and contrast their inner experiences, instead of limiting scholars of religious experience to textual analysis of the past.[44]

In addition to observing Katz's claims, Forman notes the provocative postulations of constructivist scholar Robert Gimello, who writes: "All mystical experiences, like all experiences generally, have specific structures, and these are neither fortuitous nor *sui generis*. Rather they are given to the experiences, at their very inceptions, by concepts, beliefs, values, and expectations *already operative* in the mystics' minds."[45] The problem that Forman has with these constructivist approaches is that, through the constructivist framework, mysticism "becomes a kind of delusion fostered by the indoctrination system. But it thereby loses its authenticity."[46]To better understand this argument, it deserves recognition that Forman, and likeminded neo-perennialists, do not necessarily disagree that cultural context is involved in mystical experience; they simply disagree on its time and function. To demonstrate this, let us take an example outside a Christian framework.

Katz argues that setting a "Buddhist understanding of the nature of things over against the Jewish should, in itself, already be strong evidence for the thesis that what the Buddhist experiences as *nirvana* is different from what the Jew experiences as *devekuth*."[47] However, Forman counters that such logic is fallacious, for it "implicitly denies the possibility that there may be two terms with different senses which have the same referent."[48] In other words, what Forman is saying, in promulgating a cross-cultural perspective again, is that the experience which the Buddhist calls *nirvana*, a very mystical state, can be the *same experience* that the Jew calls *devekuth* or, further, it can be the *same experience* that the Christian calls *mystical union*. However, each understands the experience differently owing to the preexistent, conceptual framework that each is operating from. The cultural context in itself does not make the individual experiences different; it simply gives *the same experience* different *forms* of interpretation and expression, according to neo-perennialist phenomenology.

Here we see that Forman, a post-constructivist, is not abandoning concepts or language that is idiosyncratic to each religious tradition, but unlike the constructivists, he is positioning the application of cultural context, and all its conceptual attributions, *after* the experience. Thus the claim is being made that the mystical experience, for it to be a genuine spiritual event, must come first and *thereafter* the mystic applies his or her cultural concepts and understanding to that experience. Another possibility would be "incomplete constructivism," wherein the content is shaped by both preexistent ideas and the "something more," thus having the combination of the mediated and the unmediated. The presence of the unmediated components in the content—thus, the *pure*, or *given*, experience—even if existing alongside mediated components, assures the integrity of the experience. Otherwise, as Forman noted, mysticism becomes a type of delusion fostered by the indoctrination system, a view that complete constructivism would promulgate, a view that challenges the very integrity of experience.

A major issue behind the debates between constructivists and neo-perennialists is the question of epistemology. Here, the influence of Immanuel Kant's ideas have been central in formulating modern hermeneutics of understanding religious and mystical experiences. However, the validity of Kantian epistemology in this specific discourse has been called into question, notwithstanding the fact that it is the predominant epistemological model underlying the debate. Let us, therefore, turn to this issue.

The Epistemological Question: A Kantian Hermeneutic or a "Kantian" Misreading of Kant?

Anthony Perovich Jr. explains that the "fundamental tenet of Kant's epistemology is that the knower plays an active role in the production of experience. . . . On this view, no experiences are simply given, but rather are always mediated through the organizing structures that knowers bring with them."[49] Thus, all human experiences are mediated by the preexistent structures, external and internal, affecting the mind and, therefore, there is no such thing as an unmediated experience, according to Kant's epistemology. This is important to realize because Kant's epistemology plays a central role in formulating the basis for a constructivist understanding of religious and mystical experiences, and constitutes the underlying framework of cognition responsible for fueling the debate between perennialists and constructivists.

Steven Katz, Peter Moore, Robert Gimello, H. P. Owen, John E. Smith, and a number of other constructivist scholars have used Kant's epistemological framework as a hermeneutic to advance a constructivist interpretation and understanding of mystical experiences.[50] Speaking of the Kantian influence on modern constructivists, Forman notes that "Katz and his colleagues are fond of the Kantian term 'mediation,' and seem to regard his doctrines as the logical foundation of their own."[51] Kant's epistemology has had a widespread influence throughout academia, affecting disciplines in the humanities and social sciences.

In a noted essay titled "Does the Philosophy of Mysticism Rest on a Mistake?" Anthony Perovich Jr. has presented the most persuasive critique of the way that constructivist scholars have appropriated Kant's epistemology to interpret mystical experiences. Perovich uses Kant himself to show how "Kantian"[52] (or "neo-Kantian") constructivists have misunderstood and misapplied Kant's epistemological model with regard to mystical experiences. He argues that the philosophical foundation on which the constructivist hermeneutic rests does not provide the grounds to critique mystical experiences the way that constructivists have been doing, perceiving a misapplication of Kant's ideas in their approach.[53]

Perovich explains how the pluralism thesis, as promulgated by constructivists to deny a shared universal core in mystical experiences, is based on Kant's epistemology.

The method of attack [against the perennial idea of universality] consists in declaring one's allegiance to the Kantian epistemology . . . affirming that the intellectual and practical context of each religious tradition performs the function of Kant's categories in shaping the religious experience of the adherents of that tradition and pointing out that these claims are incompatible with the view that the experience of mystics from different traditions can be phenomenologically identical.[54]

This constructivist argument—that religious experiences are the products of a culturally conditioned and preexistent framework of thinking leading to different experiences among different cultures—is, when promulgated, "often conjoined with an account of the reports by mystics from one or more traditions, along with the suggestion that the clearly tradition-specific character of these reports offers empirical evidence in support of the conclusions already deduced on philosophical grounds."[55] Here, Perovich is deconstructing the constructivist approach by noting that an adherence to Kant's epistemological framework can set up predetermined conclusions on the basis of a preestablished philosophical structure. It is true that there is an empirical base in the scholarship of constructivists, particularly through textual analysis of mystical writings in documenting obvious differences between mystics of various traditions. However, the notion that there may be various terms with different senses in such writings that refer to the same experience is inherently rejected in favor of the epistemological presuppositions of Kantian thinking. This is what Perovich and other perennialists are pointing to.[56] Perovich articulates three main points that form his thesis. He writes that:

1. the Kantian epistemology seems singularly inapposite when applied to certain sorts of mystical experience;
2. that, ironically, Kant was himself no "Kantian" in this area; and
3. that Kant's own position reveals the mistake on which the "Kantian" philosophy of mysticism rests and helps us to orient ourselves toward more promising paths in this area of study.[57]

Let us consider the strength or weakness of each point, starting with the first.

When writing of "certain sorts of mystical experience" that are not conducive to Kantian epistemology—not fitting into the analytical framework of the hermeneutic (or, one can say, being impervious to its filtering lens)—Perovich is primarily referring to the PCE; although he articulates the experience using classical ideas through the invocation of Neoplatonic tradition, using Plotinus to describe such a mystical experience. Perovich emphasizes "the description left by Plotinus of the One with which the mystic unites: it is formless and precedent to all being, not in space or time, without multiplicity."[58] Such a Neoplatonic understanding of mystical experience, which aligns with the PCE experience as being formless, "cannot be represented as a product of formal, conceptual shaping," according to Perovich.[59] In order to understand why this is the case, we need to consider the ways that content and form play a role in influencing mystical experiences.

In philosophical understanding, one of two things can happen in the interaction between content and form. First (and this is how Kant understands it), we could have a manifold intuition (this is, the content) that is filtered and shaped into a unified whole (the form); "this is one way in which the conceptual context may intelligibly shape experience."[60] Another way is the inversion, wherein we begin with an undivided whole in content, which is "sliced up"; the "task of concepts [the forms], then, is not to unify, but to cut up this continuum."[61] In either case, however—whether the manifold intuition (as content) is shaped into a unified whole (form), or whether a unified whole (as content) is shaped into sliced elements (form)—neither of these operating frameworks makes sense when considering the type of mystical experience that Plotinus invoked, or that neo-perennialists invoke with the PCE. "It is implausible to regard the Neoplatonic experience of the One, formless and without multiplicity, as the result of slicing a whole or unifying a manifold. Hence, there are some mystical experiences, at least, for which the claim that the mystic's conceptual scheme shapes his or her experience—if understood formally—is implausible."[62]

Although Perovich does not use the expressions "incomplete constructivism" and "complete constructivism" (these are terms applied by Forman), he speaks to their meaning by noting the various problems that arise from the ways that such lenses of interpretation are applied. In the aforementioned example, Perovich was essentially pointing to the dilemma of an "incomplete constructivism" that cannot account for a formless mystical experience. Regarding "complete constructivism," Perovich articulates a newly present dilemma, or challenge, explaining: "The attempt to locate the conceptual contribution of the tradition in the content rather than the form represents the suicide of the Kantian epistemological model. . . ."[63] Perovich makes a sophisticated argument here:

Once the "given" evaporates from one's account, a Kantian theory of knowledge is no longer appropriate: if there is nothing to be mediated, then there is no point in insisting on the mediated character of all experience. One does not require the intricacies of Kantian epistemology (or even "Kantian" epistemology) to represent mystical experience as fabrication.[64]

The main idea is this: the central component of Kantian epistemology is *mediation*: a pure experience is mediated through concepts which filter and give shape to that experience. The implication is that the original experience (the content), before it was subjected to the mediation of conceptual structures, was a pure and "given" experience. Complete constructivism, on the other hand, argues that the source of experiential content is already shaped by preexistent factors. Therefore, a pure, unmediated "given" is fully eliminated from the picture. In this regard, Perovich is not wrong in using the forceful language of "fabrication" when describing the way complete constructivism understands mystical experiences, because the implication is that there was never anything pure *to be mediated* but that the very beginning constitutes a fabrication or, at best, a distortion. For mediation to happen there must be an experience that is being mediated.

The process of mediation does not transform the experience into something else—for example, cultural mediation of a mystical experience would not change that mystical experience into an ontologically different reality, such as a hallucination, but would require processing and interpreting the mystical experience into forms of cultural expression. If the mystical experience is deemed to be a fabrication, or a hallucination, then there was no mystical experience that was being *mediated*—there was only a lie or a pathology that was being communicated. Hence, if scholars want to use a model of mediation, such as Kant's approach, they need to recognize the proper function of mediation: it is filtering and processing the content of a given experience, and not changing the given experience into an ontologically different reality, such as pathology or delusion.

Perovich explains that the process of shaping the content of an experience "does not transform that content except to add connections or divisions that are not present in the content itself: the manifold may be synthesized, but the result is still a synthesized *manifold*."[65] When the core is *not mediation* but fabrication, then the epistemological framework is far from Kantian. Perovich adds that beyond these dubious usages of Kantian epistemology, the constructivist position has little to fall back on other than "unexplicated metaphors of shaping," offering that this "is enough to suggest that there is something fundamentally misguided with the employment of 'Kantian' ideas in this sphere."[66]

The second main point of Perovich's thesis is to show that Kant himself was no "Kantian" in regard to mysticism, meaning that in interpreting mystical experiences Kant would not use the hermeneutic that constructivists have applied on the basis of his epistemology toward mystical experiences. Kant's own perspective toward mysticism was more apophatic, Perovich argues, believing that the mysteries of mystical knowledge transcend human comprehension, existing beyond the grasp of human cognition. However, this does not mean that Kant believed in the experiences of the mystics. Perovich explains that Kant was distrustful of the claims of mystics, believing them to be false not because God and the spiritual mysteries that mystics report to reveal are not true but because Kant believed that human beings do not possess the cognitive faculty to comprehend such mysteries in this life. "He insists that the claims of the mystics are false, that mystical 'inner illuminations' are merely 'pretended,' because mystical cognition presupposes a faculty which we in fact lack."[67] Thus, to quote Kant, "this feeling of the immediate presence of the Supreme Being . . . would constitute a receptivity for an intuition for which there is no sensory provision in man's nature."[68]

Here, it is interesting to contrast Kant's epistemological perspective with that of William James. As previously noted, James was challenging a rationalistic skepticism about mystical experiences whose underpinnings were based on Kant's epistemology. James believed in a faculty in human beings that transcends the senses and *is able* to comprehend deeper, spiritual mysteries. This was, of course, the "mystical consciousness" for James. Kant, on the other hand, reduced all knowledge to sense perception. Since the mystical consciousness, as James understands it, transcends the human senses, then it is impossible, in Kant's framework, to use this epistemological model as a means to gain knowledge: nothing beyond sense perception is capable of cognitive comprehension, according to Kant.

But Perovich makes an extremely important distinction that cannot be overlooked. While Kant denies the experiences that the mystics report, believing that human beings do not have the cognitive faculty to comprehend such mysteries, he does not deny the possibility of such content that the mystics report. Perovich explains that Kant "is not utterly opposed to faculties of mystical intuition, only to claims that we can employ them in the present life. He holds that after death we might know in just the way the mystics describe is possible, but we can have no certainty in the matter."[69] Therefore, what Kant takes issue with is the claim of mystics having access to such transcendent knowledge in this life, but not to the possibility of such knowledge being true, a realization that can only be known in the afterlife, according to Kant. Perovich explains how Kant's understanding of mystical experiences set him apart from the "Kantians" who have applied his epistemological framework to advance a constructivist approach:

> We are able, therefore, to distinguish Kant's view from that of the "Kantians." According to Kant, mystical knowledge is to be distinguished from ordinary empirical knowledge not only by its object, but also by its epistemological structure: mystical knowledge consists in a communion with God and a sharing in divine self-knowledge of His Ideas. Such intellectual intuition may be possible for us in the future, but it demands a cognitive faculty different from those employed in empirical knowledge and so, Kant believes, is not available in this life. The "Kantians," on the other hand, make no distinction between the conditions of mystical cognition and the conditions of ordinary cognition. In doing so, they not only depart from Kant's own view but also, I believe, err in doing so.[70]

Thus, Perovich's second main point to his thesis, that Kant was no "Kantian" when it comes to mystical interpretation, is clear. The reason why this is the case is further revealed in Perovich's third main point: that Kant's own position reveals the mistake on which the "Kantian" philosophy of mysticism rests. The mistake is present in applying Kant's epistemological model toward interpreting mystical experiences—something that Kant himself would never do.

In other words, "Kantians" (or neo-Kantians) apply Kant's epistemological model, which the latter intended to interpret ordinary experiences, to try to comprehend mystical experiences, misapplying the hermeneutic, as the model was meant solely for ordinary, and not mystical, cognition. Kant would argue, according to Perovich, that his epistemological framework cannot be applied to understanding mystical intuition because such intuition transcends the capacity of any human faculty of comprehension that this life offers.

Perovich notes that many perennialists are criticized by constructivists as roughly forcing mystical texts "to conform to preestablished ideas of experiential uniformity" but, adding his own challenge to the constructivist hermeneutic, Perovich explains that "neither must one force them [mystical texts] to conform to preestablished ideas of epistemological uniformity."[71] According to Perovich "no *presuppositions* about the mediated, shaped, conceptualized character of 'human experience,'" which is what the Kantian epistemological hermeneutic is meant to analyze, are relevant to "the sorts of 'nonhuman experience' being reported" in mystical experiences by mystics.[72] As a solution to the apparent misapplication, and consequent misunderstanding, that Kantian constructivists have conveyed through their epistemological usage of a misused hermeneutic in interpreting mystical experiences, Perovich proposes better epistemological understanding as a path for clarity in this area. He writes of the need for a "mystical epistemology"[73] that can lead to a more appropriate hermeneutical understanding of mystical experiences:

> it seems to me the recent "Kantian" philosophy of mysticism rests on a mistake, the mistake of assuming that mystical experience is narrowly "human" experience and, so, is subject to the same treatment as is "human" experience generally. But the mystics insist that their experiences result from ecstasy, that their knowledge is gained as the result of employing faculties which are not ordinary "human" ones. At the very least, these claims translate as denials of the validity of "Kantian" epistemology in the mystical sphere. By studying their reports, we can also hope to learn something about the sort of epistemology that *is* appropriate here, given that we have once learned to avoid the pitfalls of a "Kantian" analysis of mystical experience. This last lesson—of course, the point is not without irony—could have been easily learned from Kant himself.[74]

There are many strong points in Perovich's thesis, and it is clear that he makes a persuasive argument for it. However, it is not an argument without flaws, for shortcomings are also present. Perhaps the strongest shortcoming is alluded to in Perovich's final sentence, highlighting that the lesson of epistemological fallacy could have been learned from Kant himself. However true this is as a critique of "Kantian" constructivist epistemologies, the argument can also be turned upside down and be used inversely against Perovich's thesis. Let us briefly explore this option.

If we look to Kant himself as a model and consider his personal convictions, then it is not difficult to argue that Kant's own perspective in this debate may be closer to *complete constructivism* than to perennialism. It is true, and not unfair to deduce (given the evidence), that Kant would consider his epistemological framework as inadequate at getting to the root of mystical truths, as he perceived such truths to be beyond the comprehension of any human faculty of perception. However, Kant considered the experiences of the mystics to be *false* for the very reason that no human faculty, in this life, could grasp and make claims to transcendent truths the way the mystics do, he believed. Therefore, if the experiences of the mystics according to Kant are false and, thus, *human*, then Kant would argue that they are completely constructed and, as a result, conducive to study and examination through his epistemological framework.

This is not to say that Perovich's thesis is false. It is simply saying that if Perovich is going to use Kant's own personal example as support for his thesis, then he needs to consider how that personal example can, in fact, work to disprove the very argument that Perovich hopes to advance: the inapplicability of Kantian epistemology to mystics and their experiences. To consider the veracity of Perovich's thesis, one needs to perceive Kant's example selectively, choosing where to agree and where to disagree with the renowned philosopher. At first, it appears that Perovich's thesis only works if a paradox is present: if Kant is *right* in saying that mystical truths cannot be grasped by human faculties, therefore excluding his epistemological model from interpreting such truths; and on the other hand, if Kant is *wrong* in saying that mystical truths cannot be grasped by human faculties, therefore allowing the mystics to grasp such higher truths through their experiences.

Of course, in this scenario one argument contradicts the other and presents a paradox that seems irreconcilable, showing a self-defeating contradiction in Perovich's thesis. However, there is a way to reconcile the paradox, and it is this way that Perovich upholds his thesis as viable. The paradox is reconciled if we consider that Kant is right in saying that mystical truths cannot be grasped by human faculties, therefore excluding the usage of his epistemological model while, at the same time, if we consider that the experiences of mystics do not qualify under this epistemological criterion that restricts the attainment of mystical truths to the human faculties. For a mystical experience to be genuine at the heart of such an experience there must be the intrusion of grace into the natural world. Therefore, in this regard, it is not the human faculties but something other, something "more"— divine intervention—that can make the grasp of mystical truths attainable in extraordinary experiences through a faculty of perception that transcends human senses.

This is ultimately what Perovich is saying in articulating that mystics report to receive their experiences through spiritual ecstasy and, therefore, "their knowledge is gained as the result of employing faculties which are not ordinary 'human' ones."[75] As a result, to advance his thesis, Perovich must use Kant selectively, agreeing with certain Kantian tenets while disagreeing with others. Thus, Perovich agrees with Kant in enunciating that Kantian epistemology is inadequate in interpreting mystical experiences; however, he disagrees with Kant in the belief that the experiences of mystics must be false. How can Perovich reconcile the paradox of acknowledging that our human faculties are inadequate in perceiving mystical truths while allowing that the mystics did, in fact, perceive mystical truths? He can only do this by stepping outside the realm of philosophy, meaning the realm of reason, and entering the realm of theology or spirituality, meaning the realm of revelation.

The logic of the thesis, therefore, could be understood thus: the mystic reports that his or her experience is *supernatural,* and *that is why it works,* because it is not subjected to the same measures of perception as natural experiences. Therefore, in the case of the mystics, it is not their natural human faculties that allow the perception of mystical truths, but (in Christian terminology) it is supernatural grace that affords the experience, or (in more ecumenical, Jamesian language) it is the mysterious something "more" that allows higher perception. By themselves, human faculties cannot perceive such immediate higher truths—without mediation, that is. But here, in the case of mystical experiences, such higher epistemological grasp is possible because the faculties are not acting on their own accord but through grace, which expands the windows of perception. Kant was studying religion "within the limits of reason," and there is much to gain from such a study. However, for Perovich's thesis to make sense, religion cannot be limited to reason but must, in essence, transcend those epistemological boundaries and enter the realm of revelation, opening the doors to a "mystical epistemology."

The Bigger Picture

Within the perennialist–constructivist debate it is important to recognize that there is a "bigger picture" that is in play, and it is vital to understand the implications of this bigger picture. In debating the matters of extraordinary religious and mystical experiences, both neo-perennialists and constructivists are not simply partaking in discourses whose ultimate purpose is to defend or critique the integrity of such experiences, or simply to have a debate that affects religious studies; there is more to it than that. Their debate is one whose consequences affect not only questions about religion but, moreover, about *institutional frameworks of thinking* that have

influenced and permeated academia and thus the world of intellectual culture. Let us look at this in detail.

Ann Taves explains that in the nineteenth and twentieth centuries,
many religious scholars advanced the idea that religious experiences exist
in a category or class of their own, as something unique or *sui generis*,
which cannot be explained through psychological, sociological, or biological terms.[76] *Sui generis* is a Latin phrase referring to an object or person
that is unique, or in a class of its own, literally meaning "of its own kind."[77]
The idea, of course, is that religious and mystical experiences are special
subjects whose depths cannot be fully comprehended by the social or natural sciences. Within this framework of thinking, another point is made, an
apprehension of sorts: the fear that sciences like psychology, sociology, or
biology may "reduce" religious experiences to something else if an attempt
is made to apply these disciplines to study such extraordinary experiences.
In other words, what is being criticized, and avoided, is an *epistemology of
reductionism* that denigrates extraordinary religious experiences into natural or pathological categories, stripping them of their integrity.[78]

The *sui generis* approach toward religious experiences has been largely
promulgated by classic perennialist thinkers, significantly affecting religious studies in the West. Wayne Proudfoot traces the influence of this
model of thinking to the German philosopher of religion Friedrich
Schleiermacher (1768–1834), particularly to Schleiermacher's 1799 work
On Religion: Speeches to the Cultured Among its Despisers. Proudfoot
explains that the "influence of this book has been enormous" and
notes that, as a result of this work and a later publication (*The Christian
Faith*), Schleiermacher has become recognized as "the seminal figure in
nineteenth-century Protestant thought" by both critics and supporters.[79]

There were two goals to Schleiermacher's project, Proudfoot explains.
The first was to present an accurate picture of true religion, or "the religious consciousness."[80] In this regard, Schleiermacher argued that both
orthodox religionists (Christian and Jewish, in Schleiermacher's study)
and their Enlightenment critics have produced an erroneous representation of religion in depicting it (whether pro or con) in a moralistic manner
as a system of beliefs and doctrines that must be, legalistically, adhered to
in order to promote proper behavior.[81] Such an understanding abides by
the Law but kills the Spirit, Schleiermacher claimed, arguing that the core
of true religion is not found in moralism or doctrines but in the *experience*
of the transcendent. Thus, with a mystical bent, Schleiermacher was promoting a unique experientialism that transcends the pursuit of knowledge

and morality with a concentration on a deeper dimension of faith, enunciating that experience possesses an integrity of its own and is the basis of true religion.[82] It is not difficult to see how such a framework has influenced the thought of thinkers like James and Underhill.

The second goal of Schleiermacher's work was more theoretical and, according to Proudfoot, apologetic. "Schleiermacher hopes that by presenting religion in its original, characteristic form he will demonstrate the inapplicability of Enlightenment criticisms of religious belief, particularly of the Kantian critique of speculative metaphysics, to the actual phenomena of religion."[83] Here, the implications are great, from Schleiermacher's perspective, as they postulate that extraordinary religious experiences transcend history and standard epistemology, thus transcending historical conditioning and criticism, existing not in another category of study which could be understood through anthropological, sociocultural, linguistic or historical methods but, rather, on a higher plane of meaning, being autonomous, unmediated, essential, and unique.[84] The implications of such a framework of thinking regarding extraordinary experiences affect not only academia but also dynamics of belief, devotion, and spiritual authority in various church and ecclesial traditions. In considering the "bigger picture," Taves explains how theologians used the purported uniqueness of religious experiences as a source of authority against skepticism and as a means to promote religious revival:

> This spilled over into theology and the emerging academic study of religion where thinkers with a liberal or modernist bent, mostly Protestant and a few Catholic, turned to the concept of religious experience as a source of theological authority at a time when claims based on other sources of authority—ecclesiastical, doctrinal, and biblical—were increasingly subject to historical critique. For modernist theologians who followed in the steps of the liberal Protestant theologian Friedrich Schleiermacher, the self-authenticating experience of the individual seemed like a promising source of religious renewal, less vulnerable to the acids of historical critical methods.[85]

While such is the intellectual and religious context in which the works of James, Underhill, and other perennial thinkers of the early twentieth century, like Rudolf Otto, Nathan Soderblom, and Friedrich Heiler,[86] flourished, the "tide began to shift," according to Leigh Eric Schmidt, in the late twentieth century with the advent of constructivist scholarship.[87]

Schmidt locates the beginnings of the hermeneutical turning point in the 1978 publication of Katz's *Mysticism and Philosophical Analysis*, and emphasizes that "by 1983 Katz's colleague Hans H. Penner openly dismissed 'mysticism' as 'a false category,' an essentialist 'illusion.' ... Penner, in effect, set perpetual quotation marks around the term to signal the emptiness of its *sui generis* pretensions to universality and transcendence."[88] From here religious and mystical experiences were to be subjected to "a radically historicist perspective" that did not consider such subjects to be universal, unique, or essential, but constantly changing and shifting, being the products of historical and social construction and not of an unreachable and unknowable transcendent sphere.[89]

This significant shift, however, was not limited to the study of religion or mysticism but also constituted a larger, paradigmatic shift in academia, particularly within the humanities and social sciences, that transpired in the twentieth century and is understood as the "linguistic turn."[90] Taves explains that in "the wake of the general linguistic turn within the humanities" the entire approach of the *sui generis* model was called into question.[91] "Many scholars of religion, eager to deconstruct an essentialist understanding of religion and religious experience, abandoned the focus on religious experience and recast the study of religion in light of critical theories that emphasize the role of language in constituting social reality in the context of relationships of power and inequality."[92] Forman explains that this larger paradigmatic shift in academia is "the real reason perennialism came into disfavor ... the underlying cause was the broad paradigm shift in the humanities and social sciences toward constructivism."[93]

The linguistic turn ultimately constitutes a constructivist framework of thinking, as its central tenets stress linguistic and cultural mediation instead of pure, unmediated experience, as necessary filters to understanding all experiences. "This notion has become so dominant that it has taken on the status of a self-evident truism," Forman explains.[94] Forman provides a quick overview of how the humanities and social sciences have been affected by this epistemological framework:

> The sociology of knowledge and anthropology have both detailed how a culture's worldview structures and controls perception and beliefs. Psychologists since Freud have argued that past experiences—especially those of childhood—control, shape, and determine adult emotions, behavior patterns, and perceptions. Constructivism may be viewed as the controlling model in linguistic

analysis; in other words, that a person's language constrains, determines, and informs the judgments one makes about oneself and others. . . . Historians of culture, ideas, and religion all base their work explicitly on this model. Even the study of modern art and art criticism may be viewed as grappling with the implications of this constructivist picture.[95]

Here, therefore, is the bigger picture: the fact that when contemporary perennial scholars, neo-perennialists, are debating the merits of constructivist hermeneutics in understanding extraordinary religious experiences, they are not only challenging other religion scholars but also an entire, institutional framework of thinking whose established precepts have, as Forman put it, reached the level of self-evident truisms throughout academia. In other words, an entire institutional system of thought is on the line in the consequences behind the ongoing perennialist–constructivist debates, transcending implications that concern only religious studies or the understanding of religious experiences.

Taves explains that in "arguing for the cross-cultural stability of certain types of experiences that they construed as mystical, the neo-perennialists bucked the dominant trend in the humanities."[96] Forman confirms: "This was the underlying conceptual paradigm at the heart of the complaint about perennialism. Insofar as it seemed to deny that the linguistic background played a role in the shaping and perception of the mystical experience (during, not after), perennialism seemed to deny this 'self-evident' truth" that constructivism, fueled by the general linguistic turn, proposed throughout academia.[97]

An Attributional Approach

In addition to the work of Katz and his fellow constructivists with their multi-volume publications on mysticism and interpretation, an influential book affecting the debate was Proudfoot's *Religious Experience* published in 1985. In his book Proudfoot advances the thesis that purported extraordinary religious experiences exist *not* apart, as *sui generis*, from other disciplines of study but as historical categories of study within religious studies. Attempts to promote sui generis interpretations of religious experiences have been used to advance a larger "protective strategy," Proudfoot claims, that is "designed to seal off a guarded domain for religious experience amid modernity—one in which religious feelings would be safe from reductionistic explanations and scientific incursions."[98] Thus Proudfoot identifies an ideological component, accusing perennial thinkers of producing scholarship that is designed to defend religious sensibilities.[99] Proudfoot applies a hermeneutic that an initial *sui generis* framework would categorize as reductionist; Proudfoot's approach portraying the kind of "medical materialism" that James was highly critical of in his Gifford Lectures. Not surprisingly, Proudfoot is very critical of James's approach to religious and mystical experience, particularly James's four characteristics of mysticism. Proudfoot's own approach to experience was not void of tenets of psychology, particularly social psychology, incorporating attribution theory to form his approach. G. William Barnard explains:

> According to Proudfoot, the noetic quality of a mystical experience is merely the cerebral judgment made by the mystic that a certain experience is not solely his or her subjective creation. This judgment that an experience is "religious" is not made because the experience possesses certain identifiable, directly felt, intrinsic religious qualities, but instead, an experience is understood to be religious because the person who has the experience superimposes a ready-made label of "religious" onto any unexplained shift in his or her physical or psychological equilibrium.[100]

Compare Proudfoot's approach with the hermeneutic of reductionism that James warned of nearly a century earlier. James wrote:

> Medical materialism seems indeed a good appellation for the too simple-minded system of thought which we are considering. Medical materialism finishes up Saint Paul by calling his vision on the road to Damascus a discharging lesion of the occipital cortex, he being an epileptic. It snuffs out Saint Teresa [of Avila] as an [sic] hysteric, Saint Francis of Assisi as an [sic] hereditary degenerate.[101]

Regarding his hermeneutic of religious experience as being reductionist, Proudfoot has not denied the fact but has, on the contrary, affirmed it. Proudfoot does, however, make a distinction between two types, or forms, of reductionism—"descriptive reductionism" and "explanatory reductionism"—arguing that scholars should avoid the former but embrace the latter.[102] Proudfoot articulates *descriptive reductionism* as "the failure to identify an emotion, practice, or experience under the description by which the subject identifies it."[103] In other words, a researcher must be able to describe the experiences of subjects in a manner that the subjects would recognize, otherwise what the researcher is describing is "something other than what the subjects claimed they have experienced."[104] Proudfoot provides a couple examples of this, explaining:

> To describe the experience of a mystic by reference only to alpha waves, altered heart rate, and changes in bodily temperature is to misdescribe it. To characterize the experience of a Hindu mystic in terms drawn from Christian tradition is to misidentify it. In each of these instances, the subject's identifying experience has been reduced to something other than that experienced by the subject.[105]

Proudfoot, however, deems this to be different from *explanatory reductionism*, which he accepts and which "consists in offering an explanation of an experience in terms that are not those of the subject and that might not meet his approval."[106] Here, it is not the phenomenological description of the experience that is given new terms of meaning (as in descriptive reductionism) but the *explanation* for the experience. Thus, the "explanandum is set in a new context, whether that be one of covering laws and initial conditions, narrative structure, or some other explanatory model. The terms of the explanation need not be familiar or acceptable to the subject."[107] Proudfoot recognizes that reductionism "has become a derogatory epithet in the history and philosophy of religion,"[108] but he believes that a major reason for this is that scholarship against reductionism tends to conflate descriptive and explanatory reduction. He argues, therefore, for the importance of distinguishing between the two hermeneutical subtypes in renewing appreciation for a viable reductionist framework of interpretation regarding religious experiences.[109]

Although Proudfoot makes a sharp distinction, the question remains whether the distinction continues to be, if considering the root of the issue, superficial. *Superficial* at least to neo-perennialists and similar-minded thinkers who, in articulating the most common criticism of reductionism, argue that reductive hermeneutics attempt to *explain* away religious and mystical experiences.[110] In other words, what is being criticized as the central issue *is* explanatory reductionism, and not necessarily descriptive reductionism, even if the latter is often conflated with the former. Distinguishing the two, and advocating for one approach over the other, does not diminish the concerns that *sui generis* thinkers have had about reductionism, which is most recognized for its alternative *explanations*. Proudfoot's distinction, in embracing explanatory reductionism and dismissing descriptive, is at best a call for honest scholarship (as descriptive reductionism boarders on distortion of its subject, posing dubious ethicality), but it is far from an alleviation of concerns that reductionist theories of religion have evoked in those who perceive integrity in extraordinary religious experiences.

Proudfoot's work has had a great influence on the scholarship of Ann Taves, who uses attribution theory to study why individuals attribute religious meaning to their experiences—experiences that Taves does not call "extraordinary" or "mystical," but "unique," thus postulating that such experiences may, in fact, be subject to naturalistic explanations, arguing that it is often unintended and unusual experiences which receive the ascription "religious," or lead "people to make religious attributions."[111] Taves is critical of the *sui generis* model and, as a counterpoint, advocates for the "ascription model" as a hermeneutic better suited to grasp the subject. She distinguishes the two models thus: the *sui generis* model assumes implicitly or explicitly that there are uniquely religious or mystical experiences while the ascriptive model, on the contrary, claims that "religious or mystical or spiritual or sacred 'things' are created when religious significance is assigned to them."[112] Therefore, in the ascriptive model an experience is not inherently religious or mystical in its essence but is understood as "religious" or "mystical," and therefore subjectively created as "thus," by the subsequent ascription assigned to it. "One of the ways that ambiguity is maintained with respect to the two models is by referring to 'religious experience,' as if it were a distinctive thing, rather than using the more awkward, but clearly ascriptive, formulation, 'experiences deemed religious.'"[113]

At first, it is easy to see parallels here between perennialism (as *sui generis*) and constructivism (as ascription), but eventually Taves clarifies—and we'll look at those clarifications—of how her ascription model differs from traditional interpretations. The ascription model is an attribution formulation, meaning it is a hermeneutic that is grounded in attribution theory. Attribution theory, which refers to the study of the phenomenological process by which persons ascribe meaning to their experiences, came into prominence in the 1970s and '80s through social psychology. Since then, attribution theory has been adopted by other disciplines of study and has even influenced the creation of new subfields of study within social psychology, cognitive theory, and neuroscience, specifically giving birth to the subfields of social cognition and social neuroscience.[114]

Attribution theory was incorporated into the study of religion as early as 1975 through an influential article coauthored by Proudfoot and Phillip Shaver, and the subject was subsequently expanded and developed through the work of other religion and psychology scholars.[115] Proudfoot's *Religious Experience*, published ten years after his article, was also highly informed by attribution theory, to the point—according to Taves—that "both constructivists and neo-perennialists overidentified constructivism with attribution theory, in large part because Wayne Proudfoot was centrally identified with both."[116] Taves makes important distinctions between a constructivist hermeneutic and one that applies attribution theory to religious experiences. A major part of her project, in this regard, is to articulate the need "to abandon the constructivist axiom that beliefs and attitudes are always formative of, rather than consequent to, experience in any very strong sense, in favor of a model that takes 'bottom-up' or unconscious processing more seriously."[117] Yet, while Taves argues for a hermeneutic that abandons an absolute adherence to a constructivist phenomenology of experience in favor of "unconscious processing," the conclusions of her approach are more in line with constructivist, rather than perennialist, interpretation, even helping to support constructivist conclusions with greater viability than a traditional constructivist phenomenology would. Let us consider this.

A good way to illustrate Taves's method is to use the argument and personal testimony of G. William Barnard. Barnard, who has criticized perceived limitations in the constructivist hermeneutic, shared his own testimony in an academic publication (a book he authored on the mystical philosophy of William James) to display how a mystical experience that he—Barnard—experienced as a boy contradicts, and ultimately disproves, such an epistemological approach as constructivism.[118] It is specifically "complete constructivism" that Barnard is criticizing—the belief that mystical experiences are fully constructed by a particular culture's preexistent set of beliefs and interpretive framework.[119] Barnard shares an out-of-body experience that he had as a thirteen-year-old, an experience that, in his analysis, undermines the tenets that encapsulate complete constructivism:

> When I was thirteen years old, I was walking to school in Gainesville, Florida, and without any apparent reason, I became obsessed with the idea of what would happen to me after my death. Throughout that day I attempted to visualize myself as not existing. I simply could not comprehend that my self-awareness would not exist in

some form or another after my death. I kept trying, without suc-
cess, to envision a simple blank nothingness. Later, I was returning home from school, walking on the hot pavement next to a
stand of pine trees less than a block from my home, still brood-
ing about what it would be like to die. Suddenly, without warning,
something shifted inside. I felt lifted outside of myself, as if I had
been expanded beyond my previous sense of self. In that exhilarat-
ing, and yet deeply peaceful moment, I felt as if I had been shaken
awake. In a single, "timeless" gestalt, I had a direct and powerful
experience that I was not just that young teenage boy, but rather,
that I was a surging, ecstatic, boundless state of consciousness.[120]

Barnard goes on to suggest that "an epistemology of mystical experience
that is based on 'complete constructivism' does not adequately reflect the
dynamics of this experience."[121] He explains that as "a child of thirteen"
he had no words, or previous framework of understanding, with which
to make sense of his experience, realizing that he "just knew that 'something' profound had occurred"[122]—that "something profound," however,
was not informed nor inspired by any theological, religious, or cultural
content that was preexistent in Barnard's mindset in his youth. Barnard
admits that the "little religious training I had been exposed to during my
brief, and to me incredibly boring, Sundays in church did not help me in
my subsequent attempts to come to grips with this mysterious and yet
powerful event."[123] In fact, it was not until many years later, when in adult-
hood Barnard started "studying Eastern philosophical scriptures" and
spending several years practicing meditative disciplines that he "was able
to give this experience a viable interpretative structure," examining the
experience within a framework that was *different* from the religious knowledge (no matter how limited) of his youth.[124] Thus, Barnard suggests how
a complete constructivist hermeneutic that attributes *preexistent* cultural
influence as the formative factor in triggering mystical experiences is fully
inadequate in explaining his experience:

My previously religious and cultural conceptual background was
not sufficiently dense and nuanced enough to constitute completely
this experience. Instead I first had an experience, without any real
religious preparation, that possessed inherently "mystical" qualities; then *after* having this experience (because it was sufficiently
puzzling), I began to search for an intellectual framework that could

accurately reflect the content that was latent in that experience. Undeniably, at thirteen years of age, I was not a completely blank slate: I knew that experience had something to do with awareness (and I knew enough to remain quiet about this experience with my parents and even friends). But to claim, as complete constructivists would, that this highly rudimentary conceptual framework created that experience seems woefully inadequate.[125]

In examining Barnard's experience and his epistemological conclusions about the experience, Taves notes, in agreement, how inadequate the constructivist view that Barnard criticizes *is* in providing a viable explanation for the dynamics behind his experience. Taves articulates that there are "some experiences"—noticeable is her refusal to use Barnard's terminology of "mystical experiences"—that indeed cannot be explained by a "thoroughgoing constructivist view,"[126] but need to be understood, on the other hand, through an attributional lens of interpretation. Taves writes:

Barnard's previous [religious and cultural] views could not adequately explain the novelty of his experience, which suggests that a thoroughgoing constructivist view is not adequate. Although Barnard acknowledges that he was not "a completely blank slate" culturally, he is right to insist, especially in light of the cross-cultural similarity between experiences of this type, that culture cannot adequately account for the shape of his experience. Barnard is also right to insist, following William James, that puzzling, inexplicable experiences (which he and James both view as upwellings from the unconscious) may introduce novelty and precipitate radical changes in individual lives and belief systems.[127]

An attributional approach, however, can, according to Taves, provide a naturalistic interpretation for Barnard's experience because attribution theory considers both top-down (culture sensitive) and bottom-up (culture insensitive) processing in considering and analyzing particular experiences.[128] Taves explains that a constructivist hermeneutic operates mainly under the former—culturally sensitive—top-down approach while it is the latter—culturally insensitive—bottom-down approach that takes the idea of "unconscious processing" more seriously and affords, therefore, the possibility of natural explanations for unique experiences that do not need to be culturally conditioned.[129]

Deconstructing Barnard's narrative of his experience, Taves argues that an interweaving structure of cultural ideas, physical symptoms, and the practice of visualization are present to shape the experience, though she admits that the cultural aspects are not as apparent as in other cases, hence the reason that a complete constructivist hermeneutic would not work in explaining the experience.[130] Taves articulates her attributional approach by dissecting Barnard's experience into five stages, deconstructing his encounter with a naturalistic phenomenology. Let us consider the five stages of her deconstruction.

The first important stage of the experience, Taves observes, is present in Barnard's thinking about what would happen to him after his death, and thus Barnard's attempt to visualize himself as not existing. Already in this rudimentary part of the experience Taves sees cultural influence— interestingly, not religious but secular. She explains that Barnard "spontaneously initiated a practice in which he tried to imagine a counterfactual situation [not existing after death] that accorded with a secular cultural script."[131] This led to the second stage of the experience, according to Taves, wherein a paradox was produced in his mind as Barnard continued to visualize himself as not existing—"that is, asking self to imagine self not being able to imagine."[132] This mental paradox led to the third stage, Taves explains, wherein something inside of Barnard shifted and the seemingly out-of-body experience was triggered. To explain this unique phenomenon Taves poses a hypothesis, postulating that "the paradox [in thinking] triggered an altered state of consciousness in which self-other boundaries dissolved and perception of self-body relations were altered."[133] Since Barnard described the experience as "a surging, ecstatic boundless state of consciousness," Taves hypothesizes that, as the fourth stage of the experience, "alteration of self-body-other relations triggered feelings of ecstasy and exhilaration."[134] Finally, bringing all these factors together, Taves articulates her conclusion in considering the fifth and final stage of the experience, enunciating: "The novelty and intensity of the experience triggered a need for explanation. No satisfying explanations surfaced, so the experience was protected and preserved for further reflection. Later meditation practice and the reading of spiritual texts led to his describing the experience as mystical and attributing it to a higher power."[135]

Taves explains that this phenomenology of attribution can also be schematized as an interaction between ideas (thoughts), visual practices, physiological symptoms, and feelings, articulating the schema of Barnard's experience thus:

1. Thoughts led to a spontaneous visualization practice.
2. Practice generated a mental paradox.
3. Paradox resolved itself in the dissolution of self-other boundaries.
4. Dissolution of self-other boundaries triggered feelings of ecstasy and exhilaration.
5. The novelty and intensity of the experience required explanation.[136]

Of course, the biggest leap that Taves makes—and she purposely uses the terminology of "hypothesis,"[137] hinting at the apparent ambiguity behind her theory—is going from phase 2 to phase 3, suggesting that the act of *thinking* (even if turned into an effort at visualization) would trigger such a powerful and ecstatic, out-of-body experience of altered consciousness as Barnard experienced as a boy and later identified as "mystical." Taves supports her hypothesis with a reference to the recent work of neuroscientists[138] who have "identified the regions of the brain that govern the sense of embodiment" and "are now able to experimentally induce rudimentary out-of-body experiences."[139] However, notwithstanding these intriguing findings, Taves concedes that "there are as yet no studies that link practices [such as visualization or meditation] with the manipulation of those brain areas" that can induce rudimentary out-of-body experiences.[140]

Moreover, Taves admits that in contrast to such studies, relatively little research has been done "on the role of practices (visualization, meditation, chanting, fasting, et cetera) in triggering unusual experiences," although, she explains that there is "considerable historical and anecdotal evidence to suggest that this is often the case."[141] Taves thus references the works of psychologists and anthropologists "who have focused attention on the effects of cultivating imagery" and "self-injurious behaviors, such as fasting, sleep deprivation, and flagellation."[142] No matter how relevant such studies are between the cultivation of images and "injurious behavior," the connection to Barnard's experience (especially as evidence against his interpretation) remains rather superficial, as Barnard did not report partaking in such "injurious behavior" like the spiritual practices that Taves references. His experience was spontaneous, not premeditated with intensive spiritual disciplines. Furthermore, when looking at some of the sources that Taves references in regard to studies on the cultivation of images, it is evident that reference is being made here to the cultivation of visions.[143] Yet, again, in this regard making connection to Barnard's experience still constitutes a stretch of the imagination, as Barnard did not report experiencing a vision of any object, but encountering an out-of-body experience—thus a phenomenologically different experience than vision-ary phenomena.

One source that Taves lists to support her hypothesis includes a study performed on the cultivation of visions in shamanism, wherein individu-als deliberately partake in intensive, premeditated practices to cultivate certain images or visions.[144] Again, this is a great contrast to Barnard's comparably spontaneous experience as a lukewarm, and for the most part religiously illiterate, thirteen-year-old boy. The other sources that Taves incorporates could perhaps make a stronger case for her argument, refer-encing the works of anthropologist Tanya M. Luhrmann,[145] whose research focuses on trances and dissociative disorders; but again, such phenomena are not the same as out-of-body experiences and may be more applica-ble to explaining away (or naturalizing) other alleged occurrences, such as demonic possession.[146]

Although Taves would not label herself as a constructivist or a neo-perennialist, reading her work it is evident that Taves's conclusions lean toward constructivism, at least in the sense that she is critical of the *sui gene-ris* model and believes in natural, preexistent factors that not only shape but also trigger unique experiences deemed "religious" or "mystical" by those who undergo them. Using an attributional model, Taves would not even label such experiences as "religious" or "mystical," but solely consid-ers why such ascriptions are given to unique experiences after they occur, posing the presupposition in her epistemological approach that, at their core, such experiences are not what they seem to their subjects. Evident traces of Proudfoot's explanatory reductionism are present throughout her approach.

Despite discernable limitations present in Taves's attributional approach, her ultimate project is to provide an empirical, and purely nat-uralistic, understanding of religious experiences by using comparative study with other disciplines that examine experience, and by formulat-ing an attributional epistemology that can account for more explanatory accounts of such experiences than traditional interpretations. Taves argues that insofar as scholars in religious studies resist comparative work with other disciplines, considering the resistance to integration that the *sui generis* model has historically been responsible for, they inhibit a much needed interdisciplinary integration.[147] This is a major reason why Taves is a proponent of an ascription model and an opponent of a *sui generis* model—because of the major methodological implications present within each framework. Of primary concern to Taves is the resistance that the *sui generis* model has toward studying religious experiences in nonreligious terms, thus the resistance present therein toward incorporating nonreligious disciplines into the study of religion. "Stated positively, it [the *sui generis* model] asserted that religious things must be explained in religious terms; negatively, it prohibited 'reducing' religion to something else by explaining it in *nonreligious* terms."[148] It is the ascription model, according to Taves, that is conducive to interdisciplinary integration and provides a better hermeneutical approach.

Taves's interdisciplinary call is very noble, but given her own epistemological approach and its reductive tendencies, the question remains whether such integration would, in fact, help to establish greater understanding of extraordinary religious experiences or, on the contrary, simply add new flavor to old models of reductive thinking. Such a concern is far from mere speculation, as Taves has admitted that her epistemology on experience is an extension and development of Proudfoot's approach, an approach that relies on attribution theory to justify an explanatory reductionism of religious experiences.[149]

Of course, Taves's criticism of the *sui generis* model is valid in articulating that the model inhibits necessary, interdisciplinary attention by isolating religious experiences from other disciplines of study. However, the call for greater interdisciplinary focus, as a means to reaching greater comprehension of religious experiences, would be better suited under a more holistic model of interpretation—we will examine one such model in a later chapter—as opposed to the attributional (or ascriptive) model that Taves advances. The problem with Taves's model is that its very foundation is based on a presupposition that leads to predetermined conclusions about the subject. In other words, the approach begins with the presupposition that extraordinary experiences are not inherently religious or mystical, but that it is subsequent interpretations and ascriptions that give the experiences such meaning, hoping therefore to study the process (or phenomenology) of attribution. The issue, therefore, exists in the foundational principle: by claiming that extraordinary experiences are not inherently religious or mystical this approach is, from the very beginning, eliminating significant possibilities for the experience—possibilities which should be considered.

An important point here can be made with reference to Proudfoot's view on reductionism. Proudfoot distinguished between an acceptable reductionism (in what he terms "explanatory reductionism") and an unacceptable reductionism (in what he terms "descriptive reductionism").

Similarly, it would not be unreasonable to distinguish between the usage of an acceptable attributional approach and an unacceptable attributional approach in regard to the study of religious experiences. Perhaps one way to formulate this distinction is in the categorization of an "inductive" and a "deductive" attributional approach. The difference can be seen in the way that Taves analyzes Barnard's out-of-body experience.

In considering Barnard's out-of-body experience, Taves does not show through an attributional process of explanation that the experience is not inherently mystical—doing this would be an inductive approach. Instead, Taves does the opposite: she presupposes from the beginning that Barnard's out-of-body experience cannot be mystical (as he understands it) and, thereafter, she proceeds, through an attributional process of explanation, to advance a hypothesis that fits the predetermined conclusion of her starting premise. This is a deductive approach. In other words, she is not using attributional phenomenology to grasp the essence of Barnard's experience but to justify her pre-established conclusion about his experience.

The problem in taking this epistemological approach for granted is that there is the serious possibility of setting one's research upon a flawed premise, thus upon a flawed foundation. Of course, this is something that the *sui generis* model also needs to account for. However, here it is important to emphasize that the call for interdisciplinary integration, no matter how noble and necessary, cannot by itself be used as a justification for a deductive attributional approach. This means that it does not matter if Taves is making the noble calling for interdisciplinary integration, and more specifically if she is delving into such integration herself, if the various disciplines that are being integrated are used to support research that is based on an erroneous premise, a flawed starting point. Such interdisciplinary integration, in essence, becomes not only meaningless but, moreover, *detrimental* to progress in scholarship because it may be using the application of diverse disciplines to advance erroneous ideas.

Proudfoot, as noted earlier, accused perennial thinkers who apply a *sui generis* approach of hiding under a "protective strategy," a protective strategy that defends religious sensibilities against modern scholarship and criticism. Inversely, however, it is not difficult to say that the call for interdisciplinary integration may be used as a "protective strategy" by scholars on the other side of the hermeneutical divide. Here, the call for interdisciplinary integration can be used as a protective strategy that defends a deductive attributional approach against criticism, protecting itself in the name of an intellectual integration, thus in the name of advancing scholarship while avoiding the issue that the approach may be based on an intrinsically erroneous starting principle that does more harm than good to scholarship.[150]

Let us, therefore, consider the other side of the debate and, before reaching conclusions, see where the concerns arise by examining the ways in which interdisciplinary approaches to religious and mystical experiences have already been used to promulgate various forms of reductionism.

Religious Experience and Reductionism

The seeds of modern skeptical philosophies and epistemologies toward mystical experiences, whether visionary, auditory or sensory, are strongly rooted in Enlightenment philosophy and have been promulgated by Enlightenment thinkers and their intellectual heirs, who have questioned the validity and authenticity of mystical or extraordinary experiences between the human and the divine, in the process questioning not just the presence but also the very existence of the divine.

David Hume (1711–1776), arguably the preeminent proponent of philosophical skepticism in Enlightenment Europe, argued that the divine, thus God in the monotheistic tradition, is nothing more than a projection of the human being, an illusion of the mind. Inspired by the prevailing presence of hope and fear in human existence, the agitated mind "forms a species of divinity, suitable to itself," Hume argued.[151] Hume, therefore, defined Christian principles and devotional belief (very sardonically) as constituting nothing more than "sick men's dreams" and "the playsome whimsies of monkeys [sic] in human shape, than the serious, positive, dogmatical asseverations of a being, who dignifies himself with the name of rational."[152] The Dutch philosopher Benedict Spinoza (1632–1677) rejected the claims of revealed religion with a rationalism that complemented Hume's skepticism, having a seismic influence on post-Enlightenment thought. "On this view, religion must be reducible to something social, political, economic, cultural, psychological or natural, because by definition there is nothing more for it to be."[153]

Likewise, Ludwig Feuerbach (1804–1872), an intellectual inheritor of Hume's skeptical rationalism, took the psychological approach toward reproaching both the Christian faith and its alleged mysticism in his work *The Essence of Christianity*, advancing a form of psychological skepticism into post-Enlightenment thought that similarly depicted religious beliefs as desperate constructions of the human mind that, at their core, constitute nothing more than imaginary projections.[154] He argued that theology is "nothing more than an imaginary psychology and anthropology."[155] Consequently, the great theological ideas constituting religious belief—ideas about God, existence, meaning, mysticism, and so on—are all just constructions of the human mind and, therefore, the invention of human beings.[156] Such a psychologically reductionist approach toward the study of religion and religious experiences has been pervasively promulgated, highly influencing modern thinkers.[157] Similarly, Friedrich Nietzsche (1844–1900), with his influential "death of God" discourse in the early twentieth century, argued that belief in an otherworldly God is meant to give meaning to life and importance to humans as being the center of the universe, but such belief is, in its essence, "nothing more than a human projection"—in other words, a fanciful delusion meant to accommodate human desires.[158]

A significant trend to develop in the study of religious and mystical experiences is the scholarly tendency of denigrating reported supernatural experiences with dismissive reductionism in the form of alternative explanations for such experiences. Thus, in this sense, the study of religious experience has gained (perhaps unwanted) interdisciplinary attention from other areas of study, as other areas have been used to promote reductionist epistemologies concerning such experiences.

Sidney Callahan, a scholar of religion and psychology, has isolated at least three major categories to which scholars tend to reduce extraordinary religious and mystical experiences with alternative explanations, *all stemming from alternative disciplines of study*: (1) neurological/psychiatric reductionism; (2) psychoanalytical reductionism; and (3) secular-sociological reductionism. It is important to note that Callahan's attention is directed toward the more extravagant forms of mysticism, often associated with medieval and early modern female spirituality: visionary, apparitional, ecstatic, auditory, sensory experiences, and inner-locutions. Thus, here we are not necessarily dealing with simpler, cultivated spiritual experiences but, rather, with phenomena that are much more spontaneous and unique.

Neurological/Psychiatric Reductionism

Beginning with the neurological/psychiatric reductionism through which such experiences have been examined, Callahan acknowledges: "Suspicions that religious beliefs and fervent religious experiences are a form of mental pathology still prevail in our world."[159] Amy Hollywood similarly points out that extraordinary religious experiences, particularly mystical experiences, are often denigrated by skeptical scholars through neurological and psychiatric categories as simply constituting a form of hysteria, among other possible natural disorders.[160] Hollywood explains that in the nineteenth and twentieth centuries such diagnoses became prominent. She highlights the influence of the French neurologist Jean-Martin Charcot (1825–1893), who was "so important in the modern medical study of hysteria because of his insistence that hysteria is a disease of the nerves rather than a sign of moral degeneration, malingering, and laziness" and who "first introduced the reading of mysticism as hysteria in 'La foi qui guerit,' written shortly before his death. There he argues that Francis of Assisi and Teresa of Avila were 'undeniable hysterics' with the ability, nonetheless, to cure hysteria in others."[161] Thus in this interpretation, pathology is associated with the great mystics, as are, somewhat paradoxically, fruits from their alleged pathology. Here, psychologists like William James would differ in the sense of articulating that real fruits could not be produced by a pathological experience but are, in fact, indications that the experience must be authentically inspired. Taves explains that "Charcot valued the demystifying role that hysteria could play with regard to miracles, visions, and ecstatic experiences," but, she notes, later in life Charcot "wrote a little-known essay" in which he acknowledged that some of the cures reported at Lourdes were "well attested."[162] Charcot even admitted that he sent some of his own patients who suffered from "intractable cases of nervous illness" to Lourdes for treatment.[163] Yet, it is the reductive and pathological diagnosis of hysteria that Charcot is most known for in relation to interpreting extraordinary religious experiences.

Though a neurologist, Charcot's theories on religion and hysteria have reached other disciplines of study, influencing various thinkers. The French philosopher Simone de Beauvoir (1908–1986) interprets the experiences of most medieval women mystics who have claimed visionary or ecstatic encounters as constituting "a form of erotomania and hysteria," pathological categories highlighting both a Charcotian interpretation and one influenced by the French psychiatrist Gaëtan Gatian de Clérambault.[164] Such diagnoses have permeated (and continue to permeate) much of modern thought on extraordinary religious and mystical experiences. "Most scholars who have wanted to take mysticism seriously have, as a result of such dismissive diagnoses, either avoided the term 'hysteria' entirely or have reserved it for those figures seen as somehow marginal, excessive, or troubling to standard religious categories," Hollywood explains.[165]

Callahan emphasizes that temporal-lobe epilepsy "presents another popular explanation of the pathological source of rapturous religious experiences."[166] Speaking of the visionary experiences of medieval Christian mystics, neurologist Oliver Sacks articulates the hermeneutical dilemma thus: "It is impossible to ascertain in the vast majority of cases, whether the experience represents a hysterical or psychotic ecstasy, the effects of intoxication or an epileptic or migrainous manifestation."[167] Sacks is making this argument in an essay dedicated to the visionary experiences of the medieval German mystic and polymath Hildegard of Bingen. William Harmless explains that Sacks's argument is based on a theory promulgated by Charles Singer (1876–1960), a historian of science and medicine who was fascinated by Hildegard's visionary experiences.

> He noted how often she reported seeing flashing lights and having visions of concentric circles and fortress figures, and how sensitive she was to weather changes, to storms and wind. He concluded that Hildegard must have suffered from migraines, ones whose symptoms included visual auras, or "scintillating scotomata." The contemporary neurologist and popular science writer Oliver Sacks agreed and has done much to popularize Singer's diagnosis.[168]

In observing Sacks's neurological-reductionist approach we must notice at least two important weaknesses in his argument. First, he is specifically making an *assumption, a priori*, about experiences that transpired in the distant, medieval past. Thus, these are experiences that he has not directly and empirically examined. Second, in his assumption of the possible explanations responsible for such experiences, Sacks systematically omits the *possibility* of a genuine mystical experience as something to even consider. In light of his neurological (and, therefore, pathological) alternatives, Sacks ignores the option that a genuine spiritual experience may have transpired. Callahan stresses that for Sacks, significantly, "having an authentic revelation from God does not make the list of explanations. The best a visionary saint can do is to creatively mitigate her brain disease. The possibility of having nonpathological hallucinations or visions is not mentioned."[169] No doubt, a materialistic scientism may be driving Sacks's conclusions here. Yet, ironically, by abiding by such an ideological framework, Sacks's conclusions have the *unscientific* quality of omitting the applicability of certain prospects in considering a phenomenon. Thus, Sacks partakes in a direct form of neurological reductionism that not only denigrates mystical experiences but, very narrowly, refuses to even consider the *possibility* of other, meaning spiritual, alternatives, not even making his list of explanations.

Moshe Sluhovsky who, as a historian of religious experience, has concentrated on the darker forms of experience, in demonic possession and exorcisms in early modern Catholicism, likewise points to this reductionist trend in academia, acknowledging the numerous "natural" diagnoses employed by many modern scholars, including hysteria, insanity, epilepsy, and other forms of "retrospective medicine" that assume "that possession as such did not really exist, that it was always something else."[170] The point is reminiscent of how Underhill reductively dismissed every case involving the demonic as hallucinatory in nature, even in the experiences of great mystics such as Catherine of Siena and Teresa of Avila, notwithstanding Underhill's support for the "benevolent" forms of mysticism that these women reported. Today, a most common alternative theory that scholars apply to explain symptoms of what appears as demonic possession in a person is dissociative identity disorder (historically known as multiple personality disorder), an explanation which applies a psychopathological diagnosis to the experience.[171]

According to Sluhovsky, such reductionist explanations are especially popular among many contemporary scholars examining late medieval and early modern accounts of possession. However, Sluhovsky concludes that stereotyping Christians of past centuries, particularly of early modern Europe, as ignorant of medical or psychological causes for abnormal (if not paranormal) behavior constitutes an erroneous approach, if not an altogether arrogant dismissal, obstructing serious study of such cases.[172] Since matters like hysteria and epilepsy were "all classifications of afflictions that were not unfamiliar to early modern people," the assumption "that medieval and early modern people were simply not sophisticated enough to know the right meanings of the symptoms they experienced and witnessed tells us more about modern scholarly arrogance than about premodern ailments and healing techniques, or about early modern configurations of the interactions with the divine."[173]

Psychoanalytical Reductionism

The second form of reductionism listed by Callahan belongs to the discipline of psychoanalysis. Callahan specifically observes the theories of Freudian atheists interested in denigrating religious experiences. She notes that many "psychoanalytical thinkers following Freud's lead see religious experience of all kinds as rising from the unconscious mind's wishful ful-fillment and regression to infantile experiences."[174] The Freudian perspec-tive essentially is one of complete constructivism, as it postulates that all "religious beliefs are constructed in order to deny and defend against death and the powerless vulnerability of humanity in the face of a remorseless meaningless universe," Callahan explains. "For Freudian atheists, human beings regress to magical thinking and use their mental capacities to con-struct religious myths that give meaning to life."[175]

Freud's ideas are not completely original in regard to religion, but are largely inspired by the thought of Feuerbach. W. W. Meissner explains that Freud's ideas of religious beliefs as wish fulfillment, as "illusions, fulfill-ments of the oldest, strongest and most urgent wishes of mankind" are not without a precursor: "Freud was not the first to advance this idea; he follows the lead of Feuerbach, who regarded theology as a disguised form of anthropology and related religious ideas to dreams."[176] Hans Küng, like-wise, explains that before Freud it was Feuerbach who "produced a psy-chological substantiation of atheism: wishes, fantasies, or the power of the imagination are responsible for the projection of the idea of God and of the whole religious pseudo- or dream-world. Like Marx's opium theory at an earlier stage, Freud's illusion theory is grounded in Feuerbach's projec-tion theory."[177] Where Freud's originality lies is in defining the understand-ing of religion as an illusion in psychoanalytical categories.[178]

The experience of mystical union is one for which Freud applied the terminology of an "oceanic feeling,"[179] arguing that this feeling of oneness which mystical experiences describe is, in fact, a regression to an earlier, infantile experience, as he hypothesizes about a unitive feeling that infants apparently experienced—a feeling wherein the self-other dichotomy is transcended for a seeming oneness—in relation to their nurturing moth-ers. Thus, similarly, as Callahan explains:

> A religious person reporting mystical experiences of God or the Infinite is falsely identifying his or her regression into an infantile state. Experiences of a divine presence, along with beliefs in God, are actually products of regression; they represent a flight from rational reality into unconsciously dominated forms of primitive thinking. Persons will take comfort in the illusion that a benevolent deity, like a powerful parent, will fulfill their wishes to be taken care of as well as their need to be forgiven for their sins. Guilt feelings stemming from archaic and intentional lapses into wrongdoing

can be assuaged through religious rituals and belief. Finally, and most importantly, skeptics aver that superstitious religious beliefs in immortality help humankind deny the all but unbearable reality that they are going to die.[180]

In addition to the experience of mystical union as being understood, in Freudian parlance, as an "oceanic feeling" that takes one back to a regressed, infantile state, the experience of ecstasy is explained in Freudian interpretation as being based on a repressed eroticism, which constitutes the unconscious sexual origin of such states. Here, spiritual ecstasy is interpreted as a form of sexual orgasm—the spiritual ecstasy would be a substitute for sexual fulfillment for the mystic, who often is a consecrated celibate—and a major reason for this interpretation is the erotic language and imagery that many saints and mystics apply to describe their ecstatic experiences. Callahan explains that such a critique has especially been prominent in regard to female ecstatic experiences,[181] articulating that "women's purported eroticism could be seen as the unconscious sexual origin of the ecstasies of female saints. The erotic language used by mystics and the erotic quality of religious ecstasies were seen by psychoanalytic skeptics as obvious substitutes for sexual fulfillment."[182]

Meissner explains that psychoanalysis "has followed a path, with rare exceptions, of seeing religious experience in essentially reductive or, even more prejudicially, psychopathological terms. The analytic emphasis has tended to fall on the unconscious and irrational aspects of religious behavior."[183] Meissner admits that Freud's own biases were a major influence on this reductive trend in psychoanalysis. Freud's very first essay on religion, published in 1907 and called "Obsessive Acts and Religious Practices," compared the neurotically obsessive and compulsive behavior of Freud's OCD patients with religious rituals, postulating that religion at its core must be a form of neurosis.[184] This would be a foundational principle for all Freudian interpretations of religion and religious experiences. "The Freudian supposition relates more specifically to the intrapsychic aspects of religious experience; namely, it implies that all religious behavior and belief is a form of obsessive-compulsive neurosis."[185]

William Rogers has summed up Freud's main ideas on religion with great precision, explaining that Freud:

> identified a whole series of potentially neurotic functions symptomized in religious life, most having their origins in psychosexual

development. Religion from this perspective was seen as potentially obsessive-compulsive in its ritual dimensions, a return of repressed guilt or repressed fear of death, a neurotic "wish" for a longed-for father correlative with unresolved Oedipal strivings, a projection onto the cosmic screen of unacknowledged fears and longings for omnipotence, a regression to infantile forms of helplessness and dependence, or perhaps above all an illusory self-deception by which people imagine the security and solace of a loving God, a purposive history, and a stable moral base to protect them from the inevitable suffering, anguish, and death experiences in a hostile reality.[186]

Conversely, Rogers emphasizes that the criticisms of psychoanalytical reductionisms of religion have been extensive, and he stresses that the most "telling challenge" to the psychoanalytic framework has come in the form of recognizing the present "psychogenic fallacy."[187] By pointing to the error of the "psychogenic fallacy," Rogers is articulating that wishful thinking, infantile regressions, and repressed psychosexual desires in the human being, whether actually present or not, do not constitute evidence that can make the judgment whether God does or does not exist.

Secular-Sociological Reductionism

The final reductionist angle that Callahan considers is secular-sociological approaches to religious experiences. Proponents of the secular-sociological model argue that perceived mystical experiences do stem from an individual's preexistent belief system, which consequently does not only interpret but, moreover, *attributes* the individual's taught and socialized concepts and ideas to the experience. Essentially it is a constructivist idea. Thus, in this matter, human beings construct their spiritual experiences from the general cognitive beliefs of society that they have been socialized and taught to assume. According to this logic, the "erroneous attributions and internalized social judgments of a group are being projected upon internal and external phenomena, so that the internal experiences are thought of as coming from God."[188]

Where the secular-sociological model falls short is that it makes a self-defeating argument—that is, it could be inversely used against its proponents. For example, if we take a reductionist thinker like Sacks (albeit from the neurological category), could we not say that in assuming that medieval mystics must have suffered from some form of "hysterical or psychotic ecstasy, the effects of intoxication or an epileptic or migrainous manifestation," Sacks was, himself, *constructing* his explanations from the general intellectual beliefs of a society into which he has been socialized and taught to assume to be true, and, thereafter, attributing them to phenomena he does not really understand? In other words, if the secular-sociologist argument claims that medieval mystics construct God through preexistent cultural and religious indoctrination (since their medieval culture was so religious), thus succumbing to a particular socialized belief system, why not assume that secular-sociologists or *neurologists* construct their own alternative explanations for mystical experiences through preexistent cultural indoctrination (since contemporary Western culture is very secular), thus succumbing to a certain socialized belief system?

CONSIDERING ALL THE aforementioned interpretations of extraordinary religious experiences, it is not difficult to discern why many adherents of the *sui generis* model have been cautious about interdisciplinary integration as a means to better understand experience. The issue, or caution, concerning interdisciplinary integration is reductionism, as so many disciplines of study, from modern philosophy to psychoanalysis and psychology, to neurology and sociology, have been used as a means to *explain away* (a significant difference from simply *explain*) religious experiences. In this regard, distinctions that Proudfoot made between descriptive and explanatory reductionism, arguing that the former gives the latter a bad name, appear to remain superficial, as it is the *explaining away* (thus the explanatory reductionism) of religious experiences that is a central concern to those who avoid reductionist hermeneutics. Of course, this does not mean that the *sui generis* model should stand and that interdisciplinary integration should be avoided. No. Perhaps what is necessary is an interdisciplinary integration that takes a more cognitive and empirical approach toward testing extraordinary religious experiences—as disciplines like psychoanalysis, philosophy, and sociology rely highly on theory to reach their conclusions—and a hermeneutical framework that considers the possible integrity of religious experiences alongside interdisciplinary attention. This would be different from the epistemologies that Proudfoot, Taves, and like-minded thinkers have applied, which from the beginning assume the general premise that experiences are not innately religious or mystical and, therefore, hope to apply interdisciplinary attention to ascribe different meaning to such experiences.

An alternative would be the constructive-relational model, which we will discuss in detail in chapter 7, and which considers the integrity of the original religious experience, thus keeping that possibility open instead of dismissing it as a foundational principle, while applying interdisciplinary integration as a means to better understand the experience. A major difference is that this hermeneutical model does not begin with the predetermined premise that certain explanations cannot be valid, such as the experience being inherently religious or mystical; it leaves that possibility open while considering the various contributions of other disciplines in attaining a more holistic picture of the experience. Combining such a hermeneutical model with sciences whose conclusions come from highly empirical examination can help to formulate a more knowledgeable, and less presumptuous, understanding of religious experiences. Let us now, therefore, turn to a highly empirical science that has in recent years been used to directly examine religious experiences.

Moving Toward Neuroscience and New Methodology

While the foregoing models of reductionism toward studying mysticism, the neurological, psychoanalytical, and sociological may offer interesting theories for extraordinary religious experiences, their most obvious limitation is that all propose theories, *a priori*. In other words, direct examination, meaning empirical investigation of the experience, is not necessarily involved in their evaluations but solely postulations. One can argue, of course, that sociology, however, as one of the examined disciplines, is a highly empirical field. That may be, but it is an empirical field that is able to examine external measures, and a field—as we will see—that possesses its own philosophical assumptions highly based on a secular worldview. The claims of mystics and persons who report extraordinary experiences are claims about interiority, about inner phenomena. How could one measure the interiority of a spiritual experience?

In recent years, scholars have begun doing just that by applying neuroscientific technologies to the study of religious experiences. This is different from Sacks's neurological reductionism, which applies no empirical examination to the study of mystical experiences but simply postulates that such experiences cannot be authentic by offering neurological theories as alternative, pathological explanations to account for the experiences of medieval mystics. Callahan explains, on the other hand, how technologies of contemporary neuroscience have finally been able to penetrate the interior depths of altered states of consciousness (many such states occur during mystical experiences):

> In the twentieth century, scientific investigations using new brain imaging techniques have begun to explore altered states of consciousness, starting with sleep and dreaming and going on to studies of meditating adepts. One result of this is the slowly emerging understanding that altered states of consciousness and trances, whether induced or spontaneous, need not always be diagnosed as psychotic.[189]

Andrew Newberg and Eugene D'Aquili, two pioneering scholars in the neuroscientific study of religious experiences, have made the much bolder claim: "It is possible that with the advent of improved technologies for studying the brain, mystical experiences may finally be differentiated from any type of psychopathology."[190]

With the advent of neuroscience, as a discipline that allows direct study of altered states of consciousness, much methodological progress is being made and can still be made. Here, the study of extraordinary religious and mystical experience is being taken beyond textual analysis, beyond the texts left by the great mystics from hundreds of years ago, to direct scientific examination of present experiences using the human person as a document of study. James used the terminology of *documents humains* in identifying his methodology, as he concentrated on the accounts of extraordinary religious experiences of individual persons as his documents of examination in formulating his Gifford Lectures. Here, however, in the application of neuroscience, the phraseology of *documents humains* becomes even more real and immediate, as concentration is not given to *accounts* of individual experience but, rather, to the actual experiences themselves, directly examined by modern technology.

In 2010, Newberg suggested that the neuroscientific study of spiritual practices and religious experiences "may also be one of the most important areas of research that can be pursued by science in the next decade."[191] Callahan noted that neuroscientific, brain-imaging technologies have already been used to study sleep and dream states, as well as meditation states; and in recent years a lot of new scholarship has been dedicated to such studies. Of course, since such states are cultivated through preexistent efforts (whether natural or spiritual), they are easier to "produce" and, therefore, easier to study, as opposed to more unique and spontaneous states, such as visionary, apparitional, or out-of-body experiences as the type reported by Barnard, which are rarer in their spontaneity and, one could argue, *greater* in the gravity and consequentialism of their reported content. This is where the case of Medjugorje, which we turn to in the next chapter, becomes significant for scholarly research, as it constitutes a case wherein a unique and spontaneous phenomenon, an alleged Marian apparition (or, in the language of mystical theology, a corporal vision), has been reported and has been subjected to exhaustive scientific study.

Medical and Scientific Studies on the Apparitions in Medjugorje

For the first time in all the history of apparitions, science has had an opportunity to investigate extraordinary phenomena while they were actually happening. Medjugorje opened up for the scientist possibilities for research that neither Lourdes nor Fatima had been able to provide.

—MARY CRAIG

I would discover eventually that the apparitions in Medjugorje had been subjected to perhaps more medical and scientific examination than any other purported supernatural event in the history of the human race. . . .

—RANDALL SULLIVAN

MARY CRAIG'S WORDS have astutely pointed out the importance and uniqueness of the Medjugorje apparitions for scientific study. What makes the case of Medjugorje unique in contrast to earlier events is the fact that Medjugorje constitutes a contemporary phenomenon, transpiring in the technologically advanced periods of the late twentieth century and continuing into the twenty-first, and therefore has been able to be examined *while transpiring* by sophisticated means available to modern science. On a daily basis, the six visionaries of Medjugorje entered a deep altered state of consciousness, an ecstatic state, during the same time (5:45 P.M. in the winter and 6:45 P.M. in the summer) when they fell to their knees and reported experiencing their apparitions of the Virgin Mary, undergoing their visionary experiences. The frequency and timing of this phenomenon, its daily and routine occurrence, allowed scientific teams to study the experiences as they were happening in front of them.

Scientific Teams Investigate

Since as early as 1981, various scientific examinations have been conducted on the visionaries. Early important tests, René Laurentin writes, were made by "Italian doctors who came in large numbers in 1984."[1] However, the most in-depth examinations, Craig explains, were an "extremely important and comprehensive series of tests"[2] conducted by a French team that came shortly thereafter in 1984, and "an important series of tests by Italian doctors" in 1985[3]; these were followed, years later, Sullivan articulates, by "the most extensive scientific testing in more than a decade" on the visionaries by a collaborative team of Italian and Austrian doctors in 1998.[4] Instead of observing these various studies chronologically and individually, an approach that would lead to much repetition in documenting overlapping findings, the approach here will be to examine the studies in juxtaposition with one another on the basis of which particular set of data is being observed. Let us, therefore, begin with the social and psychological data, examining what conclusions these various teams reached about the mental and social stability of the visionaries, and from there continue on to the other studies.

Behavioral and Psychological Studies

Dr. Giorgio Sanguinetti, a professor of psychiatry at the University of Milan, was part of the 1985 Italian team that examined the visionaries. Interestingly, in desiring to examine the social and psychological stability of the visionaries, Dr. Sanguinetti was less concerned with studying the altered state of consciousness that the visionaries enter during their apparitions and more interested in observing their daily lives. He was "given an unusual degree of personal access to the seers" to pursue this.[5] Dr. Sanguinetti was searching for any indication of pathological patterns that were observable in "delirious people with a mystical bent." Such patterns were observed again and again in various cases, most tellingly conveyed in such delirious persons through a sense of omnipotence, which was "not necessarily expressed with noisy insistence or displayed fanatically, but coming across with a quiet, complacent silence," the doctor explained. "This hides the sense of triumph through a privileged relationship with the transcendent."[6] Such individuals have limited capacity for spontaneous communication and little interest in other people, the doctor continued. They tend to display very extravagant and theatrical behavior, and react resentfully when criticized, questioned, or contradicted, showing intolerance when challenged or when presented with opposing viewpoints.[7] After studying the daily lives and habits of the Medjugorje seers, Dr. Sanguinetti wrote a detailed report, concluding:

> I consider it of fundamental importance to emphasize that in all my conversations with the young "visionaries" of Medjugorje I have never discovered, on any occasion, any thought, look, conversation, attitude or behavior similar to these pathological states which I have listed. First of all it must be made clear that the "visionaries" live a normal life; they are integrated in their community and in their families and are treated by others as if they were no different from other people, or from themselves before they became "visionaries." . . . [T]hey differ from others only in the time they give to the practice of religion and to the visions; all this is done in a very natural way without piosity or complacency; their behavior is by preference discreet and, politely, they try to shield themselves from the overpowering pressure of pilgrims, when this is possible. They are quite often open to conversation and seem patiently resigned to having to answer the same questions; in this they are not effusive, nor are they withdrawn or exhibitionist. On the contrary they look calm and peaceful and gentle. They do not try to convince one, and they do not exceed what is asked of them; their smile is not smug or malicious, and it is not artificial. Their movements reflect only kindness and good will. They certainly are not looking for attention or for an audience; they do not offer interpretations or personal opinions about mystical experiences; all they want to do is report the facts and admit that they are happy.[8]

The apparent normalcy of the seers is something that has impressed, and at times surprised, various investigators who have met the visionaries. A year before Dr. Sanguinetti arrived with the Italian team, a French team of doctors and scientists came to Medjugorje to study the visionaries and their experiences. The coordinator of the team was Dr. Henri Joyeux, who was a professor in the Faculty of Medicine at the University of Montpellier and a surgeon at Montpellier's Cancer Institute. Dr. Joyeux explains that he and his colleagues heard of the phenomenon in Medjugorje by reading the book *La Vierge, apparait-elle a Medjugorje* (Is the Virgin Mary Appearing at Medjugorje?) by Fr. René Laurentin. "We were intrigued by this reading, but not convinced,"[9] Dr. Joyeux admitted. He moved forward, however, in contacting Fr. Laurentin to organize an investigative team of scientists to come to study the apparitions. The impression that Dr. Joyeux and his colleagues formed of the visionaries they were able to examine (most, but not all, of the visionaries were present for the testing) is noteworthy, seeing much commonality with Dr. Sanguinetti's observations:

> Vicka, Ivan, Marija, and Jakov are like any other youngsters of their age. We saw no signs of hallucination, pretense or invention. They were calm, serene and deeply serious and did not play at being celebrities. They remained normal in all circumstances in which we observed them. They did not collude with each other either before, during or after the essential event of their day [when they experience their apparitions], and they all returned home to their families.
>
> These young Yugoslavs are easy to communicate with (even in the case of strangers, a doctor and an engineer); they allow themselves to be photographed or filmed but they do not seek this out; rather, they appeared to be somewhat annoyed by all the fuss that surrounded them. They are country youngsters who do not appear to need either a psychologist or a psychiatrist. They dress in the normal fashion of other young people of their country. They give no impression of being bigoted, each seeming to have his or her own personality; we felt at ease with all of them: they are neither geniuses nor simpletons; they are not being manipulated but remain free and healthy in mind and body.[10]

One of the earliest doctors to examine the visionaries was Ludvik Stopar, a professor of psychiatry at the University of Maribor and a member of the prestigious International Commission of Doctors. "Dr. Stopar had been permitted to examine the six young seers over a period of weeks during late 1982, conducting a battery of neurological, psychological, intelligence, and personality tests on each of them," Sullivan explains.[11] Although he did not provide in-depth details of the examinations, in his final report Dr. Stopar wrote: "Scientific and sociological tests, including (respectively) neuropsychiatric, medico-psychological, somatic, adolescent and young-adult profiles, lifestyle characteristics and intelligence and educational standards, show the children to be *absolutely normal* and free from all psychopathological reactions."[12]

Dr. Enzo Gabrici, a neuropsychiatrist who was one of the Italian doctors to examine the visionaries in 1984, similarly concluded: "The subjects are very normal in their ordinary lives (family, school and church). Jakov was somewhat tired after the long ceremony which followed the apparition and went out for a few moments to play with Dr. Frigerio's children. Vicka is an equally normal subject with no traces of neurosis or psychosis."[13] Dr. Gabrici "saw no indication of neurosis or psychosis in any of the other three seers he tested either," Sullivan notes.[14] Furthermore, according to Dr. Gabrici's report:

Clinical observation has also excluded hallucinatory phenomena as well as the normal components of epilepsy or of any other malfunction capable of producing the alteration of consciousness. There are no symptoms which would suggest that the subjects are living out something which was previously suggested under hypnosis. The visionaries can recall with absolute lucidity what has happened to them.[15]

Although Dr. Gabrici examined Ivan, Jakov, and Marija, he "found Vicka particularly impressive; the girl's ease and spontaneity mitigated strongly against an interpretation of hysteria."[16] He wrote that Vicka "shows no signs of emotional hardship, human misunderstanding or previous traumas. The apparition does not tire her as is the case with hysterical trances; on the contrary, she feels more invigorated."[17] Curiously, Dr. Gabrici even noticed a discernable distinction between the behavior of the visionaries during their apparitions and that of spirit mediums. He explained that the visionaries "are, as it were, rapt, at the moment of the apparition. They differ from mediums who are taken over by a different personality; the visionaries retain perfect consciousness of their identity."[18]

In late 1989, a little-known examination of all six visionaries took place with a team of physicians, psychologists, and sociologists who were brought together by the Vatican in order to study the seers and their experiences. The testing took place in a monastery near Split, and—Sullivan explains—although "no details were released, the French-Canadian priest who headed the Vatican team offered the final paragraph of his report for publication."[19] That final paragraph, like previous reports, highlighted the normalcy, mental stability, and moral integrity of the visionaries, stating: "The conclusion we draw is that the visionaries' behavior patterns, both socio-cultural and socio-religious, do not give the least indication of any tendency to fraud, hysteria or self-deception."[20] This was similar to a conclusion that the 1985 Italian team reached, explaining: "On the basis of the psychological tests, for all and each of the visionaries it is possible with certainty to exclude fraud and deception."[21]

Many years later, in 1998, when the collaborative Austrian-Italian team had the chance to examine the visionaries as adults, the psychological testing was extensive and the results, once again, supported the psychological and moral integrity of the visionaries. Sullivan notes the depth of the studies that were conducted by the team:

> Their specialties ranged from internal medicine, neurology, and gynecology to psychiatry, psychophysiology, and hypnotherapy. The psychological tests alone were smothering in their scope: MMPI, EPI, MHQ, Tree test, Person test, Raven Matrixes, Rorschach, Hand test, and Valsecchi truth detection. Physiological tests that included an electrocardiogram and computerized polygraph were conducted concurrently. Four separate states of consciousness had been tested: waking state, visualization of mental images, hypnotically induced ecstasy, and the raptures of the three seers who still reported daily apparitions.[22]

The scientific team was led by the Austrian psychologist and theologian Dr. Andreas Resch and by the Italian psychiatrist Dr. Giorgio Gagliardi.[23]

In a documentary film recording the 1998 scientific tests on the seers, Dr. Andreas Resch commented openly about his impressions of the visionaries. He was able to interview each visionary with questions about the initial days of the apparitions. About Marija Pavlović, he has said: "Marija was very open and very profound. I often repeat that it was almost overwhelming. We felt that we were faced with a person who completely faces up to what she is going through and for whom the experience becomes something of an all-encompassing commitment."[24]

About Ivanka Ivanković, who was the first visionary to see the apparition and who, since then, has become the most reclusive visionary, Dr. Resch said: "My impression was that she is someone who lives a life away from the public, a sensitive woman full of empathy who speaks quite openly about her experience but who today simply wants to be left to live in peace."[25]

Dr. Resch's impression of one of the male visionaries, Ivan Dragičević, was initially negative but gradually the impression changed. He explained: "At the beginning of Ivan's interview, I feel I had a negative atti-tude. I had to fight the idea that he wanted to deceive and lie. This is why in the beginning the questioning was rather formal. Then the atmosphere became relaxed. In the end I understood that in Ivan there was such a pro-found inner depth that I was very impressed, and had to completely review my initial judgment."[26]

Regarding his interview with Mirjana Dragičević, the most educated of the visionaries,[27] Dr. Resch commented: "The interview with Mirjana was probably among the most peculiar. This young woman is very critical and has strong reservation where this kind of interrogation is concerned but she finally agreed to it freely. At first she gave short answers then she expressed herself freely. My first impression was that I was talking to a person who expects a lot from herself, as much as in terms of behavior as what she expresses freely to outsiders. In any case, she spoke openly."[28]

About his interview with Vicka Ivanković, the most extroverted of the visionaries, Dr. Resch commented: "From the beginning, conversation with Vicka was very free and open. Vicka is very communicative and her memory's exceptionally clear. She told the story [of the beginning of the apparitions] with determination. She didn't respond aggressively to con-tradiction. For example, when I said that the bishop doesn't approve of this, she simply remarked that that was his own business and that she didn't want to voice any judgment. For her the important thing is what she has experienced and has to accomplish in her life."[29]

Here, it is noteworthy to recall Dr. Giorgio Sanguinetti's point, during his 1985 investigation of the seers, wherein he pointed to pathological pat-terns in "delirious people with a mystical bent," and emphasized that such individuals become extremely resentful and defensive when contradicted or criticized—something that the doctor did not see in the Medjugorje visionaries, similarly to Dr. Resch's latter (1998) encounter with Vicka.[30] Fr. Slavko Barbaric made the same point years earlier. Fr. Barbaric, who was a Franciscan priest and a psychologist, was initially sent to Medjugorje in 1982 by the bishop of Mostar to investigate and attempt to expose the appa-ritions.[31] After conducting his investigations, Fr. Barbaric, to the dismay of Bishop Žanić, became a believer of the integrity of the experiences of the young visionaries and, moreover, became a spiritual director to the vision-aries. What impressed him greatly, among other things, he explained, was the fact that the visionaries "do not act like fanatics. These are children, aged ten to sixteen, but when you tell them, 'I do not believe,' they do not attack you, they do not try to convince you, they do not argue with you. Like the postman, they deliver a message and they go home. They do not worry at all about what people expect of them."[32] He continued to emphasize the normalcy of the seers: "Jakov can barely wait to finish school and prayers so he has time to play soccer. These are not people sitting in a corner and waiting for the next apparition, living for the attention it brings them. They are normal children in every way. Even more than if pretending, they would be consumed by this if it was a projection. And these are not children who have a natural gift for such a thing. They are not depressive. They are not children with overactive imaginations. Far from it."[33]

According to Dr. Joyeux's final report from the French team, which agrees with the conclusions of Fr. Barbaric and takes them further: "The visionaries have no symptoms of anxiety or obsessional neurosis, phobic or hysterical neurosis, hypochondriac/or psychosomatic neurosis, and there is no indication of any psychosis. We can make these formal statements in the light of detailed clinical examinations."[34]

Neuroscientific Studies

Electroencephalogram (EEG) tests were administered on the visionaries, measuring brain waves by indicating the rhythms of brain activity according to eight diagrams that come through electrodes attached to eight parts of the skull, and the results were recorded as taking place before, during, and after the apparitions.[35] The EEG examinations were used to test whether the state that the visionaries experience during their apparitions can be identified, and therefore explained, as a hallucinatory sleep or dream state, or an epileptic state. What is most interesting is that, in neuroscience, states of consciousness are identified through some combination of alpha (receptive) and beta (reactive) impulses. "Dr. Joyeux observed that the ratio of activity in the seers' brains prior to an apparition was exactly normal: ten alpha cycles to twenty beta cycles each second."[36] Falling into a sleep or trance state would decrease the number of alpha cycles while increasing the beta. Yet, the exact opposite happened during apparitions: the visionaries' beta impulses stopped completely, showing them to be in a state that is not simply awake, but *hyper-awake*.[37]

The first visionaries that were tested with the EEGs were Ivan and Marija. What was identified in their brains from the EEG results was the "normal electrical activity associated with wakefulness" and, furthermore, the "examination shows no sign of sleep or of epileptic discharge."[38] Combined with the clinical studies, these results were also able to exclude pathological hallucination. "The electro-encephalogram also excludes epilepsy. Together with the clinical observation (both direct and on video) the test excludes hallucination in the pathological sense of the word."[39] The French team offered a three-point conclusion summing up the EEG results thus:

1. Ivan Dragicevic and Marija Pavlovic have normal and identical electro-encephalograms, before, during and after the period of ecstasy.
2. The electroencephalograms allow us to exclude totally the existence of the phenomena of dreams, sleep or epilepsy, in both subjects, on the day of the tests.
3. Intermittent light simulation during three recordings showed no electrical discharge of an epileptic type before, during or after ecstasy.[40]

The Question of Hypnosis and Self-Suggestion

The 1998 Italian-Austrian team studied the visionaries by examining four distinct states of consciousness: (1) a waking state; (2) an altered state of consciousness induced by hypnosis; (3) a state of visualization of mental images; and (4) the altered state of consciousness that the visionaries experience during apparitions.[41] The final report explained that the purpose of this testing was to "investigate whether the ecstatic state of the apparition, already registered in 1985 by the Italian doctors working group, still continue to be present or has undergone changes. In addition it was desired to investigate potential coincidence/divergence with other states off [*sic*] consciousness such as guided visualization or hypnosis."[42] The tests ended up demonstrating that during their apparitions the visionaries "entered an altered state of consciousness quite different from the other three mental states in which they were tested."[43] These findings were significant, for they were able to show that these other states of consciousness (induced hypnosis, guided visualization, or a waking state) could not be used as alternative, natural explanations for the state that the visionaries experience during their apparitions, as the state that the visionaries entered was proven to be distinctly different.

Sullivan explains that to the scientific team and to Vatican officials, who requested the results of the studies, the most interesting conclusion from the 1998 examinations of the visionaries was that the psychiatrists who had examined the seers "were able to induce a hypnotic trance in each instance, but were unsuccessful in producing any visions of the Virgin

Mary, despite repeated attempts."[44] This was significant for a couple of reasons; one can be seen in the way that the attempt at producing visions of the Virgin Mary was orchestrated. For example, at one point the visionary Marija, who is one of the three visionaries who claims to continue experiencing daily apparitions, was hypnotized for 28 minutes. Under hypnosis she was asked by Dr. Gagliardi to re-experience an apparition. "The Virgin Mary is now appearing to you," suggested Dr. Gagliardi. "You will soon be able to see her face, as you have seen it so often."[45] These kinds of guided visualizations under hypnosis were not able to produce, or perhaps more aptly *reproduce*, the kind of altered state of consciousness that the visionaries encounter during their apparitions.

"The aim of the hypnosis was to determine whether or not the apparition, linked with the ecstasy, can be provoked by suggestion and therefore dismissed as self-suggestion and imagination. This would've led to labeling the visionaries as simulators. However, if the ecstasy cannot be provoked by hypnosis then the apparition, the ecstasy, cannot be passed off as self-hypnosis, self-suggestion, or imagination."[46] Computerized polygraphs—examining "skin electrical activity; peripheral cardiac capillary and heartbeat activities; skeletal and diaphragmatic pneumography"[47]—were applied to measure the interior state that the visionaries entered during hypnosis and during their apparitional experiences to make the comparison between the states.

Dr. Mario Cigada, an Italian specialist on hypnosis who was a psychotherapist and oculist on the 1998 team, explained the results. He emphasized that the results for both Marija and Ivan were nearly identical, and therefore (when interviewed) he used the results of Marija's tests to articulate what both visionaries were experiencing. "These are the results of the research made in 1998 on Marija and Ivan. The differences between hypnosis and ecstasy, which we demonstrated, have been exposed," Dr. Cigada explained.[48] In this regard, electrical activity on the surface of the visionaries' skin was recorded "in order to gain information about the functionality of the neurovegetative system and the state of awareness of the visionary."[49] Dr. Cigada explained that a vegetative nervous system is split into two parts—the sympathetic system and the para-sympathetic system. During Marija's apparition, the sympathetic nervous system was active and her heart activity went up to 135 beats. Under hypnosis, however, "where we suggest that she recall previous ecstasies [previous apparition experiences through visualization], the graph shows the highest peak of activity in a totally different place," the para-sympathetic nervous system.

This system (unlike the sympathetic) is characterized by relaxation, and the heart rate, therefore, slowed down to 70 beats per minute. According to Dr. Cigada this "shows that there is a radical difference between the state of hypnosis and ecstasy."[50]

These findings were instrumental, as they were able to show that hypnosis and guided visualization were not able to reproduce the same state of consciousness that the visionaries experience during their apparitions, in fact pointing to a completely different state in the distinctions that were recorded. The results, thus, were able to demonstrate that hypnosis (and thus self-suggestion), visualization, and imagination were not responsible for the apparitional experiences of the visionaries. This came alongside the findings of the EEG tests, which showed that pathological hallucination, an epileptic state, a sleep or a dream state, also were not responsible for the experiences of the visionaries.

Studies on Ocular and Visual Functions

Dr. Jacques Philippot, an ophthalmologist on the French team, undertook the study of ocular and visual functions on the visionaries, examining the back of their eyes, photomotor and blinking reflexes, and the frequency of blinking before, during, and after ecstasy, as well as conducting screening tests and studying the mobility of the eyeballs by using electro-oculographic recordings before, during, and after their apparitions.[51] The examinations on the back of the visionaries' eyes "were normal and were identical before and after the ecstasy."[52] These tests excluded any "organic anomaly (either ocular or cerebral, whether due to swelling or not)" and, furthermore, they excluded the possibility of visual hallucination since the "ocular system is anatomically and functionally normal."[53]

The reflex of blinking, interestingly, was absent from the eyes during their apparitions when extremely strong lights were flashed in front of the visionaries, having no effect on them. And yet reflexive blinking was present both before and after ecstasy in the face of dazzling lights.[54] "Examination of the inner eye indicated a normal state, identical before and after ecstasy. The pupils contracted normally in the presence of light, but it was noted that while Marija and Ivanka blinked in the bright light before and after the apparition, during it they did not blink even once."[55] This was the same result that the 1985 Italian team would reach a year later, as during apparitions "a 100-watt bulb shone full in their [the visionaries'] faces [but] produced no ocular reaction."[56] Moreover, during apparitions the number of eyelid movements—thus blinking—was significantly less than what was observable before and after an apparition. Two of the visionaries had no eyelid movement whatsoever during apparitions when examined by the French team.[57] These results agreed with earlier tests that were performed by Dr. M. Frederica Magatti, a member of an earlier 1984 Italian team.[58] Dr. Magatti tried "shouting at, jabbing, and pinching the seers during an apparition, without obtaining 'any observable reaction.' "[59]

> Finally, after noting that the eyes of each child had become "hugely dilated" during their apparition, Dr. Magatti used a film projector with a 1,000-watt bulb to blast their pupils with light. None of the five* had reacted, Dr. Magatti wrote; not only did their pupils remain unusually dilated, but the eyelids of each seer continued to blink at a normal rate. Her tests were preliminary, Dr. Magatti noted; nevertheless, she was prepared to assert that the Medjugorje visionaries, during their apparitions, were demonstrating the most complete "suspension of consciousness of their relationship with the exterior world" she had ever observed in a subject.[60]

Furthermore, according to the electro-oculogram tests, as the apparitions began, the eyeballs of the visionaries become immobile, their eye movements "ceasing simultaneously almost to the second."[61] This graphic recording of the uncanny synchronization in the simultaneous movements of the eyeballs "indicates simultaneity to the second in cessation of movement at the beginning of the ecstasy and, again, simultaneity to the second in the return of movement at the end of the ecstasy."[62] Dr. Philippot would notice that, actually, at "the beginning of the ecstasy there is a simultaneity to *one-fifth of a second* in the cessation of eyeball movement which begins again simultaneously at the end of the ecstasy."[63] Such synchronism, for Dr. Philippot, "was so far beyond the capacity of normal human functioning that no form of collusion or manipulation could account for it."[64]

Video recordings, photographs, and firsthand examination by the French team further showed that during apparitions, the visionaries' eyes converge on the same point, a spot a few feet above their heads where they report to see the Madonna.[65] "For anyone who has seen the ecstasy or a photograph of it, it is evident that the visionaries look intently at the same

---

* Mirjana, the sixth visionary, was absent during the examinations, as she was residing with her family as a teenager in Sarajevo.

object. On all levels (visual, auditory, tactile) they relate in such a coherent manner to this same object that it seems impossible to explain the fact through a pre-established harmony of their subjective dispositions."[66] However, when an opaque screen was placed in front of the visionaries' eyes to test whether the experiment would interfere with, or disrupt, their apparitions, it had no effect on them or their visionary experiences. This has led to questions surrounding the nature of their experiences, asking whether the experiences of the visionaries can be categorized as objective or subjective, or perhaps as an admixture containing both components, a matter we will discuss in greater detail shortly hereafter.

Studies on Auditory and Voice Functions, and Sensitivity to Pain

Dr. Francois Rouquerol, a member of the 1984 French team, conducted tests measuring the auditory functions of the visionaries to determine whether an auditory hallucination is taking place. Dr. Rouquerol concluded that during apparitions there is an absence of normal objective clinical reactions to the presence of violent noise. In other words, when a 90 decibel sound—the "equivalent to the noise of a combustion engine at high speed"—was fed into the right ear of visionary Ivan Dragičević during an apparition, the visionary did not convey a single reaction to the noise, as if being oblivious to it. "At the end of the ecstasy Ivan confirmed that he heard nothing."[67] This was a great contrast to his pre-ecstasy reaction, wherein the injection of a lesser, 70 decibel sound, visibly startled the young visionary. "The boy jumped, as was to be expected, when exposed to a seventy-decibel noise. During the ecstasy, however, although the sound was conducted along the auditory passages in the same way, Ivan did not react to a ninety-decibel noise, and afterwards said he had heard nothing at all. It would appear that, at this time, the sound had not reached the cortex of the brain."[68]

In addition to concluding that there is a clear disconnection of auditory pathways during the apparitions, making the visionaries as impervious to exterior noise as they are to strong blasts of light, in "the same way [it was determined that] the visionaries do not feel pinching, prodding or other interventions," thus being impervious to pain as well.[69] These findings on the visionaries, their imperviousness to pain during apparitions, were confirmed by the 1985 Italian team as well. One of the doctors[70] on the Italian team used an algometer, "an electric instrument for measuring resistance to burns,"[71] to test the visionaries' sensitivity to pain. The test showed that "prior to the apparitional experience their reaction to pain was normal (between 0.3 to 0.4 seconds), [yet] during the apparition they did not perceive any pain."[72] Mary Craig provides details behind the test, explaining:

> When a heated silver disc was applied to Marija and two of the other visionaries before ecstasy, they reacted within three or four tenths of a second—in other words, normally. During ecstasy, however, they did not react at all. The test was limited to seven seconds, for fear of inflicting serious burns if the period was extended. During that time, the visionaries appeared to be completely insensitive to pain.[73]

The doctor who performed the experiment wrote that this proved without a doubt that the visionaries were not faking their experiences or trying to deceive.[74] Dr. Luigi Frigerio, another member of the Italian team, explained that these results combined with the EEG testing, which determined that the visionaries were not only awake but hyper-awake during their apparitions, presented a contradiction that "cannot be explained naturally, and thus can be only preternatural or supernatural."[75] In other words, in a state of hyper-wakefulness a person would be very sensitive and vulnerable to pain, unlike the unexplainable paradox that encapsulates the state of consciousness that the visionaries enter into: being vividly awake yet impervious to pain.

Dr. Rouquerol's results additionally showed that the "auditory potential test, which studies the nervous influx from the periphery (the cochlea, part of the inner ear) to the core of the cerebral artery, indicates that the various pathways to the brain are normal. The regular and rounded shape of the graph eliminates auditory hallucination of an epileptic type."[76] Thus, in addition to the EEG examinations, these tests provided further evidence against an epileptic diagnosis in explaining the apparitions, in addition to eliminating auditory hallucination as an explanation.

Dr. Rouquerol also conducted voice function (phonation) experiments on the visionaries. It is important to note that during their apparitions the visionaries' voices become inaudible while their lips continue moving as if in conversation with someone. This is one of the key synchronisms experienced by the seers during their apparitions. As the apparition begins, first the visionaries fall to their knees and their voices immediately and simultaneously become silent without even a split second of distinction.

Curiously, the "visionaries themselves have admitted to hearing their own voices of verbal communication as normal during the apparitional experience and are surprised that others cannot hear them."[77] Dr. Rouquerol's tests showed that during the apparitions, while the lips and facial muscles of the visionaries are mobile, the larynx (where the vocal cords are present) stops. This means that while their lips are moving normally, as in communication, the act of exhaling does not vibrate the vocal cords, presenting another inexplicable paradox. Moreover, the movement of the lips, and thus the muscles controlling gesticulation on the face, provide "a further argument against catalepsy" since a cataleptic state would constitute a condition wherein rigidity and immobility of the muscles are present.[78] Dr. Rouquerol explained the results on voice and larynx functions in five points, enunciating:

1. While the visionaries recited the Rosary before the apparition[,] the needle indicating the functioning of the larynx muscles displayed ample movement.
2. At the beginning of the ecstasy, when the voice became inaudible, the needle stopped. There was no longer any movement of the larynx. When the visionary conversed with the apparition[,] there was movement of the lips only (articulation without phonation).
3. The needle moved again. This time the voices returned in the middle of the apparition to recite the Our Father which, according to the visionaries, had been started by the Virgin.
4. The voice disappeared in the final phase of the ecstasy as it did in the first phase (articulation without phonation).
5. The movements of the larynx reappeared at the end of the ecstasy as soon as the visionaries began to speak.

> This shows that the extinction of the voice at the beginning of the ecstasy is connected with the fact that there was no movement of the larynx and, though lip movement remained normal, the act of breathing out no longer caused the vocal cords to vibrate.[79]

Another important connection has been made between the first word that is uttered by the visionaries once their voices return the moment their apparition ends and the simultaneous eyeball movements of the visionaries that also return. Here, it is important to note that at the end of each apparition "one visionary, or more, utter more or less simultaneously the word 'Ode,' which [in Croatian] means 'she is gone.' "[80] Craig explains the connection:

> The French professor, [Jean] Cadilhac, who later conducted psycho-
> logical and psychiatric tests on the children, attached great impor-
> tance to the fact that the word *ode* was uttered (by one or more of
> the visionaries) *after* they had lowered their eyes. Had they spoken
> first, the word could have been interpreted as a pre-arranged signal.
> Moreover, *ode* was not always synchronized. Out of fifty apparitions
> studied by the French team, Jakov came in first with it fourteen
> times, Vicka eight, Marija four, and Ivanka only three.[81]

Subjective or Objective Experiences?

What does it mean to ask whether the experiences of the visionaries are subjective or objective? It is a question that has come up often in the writings of both scholars and journalists in regard to the Medjugorje visionaries.[82] The vocabulary of mystical theology that we examined in an earlier chapter regarding visions provides an appropriate means of explanation for this question. Essentially, the question of subjective or objective experience is asking whether the visionary experience possesses the characteristics of an imaginative or a corporal vision. The latter, the corporal vision, would constitute an "objective" experience, as it points to the presence of a three-dimensional entity (the apparition) that is externally perceivable by each visionary, thus objectively experienced as the phenomenon is perceived *in the same way* by the external senses of each seer. The former, the imaginative vision, would constitute a "subjective" experience, as it points to the presence of an entity that is perceivable through the "inner senses" of each visionary, being filtered and manifested through the inner, imaginative faculties of each individual seer, independent of the other seers. In such a case, each visionary may have a subjectively experienced encounter whose content, although (possibly) similar, can possess different characteristics.

However, in the case of Medjugorje the answer does not seem entirely black or white, as the experiences of the visionaries signify the presence of both subjective and objective elements, even to the point of paradox. James Paul Pandarakalam, a psychologist who examined the visionaries on various occasions, explains: "Medical tests with Medjugorje visionaries at the time of the apparitional occurrence point toward an objective and subjective or nonobjective visionary experience."[83] There are two pieces of evidence from the medical tests that point to a subjective experience. "The screening test does not impair the vision; therefore, the normal visual pathways are not used, and the evoked auditory potential tests proves [*sic*] that during the apparitional experience the auditory pathways remain normal but are not used."[84] In other words, both these tests point to the presence of an inner experience, one whose manifestation is not altered or disturbed by exterior factors such as blocking the view of the visionaries with a screen or attempting to affect their hearing with loud noises. These experiments point to the reality that the apparition is filtered and manifested through the imaginative faculties (not externally) and that this may be an imaginative—in other words, subjective—experience that the visionaries are undergoing.

Other evidence, however, points to the opposite conclusion, signifying the presence of a corporal vision, or an objective experience, in the apparitional encounter of the visionaries. René Laurentin stresses three pieces of evidence that point to an objective experience. First, what is significant during the apparition is the convergence of the gaze of the visionaries' eyes that is directed toward a spot above their heads, as if all were perceiving a nonvisible entity that is externally (and thus objectively) present. Second, the electro-oculograph testing showing simultaneity of the cessation of eyeball movements points to an objective experience, as it shows that the visionaries are experiencing the same phenomenon at the same moment, instead of having intersubjective or personal experiences. Third, Laurentin points to the "simultaneous raising of their eyes and hands as the apparition disappears upwards" as a final sign of objectivity, again evidence that signifies behavior responding to an external (and, therefore, corporal, or objective) vision or presence.[85]

Of course, an apparent paradox is present in the evidence here, as elements of both the subjective and the objective are observable, presenting an admixture of characteristics behind the experience that are not easy to categorize into one definition. Therefore, on the matter of subjective or objective experiences, the French team concluded by emphasizing the apparent ambiguity, or mysteriousness, of the case: that this "is an essential question which the tests do not answer with certainty."[86] However, their report further postulated that if "the vision is objective, and the above points [referring to the three points that signify objectivity] would seem to indicate this, the modalities of the vision are not those of ordinary perception; they belong to another mode of perception, itself objective, but not measurable by our tests (which nevertheless do not exclude it)."[87]

The point here, interestingly, can be seen in comparison to what was previously said about Kant's epistemological framework and mystical experiences in Perovich's essay. Perovich stressed that Kant would consider his epistemological model to be inadequate in analyzing mystical experiences, as the Kantian epistemology was intended for, and therefore limited to, ordinary human perception. Mystical perception, on the other hand, transcending normal human cognition, could not be measured by, and therefore subjected to, the Kantian epistemological framework. This is similar (though not identical) to what the French team was stating about the experiences of the Medjugorje visionaries. The experiences indicate a mode of perception that is not ordinary and whose essence is not measurable by their scientific tests. Important distinctions, however, need to be made here, as the foregoing point could be too easily misinterpreted. What the scientific team is saying essentially comes down to an *epistemological* issue: that the *mode of perception*, and *not* the psychological and neurophysiological mechanisms, of the experiences cannot be determined by their scientific examinations. In other words, there was a lot that could be measured and *was* indeed determined by the scientific testing—primarily the negative criteria of distinguishing what the visionaries are *not* experiencing—through the various pathological symptoms and theories of fraud that were excluded as untenable alternative explanations by the scientific examinations. Once again, the issue was the mode of perception, the question of how the visionaries are able to experience their encounter in a way that transcends standard subjective-objective dichotomies of perception that are essential to normal human cognition.

An understanding of the state of ecstasy may help clarify the experience of the visionaries here. When a visionary enters an ecstasy, the individual can be suspended above his or her time-space reality, meaning they are (at the moment of the experience) lifted up into the time-space reality of the apparition, thus the heavenly sphere of the Virgin Mary in this case. This means that, while their experiences may be objective, and while the visionaries do look up at the same spot above their heads, the object of their apparition—the Virgin Mary—is not actually present in that spot, meaning in their time-space reality, but rather they are in that moment being enraptured and thus lifted into her time-space reality, into heaven. Therefore, to illustrate with another famous case, this understanding suggests that the Virgin Mary is not present, for example, in the historical time of 1858 and in the space of Lourdes, France—meaning, in our time-space reality—but that the visionary, Bernadette Soubirous, at the moment of the apparition was taken up into the time-space reality of the Virgin Mary, being lifted up into heaven at the moment of the apparition. This under-standing of ecstasy explains why visionaries can be impervious to pain during their apparitions: their bodies have remained on earth while their souls (thus their consciousness) have transcended their bodily senses, being in the moment of the ecstasy taken up into another realm of exist-ence. This would also explain how the sight and hearing of the Medjugorje seers can be interfered with during the apparition, yet because they have "left" their bodies during ecstasy, it has no effect on stifling their visionary experiences. The experiences, in this understanding, because they are not filtered by the internal faculties of the visionaries but have transcended the normal modes of human perception, are objective, but the subjectiv-ity comes into play when the visionaries must report on, and transmit the content of, their experiences after they occur.[88]

The Results

The final results of the various scientific teams that examined the visionar-ies highly correspond with one another's findings. Let us begin with the final report of the 1984 French team written by Dr. Henri Joyeux. It states:

> The phenomenon of the apparition in Medjugorje, which was stud-ied during five periods of 1984 with five visionaries as subjects, is scientifically inexplicable. Clinical observation of the visionaries leads us to affirm, as our Yugoslav colleagues have already affirmed, that these young people are healthy in mind and body.
>
> Detailed clinical and paraclincial studies completed before, dur-ing, and after the ecstasies of 24–25 March, 9–10 June, 6–7 October, and 28–29 December allow us to affirm scientifically that there is no pathological modification of the parameters studied: electro-encephalogram, electrocardiogram, evoked auditory potentials.

- There is no epilepsy, as electro-encephalograms demonstrate.
- They are not asleep, again the electro-encephalograms demonstrate this.
- There is no question of any hallucination in the pathological sense of that word:
  - There is no auditory or visual hallucination that would be linked to the peripheral auditory or visual receptors (normal visual and audi-tory pathways).

- There is no paroxystic hallucination: the electro-encephalograms demonstrate this.
- There are no hallucinations that would have their origins in dream such as one would observe in cases of extreme mental disorder or in the course of the development of atrophic dementia.
- There is no question of catalepsy, because, during the ecstasy the muscles controlling gesticulation are not inhibited and function normally.[89]

Given all the examinations and their results, the final report of the French team would conclude that the visionaries' regular "behavior is always non-pathological," emphasizing that the seers do not possess any symptoms of anxiety, neurosis, or hysteria, and that the "ecstasies are not pathological nor is there any element of deceit. No scientific discipline seems able to describe these phenomena."[90]

The 1985 Italian team reached similar results, although their final report, issued as a twelve-point conclusion, highlighted not only the medical and psychological findings but also observations about the visionaries' growth in virtue due to their apparitions, as well as making numerous theological claims about the nature of the experiences. The report stated:

1. On the basis of the psychological tests, for all and each of the visionaries it is possible with certainty to exclude fraud and deception.
2. On the basis of the medical examinations, tests and clinical observations etc., for all and each of the visionaries it is possible to exclude pathological hallucinations.
3. On the basis of the results of previous researches for all and each of the visionaries it is possible to exclude a purely natural interpretation of these manifestations.
4. On the basis of information and observations that can be documented, for all and each of the visionaries it is possible to exclude that these manifestations are of the preternatural order, i.e. under demonic influence.
5. On the basis of information and observations that can be documented, there is a correspondence between these manifestations and those that are usually described in mystical theology.
6. On the basis of information and observations that can be documented, it is possible to speak of spiritual advances in the theological and moral virtues of the visionaries, from the beginning of these manifestations until today.

7. On the basis of information and observations that can be documented, it is possible to exclude teaching or behavior of the visionaries that would be in clear contradiction to Christian faith and morals.

8. On the basis of information and observations that can be documented, it is possible to speak of good spiritual fruits in people drawn into the supernatural activity of these manifestations and in people favorable to them.

9. After more than four years, the tendencies and different movements that have been generated through Medjugorje, in consequence of these manifestations, influence the people of God in the Church in complete harmony with Christian doctrine and morals.

10. After more than four years, it is possible to speak of permanent and objective spiritual fruits of movements generated through Medjugorje.

11. It is possible to affirm that all good and spiritual undertakings of the Church, which are in complete harmony with the authentic magisterium of the Church, find support in the events in Medjugorje.

12. Accordingly, one can conclude that after a deeper examination of the protagonists, facts, and their effects, not only in the local framework, but also in regard to the responsive chords of the Church in general, it is well for the Church to recognize the supernatural origin and, thereby, the purpose of the events in Medjugorje.[91]

The Italian anthropologist Paolo Apolito has been critical of certain conclusions that the Italian team reached about the experiences of the visionaries. Although he acknowledged that the team was "carrying out serious and reliable investigations and tests,"[92] Apolito was critical of two aspects of the results that provided a "theological analysis" and a "scientific and theological judgment" about the apparitions.[93] Apolito's criticisms, when considering the twelve-point conclusion just given, are not without merit, as Apolito voiced reservations about the way that matters of scientific empiricism were intertwined in the results with matters of faith and theological speculation.[94]

It is, in fact, not difficult to see when considering the twelve-point conclusion that the first couple points, which speak to psychological and medical tests that determined the absence of pathological hallucinations, as well as fraud and deception in the experiences, belong to the area of science, while other points, which speak to "the supernatural activity of these manifestations" (point 8) or their "supernatural origin" (point 12), belong to the area of faith and theological speculation. The distinction is important to recognize and, therefore, Apolito's criticism is substantial. However, it is also important to recognize that the investigative team was made up of "seventeen renowned natural scientists, doctors, psychiatrists and theologians."[95] Theologians can, in their competence, make theological judgments about alleged mystical phenomena—judgments that scientists, doctors, or psychiatrists would not be able to make professionally because it is outside the purview of their fields of expertise. Yet again, it is also important to note that the authenticity, or lack thereof, of the purported apparitions of Medjugorje will not necessarily come through a theological judgment but, rather, an *ecclesial* decision. In other words, it is up to the Church, and not individual theologians, to make the statement that the apparitions are, or are not, of supernatural origin. The Church does take into consideration the findings of both scientists and theologians in making a decision on such matters, but can also disregard the conclusions of scientists and theologians, as it is ultimately an ecclesial decision when it comes.

The belief that the Virgin Mary is appearing to the visionaries of Medjugorje in the form of supernatural apparitions does require (and, therefore, constitutes) an act of faith. The scientific studies cannot *prove* this reality. They can, however, help *support the possibility* by strengthening the visionaries' claims and personal integrity through empirical evidence that eliminates other, alternative, natural, or pathological explanations for the phenomena. But the scientific studies cannot show that the spiritual and theological content of the visionaries' experiences are true as believing in the veracity of those claims still necessitates an act of faith.

The 1998 Austrian-Italian team also concluded in their final report that the visionaries—tested by them as adults, this time—"do not exhibit any kind of pathological symptoms" while admitting, however, that they did exhibit "symptoms that are related to justified stress that occurs through very high levels of exogenous and endogenous stimulation as a consequence of everyday life."[96] Furthermore, the report continued: "From their personal testimonies it follows that the initial and subsequent altered state of consciousness occurs due to their unusual experiences which they themselves recognize and define and still continuously recognize as a vision/apparition of Our Lady."[97] Psychophysical investigations were carried out on the four distinct states of consciousness that were previously mentioned: a waking state, a state of hypnosis, a state of visualization of mental images, and an apparition state. The conclusion reached was that during their apparitions the visionaries entered an altered state of consciousness that was different from the other (tested) states, excluding the possibility of self-suggestion, imagination, or hypnotic simulation for their experiences.[98] "The hypnotically induced state of ecstasy did not cause the phenomenology of spontaneous experiences and therefore it can be deduced that the ecstatic states of spontaneous apparitions were not states of hypnotic trance," the final report concluded.[99]

At the request of the Vatican, one of the most recent sets of scientific examinations on the visionaries was performed on June 25, 2005, commemorating the twenty-fourth anniversary of the apparitions. Agreeing to the Holy See's request to be examined were the visionaries Marija Pavlović and Ivan Dragičević, two of the three Medjugorje seers who still report to receive daily apparitions. The investigation was led by Dr. Henri Joyeux, the physician who conducted tests on the visionaries two decades earlier with his French team. In a report send to Pope Benedict XVI, Dr. Joyeux concluded that twenty years later, the conclusions were still the same.[100]

6

Medjugorje's Uniqueness

A DIFFERENT CASE STUDY FOR NEUROSCIENCE

*Like patients in the wards, mystics had become hysterics: their
phenomena were symptoms, and their messages, ramblings.*

—SOFIE LACHAPELLE, on medical trends in rediagnosing
the experiences of mystics toward the end of the nineteenth
century

*It is possible that with the advent of improved technologies
for studying the brain, mystical experiences may finally be
differentiated from any type of psychopathology.*

—ANDREW NEWBERG AND EUGENE D'AQUILI, on scientific advancements in understanding mystical experiences
toward the beginning of the twenty-first century

THERE HAVE BEEN scholars who have studied the relationship between
neuroscience and religious experiences. That reality is not rare. However,
what distinguishes the case of Medjugorje and the contribution that it can
make to scholarship is how rare are the particular religious experiences
that the visionaries report. Such experiences have yet to be subjected to
similar in-depth scientific study before Medjugorje.

Judging by their work, it is evident that few religion scholars (and this
includes scholars of religious experience) are familiar with the scientific
examinations on the Medjugorje visionaries. For example, in a 2008 article on EEG activity in Carmelite nuns, Mario Beauregard and Vincent
Paquette write that to "date, no electroencephalography (EEG) study has
been conducted to identify the neuroelectrical correlates of a mystical
experience," although admitting that several EEG studies have been performed on deep meditation and absorption states.[1] Yet, the experiences
of the Medjugorje seers are better identified as the former (thus, "mystical"), rather than put in the latter ("meditative" or "absorptive") categories

of religious experience, as the visionary experiences pertain to a type of experience identified in mystical theology. Granted that, as Beauregard and Paquette might not recognize or appreciate the unique quality of the Medjugorje experiences, to say that to date EEG studies have been conducted *only* on meditative or absorptive experiences is to ignore the important studies performed on the Medjugorje visionaries; although in this case, as in similar cases,[2] the issue does not seem to indicate any dishonesty in scholarship on the part of the authors; it is simply academic ignorance of the fact that these studies have been performed in Medjugorje.[3]

Another issue arises. A similar claim from Sidney Callahan mentioned in chapter 4 is that in "the twentieth century, scientific investigations using new brain imaging techniques have begun to explore altered states of consciousness, starting with sleep and dreaming and going on to studies of meditating adepts."[4] There has been a prevalent trend in scholarship on neuroscience and religious experiences or altered states of consciousness, where most often it is simpler, cultivated experiences that are examined for the reason that they are more common than extraordinary or unique experiences (like apparitions) and, therefore, they are easier to "produce" and study. This reality, however, has led to the study of "religious experiences" that, under closer scrutiny, appear to be less than religious experiences. Let us consider two examples.

While Beauregard and Paquette titled their 2008 article "EEG Activity in Carmelite Nuns during a Mystical Experience," from their methodology it becomes evident that what the authors were actually examining in a group of Carmelite nuns was far from a "mystical experience." The authors measured EEG activity inside "a dark, soundproof room (isolated acoustically and electromagnetically) during a Mystical condition, a Control condition, and a Baseline condition," they explain.[5] The experiments always began with a baseline condition, which was understood as a normal, restful state lasting five minutes during which the nuns were asked to have their eyes closed. During the control condition, "subjects were instructed to remember and relive (eyes closed) the most intense state of union with another human ever felt in their lives as a member of the Carmelite Order."[6] And finally, during the mystical condition, "subjects were asked to remember and relive (eyes closed) the most intense mystical experience ever felt in their lives as a member of the Carmelite Order. This strategy was adopted given that the nuns told us before the onset of the study that 'God can't be summoned at will.'"[7] And herein lies the problem: the authors were not able to study the EEG activity of an actual mystical experience in Carmelite nuns, as the title of their article misleadingly suggests, but that they were, on the other hand, studying the EEG activity of *mental reenactment* that uses imagination, memory, and self-suggestion to try to reproduce the state of a "mystical condition"—as if such a state were voluntarily reproducible, disregarding the gifted nature of such experiences.

Yet, as we saw in the studies on the Medjugorje visionaries, when psychiatrists tried to hypnotize the seers and lead them, through a process of visualization and imagination, to relive their apparitional experience, attempting to reproduce it, the state of consciousness that the seers entered was entirely different from their apparitional state. Thus, by contrast, the authors provide no proof that the "mystical condition" that the Carmelite nuns were asked to relive and reproduce can be the same state (or even similar) to the one that the nuns experienced individually when they did undergo intense religious or mystical experiences in their lives. No proof that such states can be volitionally "relived" or "reproduced" is given, although empirical evidence pointing to the opposite conclusion—that such states cannot be reproduced—is present, as the tests performed on the Medjugorje visionaries show. The nuns rightly explained to the authors that God cannot be summoned at will; that in itself speaks to the reality that a spontaneous, mystical experience of God cannot be summoned voluntarily and, further, that what the authors studied through the EEG tests was not an actual mystical experience.[8]

A similar problem is evident in the method of an earlier, albeit more influential, study published by the *European Journal of Neuroscience*. The article, titled "Neural Correlates of Religious Experience," was published in 2001 by neuroscientist Nina P. Azari and a number of co-authors.[9] Azari has been recognized for her important work in religious experience and neuroscience.[10] Like Ann Taves, she is highly influenced by Wayne Proudfoot's work in attribution theory in studying religious experiences.[11] However, while the article is titled "Neural Correlates of Religious Experience," after examining the methodology and the subjects that were used in the study, it becomes evident, again, that like the Beauregard and Paquette study on Carmelite nuns, the so-called religious experience in this case is less than what it is conveyed to be.

What kind of religious experience were Azari and her colleagues examining with neuroimaging technology? "We studied a group of self-identified religious subjects, who attributed their religious experience to a biblical psalm, in order to explore for the first time using functional neuroimaging the brain areas involved in religious experience."[12] In other words, Azari and her colleagues studied religious subjects who read (and possibly meditated on) a biblical psalm. These subjects were members of a Free Evangelical Fundamentalist Community in Germany, all of whom had reported a conversion experience in their lives and for whom the first verse of Psalm 23 was important.[13] "According to their responses in prestudy interviews, the religious subjects regarded the induction of repeated, transient religious states in a single scanning session as antithetical to religious experience (and disrespectful to their faith)."[14] However, "they found it acceptable (and were asked) to induce in themselves, and then sustain for the duration of a given scanning session a unique religious state."[15]

The experiences that were studied, in other words, were admittedly self-induced; they were cultivated through the reading and recitation of biblical psalms. Although such experiences may be *religious*, for the act of reading and reciting biblical texts is known in Christianity as a form of prayer, they are far from being *extraordinary* religious experiences. This is something that the authors have acknowledged, admitting that they used a very standard "stimuli to identify a neurobiological correlate of the concept of 'religious experience' in this initial study. A challenge for future work will be to explore transient religious states and the evolution of other varieties of religious experience."[16]

Notwithstanding the limitations of studying such ordinary "religious experiences," there has been important work done on the relationship between prayer, meditation, and neuroscience. Andrew Newberg, Eugene D'Aquili, and Vince Rause have studied the experiences of Franciscan nuns in prayer and Buddhist practitioners in meditation, documenting the effects on the brain through SPECT scans.[17] A SPECT camera is an imaging-tool that scans inside the head and is used to detect radioactive emissions in the brain, therefore being able to notice distinct conditions of areas of the brain during different states of consciousness.[18] Such studies have been able to detect the beneficial influence that prayer and meditation have on such factors as reducing stress and anxiety while enhancing compassion and social awareness.[19] Although such studies are highly significant, they are, once again, using neuroscience to study *cultivated* experiences in the form of spiritual practices that affect the brain. While acknowledging that in recent decades (since the 1960s) there has been a growing interest in meditation and in research on meditation, Edward F. Kelly and Michael Grosso recognize that the study of such spiritual practices have yet been able to allow access to, and therefore the study of, higher mystical experiences. "We have barely scratched the surface, however, in terms of using meditation to gain experimental access to the higher forms of transformative ecstatic and mystical experience that comprise its principal long-term objective."[20]

Compared to such studies, it is not difficult to see what makes the Medjugorje studies unique. The religious experiences of the Medjugorje visionaries are not standard, ordinary, or simple experiences; rather, they are *extraordinary* religious experiences. They are not, as scientific investigations have shown, cultivated or self-induced by preexistent efforts such as visualization, memory, the reading of biblical psalms, or prayer and meditation but, instead, are spontaneous experiences whose presence is not dependent on the actions of the visionaries. It is true that the visionaries often pray the rosary before experiencing their apparitions; however, so do millions of other Catholics around the world, without ever experiencing an apparition or such an instantaneous, deep state of altered consciousness that the visionaries enter. Thus, it would be unreasonable to conclude through causality that it is the prayer that functions as a stimulus to lead to the experience. Furthermore, there have been instances when the visionaries have experienced apparitions unexpectedly, in environments where prayer was absent, further pointing to the reality of spontaneous experiences.[21]

Much recent scholarship has been dedicated to applying cognitive sciences such as neuroscience to the study of various types of alleged religious experiences. But, unfortunately, very little attention has been given in academia to the scientific studies on the experiences of the Medjugorje visionaries. This is the reality, notwithstanding the fact that the uniqueness of the experiences in Medjugorje, as experiences that are spontaneous and visionary in character, affords scholars of religious experience the opportunity to study a much rarer, and possibly more significant, phenomenon than more common, cultivated, and self-induced experiences.

Contribution to Discourses on Religious Experience

Having examined the major scientific studies on the experiences of the Medjugorje seers, let us consider what contributions these studies can make to discourses and debates about religious experience. Regarding the modern perennialist–constructivist debate, a major issue that was discussed, to which the Medjugorje studies may bring greater clarity, is the question of reductionism. As we have observed, many classic perennial thinkers subscribed to a *sui generis* framework of thinking that elevated religious experience into a special category of its own that isolated the subject from interdisciplinary analysis, partially in light of fears that such analysis can lead to reductionist interpretations of experience. The fears were not without merit, as various academic disciplines have been used to theorize that purported mystical and religious experiences can be explained away through natural or psychopathological categories of understanding. Yet, in this regard, when considering the results of the Medjugorje studies, a powerful point briefly referenced in the previous chapter, which was articulated by Newberg and D'Aquili, comes to mind: "It is possible that with the advent of improved technologies for studying the brain, mystical experiences may finally be differentiated from any type of psychopathology."[22] Herein the scientific studies on the experiences of the Medjugorje visionaries present a significant contribution to discourses and literature on religious and mystical experiences. Let us expound on this in detail.

Epileptic-Seizure Interpretations

Newberg and his colleagues explain that:

> Many researchers have found the link between epilepsy and spirituality very compelling. Some researchers have even gone so far as to posthumously diagnose history's greatest mystics as victims of epileptic seizures. Some of these diagnoses suggest, for example, that Mohammed, who heard voices, saw visions, and sweated profusely during his mystical interludes, may have suffered from complex partial seizure. The same type of seizure may have been the source of the blinding light that struck St. Paul on the road to Damascus and caused the auditory hallucinations that led him to believe he had heard the voice of Jesus. Joan of Arc, who also saw a spiritual light and was transfixed by beatific voices, may have suffered ecstatic partial seizures and perhaps an intracranial tuberculoma. Various epileptic states may have been responsible for the visions of the Catholic mystic Saint Teresa of Avila, the conversion experience of Mormon patriarch Joseph Smith, the ecstatic trance states of Emmanuel Swedenborg, even the hyper-religiosity of Vincent Van Gogh.[23]

This modern reasoning that uses epileptic diagnoses to find a natural and/ or pathological explanation for alleged extraordinary religious experiences is an instance of the "medical materialism" that William James warned about a century earlier. Furthermore, it is important to recognize that given the diversity of the religious figures which Newberg et al. present, ranging from various religious traditions, and the diversity of their experiences—visionary, auditory, sensory, ecstatic—there is both a generalization and a reductionism in play here. A lot of modern scholarship tends to use epileptic diagnoses not to discredit one form of religious and mystical experience (such as visionary, for example) but all forms of experiences (visionary, auditory, unitive, out-of-body, etc.). There is thus a gross generalization that permeates this reductionist hermeneutic which looks to epileptic diagnoses to form a basis of understanding.

Newberg and his colleagues are of the *opinion*,[24] one based "on some very simple observations," that certain epileptic symptoms can be differentiated from mystical experiences, although admitting that similarities also exist, and they argue therefore that these (the epileptic and the mystical) should be recognized as two distinct types of phenomena: one as pathological and the other as spiritual.[25] Significantly, if we consider the scientific studies on the experiences of the Medjugorje visionaries, it becomes evident that this opinion is no longer simply an opinion but an empirically observable and proven fact.

As was observed, EEG testing indicated no signs of epileptic discharge in the brains of the visionaries during their experiences. The conclusion that no signs of epilepsy were present was also supported by auditory and clinical testing. Dr. Henri Joyeux's French team concluded that there "is no epilepsy, as electro-encephalograms demonstrate."[26] Additionally, Dr. Francois Rouquerol's auditory potential test indicated "that the various pathways to the brain [in the visionaries] are normal. The regular and rounded shape of the graph eliminates auditory hallucination of an epileptic type."[27] This is important to note, as epileptic hallucinations can be present in both visual and auditory modes.[28] Even before the French doctors, the Italian physician Dr. Enzo Gabrici observed in the visionaries: "Clinical observation has also excluded hallucinatory phenomena as well as the normal components of epilepsy or of any other malfunction capable of producing the alteration of consciousness."[29] In sum, there was no empirical evidence that the altered state of consciousness that the visionaries enter during their apparitions was an epileptic state, nor did it possess any symptoms of an epileptic state—thus challenging the application of this popular, reductive theory as a universal explanation for all forms of extraordinary religious or mystical experiences.

Interpretations of Hysteria

As observed in a previous chapter, another popular theory of reductionism that has permeated much critical thought about extraordinary religious experiences is the psychopathological interpretation of hysteria. In writing a hermeneutical history of hysteria, historian Mark S. Micale notes how the tendency to substitute hysteria as an alternative explanation for extraordinary religious experiences spoke to a deeper, historical conflict between the worldviews surrounding the cultures of psychiatry and those of religion. He explains:

> In nearly all historical writing about psychiatry, the religious and psychiatric worldviews are presented at sharp variance with one another. In the 1800s, introductory historical chapters to psychiatric textbooks and dissertations often pointedly contrasted the current state of enlightened medical knowledge with past religious obscurantism and philosophical mysticism. During the 1930s and 1940s, the first full narrative histories of psychiatry retailed similar scenarios. In his influential *A History of Medical Psychology* (1941), Gregory Zilboorg presented psychiatric history in almost Manichean terms, as the world-historical clash of the religious/supernatural and medical/naturalistic models of the mind. This view was then subsequently bolstered by the biographical literature on Freud. With his outspoken and uncompromising personal atheism, his interpretations of piety as psychopathology, and his polemical antireligious statements *The Future of an Illusion* and *Moses and Monotheism*, the founder of psychoanalysis seemed to exemplify the opposition between institutional religion and psychiatry that has existed throughout history.[30]

The neurologist Jean-Martin Charcot was an eminent thinker who, as previously mentioned, has been known for identifying extraordinary religious and mystical experiences with hysteria. Charcot, as noted in chapter 4, was a pioneering figure in the study of hysteria and in associating it with religious experience; his work did influence the anti-religious convictions of the psychiatric worldview even before Freud.[31]

In the late nineteenth and early twentieth centuries, France was at the center of major cultural and intellectual debates surrounding science and religion, particularly religious experience, because of two major events

that took place in the country. On the one hand, there was the revolu-
tionary work of Charcot and fellow doctors at the Neurology Clinic at La
Salpêtrière Hospital in Paris, rediagnosing alleged mystical experiences—
which included cases of purported miracles, apparitions, visions, stigmata,
and even darker spiritual manifestations like demonic possessions—as
pathological cases associated with hysteria, a practice which came to be
known as "retrospective medicine."[32] On the other hand, the reported
Marian apparitions in the village of Lourdes to the French peasant girl
Bernadette Soubirous in 1858, which led to Lourdes becoming a major
pilgrimage and healing shrine that culminated in the formation of the
Medical Bureau of Lourdes established to medically investigate miraculous healings at the site, constituted the other major phenomenon that
fueled debates between science and religious experience in the culture.[33]

Sofie Lachapelle explains how deeply connected, even conflated,
the cultures of religious mystics and the those of hysteria and insanity,
from the perspectives of psychology and psychiatry, became during this
period: "With the rise of psychology and psychiatry, the subjects [both
alleged mystics and demoniacs] were made to leave their homes or sanc-
tuaries for the more sterile and controlled hospital ward."[34] In fact, the
cultures of mysticism and the medical milieu studying pathology were
so deeply intertwined, Lachapelle emphasizes, that accounts of mystical
experiences contributed to the development of theories of pathology in the
medical establishment at the turn of the century:

> The stories of mystics fill the pages of scientific journals of the *fin
> de siècle*. Living in hospital wards or surrounded by devout followers,
> portrayed as hysterics or saints, as manipulated or manipulators,
> these men and (more often) these women played a significant role
> in the developments of theories of pathological behavior. Though
> historians have acknowledged this role, it remains little explored.[35]

Charcot's followers did much to advance the work of rediagnosing
alleged mystical phenomena into pathological categories. Desire-Magloire
Bourneville, "a disciple of Charcot," looked "at both contemporary and
past instances of mysticism, possession, stigmata, and ecstasies, [and]
he encouraged a new understanding of such phenomena in pathological
terms."[36] Bourneville began publishing the series *La bibliotheque diabolique*
in 1883, "comprised of texts that reinterpreted neuropathologically past
religious events and personalities."[37] The Marian apparitions at Lourdes

were not impervious to such reinterpretation. Auguste Voisin, "an alienist at the Salpêtrière, argued that Bernadette's ecstasies had only been hallu-cinatory deliria that presaged an acute psychiatric deterioration. The cel-ebrated inspiratress [*sic*] of Lourdes, added Voisin, was in fact currently being cared for at the Ursuline convent of Nevers, where she was now quite insane—a charge that Catholic commentators denied vociferously."[38] Not only was the famous seer of Lourdes being rediagnosed, notably by doctors who were not present at her apparitions, but so were the masses of people who traveled to the Marian shrine. "Dr. Paul Diday (later known for his work in venereology) applied Voisin's pathologizing line of analysis to the pilgrims of Lourdes as a whole."[39]

In 1886, Hippolyte Bernheim, an internist from the University of Nancy in Alsace-Lorraine, who became the leading figure of the "Nancy School," a rival to Charcot's "Salpêtrière School,"[40] posited a parallel "between the hypnotic psychotherapeutics pioneered in his clinic and what he called the 'miraculous therapeutics' of Lourdes. Both phenomena, contended Bernheim, were fully explicable as the result of exaggerated impression-ability in susceptible individuals. Piety and hysterical psychopathology resulted equally from excessive autosuggestion."[41] Micale explains that the following decades would find the work of several physicians repeating "with minor variation the Bernheimian analysis."[42]

The noted psychologist Pierre Janet, who was a student and colleague of Charcot,[43] began publishing in the final years of the nineteenth cen-tury "on possession, ecstasy, and stigmata, using his previous work on the disaggregation of the personality to understand these religious phenom-ena in physiological terms."[44] Thomas Acklin explains that Janet's "chief work pertaining to religion was *De l'angoisse à l'extase*, in which he came to describe thought during ecstasy as inferior, regressive, analogous to the thought of small children and infants. Janet found an ensemble of char-acteristics common to much mystical experience which for him indicated a specific syndrome that he termed 'mystical delirium.' "[45] Among the patients that Janet examined there was the case of Madeleine, a devout, middle-aged woman who entered Paris's Salpêtrière Hospital in February 1896.[46] Amy Hollywood explains that for "Janet, Madeleine was 'a poor contemporary mystic' whose ecstasies, crucifixion postures, and bleed-ing wounds (stigmata) were signs of delirium and other pathologies."[47] Lachapelle makes the interesting observation that a "geographical dimen-sion" began to determine whether a mystic's unique experiences should be understood as sacred or pathological. Thus, in the case of Madeleine,

"Janet diagnosed her as having suffered from a neurosis since her child-hood that had developed into a severe religious delirium with ecstatic crises. There is thus a geographical dimension to the experience of a stig-matic: in the hospital, all phenomena become symptoms, and Madeleine's love for God was turned into pathology."[48] The geographical dimension of taking purported mystics and analyzing their experiences in the hos-pital ward during this period carried with it, therefore, the *epistemological shift* of perceiving what religious devotees considered signs of the sacred and supernatural as symptoms of the pathological. "Like patients in the wards, mystics had become hysterics: their phenomena were symptoms, and their messages, ramblings."[49]

Historians have acknowledged that there were major ideological battles—religious, political, cultural—in nineteenth-century France that fueled the debates on science and religious experience. Jan Goldstein explains that in the 1870s and '80s there was an "anti-clerical crusade, and the psychiatrists of the Salpêtrière school participated in it enthusiasti-cally."[50] Micale expounds on these matters:

> Nineteenth-century French physicians, from Calmeil to Charcot, working self-consciously within an anticlerical Enlightenment tra-dition, produced authoritative-sounding commentaries that diag-nosed past religious behaviors as signs of hysterical pathology. Similarly, Veith's *Hysteria: The History of a Disease* . . . highlights the struggle of modern science to free itself from mystical, spir-itistic, or demonological readings of the disease. Most recently, Goldstein . . . has written extensively about the relation between hys-teria doctors and clericalism during the age of Charcot. In France during the final quarter of the nineteenth century, the long-running conflict between the Catholic Church and political republicanism entered a particularly antagonistic phase. The school of Salpêtrière, Goldstein has established played a significant part in this confronta-tion, laicizing hospital nursing staffs, establishing new chairs on the Paris Medical Faculty, and publishing the *Bibliotheque Diabolique*, comprised of texts that reinterpret neuropathologically past reli-gious events and personalities. In the theoretical realm, Charcot integrated into his work elements of demonological hysteria refor-mulated in the terms of positivist medicine. Charcot's newly scien-tized theory of the disease, Goldstein has contended, was a classic

episode in the historical clash of the religious and the scientific mentalities, with the latter emerging triumphant.[51]

Lachapelle explains how the development of both psychology and psychiatry saw with it ideological interests for these sciences in explaining matters that have historically been the purview of the Church, such as mystical phenomena. "Not only were physical manifestations of religiosity—possession, visions, cures, and stigmata, amongst others—of interest to them, but they were potentially problematic for sciences constructed on the assumption that the human mind and its productions could be explained physiologically."[52]

Psychopathological reductionism toward religious experiences, although having historical roots in the development of sciences such as psychiatry, is not a reality of the past but, rather, one that continues to find advocates in the present. It is also perceivable, for example, in the reductionism articulated by Oliver Sacks, as he comments about the extraordinary experiences of medieval mystics as representing either "a hysterical or psychotic ecstasy, the effects of intoxication or an epileptic or migrainous manifestation."[53]

In light of such reductive theories, and those that have come before, the scientific studies on the Medjugorje seers make an extremely significant contribution toward reaching greater clarity regarding the universalism of these and similar interpretations; Medjugorje psychological and clinical studies, performed by various doctors throughout the years, have consistently shown the visionaries to be mentally healthy individuals who do not possess any symptoms of hysteria or any indications of psychosis.[54] Thus, the *universal application* of the hysteria diagnosis, as an all-encompassing explanation for extraordinary religious or mystical experiences, is undermined, as are the other diagnoses promulgated by Sacks as alternative theories of explanation: psychosis, intoxication, epilepsy, or migraine-induced manifestations (as the Medjugorje visionaries did not possess any of these conditions, nor related symptoms, either). This does not mean that any past report of mystical experience could not fall into any of these categories; of course, such reports could, as not all experiences are authentic. However, the case of the Medjugorje seers, empirically examined for such natural and pathological conditions, does pose an exception to the reductionist rule in terms of applying an all-encompassing epistemology that would categorize every extraordinary religious experience as either natural or pathological.

Interpretations of Hallucination

Other variations of an all-encompassing reductionism have been used to reinterpret such phenomena as visionary experiences. Richard Dawkins, the evolutionary biologist at Oxford and popular atheist author, writes in his best-selling book *The God Delusion* about the subject of extraordinary religious experiences, making reference to Marian apparitions. Dawkins argues:

> Constructing models is something the human brain is very good at. When we are asleep it is called dreaming; when we are awake we call it imagination or, when it is exceptionally vivid, hallucination.... If we are gullible, we don't recognize hallucination or lucid dreaming for what it is and we claim to have seen or heard a ghost; or an angel; or God; or—especially if we happen to be young, female and Catholic—the Virgin Mary. Such visions and manifestations are certainly not good grounds for believing that ghosts or angels, gods or virgins, are actually there.[55]

While Dawkins may be unwittingly promulgating a sexist argument in articulating that young Catholic females would especially be prone to having hallucinations or vivid dreams of the Virgin Mary, he is essentially making a constructivist claim in enunciating that such visions, or apparitions, are either natural or pathological and, therefore, a product of the mind. An all-encompassing reductionism is also present in the way that Dawkins dismisses all forms of religious or spiritual visionary experience as a case of either lucid dreaming or hallucination, akin to the hermeneutical trends that Underhill criticized in rationalists and that James criticized in medical materialism.

The EEG tests on the Medjugorje visionaries again make a significant contribution here in presenting a case that empirically calls into question the universality of this reductionist argument, as the tests showed that the visionaries are hyper-awake during their apparitions—thus the experiences cannot be a case of lucid dreaming—and as the EEG exams, combined with visual and auditory tests, showed that the visionaries are not suffering from any kind of hallucination during their experiences. Lucid dreaming, pathological hallucination, visual hallucination, and auditory hallucination were all discredited as possible alternative explanations for the apparitions, the visionaries being free of all such natural and pathological symptoms. Yet, they still enter an inexplicable altered state of consciousness during their apparitions and report to see and encounter the Virgin Mary, having experiences that transcend the interpretative framework of Dawkins's explanatory reductionism.

Dawkins is not, by any means, the only author who has dismissed all visionary experiences like Marian apparitions as hallucinations. Many have adopted this approach. Another prominent example of this, coming from a psychoanalytical model, is a book published by Princeton University Press in 1986, Michael P. Carroll's *The Cult of the Virgin Mary: Psychological Origins.*[56] Sandra L. Zimdars-Swartz explains that Carroll's book "attracted a considerable amount of attention," while admitting, however, that "Carroll's attempts to explain Marian devotion in terms of classical Freudianism have not been very convincing to most reviewers," although the work, according to Zimdars-Swartz, should still be high-priority reading for those interested in Marian apparitions.[57] Using psychoanalytical theories, Carroll dismisses all reported cases of Marian apparitions as constituting either illusions or hallucinations or, in some cases, a combination or admixture of each. Applying an elaborate, psychoanalytical hypothesis, Carroll argues, using Freudian Oedipal-complex ideas, that father-ineffective families affect the sexual desires of sons for their mothers, and that fervent "devotion to the Mary cult on the part of males is a practice that allows males characterized by a strong but strongly repressed sexual desire for the mother to dissipate in an acceptable manner the excess sexual energy that is built up as a result of this desire."[58] Inversely, Carroll argues that identifying "strongly with the Virgin Mary allows women to experience vicariously the fulfillment of their desire for sexual contact with, and a baby from, their fathers."[59]

It is not difficult to discern why most reviewers did not take Carroll's classical Freudianism seriously as a phenomenological explanation for Marian devotion, given that repressed, unconscious sexual desires that children allegedly have for their parents (in itself a controversial Freudian claim) are possibly the last thing that Marian devotees cogitate when considering their veneration for the *Virgin* Mary.[60] However, an aspect of Carroll's thesis that more readers would take seriously, given how much skepticism exists on the subject, is his conclusion that all Marian apparitions can be explained as either illusions or hallucinations, or an admixture that combines these explanations.[61]

Carroll analyzes the major Marian apparitions such as Lourdes, Fatima, Medjugorje, and others. He argues that there were three sets of Marian apparitions wherein hallucinations were preceded by illusions. In this grouping he includes Medjugorje, writing: "The third set of Marian hallucinations probably preceded by an illusion were the apparitions at the village of Medjugorje in Herzegovina [sic], Yugoslavia."[62] In this regard, Carroll further writes: "From the start, one or more of the Medjugorje seers reported both seeing and hearing the Virgin. Since other observers present heard nothing, it seems clear that at least the auditory components of these apparitions (assuming sincerity on the part of the seers) were hallucinations."[63]

But, as we have already seen, the scientific studies on the seers have disproven this argument, as auditory tests showed that the auditory pathways of the visionaries are completely normal and that they are not experiencing any auditory—nor, for that matter, visual or pathological—hallucination during their experiences. Carroll further attributes the fact that a bright light was seen by many observers during the first days of the apparitions (while the seers were reporting their encounters with the Virgin Mary) with the theory that the apparitions began as an illusion.[64] Thus, he speculates that "the first few apparitions at Medjugorje, or at least the visual component of these first few apparitions, were probably illusions. Once the local community accepted the reality of the apparitions, however (which seems to have occurred relatively rapidly), the children began having true hallucinations on an almost daily basis."[65] If one were to take Carroll's hypothesis seriously, then the conclusion would have to be that three of the visionaries—the three who as adults claim to continue experiencing daily apparitions—have been experiencing *daily hallucinations for over thirty years now since their teenage years.* The fact that clinical and psychological testing has consistently shown the visionaries to be mentally healthy people without any traces of hallucinatory or hysterical symptoms, in addition to the neuroscientific, auditory, and visual exams that proved the visionaries are free of every form of hallucination, highly undermines the probability and validity of Carroll's thesis.

Methodological Considerations

In his defense, Carroll's book was published in 1986, which means that he was writing the work around the same time as the first major scientific examinations were being carried out on the Medjugorje visionaries. His conclusions, therefore, were based more on theoretical speculation than on scientific examination. The subsequent publication of the scientific studies on the visionaries, however, would contain empirical evidence disproving significant components of Carroll's thesis.

There is also a methodological issue that arises in considering Carroll's treatment of Marian apparitions. Carroll explains his method: "If we approach the study of Marian apparitions (or any set of religious apparitions) on the premise that they are produced by natural causes, then it is evident that they are either *illusions or hallucinations.*"[66] The problem with Carroll's approach is that the starting premise on which he bases his research can be false and it can, therefore, lead to faulty conclusions. Carroll begins with the general principle that Marian apparitions are caused by natural causes and, thereafter, proceeds to employ a psychoanalytical phenomenology as the underlying explanation for understanding those natural causes, pointing to the conclusion of "Marian hallucinations."[67] However, as the scientific studies on the visionaries display, Carroll's conclusions, at least in the case of Medjugorje, were faulty, pointing to the reality that his research was based on a false premise.

This fact is further supported by the combination of the algometer and EEG studies performed by the 1985 Italian team on the visionaries; the algometer, again, showing that the visionaries were impervious to pain during their apparitions while the EEGs showing, among other things, that they were in a state of consciousness that is hyper-awake. Dr. Luigi Frigerio, as quoted in chapter 5, articulated that these results presented a contradiction that "cannot be explained naturally, and thus can be only preternatural or supernatural." [68] It is important to note that this is not a theological judgment, as the doctor is not saying that the Virgin Mary is appearing; rather, it is a scientific judgment, as the doctor is articulating, through the usage of scientific instruments, that the phenomenon presents a paradox, in the combination of the state of hyper-wakefulness and the imperviousness to external pain, that cannot be explained naturally. Thus, here we have further empirical evidence that suggests how faulty the hypothesis can be that all Marian apparitions may be explained through natural means, as Carroll promulgated, leading to research that is dangerously set up to attain questionable conclusions. Here, it is important to recognize that the scientific studies on the visionaries help us to make hermeneutical judgments, a significant contribution to discourses on religious experience. Those hermeneutical judgments substantially challenge an all-encompassing reductionism that epistemologically reduces all extraordinary religious experiences to natural, psychological, or pathological categories.

It is ironic, for there is an inversion to classical perennialism in what is being challenged here. Classical perennialists argued for the presence of universal, underlying core characteristics that are cross-culturally present in all authentic religious and mystical experiences. Inversely, many critics who have subscribed to an all-encompassing reductionism on extraordinary religious experiences (such as Dawkins, Carroll, Sacks, complete constructivists, or the various researchers who apply an epileptic-seizure diagnosis as a universal alternative explanation) also argue for certain core characteristics that encapsulate all claims of extraordinary religious experiences. These core characteristics, however, have the reductive quality of constituting natural and psychopathological categories of interpretation, such as visualization, self-suggestion, hypnosis, hysteria, epilepsy, hallucinations, psychosis, unconsciously repressed sexual desires, obsessional neurosis, and so on. The scientific results on the Medjugorje visionaries substantially challenge and undermine the universality of such reductionist theories.

It is interesting how eclectic the challenge is that the Medjugorje studies offer to reductionist theories of interpretation. Some of the tests performed on the visionaries, as previously observed, very directly eliminate the possibility of conditions like epilepsy or hallucination. There is also the hypnosis test, however, which challenges the universalism of reductive theories of self-suggestion and visualization. It was shown that the altered state of consciousness the visionaries enter during their apparitions is radically different from the state of consciousness they entered under hypnosis when, through suggestion and visualization, an attempt was made to "re-create" their apparitional experiences. This brings to mind Taves's treatment of Barnard's out-of-body experience. Although it was pointed out that visionary experiences and out-of-body experiences are two phenomenologically different occurrences, thereby questioning whether Taves was right to use the reductive logic often applied to explain one (visualization as causing visionary experiences) as a way to explain the other (visualization as causing out-of-body experiences), such experiences may share at least a single major similarity: both experiences constitute states of altered consciousness. Taves explained that relatively little research has been done "on the role of practices (visualization, meditation, chanting, fasting, et cetera) in triggering unusual experiences," although she also explained that there is "considerable historical and anecdotal evidence to suggest that this is often the case."[69] Using such evidence,[70] she hypothesized that Barnard's out-of-body experience was triggered through a process of visualization—thus, the visualization triggered a state of altered consciousness.

However, in the case of the Medjugorje studies, we have an empirical challenge to such theories of reductive thinking that would consider visualization as an ultimate triggering cause for altered states of consciousness that are understood as mystical experiences. With the Medjugorje visionaries, visualization techniques through suggestion and imagination were used under hypnosis in an attempt to re-create their apparitional experiences, and the state of consciousness that was reached was incredibly different from the apparition state, showing that visualization does not constitute an explanation for their experiences. Here, one wonders whether the same could be the case for Barnard's out-of-body experience, as well as other reported religious or mystical phenomena that have been dismissed by scholars as simply being the natural products of suggestion, imagination, and visualization.

The underlying issue here is methodology—the danger of allowing the application of a hermeneutic in studying religious experiences whose structure necessitates the formulation of theories that satisfy a predetermined conclusion. To take this point further, let us consider the experiences of the Medjugorje visionaries in light of Carroll's treatment of them in comparison to that of the scientists who empirically examined the visionaries.

It is one thing to say that the Medjugorje visionaries are hallucinating and then employ psychoanalytical theories that try to justify this premise; it is another thing to leave open the question of what the visionaries are experiencing, and through a process of discovery, use cognitive sciences to ascertain that the visionaries are not hallucinating and, thereby, come closer to the correct answer by empirically eliminating false possibilities. The former method was employed by Carroll; the latter was used by the doctors who examined the visionaries. Here, again, the issue is methodology. The former method attempts to justify a predetermined conclusion through theoretical speculation within the intellectual framework of psychoanalysis. The latter method attempts to attain a conclusion through empirical examination without limiting the possibilities to the interpretive framework of a single intellectual system.

It is important to reiterate here that the issue, meaning the problem, is not psychoanalysis but, rather, methodology. In other words, there are various things that psychoanalysis can contribute to an understanding of religion. However, if psychoanalytical theories are used to form the *dominant* hermeneutical framework that tries to justify reductionist conclusions about religious experiences, while ignoring the contribution of other sciences that help grasp a fuller picture of the subject, then the complexity and multifariousness of many religious experiences are not given their due. This, as the example of Carroll's interpretation of the Medjugorje apparitions shows, can lead to misguided conclusions about such phenomena.

Interpretations of Freud

Let us also consider the original Freudian interpretation. As mentioned in chapter 4, Freud first articulated his connection between neurosis and religion in his 1907 essay "Obsessive Actions and Religious Practices," wherein Freud compared common religious practices with the "rituals" that his OCD patients compulsively performed to control their neurotic obsessions. His later writings would attempt to take the argument further. Küng explains:

> Freud was at first concerned simply to corroborate from the history of religion the thesis he had put forward as early as 1907, that religious rites are similar to neurotic obsessive actions. This he did in four essays published as a book under the general title *Totem and Taboo* (1912). Whether investigating the horror of incest (first essay), taboo prohibitions as a whole (second essay), animism and magic (third essay), or even totemism (fourth essay), he finds everywhere a similarity between the customs and religious attitudes of primitives, on the one hand, and the obsessive actions of his neurotic patients on the other, everywhere a survival of primitive mental life up to the present time. Nevertheless Freud now modifies his former provocative statement to the effect that religion is a universal obsessional neurosis.[71]

While through his comparative study of the religious attitudes of primitive peoples and his neurotic patients Freud came to the theoretical conclusion that religion is, in its essence, a universal obsessional neurosis, there has been important work done undermining the tenets of this hypothesis. Critique has particularly been aimed toward the dependence of this hypothesis on Freud's 1907 essay, as the foundational work establishing a connection between religion and neurosis.

In his dissertation *Freud on Ritual: Reconstruction and Critique,* Volney P. Gay makes a strong argument, supported by linguistic and psychoanalytical analysis, that scholars have accepted Freud's psychology of religion without realizing that it, and their acceptance of it, is based on an erroneous reading of "Obsessive Actions and Religious Practices." "It is my thesis," Gay explains, that "in opposition to his rhetorical expressions and to the usual acceptance of their psychoanalytic validity, Freud never demonstrated and in fact never claimed (in the 1907 essay) that religious rituals shared with obsessive actions a common genesis in the workings of repression."[72] Gay argues that the popular Freudian notion that religion and neurosis have an intrinsic connection in the form of repression, as the psychopathological mechanism that "secretly linked obsessional acts with religious practices," is undermined when Freud's essay is studied closely and it becomes clear that in his language Freud is describing *suppression* and *not repression* as the mechanism underlying religious practices. The distinction is monumental, Gay explains, because if "neurotic anxiety is a function of repression, and if the anti-instinctual mechanism typical of religious acts is suppression (and not repression), then it would seem to follow that the 'anxiety' which Freud ascribes to pious individuals who perform certain religious rituals cannot be neurotic anxiety."[73] The importance of this argument is further highlighted in a fundamental distinction between repression and suppression: the former implies pathological behavior while the latter does not. Repression, in psychoanalytical thought, is a mechanism that "entails or implies the presence of psychopathology" while suppression, on the other hand, "only implies the presence of instinct control" and, therefore, is not associated with psychopathology but denotes behavior that is healthy.[74]

The central foundations of Gay's thesis are based on a close linguistic reading of Freud's text. Gay explains:

Throughout most of the essay, Freud carefully describes the anti-instinctual mechanism typical of obsessive acts as *Verdrangung* (repression) and that which is typical of religious acts as *Unterdruckung* (suppression) or as *Verzicht* (renunciation). The linguistic distinction seems significant in light of the crucial topographic and dynamic differences by which Freud distinguished the two processes. Since even in the earliest analytic literature "repression" was said to be one of the main features in the genesis of neurotic disorders, and since Freud's goal in this essay is to demonstrate an underlying similarity between obsessional acts and religious behavior, we would expect him to demonstrate that repression is the fundamental mechanism responsible for the formation of religious ceremonies. However, he does not.[75]

In fact, in his study of Freud's text, Gay notes that Freud equates the word *Verzicht* with *Unterdruckung*—that is, "renunciation" with "suppression"— and that it is these terms that Freud associates with religious rituals and behavior.[76] Gay further notes that Freud would not conflate the meaning of "suppression" with "repression," nor use the terms interchangeably, as his writing displays that "Freud's technical description of the anti-institutional processes typical of both kinds of behavior reveals that he consistently distinguished the mechanism of *repression* which he says operates in the formation of obsessional neurosis from that of *suppression* or renunciation which he ascribes to religious behavior."[77]

In addition to the claim that Freud would not equate "repression" with "suppression," textual analysis provides evidence that neither would Freud equate "repression" with "renunciation" (the other term that is applied in his essay in association with religious practices). This point becomes evident when considering the very meaning of the term "renunciation," Gay argues, as a word that denotes a fully conscious act of resignation. "Clearly, one can only renounce a desire or resign from an attempt to fulfill it if one is fully conscious of entertaining it as a wish which is either to be granted in the future or fulfilled, through fantasy expression, in the present."[78] Gay's point is that *the deliberate consciousness* that is required of renunciation further supports his thesis that Freud was not referring to repression when writing of the mechanism that underlies religious behavior (which Freud described in the language of "suppression" and "renunciation"[79]), as repression, in Freud's meta-psychological essays, "involves *unconscious processes* which are not available to deliberation or judgment"[80]—in other words, constituting phenomenologically different (in fact, polar opposite) processes.[81]

If correct, the implications of Gay's arguments are significant for, as Küng previously explained, with his subsequent writings on religion, Freud tried to corroborate and develop further the theory established in his 1907 essay, seeing similarities behind neurosis and religious rituals; however, the basis of his subsequent work on religion may have been founded on a theory that was misapplied; Freud's rhetoric on religion and universal neurosis were based on a work that possibly never actually established the connection between the two. "If I am correct," Gay writes, "it follows that Freud and his followers misapplied the full-fledge metapsychology of psychoanalytic theory."[82] This bold thesis is not dissimilar from the one made by Anthony Perovich, claiming that constructivist scholars may have misread and misapplied Kant's epistemology as the foundational framework for developing their hermeneutical ideas. Gay's point takes it a step further, however, as it associates the misapplication of the original idea not simply with subsequent scholars but also with the original author. He argues, therefore, that Freud got carried away with the overt rhetoric of his 1907 essay, which implied a connection between religion and neurosis, to the point that Freud failed to see in his later work that he never *technically* established a connection between religion and neurosis in the psychoanalytical reasoning of his 1907 work. Gay concludes that "because the clinical model of obsessional neurosis entails the repression hypothesis and because, as we have seen, Freud never showed that religious rituals exemplified repressive behaviors, it follows that when he uses the model of obsessional neurosis to explain religious behavior he does so on inadequate metapsychological grounds."[83]

The case of Medjugorje provides further empirical evidence challenging the religion–neurosis connection *on the basis of psychological grounds*. Therefore, in addition to Gay's use of linguistic and psychoanalytical analysis that has been able to identify the central missing link (the mechanism of repression) between religion and obsessional neurosis in the foundational psychoanalytic literature, in Medjugorje the application of firsthand clinical studies on the visionaries has identified an absence of neurosis through psychological examination. In Medjugorje we have a case study wherein a group of people are purportedly experiencing one of the most extraordinary forms of religion imaginable—an alleged apparition of the Mother of God—and, according to clinical studies, they do not possess any symptoms of neurosis; this undermines the Freudian notion that neurosis and religion must have an intrinsic connection, whether analogously, or that the two, in fact, refer to the same phenomenon. The concluding clinical report of Dr. Joyeux's French team, once again, read: "The visionaries have no symptoms of anxiety or obsessional neurosis, phobic or hysterical neurosis, hypochondriac/or psychosomatic neurosis, and there is no indication of any psychosis. We can make these formal statements in the light of detailed clinical examinations."[84]

A distinction can be made that in his major writings on religion Freud is, however, studying *rituals*, and *not* extraordinary experiences, to which he attributes neurotic behavior. The distinction is not without merit, as Bernard McGinn explains that "Freud paid tribute to [his friend Romain] Rolland as a representative of the difference between higher, mystical religion and the religion of the common people he had attacked in *The Future of an Illusion* (1927)."[85] Rolland, as noted, was the friend of Freud's who wrote about mystical experiences in the terminology of encountering an "oceanic feeling." Here, Freud had to address something higher than the common religious rituals and practices that he was criticizing in his writings. These matters of mystical experience were not easy to dismiss for Freud, who admitted that the "views expressed by my friend whom I so much admire . . . caused me no small difficulty. I cannot discover this 'oceanic' feeling in myself. It is not easy to deal scientifically with feelings."[86]

McGinn emphasizes that in "his letters to Rolland, Freud admitted the complexity of the nature of mystical experience and the tentative character of his own analysis."[87] McGinn further speculates that there "may be hints in these letters and even in the first chapter of *Civilization and its Discontents* that transient forms of mystical experience can have a positive, cathartic value."[88] Here, McGinn uses the ambiguous language that there "may be hints" as he admits that Freud actually wrote very little, and with ambivalence, about mystical experiences.[89] Notwithstanding the fact that Freud's writings reveal hints that mystical experiences can have positive and cathartic effects, this does not mean that Freud would consider such experiences to be authentic, as for him all forms of religion stem from the same psychological origins of the mind.

> Of course, even if there are the germs of a more positive view of mysticism in Freud, there can be no question of any transcendental dimension to mystical consciousness. On the whole, Freud clearly emphasized the regressive aspects of all religion and this is the view that has become canonical in the Freudian school, although some recent psychoanalysts have begun to suggest other possibilities.[90]

Therefore, while it is not improper to make a distinction between the predominant (or "common") forms of religion that the majority of Freud's writings criticize, in terms of piety and ritualism, on the one hand, and higher forms of mystical religion as Freud acknowledged in his friend Romain Rolland, on the other, it is improper to take the distinction too far, as if separating the ontological origins of the two. Freud's approach toward religion was fixed, in the sense that in Freud's psychoanalytical phenomenology *all religion,* without distinction (therefore, the common expressions and the higher, more unique expressions), were man-made experiences whose underlying causes were rooted in repressed neurosis stemming from the mind.

This is not to say that Freud's writings have not made insightful contributions to understanding facets of religious experiences; they have, particularly in regard to such issues as sublimation in religious experiences or more deviant forms of religious behavior. Much can be gained from Freud's insights.[91] However, in the case of the Medjugorje seers who, despite experiencing extraordinary religious experiences on a daily basis, are free of all forms or symptoms of neurosis, we see a significant challenge to a dominant theme underlying Freudian understandings of religion: the rooted connection to neurosis.

The thesis proposed by Gay through linguistic and psychoanalytical analysis, arguing the absence of an intrinsic connection between religion and neurosis in the foundational psychoanalytic literature, is developed[92] and empirically advanced here. It is done so in another, albeit still psychological, manner through clinical studies on visionaries and their extraordinary religious experiences. Their experiences have been tested and found to be completely free of a diagnosis that could link religion to neurosis.

7

Learning from Shortcomings, Moving Forward with New Methods

Scholars of religion today do not avow naturalist meta-physical commitments because presumably they do not need to. Such beliefs constitute part of the assumed back-ground convictions of secular academia, in which ostensibly it is simply "obvious" that claims about miracles or the afterlife, for example, are "not to be taken seriously."

—BRAD S. GREGORY

Surely we cannot take an open question like the supernatural and shut it with a bang, turning the key of the madhouse on all the mystics of history. You cannot take the region of the unknown and calmly say that, though you know nothing about it, you know all the gates are locked. We do not know enough about the unknown to know that it is unknowable.

—G. K. CHESTERTON

IN AN 1890 essay called "The Hidden Self," which he wrote for *Scribner's Magazine*, William James acknowledged that no subject "has usually been treated with a more contemptuous scientific disregard than the mass of phenomena generally called *mystical*."[1] He noted that when it comes to mystical phenomena:

Physiology will have nothing to do with them. Orthodox psychology turns its back upon them. Medicine sweeps them out; or, at most, when in an anecdotal vein, records a few of them as "effects of the imagination," a phrase of mere dismissal whose meaning, in this connection, it is impossible to make precise. All the while, however, the phenomena are there, lying broadcast over the surface of history. No matter where you open its pages, you find things recorded under the name of divinations, inspirations, demoniacal possessions, apparitions, trances, ecstasies, miraculous healings . . .[2]

James then continued to make important epistemological observations, noting that mystical phenomena are considered by many to be unusual and inexplicable occurrences and, therefore, they pose a problem for various systems of thought whose interpretative frameworks cannot account for such phenomena. "The ideal of every science," James explains, "is that of a closed and completed system of truth."[3] In this regard, James notes the evident, epistemological clash between various sciences and inexplicable phenomena like the mystical:

Each one of our various *ologies* seems to offer a definite head of classification for every possible phenomenon of the sort which it professes to cover; and, so far from free is most men's fancy, that when a consistent and organized scheme of this sort has once been comprehended and assimilated, a different scheme is unimaginable. No alternative, whether to whole or parts, can any longer be conceived as possible. Phenomena unclassifiable within the system are therefore paradoxical absurdities, and must be held untrue.[4]

Here, James spoke to an epistemological reality or outlook, or—one could even venture to say—*ideology* that many scholars, including Freud, would turn to.

Epistemological and Hermeneutical Considerations

It would not be inappropriate to use the word *ideology* if we understand the term to refer to a strict abidance to a certain way of thinking, thus to a certain system of thought, as if anything that contradicts or transcends that system of thought must be disregarded as untrue. Essentially, this is what Freud's method came down to in regard to the "oceanic feeling." He contemplated the enigma of the phenomenon of the oceanic feeling and came to the conclusion that it is so alien to the fabric of the science of his psychology, to its framework of understanding, that it is justifiable to call into question the authenticity of this type of experience and deliberately look to explain it away in natural (thus psychologically friendly) ways. Freud wrote thus of his approach toward interpreting the oceanic feeling:

> From my own experience I could not convince myself of the primary nature of such a feeling. But this gives me no right to deny that it does in fact occur in other people. The only question is whether it is being correctly interpreted and whether it ought to be regarded as the *fons et origo* of the whole need for religion.
>
> I have nothing to suggest which could have a decisive influence on the solution of this problem. The idea of men's receiving an intimation of their connection with the world around them through an immediate feeling which is from the outset directed to that purpose sounds so strange and fits in so badly with the fabric of our psychology that one is justified in attempting to discover a psychoanalytic—that is, a genetic—explanation of such a feeling.[5]

Here, we see an epistemological precursor to modern constructivist, attributional, and reductionist hermeneutics of interpretation. Freud attempted to promulgate the theory that the oceanic feeling is a human *construction* to which individuals *attribute* religious meaning, while himself applying a psychoanalytical interpretation to the genesis, therefore to the meaning, of the feeling. In the process, Freud stripped it of any religious or spiritual foundations with his explanatory *reductionism*.

The epistemological issue, however, lies in the penetrating points that James's essay invoked regarding established systems of thought. He argued that the ideal of each science is to reach a complete system of truth, a synthesis of holistic understanding, and that therefore the presence of any anomaly that is not explainable by the interpretive structures of a given science is often dismissed as inauthentic or untrue by adherents of the science. Such is the dilemma that Freud encountered in considering the question of Rolland's "oceanic feeling." Freud understood that the experience of the oceanic feeling, essentially the mystical experience (as that is what Rolland was referring to), "sounds so strange and fits in so badly with the fabric of our psychology" that Freud thought it would be justifiable to look for a natural, psychoanalytical theory that can explain away the spiritual understanding of the experience. In other words, Freud was not using his science to openly consider the possibility of the experience, an experience that Freud admitted did not fit into the interpretive para-digm of his science, but to justify his predetermined conclusion that such an experience must be false because it does not fit into the interpretive structures of his science. The issue here is twofold.

First, such an epistemological approach rests on the grounds, or more aptly on the presupposition, that one system of thought has a monopoly on the truth and that if a phenomenon is introduced that is outside the cognitive purview of that system, then it must be dismissed as inauthentic, as something that is not possible for it violates the interpretive assump-tions of the accepted system. James writes that "if there is anything which human history demonstrates, it is the extreme slowness with which the ordinary academic and critical mind acknowledges facts to exist which present themselves as *wild* facts with no stall or pigeon-hole, or as facts which threaten to break up the accepted system."[6]

The second issue, one that has already been observed in the psycho-analytical approach of Carroll, is that Freud's method begins deductively with a general principle, or premise, that essentially constitutes a prede-termined conclusion about the object of study. Thus, Freud does not try to ascertain whether or not the oceanic feeling can be authentic but begins with the starting premise that it is not authentic (again, because it does not fit into his established structure of thought) and, therefore, attempts to articulate a psychoanalytical theory that can justify his preestablished conclusion. Freud does acknowledge that people experience what Rolland describes as oceanic feelings; however, he refuses to consider the option that such experiences can be genuine, attempting to ascribe different meaning to them through a psychoanalytical form of explanatory reduc-tionism. Therefore, considering these epistemological decisions, the prob-lem is twofold: the object of study is never considered on its own terms and the reductive conclusions about it are already predetermined.

Deconstructing Taves's Naturalistic Approach: Important Implications

If we consider the first issue just observed, as displayed by Freud's method and critiqued by James's essay—the idea that one system of thought has a monopoly on the truth and that any phenomenon that does not fit into the system's interpretive framework must be dismissed as untrue—it is evi-dent that, although this thinking is faulty, if it were replaced by interdisci-plinary integration, then the methodological problem, although improved, would not yet be fully resolved. The reason that full resolution would still be lacking is the presence of the second mentioned problem: the methodological decision of studying religious or mystical experiences through a deductive approach that has a predetermined conclusion as its starting premise. A critical observation of Ann Taves's work can clarify this point.

It is important to recognize that Taves's book *Religious Experience Reconsidered* has been very influential in the study of religion, especially in advancing Taves's naturalistic ascriptive model as a hermeneutic for interpreting religious experiences. A detailed focus on Taves's approach can clarify much regarding hermeneutical and epistemological issues about studying religious experiences and can point to important implications that need to be considered for future study.

Taves focuses her project on the goal of interdisciplinary integration. Thus, unlike Freud, she is not restricting truth claims to the hermeneutical categories of one system of thought, such as psychoanalysis. On the contrary, Taves believes in the integrity of using various disciplines of study to pursue a greater understanding of the subject of study. The ascriptive approach that Taves uses within her interdisciplinary method claims that "religious or mystical or spiritual or sacred 'things' are created when religious significance is assigned to them."[7] In this ascriptive approach, an experience is not inherently religious or mystical in its essence but is understood as "religious" or "mystical," and therefore subjectively created as "thus," by the subsequent ascription assigned to it, implicitly advancing the notion that the essence of the experience may be different from the ascription that has been applied to it.[8]

James V. Spickard highlights this point in Taves's work by explaining that in *Religious Experience Reconsidered* there are three presented perspectives, yet it is one—which is a conflation of two—that dominates: for Taves experiences "can be religious in themselves, they can be deemed religious, or they can be mistakenly identified as religious. Taves too often equates these last two. Though she claims to focus on 'deeming' experiences, in fact she focuses on explaining them naturalistically and as something other than what they appear to be."[9] Spickard explains why this approach presents a problem, particularly if one is advocating a naturalistic hermeneutic, as Taves is: "Taves recognizes that treating religious experience as *sui generis* involves a metaphysical commitment—one opposed to her own commitment to naturalistic inquiry. Focusing on experiences that people deem religious is supposed to let naturalism do its work."[10] However, where the issue lies, Spickard continues, is in the philosophical assumptions that Taves's methodology makes, a methodology that is not free of a meta-physical commitment, undermining her own goal of a purely naturalistic hermeneutic. He looks at Taves's treatment of Barnard's out-of-body experience, which we observed in chapter 4, to articulate the issue:

> For example, her lengthy account of William Barnard's rather ecstatic state of consciousness hypothesizes that "the mental paradox involved in [his] visualization triggered the dissolution of self-other boundaries . . . [which] triggered feelings of ecstasy and exhilaration.". . . She posits that the first triggering was "unconscious," without recognizing that this claim puts her naturalism beyond examination every bit as much as [Rudolf] Otto's claim for "the numinous" puts religion beyond scientific scrutiny. Each depends on unexaminable entities. Her universe is populated by "the unconscious" and by "self-other boundaries"; Otto's is populated by God (and perhaps by other beings). Each posits a metaphysic that sets the rules for explanation, then reads the results back from the rules it has set.[11]

Here, Spickard identified a fundamental flaw—a contradiction, in fact—with Taves's hermeneutic, one that could easily be overlooked. Taves is advocating a naturalistic approach to the study of religious experiences, one that is free of metaphysical commitments, in order to study that which can be naturally known about such experiences. However, by *hypothesizing* natural explanations for religious experiences that root the cause of such experiences in unconscious mental processing,[12] Taves is transcending the epistemological confines of a naturalistic approach and making metaphysical claims, which cannot be empirically proven, about the origins of such studied experiences.[13]

Spickard explains the hermeneutical dilemma in greater detail, expounding why Taves's approach transcends naturalism by contrasting it to his own work on religion. He writes:

> If Taves wants to focus on "experiences deemed religious" without taking such a metaphysical stance, she must give up trying to explain them. For example, my own fieldwork with the American members of the Japanese new religion *Sekai Kyusei-kyo* (Spickard, 1991a, 1995b) required me to experience their core healing practice, *johrei*. It involved channeling invisible "divine light" to "clean the clouds from people's spiritual bodies." They certainly deemed

this "religious," and I could certainly experience it, though I have (frankly) no idea what they were "really" doing. Nor do I care. What interested me as an ethnographer was the meaning that my inform-ants made from it, how it shaped their social lives, their decisions, their factional fights, and so on. These were not epiphenomenal, and they were informed by their collective metaphysical interpre-tations of their *johrei* practice. My inquiry was naturalistic, and it was grounded in experiences deemed religious. It worked precisely because I made no metaphysical claims about those experiences, on any side.[14]

Taves has responded to Spickard's critique by pointing to Proudfoot's distinction between descriptive and explanatory reduction, and also by emphasizing how her own cultural influences in the feminist movement have shaped her methodological approach as a scholar, thus noting the importance of a scholar's personal voice in interpreting experiences.[15] Proudfoot's distinction between explanatory reduction as an acceptable form of reductionism and descriptive reduction, again, highlights that a scholar needs to accurately describe an experience but does not necessar-ily have to agree with the given interpretation of the experience. It is "a distinction," Taves explains, that she "internalized in the eighties at the height of the feminist movement and assimilated to a feminist insistence on the importance of women having a voice. As a researcher, I have been committed both to the voices of my subjects and to my own voice."[16]

Taves's reply, however, does not fully satisfy, or answer, the claim that Spickard is making about her approach. Spickard's point, as he empha-sized in his own field work with American members of a new Japanese religion, is that his approach was "naturalistic" because it did not offer a metaphysical interpretation of the subject but simply observed the various mechanisms surrounding the religion and its devotees, thus observing that which can be naturally ascertained. Taves is emphasizing the impor-tance of a scholar's unique voice and interpretation, which do not have to agree with traditional explanations of religious experiences, as long as the experiences are accurately described. She writes: "Though in this book I wanted to speak in a 'naturalistic' voice, I took pains throughout to rep-resent the voices of those with whom I disagreed as accurately as I could, even checking with them in some cases."[17] The issue, however, is that this response misses the underlying point Spickard is making. He is not say-ing that Taves cannot provide her own naturalistic explanation, her own naturalistic voice, *if it is empirically established*, thus naturalistically ascertained. He is saying that she cannot call her approach "naturalistic" if her explanations are reached through metaphysical speculation rather than means which can be empirically (thus naturally) proven. Thus, scholars can have their own interpretations of claimed mystical or religious experiences, whether that interpretation is framed in a feminist voice, a Marxist voice, a religionist voice, or any other hermeneutical "ism." But if the methodological means of reaching such conclusions take metaphysical (instead of purely empirical) means, then such hermeneutical voices cannot be called "naturalistic," as they betray the fundamental tenets of naturalism. In this regard, the personal voice becomes a metaphysical voice.

The presence of a metaphysical voice in Taves's claimed naturalism becomes evident even in Taves's own explanation of her methodological goals:

> As I have indicated elsewhere . . . the term "naturalism" is used in a variety of senses, ranging from the belief that the physical sciences can provide a complete account of human behavior, on the one hand, to non-supernaturalism, on the other. I am assuming that collaboration between scholars of religion and natural scientists will be most fruitful if scholars of religion set aside supernatural explanations, as most already do, and scientists are open to the possibility that we need more than the physical sciences to give an adequate albeit still naturalistic account of human behavior."[18]

There is a subjectivity in this perspective that betrays deeply rooted philosophical assumptions, as Taves is asking scholars of religion to set aside supernatural explanations while encouraging scientists to be open to the possibility that more is necessary than the physical sciences (albeit keeping to the exclusion of the supernatural). The latter point—explaining that more is necessary than the physical sciences—opens the door to the methodological incorporation of the unconscious, as the unconscious does not belong totally to the strict empiricism of a physical science but is, in its essence, *meta*-physical; therefore, it opens the path to Taves's hermeneutical emphasis on unconscious processing in interpreting religious experiences, constituting a metaphysical commitment. The former point, however, explaining that scholars of religion should set aside supernatural explanations, closes the door to other metaphysical considerations, thus making a case for one form of metaphysics against others in a hermeneutic whose ontological subjectivity betrays the deontological expectancy of a purely naturalistic perspective. This is the case not necessarily as a result of the unconscious processing that is at the center of Taves's hermeneutic, but because Taves takes it a step further and associates the unconscious not simply with the processing of experience but also with *the ontological roots of experience*: once the unconscious becomes the ontological key toward explaining the source of a phenomenon, we are no longer dealing with naturalistic, meaning purely empirical, claims but, rather, those that are rooted in philosophical presuppositions.

Taves's analysis of Stephen Bradley's and William Barnard's experiences speaks well to this reality. While Taves is able to naturalistically analyze unintentional behavior and tacit thoughts in their behavior—therefore, study unconscious processing—she goes further by hypothesizing ontological claims to the sources of their experiences as being something other than what they believe. A great example of such metaphysical methodology and its underlying presumptions is also seen in a recent documentary on Joan of Arc that attempts to explain the purported mystical experiences Joan reported, both her locutions and visions, in naturalistic ways. Not being able to dismiss Joan's experiences through a pathological explanation, given the fact that there is no trace of a history of insanity in Joan's life or that of her family, scholars in the documentary turn to the unconscious in order to find a "natural" explanation for Joan's mystical experiences and achievements. Explaining that Joan came from a medieval religious culture wherein claims of visionary and mystical experiences were not scarce, the documentary concludes that Joan was heavily influenced by her surrounding culture, to the point that she did hear voices and see visions, as culturally influenced phenomena stemming from the unconscious. Therefore, Joan's voices and visions, according to the documentary, came not from God but from her unconscious mind. What is noteworthy is that the experienced phenomena—the voices and visions—are not denied; what is denied are *the ontological origins*, as supernatural experiences coming from God, of the phenomena in favor of another metaphysical explanation in the form of the unconscious. This, observed superficially, can be construed as a "natural" explanation of phenomena which the subject (Joan of Arc) understood as supernatural. Yet, examined carefully, it becomes evident that the given explanation is not reached through empirically established natural means but is, in fact, an unproven, and therefore speculated, claim of the metaphysical origins of the phenomena, speaking more to the philosophical and ideological biases of those making the arguments than to the ontological essence of Joan of Arc's experiences.[19]

Spickard is not the only scholar who has pointed to philosophical motivations in Taves's approach. Finbarr Curtis argues that "Taves and other proponents of cognitive approaches to religious studies fashion a kind of secular praxis in which breaking taboos is a crucial attribute of scholarly integrity and intellectual heroism."[20] Essentially, Curtis sees an underlying agenda in play that, under the guise of advancing "scholarly integrity" and displaying an "intellectual heroism," is in fact promoting a secular ideology through its hermeneutical methodology. Curtis is especially critical of how Taves's approach calls for the violation of *sui generis* taboos—in her promotion of an ascriptive model that tends toward explanatory reductionism in interpreting religious experiences—that, in his view, transcends the boundaries of objective scholarship through ideological motives.[21] "In calling scholars to violate taboos, Taves alludes to social and institutional ambitions that reach beyond the methodological guidelines for cognitive research."[22] The critique that Curtis is voicing here reads like an inversion of Proudfoot's critique of *sui generis* thinkers who, through "protective strategies," he argued, defend religious sensibilities against critical scholarship: Proudfoot, therefore, identifying an ideological component in their hermeneutical goals. Curtis points to scholars on the other side of the ideological spectrum and, instead of seeing an objective sphere of secular neutrality in their hermeneutical positioning, identifies the presence of hermeneutical assumptions championing another—although, perhaps more subtle—ideological agenda.[23]

Timothy Fitzgerald similarly notes ideological components, even in Taves's call for interdisciplinary integration between social and natural sciences in studying religion, which in his view undermines a sense of objectivity with its one-sided emphasis. He notes that Taves's "discussion forges an alliance with those scientists in biological and psychological disciplines who, from their own assumed standpoint of natural and secular knowledge, themselves have a strong investment in discourses on religion and the supernatural."[24] Fitzgerald is arguing that one cannot simply critique religious perspectives without considering the other side of the ideological spectrum—the secular, from which the critique originates. "Taves seems uninterested in the secular positionality of the scientists and their research agendas. Nor, for that matter, does she look at her own positionality. I suggest that any critique of 'religion' as a modern category must simultaneously be a critique of the non-religious secular as the other half of one ideological discourse." He expounds on the issue in detail:

> The implication of Taves' text seems to be that scientists who investigate "religious" phenomena such as special experiences are not themselves engaged in following a special path to a special goal of knowledge, a path imbued with ideals and values, surrounded by prohibitions and taboos, predicated on some very basic metaphysical constructions, and developed within a historically longer term ideological project of progressive liberation from existing conditions of ignorance and superstition. Whatever individual scientists may believe motivates them as individuals at conscious or unconscious levels, their work is located in a historically constructed ideological domain of enlightenment rationality and universal progress.[25]

Taves, in response, has written that she agrees "with Fitzgerald that we can't understand things deemed religious in isolation."[26] Taves highlights a section in Fitzgerald's article wherein he emphasizes justice, courts, and judicial procedures as having specialness in value analogous to religion, and agrees with his point that the domain of science, and particularly the practices and goals of scientists, should be treated with the same analysis that spiritual and religious paths receive, thus doing justice to a holistic analysis of a religious–secular binary.[27] However, Taves completely ignores a very important section in Fitzgerald's article, providing no adequate response to it, which gets into a deeper dimension of what Fitzgerald means in terms of providing a holistic critique of a religious–secular binary, particularly in acknowledging the ideological presuppositions that are embedded in a secular/naturalist perspective that says more than can be empirically established.[28]

Specifically, like Spickard, Fitzgerald is very skeptical about the assumptions that Taves's analysis of Barnard's out-of-body experience makes. Fitzgerald explains that he feels "a strong empathy with Barnard's dilemma. . . . I do not doubt that something of profound significance happened which retrospectively has been classified as 'religious.' "[29] The dilemma, however, according to Fitzgerald, is how to convey such an extraordinary experience within the conceptually limited confines of language without distorting the essence of the experience.[30] Like Spickard, Fitzgerald sees a problem with Taves's ontologically laden analysis that is able to look at a unique experience as Barnard's and claim that it is not religious but could, through a naturalistic inquiry, be explained naturally. Such a conclusion, according to Fitzgerald, extends beyond what can be scientifically examined, pointing to the ideological undercurrent that encapsulates the perspective.[31] He points to Taves's goal of extending the work performed by scholars in attributional theory that, as Taves writes, "looked at meaning making in relation to the entire range of life events in order to explain when and why events are attributed to religious as opposed to non-religious causes."[32] He expounds:

> It would be one thing to investigate reports of *special* "experiences," something which has been done historically and, within the terms of its own criteria, authoritatively by the Catholic church-state, for example. But I cannot see how, to classify them as "religious" as distinct from "non-religious," can be part of the data derived from tracking brain functions. It is the utilization of a modern Anglophone scheme of classification which itself functions in a wider ideological context of power. It seems to me that the distinction between religious and secular or natural causes cannot itself be derived from any amount of scientific observation or experiment. There seems to be an in-built circularity where the natural sciences investigate in terms of categories which are already implicated in their own self-designation.[33]

Particularly striking is Fitzgerald's claim that, in his view, it appears that the distinctions between religious, secular, or natural causes "cannot be derived from any amount of scientific observation or experiment."[34] Fitzgerald's claim here, in critiquing Taves's approach, possesses both merit and shortcoming. On the one hand, Taves would partially agree with Fitzgerald in explaining that an experience cannot be authentically identified as "religious" if one is analyzing the experience from an etic perspective, meaning outside of the tradition (such as Catholicism, with its own criteria for evaluation) from which the purported theological content of the experience stems.[35] On the other hand, Fitzgerald makes the claim that the designations of "secular" or "natural" also cannot be ascertained through any form of scientific examination. In his article, Fitzgerald makes this claim after voicing hesitation about Taves's treatment of Barnard's experience. To be sure, in such an example as Barnard's experience, Fitzgerald's statement has great merit; however, it may be a claim that is not as universally applicable as Fitzgerald assumes. Let us consider both points.

First, similar to Spickard, it seems that Fitzgerald is saying that scientific observations cannot make ontological claims about whether an experience has religious, natural, or secular causes, for such claims extend beyond what is empirically verifiable. This, again, as Spickard agreed, is the case with Barnard's experience. An important distinction is vital to highlight, however, here in considering Taves's approach with respect to unconscious processing in regard to Barnard's experience. The distinction is this: Taves can, in a naturalistic way, make observations about unintentional behaviors and thought patterns that Barnard's experience conveys, thus record the phenomenology of unconscious processing, as she has, in fact, done.[36] She cannot, however, make the ontological claim that the unconscious is the source of the experience, as she has done, for that is a metaphysical claim that is beyond empirical examination, undermining her claimed naturalism and critique of metaphysics.[37] In short, if Taves wants to be true to a naturalistic hermeneutic that avoids metaphysics, then she can analyze the unconscious behaviors associated with purported religious experiences but she cannot ontologically designate the unconscious as the source of such experiences, as such a claim is not empirically verifiable. This is the issue that Spickard and Fitzgerald are getting at, presenting a valid critique of Taves's hermeneutic.

On the other hand, Fitzgerald's claim that the ontological designation for extraordinary experiences as being religious, secular, or natural cannot be reached through any form of scientific experimentation is taking the argument too far—specifically, with the claim that scientific examination cannot prove secular or natural conclusions. The example of the usage of scientific studies on the Medjugorje visionaries can, for instance, undermine the totality of this point. For instance, while the scientific studies are not able to verify the purported theological content of the experiences—in that sense, Fitzgerald is correct—if they were to find a natural or pathological explanation for the phenomenon, such as epilepsy, hallucination, or fraud, then scientific experimentation would, in fact, be tracing the origins of the experiences to secular or natural sources with a natural empiricism that deserves its due. That was the purpose of the studies—to see whether natural, thus alternative, explanations could be located. This has not been the case with Medjugorje, since the experiences of the visionaries have, as observed, endured scientific scrutiny with integrity; but such could be the case with other alleged mystical experiences: scientific experimentation used to purify religion of false experiences. In this regard, Fitzgerald's critique has only partial merit.

In response to Curtis's concern that Taves is partaking in a form of "intellectual heroism" whose ideological goals are to promote a secular agenda through her call for scholars to violate taboos, Taves has replied that she does not think that her call is a form of secular heroism because she does not believe that taboos are strictly religious; thus, their violation (and her advocacy for the goal) is not an exclusively secular enterprise.[38] Taves, of course, is correct in this fact: taboos are not exclusively religious and, therefore, their violation is not exclusively secular. However, this response may be an unfair generalization of Curtis's point, as Curtis's article states: "I will argue that many of the prominent advocates of the cognitive science of religion are arguing for more than just a new sub-field of religious studies. . . . In particular, *cognitive approaches to religion* draw their rhetorical force from their participation in a critique of what-ever institutional boundaries and limits are perceived to restrict secular freedom."[39] This concentration of Curtis's, specifically on the institutional aims of many cognitive approaches to religion, leads him to an interest "in how Taves and other proponents of cognitive approaches to religious stud-ies fashion a kind of secular praxis in which breaking taboos is a crucial attribute of scholarly integrity and intellectual heroism."[40] In other words, Curtis is not denying the fact that taboos are not strictly religious and their violation, therefore, not an entirely secular enterprise; he is, however, spe-cifically concentrating on cognitive approaches *to religion* (as Taves's work is pursuing) whose underlying goal of violating *sui generis* taboos he sees as an attribute of an ideologically inspired, secular heroism. This is not a negation of the existing universalism of taboos (beyond the religious), but is a specific concentration on the call to violate taboos within the context of the study of religion through various cognitive approaches, as Taves is advocating in her book; even if her advocacy transcends religious catego-ries, such categories do remain the central focus of her concentration.

Spickard juxtaposed Taves's categories of interpretation with Rudolf Otto's, showing that both use terminology—such as Taves's "the uncon-scious" and "self-other boundaries," and Otto's usage of "the numinous," God, or other spiritual agents—which speak to metaphysical entities that not only transcend empirical examination but that also can be used, her-meneutically, to posit "a metaphysic that sets the rules for explanation, then reads the results back from the rules it has set."[41] This is akin to Freud beginning with the unproven, albeit predetermined, conclusion that oceanic feelings are not inherently religious or mystical but simply receive those ascriptions by those who experience them. A metaphysical

commitment sets the rules for explanation, then reads the results back
from the rules it has set.

In comparing Freud and Taves, it is important to note that the means
to their approaches are completely different—the opposite of each other, in
fact—as Freud monopolizes truth for one system of thought, restricting his
thinking to the interpretive structures of psychoanalysis, while Taves applies
interdisciplinary integration to support the conclusions of her approach,
expanding her thinking to multiple disciplines. Notwithstanding, while the
means are so different—opposite from each other—the general conclusions
become similar in the sense that each approach is set up to lead to a naturalistic account articulated within a framework of a phenomenology of explanatory reductionism.[42] It is not a perfect comparison, as Taves's explanatory
reduction does not match the all-encompassing totality of Freud's, but it is
important to convey how a single intellectual system, on the one hand, and
an interdisciplinary integration of a number of systems, on the other hand,
can lead to similar general conclusions belonging under the umbrella of
"explanatory reductionism."[43] Freud did it one way, theorizing psychoanalyt-
ically that persons who report oceanic feelings are probably experiencing a
regressive, infantile state wherein mother–child boundaries are transcended
for a feeling of oneness. Taves did it another way, theorizing through the
combination of various sciences and ideas, such as visualization, imagination, self-suggestion, and unconsciously induced states of altered consciousness, that extraordinary experiences like Stephen Bradley's and G. William
Barnard's have natural explanations not inherently religious or mystical.[44]

An important distinction needs to be made here, however. When critiquing the methodology of Freud and Taves, the central issue is not that
their methods lead to a conclusion of explanatory reductionism; the issue
is that such methods can border on leading to *nothing but* a conclusion
of explanatory reductionism. In other words, many purported religious
experiences may be false, and the only way to understand them is through
a phenomenological investigation whose procedure leads to a conclusion
of explanatory reductionism. Such an inductive method is perfectly appropriate. However, this is not the method that Freud or Taves uses. Their
methodologies apply a deductive approach, wherein from the starting
point it is presupposed that experiences are not inherently religious or
mystical but, rather, natural and therefore this leads to scholarship whose
only conclusion—no matter what the means—will be explanatory reductionism.[45] The possibility of an extraordinary religious experience being
authentic is not even considered, *nor can the possibility be considered*, as

these deductive methodologies on religious experience are structured to set up research on the premise that such experiences are not authentic but must have other, naturalistic explanations.[46]

Granted, Taves has acknowledged that she does not want to say anything about the authenticity of religious experiences because, as a scholar, she is approaching the subject from an etic perspective, thus from a perspective that is meant to say as much about the subject as can be naturalistically ascertained from an outsider's angle without considering the insider discourse of analyzing the theological content of an experience under an emic criterion of evaluation.[47] The latter approach, tackling the subject from an emic perspective, would be the only way to comment on the authenticity of such experiences. This is a valid distinction and one whose implications we will discuss later in greater detail. However, the issue remains—and this goes back to Spickard's concern—that Taves's approach does not simply say as much as can be naturally known about "experiences deemed religious"; it takes it further by making metaphysical leaps (beyond empirical naturalism) to reinterpret such experiences as mistakenly identified as religious.

Yet, the possibility of a religious experience being authentic can be respected and, out of an intellectual openness that does not close the door to any cognitive consideration, *should* be respected, even if one is approaching the subject from an etic perspective that cannot comment on authenticity. The Jamesian approach of empirically studying religious experiences from an outsider's perspective while respecting the possibility of the "more" in such experiences is a good example of such an approach.[48] By leaving the question of the ontological origins of extraordinary religious experiences open,[49] instead of trying to fully explain such phenomena through a naturalistic metaphysic that could frame such experiences as complete constructs of the human mind, James formulated an open-ended approach that was able to be etic (exhausting how much the psychology of religion can say) without attempting to dismiss the possibility of the "more," the mystery behind such experiences—in essence, keeping all cognitive considerations available.[50] For Romain Rolland, James's approach constitutes "a model of methodological humility" and provides "an example of how psychologists should position themselves with respect to mystical phenomena."[51] Given the merits of such a model, this type of approach should not be limited to the positioning of psychologists but extended to any scholar who is studying religious and mystical phenomena from an etic perspective.

Examining these matters, we can grasp a better understanding of the important difference between Spickard's etic approach to religious experiences and Taves's etic approach, which we have briefly observed: Spickard does not make any metaphysical claims about the religious experiences he studies when such claims are beyond empirical examination, abiding by the hermeneutical parameters of a naturalistic approach and respecting (even if inadvertently) *the possibility* of the Jamesian "more" in the studied experiences. Taves, on the other hand, attempts to naturalistically explain the ontological roots of the experiences she studies, closing the door to the cognitive consideration of the "more" with an ascriptive approach that (metaphysically) presupposes that such experiences are not innately religious or mystical.[52]

Taves's approach, thus, is different from a perspective—which we will examine hereafter as the "criteria of adequacy"[53]—wherein religious experiences are studied against a naturalistic framework, utilizing the social and natural sciences, to say as much as can be said naturally about such experiences without making the metaphysical leap (when it is beyond empirical examination) that tries to naturalistically explain the totality of the phenomenon. A benign reductionism that considers the psychological dynamics of religious experiences without claiming to explain the totality of the phenomenon is necessary, as it helps to account for the multidimensionality of such experiences; it is a naturalistic hermeneutic whose aims is to explain as much as natural and social sciences can, even if it means empirically proving that an experience is not inherently religious but, rather, something else. Such methodology is crucial, and it is even beneficial to religion, for it protects religion from false experiences that do not merit the label "religious."

It is highly important, however, to make a distinction between the two approaches: one is a purely naturalistic hermeneutic that is able to reach empirical conclusions about religious experiences and the other is a *purportedly* naturalistic hermeneutic that makes metaphysical claims predominantly against religious experiences to support its predetermined conclusions about such experiences. The latter constitutes what Spickard is critiquing in Taves's approach, noting that "Taves slips so easily from naturalism to metaphysical atheism, claiming that religious experiences are other than they appear."[54]

It is at the same time important to highlight, as has been noted earlier, that Taves's approach does make a significant contribution to the debate on religious experience by incorporating the notion of unconscious processing—something that separates her approach from traditional con-structivist and attributionist hermeneutics and adds another challenge to neo-perennialist interpretations. In that sense, Taves's contribution is important and deserves recognition. However, where her methodology falls short, essentially committing a contradiction in logic, is in her advo-cacy for a purely naturalistic and interdisciplinary approach to religious experiences that is free of metaphysical commitments, whereas Taves her-self articulates an approach that is underlined, however more subtly, by a metaphysical commitment. The problem may actually be twofold. First, as Spickard highlights, by relying on empirically unexaminable sources asso-ciated with the unconscious as ontological roots[55] for mystical and reli-gious experiences, Taves is delving into metaphysical considerations that transcend a naturalistic epistemology, undermining her own critique of metaphysics. Second, as Fitzgerald emphasizes, by advocating for an inter-disciplinary integration between the work of social and natural scientists, Taves should take into consideration the very philosophical commitments that such scientists bring to the study of religion; not to do so undermines a sense of objectivity by offering a critique of religious perspectives that does not consider the philosophical presuppositions the other side of the ideological spectrum—the secular—brings to the discourse. This is not to say that all social and natural scientists are "secular," but it is to say that the social and natural sciences operate under the interpretive parameters of a metaphysic that, far from being neutral, tends to translate the sacred into the secular. Let us consider this.

The Myth of Secular Neutrality?

The British theologian John Milbank has made the argument that it is erroneous to perceive the perspectives offered by the social sciences, par-ticularly on religious phenomena, as being "objective," as if they were free of metaphysical commitments. Milbank argues that social scientific theo-ries "interpret religious phenomena by reducing their particular nature to some extrinsic, universal explanation. Although they masquerade as objective discourses of fact, these social theories . . . are none the less forms of metaphysics whose hidden agenda is to domesticate the sacred by translating it into the secular."[56] Milbank's magnum opus is the book *Theology and Social Theory: Beyond Secular Reason*, which begins with the provocative sentence, "Once, there was no 'secular.' "[57] In the very next par-agraph, Milbank expounds: "The secular as a domain had to be instituted or *imagined*, both in theory and practice."[58] Milbank's argument, that there is no such thing as a neutral, autonomous secular vantage point from which the social sciences study religion, but that the social sciences themselves possess intrinsic metaphysical assumptions, reinforces Fitzgerald's point that a critique of religion should be juxtaposed with a critique of the secular (as religion's counterpart), which far from being a sphere of objective discourse, contains its own hermeneutical assumptions. It also reinforces Curtis's point that many cognitive approaches to the study of religion possess their own ideological biases based on a secular praxis that extends beyond what the methodological boundaries of cognitive research can say.[59] The historian Brad S. Gregory articulates the issue well, pointing—like Milbank—to how social scientific and cultural-theoretical approaches that claim to be "neutral" in studying religion contain their own implicit metaphysical biases whose hidden agendas are to domesticate the sacred by translating it into the secular:

> To the extent that the modern social sciences and humanities are framed implicitly by the metaphysical naturalism of the modern natural sciences, they leave no room for the *reality* of the content of religious claims: in Christianity, for example, content concerning God, Satan, sin, grace, heaven, hell, revelation, redemption, providence, sanctity, and the rest. Consequently, spirituality, for example, can only be approached through secular psychological categories; sacraments only in terms of anthropological rituals and symbols that ostensibly construct and reinforce community identity; sin only in terms of socially and/or politically disapproved behaviors that threaten stability or some other interest. That prayer might *really* be channels of grace, or that sin might be an *objective* category of actions disapproved of *by God*, are notions that modern social-scientific and cultural-theoretical approaches to religion simply reject as incompatible with their implicit assumptions.[60]

It was the French sociologist Émile Durkheim (1858–1917), recognized as the father of sociology, who in his 1912 work *The Elementary Forms of Religious Life* advanced metaphysical naturalism to be the philosophical basis for the social sciences in studying religion. Durkheim asserted that "only a few minds" have accepted the laws of naturalism during his time, acknowledging that "true miracles are thought possible in society" and, by consequence, Durkheim believed that "we still have the mind-set of primitives."[61] Underlying the metaphysical foundations of the social sciences is a naturalism that rejects, from the outset, the possibility of the miraculous and supernatural, as Durkheim did, being informed by a strongly rooted ideological assumption.

If we understand the "secular" as an imagined construct—Milbank traces the historical origins of this construct to the year 1300[62]—as opposed to the common understanding of the secular as a realm of hermeneutical objectivity, then, the "secular" becomes another perspective, among others, that is able to impose its own constructed philosophical assumptions onto the object of study instead of being understood (ironically, in a *sui generis* fashion) as an elevated and autonomous sphere of objective discourse.[63] Spickard's critique of Taves's method—that too often she equates the perspective of studying "experiences deemed religious" with "experiences mistaken as religious"—implicitly locates the philosophical presuppositions of a secular ontology in Taves's approach, alluding to Milbank's point about sociological theories that can constitute forms of metaphysics whose underlying agenda is to domesticate the sacred into the secular.[64] Spickard writes: "Taves clearly wants more [than a naturalistic perspective]. Throughout the book, she speaks of religion as a faces-in-the-clouds phenomenon . . . in which the (postulated) human tendency to find patterns in random events imagines supernatural agents to be active in the world. Naturalistically, she can explain those agents as category mistakes. But this interpretation depends on metaphysical claims as much as do religious views."[65]

Gregory similarly emphasizes, "In this conceptualization, the adoption of secular theories that overtly or tacitly explain religion by reducing it to something else would constitute a form of confessional history—a secular confessional history—one that in important ways mirrors traditional, religious confessional history."[66] By "mirroring" religious confessional history, Gregory means that both religious and secular confessional histories contain metaphysical claims that cannot be proven but, nevertheless, are assumed to be true by the authors embracing these individual approaches. It would be erroneous, however, to presume that one, a secular confessional history, is more objective than the other, a religious confessional history. "Whereas traditional confessional historians assumed that a particular religious tradition is true and conducted their investigation accordingly, secular confessional historians assume —based ultimately on a dogmatic metaphysical naturalism, or on its functional equivalent, a thoroughgoing epistemological skepticism about all religious claims—that *no* religion is, indeed *cannot be*, what its believers-practitioners claim that it is."[67] If such an approach is conveyed as a metaphysically free, naturalistic perspective, then it becomes a misnomer, as such a designation does not account for the metaphysical means by which the hermeneutic reaches empirically unexaminable conclusions. The approach claims to be naturalistic and empirical—to the exclusion of metaphysical considerations—yet says more than can be naturally and empirically accounted for, thus becoming another, albeit more subtle, form of metaphysics.[68]

Escaping an Ontological Prison: Beyond the Dogma of Metaphysical Naturalism

In a significant article published in 2008 under the title "Abundant History: Marian Apparitions as Alternative Modernity," Robert A. Orsi uses the Marian apparitions of Lourdes as a case study displaying why scholars of history and religion need to expand their methodology, and let go of their modernistic presumptions, in studying such unique experiences as human and divine encounters. Orsi calls for a new historiography to influence modern scholarship.[69] He would elaborate on his thesis years later in his book *History and Presence* (2016). One of Orsi's central arguments is that methods that historians and religious studies scholars use to study their subjects operate with an underlying worldview, an ontology based on the assumptions of modernity. Such methodological assumptions study the subject within the confines of their own boundaries and limitations—boundaries and limitations that derive from a general metaphysic of naturalism—thus, a worldview that is at odds with the supernatural, an obvious dilemma when one is studying subjects who claim supernatural experiences.

Orsi is not the only scholar to make such observations. Amy Hollywood, who as a historian of medieval mysticism has dedicated much of her scholarship to studying the mystical and visionary experiences of medieval women, has recently written similarly about this philosophical bias in modern scholarship, explaining:

> Most importantly, I want to ask whether the methods others—in this case religious people of a particular sort, those who encounter or interact with ghosts, spirits, saints, demons, or God—use to determine what is real and what is true might challenge the ontological and epistemological presuppositions of modern history, themselves

grounded in central presumptions of modern Western philosophy. For whether we acknowledge it or not, there *is* a theory—there
are many theories—underlying contemporary historical work and
the study of religion, most prominently a kind of naturalism that
assumes everything in human history can be explained in terms
of the operations of the natural world and of human beings, themselves part of that world.[70]

Hollywood admits that her own view here is influenced greatly by Orsi. The
question that both scholars are asking is important, for when we consider
experiences like Marian apparitions or similar visionary accounts, wherein
claims are made of a personal encounter with a supernatural presence,
then are the methods of modern historiography, which implicitly assume a
naturalistic worldview, tenable to properly understand such a subject?

Hollywood cites the work of the anthropologist Saba Mahmood, who
"together with a host of other scholars in the study of religion" asks
"whether we can have a meaningful engagement with subjects whose self-
understanding we presume from the outset to be false or misguided. How
can we begin with such assumptions and ever hope to understand?"[71] Such
a question brings to mind the approach of scholars like Proudfoot and
Taves. Hollywood underscores the connection, noting that for "Proudfoot,
however, supernatural explanations are never adequate to the phenomena
and always require correction."[72] She emphasizes that such an approach
presumes, "as modern historians and others in the humans sciences like
Proudfoot tend to do, the ultimate validity of naturalistic explanations,"
and from such a perspective, "other modes of explanation (and hence of
existence) are invalidated from the outset."[73]

The language that Hollywood uses here, in reference to modes of explanation and therefore existence, speaks to an ontology. There is a singular
ontology that informs the dominant approaches of historians and religious studies scholars: a naturalistic metaphysic. From the perspective of
a naturalistic metaphysic, it is assumed by the scholar that supernatural
agents—be it an apparition of the Virgin Mary, spirits, ghosts, demons,
God—are not real and, therefore, we can only understand religious experiences in naturalistic categories. Such a limited approach, reducing
knowledge to one ontological perspective, is not satisfying to Orsi, who
in the case of Lourdes asks the question, "How is the event at Lourdes
even approachable from outside the metaphysical assumptions underlying the phrase 'the transcendent broke into time,' a metaphysics the denial

of which is fundamental to modern reason?"[74] Here, Orsi makes an important insight. How can an event that claims to be an encounter with a supernatural presence in our time be sufficiently studied by an approach whose metaphysical assumptions rest on denying this very reality?

As a historian, Brad Gregory recognizes the two unhealthy extremes that can be taken up by scholars who attempt to study and reconstruct religious history: falling into the framework of a religionist confessional history that assumes the theological truths and dogmas of the studied tradition must be true; or falling into a secularist confessional history that assumes the theological truths of the studied tradition cannot be true in favor of its own metaphysical dogma of naturalism. The first, a religionist confessional history, is largely rejected in the world of mainstream academia, whose philosophical underpinnings are innately secular in approach and worldview. The second, the secularist confessional history, is largely presumed to be true in mainstream academia; and in the process, what is taken for granted is its own undemonstrable worldview from which the hermeneutic operates. Gregory is critical of the dominance of secular theories that inform the work of historians, often to the point of presenting the religious experiences of their subjects as something else.[75] Hence, for Gregory, it is not that one side—whether religious or secular—is more objective than the other; it is, rather, that both sides assume metaphysical beliefs, whether of supernaturalism or of naturalism, that cannot be demonstrably proven as true or false—yet one is treated as implicitly true and the other as implicitly false.

Calling the secular-naturalist perspective an approach that constitutes a confessional history—meaning, one with its own ingrained assumptions about the nature of reality and how to interpret it—may come as surprising to many, Gregory writes. This is so because the metaphysical naturalism that undergirds secular approaches has become such an accepted, and seemingly self-evident, dogmatic truth that few realize they are, in fact, falling into the worldview of one subjective philosophy in adopting this hermeneutic. Gregory explains:

> If such an idea seems strange, this derives largely from the fact that the foundational beliefs of the modern social sciences and humanities, notwithstanding the linguistic turn, postmodernism, postcolonialism, and other recent intellectual trends, are by now so pervasive and so taken for granted that they are not even self-consciously regarded as beliefs at all. Rather, they are implicitly

considered in academic discourse as true, neutral descriptions of the nature of reality, although this is seldom articulated.[76]

Similar to Milbank, Gregory notes how the social sciences and humanities have been affected by this hermeneutic to the point that these disciplines, while popularly perceived as neutral and objective, undermine the metaphysical claims of religion not with "objectivity" but with their own adopted metaphysical and cultural biases. "Put bluntly, the underlying beliefs of the modern social sciences and humanities are metaphysically naturalist and culturally relativist, and consequently contend that religion is *and can only be* a human construction."[77] Orsi also points to this trend in academic culture, explaining, "Religions are *social constructions*, in modern intellectual orthodoxy."[78]

Religion and history are not the only disciplines that have seen such an epistemological trend. It has been pervasive across disciplines. Bruce Greyson has made similar observations about disciplines like psychology, neuroscience, and philosophy of mind, specifically in relation to the question of consciousness, or how the mind and brain correlate and are understood. He is critical of a materialistic reductionism that refuses to acknowledge the mind may continue to function outside the brain. Spending much of his career studying near-death experiences (NDEs), Greyson notes how systematic documentation of such experiences points to the plausibility that consciousness—meaning a person's mind—continues to function when the brain appears to be inactive or impaired, often with flat EEGs recorded. "Individuals reporting NDEs often describe their mental processes during the NDE as remarkably clear and lucid and their sensory experiences as unusually vivid, equaling or even surpassing those of their normal waking state."[79] This poses a problem for the classical mind-brain identity model, which assumes that the brain is the basis for consciousness and, therefore, the mind cannot live on once the brain stops functioning at brain death. The greatest challenge to this framework, Greyson explains, one which "is so commonly reported in NDEs, is the occurrence of normal or even enhanced mental activity at times when, according to the mind-brain identity model, such activity should be diminishing, if not impossible."[80]

A number of scholars, including Edward Francis Kelly, Emily Williams Kelly, Michael Grosso, Adam Crabtree, Alan Gauld, and Greyson among them, have contributed to the book *Irreducible Mind: Toward a Psychology for the 21st Century*. In this work they examine how much empirical evidence supports the case that the mainstream opinion claiming that all aspects of the mind and consciousness are generated from physical processes from the brain is incomplete and, in fact, is false. What is being challenged here is a physicalism, meaning a reductive materialism that reduces consciousness to physical and mechanical forces of the brain. Edward F. Kelly writes, "Quite apart from any personal or theological interests readers may bring to this subject, it should be evident that postmortem survival in any form, if it occurs, demonstrates the presence of a fundamental bifurcation in nature, and hence the falsehood of biological naturalism."[81] By "fundamental bifurcation in nature" Kelly means, of course, the possibility of the soul or, in more "neutral" academic parlance, *consciousness* leaving the body and continuing to exist; this undermines the tenets of biological naturalism, which suggest that the death of our physical bodies is the end of our existence. This is why systematic research into near-death experiences—their phenomenology, neurophysiology, and varieties of inexplicable occurrences, such as veridical NDEs—constitutes a convincing, vastly documented challenge to the materialistic model in psychology, neuroscience, and philosophy of mind that cannot see life (therefore, consciousness) as existing beyond the physical body or brain, thereby undermining the assumptions of its materialist-naturalist-physicalist reductionism.[82]

In addition to studying NDEs, the authors examine various phenomena, both ordinary and extraordinary, including memory, genius-level creativity, mystical experiences, psi phenomena, extreme psychophysical influence, psychological automatisms and secondary centers of consciousness, the unity of conscious experience, and informational capacity, precision, and depth, to illustrate, through a wide array of empirical data, the various pieces of evidence that point to the shortcomings of biological naturalism.[83] Greyson notes how at the beginning of the twentieth century, before quantum physics became the dominant and adequate paradigm as the foundation of science, it was classical mechanics that held that place. However, once advancements in knowledge were made and it became clear that there were certain extraordinary things the classical mechanical model could not explain, the transition had to be made to another explanatory model, that of quantum physics. Greyson is making the same point for other disciplines, such as psychology, noting that there are certain extraordinary circumstances, like near-death experiences, whose dynamics cannot be totally explained by a materialistic-physicalist model that dominates the field, and thus there are grounds for expanding dominant modes of explanation to other models.[84] Kelly makes a similar argument. "The point I want to make, especially to my fellow psychologists, is this: Our *a priori* commitment to a conventional physicalist account of the mind has rendered us systematically incapable of dealing adequately with the mind's most central properties. We need to rethink that commitment."[85] He agrees with the philosopher E. J. Lowe, who articulated: "Reductive physicalism, far from being equipped to solve the so-called 'easy' problems of consciousness, has in fact nothing very useful to say about *any* aspect of consciousness."[86]

Whether the discipline is religion, history, psychology, neuroscience, philosophy, or any other social or natural science or humanities field, and whether the form of reductionism is called materialist, physicalist, or metaphysical naturalism, we are essentially dealing with the same underlying issue: one metaphysical view dominating academic discourse, across the disciplines, at the expense of another major worldview that is not given its due. One worldview cannot see anything beyond the physical or natural while the other does not believe that the physical and natural tell the whole story, considering a more robust understanding of knowledge that does not exclude the spiritual or the possibility of consciousness living beyond the material world and, by consequence, the possibility of spiritual realities. Orsi categorizes these two ontologies, or worldviews, as "absence" and "presence."

In this dialectic of presence and absence, Orsi sees that for a long time individuals lived with a worldview of presence, wherein invisible, spiritual realities like the real presence of Christ in the Eucharist, or apparitions and encounters with the Virgin Mary, with angels, with the saints, with God, both extraordinary and that of ordinary life, were lived realities for people. These lived realities, Orsi explains, have not disappeared—people still claim to experience Marian apparitions and other such phenomena, as well as lived experiences of God in their daily lives (thus in more mundane manifestations). Therefore, Orsi's point is not about illustrating a narrative that frames early and medieval people as living with the worldview of presence while modern people were transitioning to a worldview of absence. This is not the case, as the Marian apparitions of Lourdes (Orsi's case study) happened in the modern world, and as our own study, that of Medjugorje, continues to unfold into the twenty-first century. Orsi further points to the fact that in addition to Lourdes, there are various claims of encounters with the supernatural outside of Europe, especially in Asia and Africa. "One could say that the parallel history of modernity, from one perspective, is the history of the ongoing eruption of presence into the spaces of its denial, to the transformation both of religious practice and imagination and the social world."[87]

Orsi's point is significant. It allows us to recognize that it is mistaken to simply reduce the supernatural to something that belongs to the ancient or medieval world, as if what is in play here is an out-of-date, superstitious worldview stemming from an unenlightened past and people, the product of the so-called Dark Ages and the periods preceding it. This is exactly the narrative that many historians have tried to convey, betraying their own discomfort with, and prejudice toward, the supernatural. Ruth Harris, in her masterful history of Lourdes, explains how this reality has touched historians of modernity:

> Understanding Lourdes requires a different approach and central to this, I believe, is a more sympathetic approach to the sustained appeal of the miraculous in religion, a topic which, on the whole historians of modern era have been wary of examining. While medievalists happily dwell on the supernatural—recounting narratives of saintly women sucking the pus of the sick, visions of nursing from Christ's breast and Eucharistic ecstasy—historians of the nineteenth century are usually ill at ease with, if not actually repelled by, the equivalent phenomena in their own period. The magical incantations of the peasant world, the pious murmurings of female devotees of the Sacred Heart and clerical communion with the Virgin, let alone miraculous cures, are usually seen as little more than superstitious remnants on the road to extinction. Relegating the study of such religious phenomena to the Middle Ages and early-modern period is one of the ways that historians have maintained a division between our "modern," "rational" age and the "irrational," ecstatic world that supposedly preceded it. The distinction allows them to erase any acknowledgement of the sustained attraction of religious mystery and adherence from more recent history.[88]

While it is true that in light of the rationalistic philosophies of the Enlightenment and post-Enlightenment, the *idea* of the supernatural has been marginalized, especially in Western European culture, the *lived reality* of the supernatural has not: as people have continued across the globe to report encounters of supernatural experiences, of the transcendent, in numerous ways. Therefore, if historians of the modern era continue to relegate such experiences to the Middle Ages, betraying their own discomfort with such phenomena in the process, they will have to ignore the lived experiences of modern people. Orsi notes that, "Presences have been marginalized and disciplined since the 16th century, in Europe and everywhere that Europeans touched, but the presence of the gods has persisted, abundantly so, and now they appear to be thriving again throughout the contemporary postmodern world."[89]

Whereas Orsi acknowledges this thriving, he also recognizes the academic dilemma associated with it. Orsi notes that "we have no idea what to make of the bonds between humans and the spirits really present to them within the limits of our critical theories."[90] Orsi realizes that in the modern compartmentalization of knowledge, it is theology that is pronounced to be the domain that examines such experiences. However, he rightfully notes that theology itself is a marginalized discipline within our modernist arrangement of knowledge. Amy Hollywood makes a similar observation in her critique of Wayne Proudfoot's method toward religious experiences, noting that the religious person's explanation of his or her extraordinary experience is never considered as one possible explanation by Proudfoot and, it goes without saying, "the theologian is almost entirely written out of the scholarly community in Proudfoot's account."[91] Orsi believes, therefore, that beyond theology, critical theory and history also need to seriously consider the study of the presence of spirits and humans to each other in their various interactions and all that those interactions inspire. This task cannot be restricted to theology but must extend to a new way and a new vocabulary in approaching critical theory and history.

Thus, as a historian, Orsi is making the call for a new historiography, naming the new approach "abundant history." He identifies events with supernatural entities such as Marian apparitions as "experiences of radical presence or realness," which he calls "abundant events."[92] These abundant events are not sufficiently studied under the current methods and tools of modern historiography. Orsi invokes the epistemology of William James, asking, "How would a history of a particular instance of the *more* (as William James named it) be written?" In response to the question, he offers the notion of abundant history as a contribution "toward such an alternative historiography, using a Marian apparition as a case study."[93]

Orsi underscores that visionary phenomena like Marian apparitions challenge the ideological presumptions of modernity's view of religion, a view that would like to restrict religion to "safe" categories of a naturalistic and private expression within the laws of nature.[94] Marian apparitions are anything but: they pertain to the supernatural, often inspire life-transforming conversions, cases of miraculous healings, a deeper spirituality of prayer and asceticism, worldwide devotion, and public pilgrimages, standing at odds with everything that modernity's view of a proper religious identity and practice, as naturalistic and private personifications, exemplify. However, Orsi sees that historians have not been freed from—and have in fact played into—modern naturalistic presumptions about religion and religious experiences in their scholarship: "Historians have inherited an ontology in which all events derive their meaning from the social and which is aligned with the modern privileging of absence. If this were not so, then we would find a place for the gods in our histories of the modern world. We would not reframe those occasions when humans and the gods come face to face with each other (as they did at Lourdes) in the registers of either function or resistance."[95]

By examining cases like Lourdes from the registers of "function or resistance," Orsi means that they are studied through the framework of social power and influence; thus, in the example of Lourdes, the apparitions have been examined within discourses that stress "power in the social worlds of modern France and global Catholicism."[96] This means that Lourdes could be studied as a symbol of power for the influence of the Church against anti-clerical authorities in France, and it could be studied in terms of promoting global Catholicism around the world, and it could be studied in terms of the consumer culture connected to a pilgrimage shrine, and through a variety of similar sociological and political dynamics. The problem is that such perspectives ignore the central element of the encounter between Bernadette and her Marian apparition, and how that encounter has influenced millions of people around the world who have been touched by Lourdes. As in this case, devotees and pilgrims are not being influenced by a desire for social power but, rather, by something deeper and purer, something "more," as William James stated. Even if power structures of church and state are somehow influenced by the phenomenon, that reality constitutes secondary or accidental circumstances associated with the phenomenon and not its core. This is what Orsi is getting at. We are missing the *core* of the experience, the essence and dynamism of the encounter: why it was so powerful for Bernadette and why it was able to inspire millions of people around the world for centuries to come. "But I am saying that our understanding of such matters will be opened in interesting and revealing ways if we do not back off, but find out way more deeply into what happened at Lourdes, in particular if we do not turn away from Bernadette's experience of the woman in white and then what happened as a result of this to those around these two figures."[97]

Orsi knows that what underlies this debate is a single ontology—one metaphysical worldview that presumes to be the basis of all truth. Modernity's worldview of naturalism and absence dominates academic culture, but it is not exclusive to it. This worldview perceives reality under the assumption that supernatural presences—and therefore the spiritual realm—are not real and that everything needs to be explained in natural terms. The call of making the transition from an approach of absence to an approach of presence, wherein the presence of supernatural forces is considered, necessitates not being "bound to a single account of human life," meaning to "a single ontology." Orsi understands, however, the prevalence of the idea that religions and, therefore, religious experiences are just social constructions. Such a notion is especially present in intellectual culture wherein it is the established dogma. In this sense, modern scholarship suffers from an "ontological 'vertigo,'" he points out, which leads to the "double intellectual tragedy" wherein the reality of people who experience extraordinary religious phenomena is constrained by the methodological limits of the scholars who study their experiences, as such experiences are studied through epistemological tools that assume from the outset that such encounters with the supernatural are not real. In the process, the individuals who undergo these extraordinary religious experiences no longer have the capacity to expand our understandings or imaginations, their voices being restricted by a modern ontology that opposes the authenticity of their experiences and, therefore, translates them into something else. "This is the price of ontological safety."[98]

Orsi acknowledges that context is, of course, important in understanding an experience; thus he is not writing against the importance of grasping the various dynamics of the cultural context of such experiences. Orsi understands the importance of studying apparitions from a psychological, cultural, sociological, or anthropological angle. But what he is arguing is that such studies, while important, are not sufficient in grasping the heart of the topic. Cultural context is certainly essential. However, cultural context cannot always account for the experience, a perspective which a lot of scholarship has attempted to advance.

"The confident translations of the stories men and women tell of their encounters with the supernatural into language that makes these stories about something else is based on the pervasive assumption in modern scholarship of the 'always already mediated nature of cultural relations.'"[99]

In this statement, Orsi gets to the heart of this ontological scandal. Two crucial points are important to highlight. First, an attempt is often made by scholars to translate the encounters that people have claimed with the supernatural into something else; the underlying assumption is that the supernatural experience cannot be real and therefore we must explain it in another way. Second, such a dominant perspective in academia is based on the assumption that everything in reality is mediated and therefore culturally constructed. Such a perspective sees the reality of the Marian apparition as being dependent on the visionary. In other words, the Virgin Mary does not actually exist in the form of a supernatural apparition or ontologically as a visitor from heaven, according to this perspective. That is, the Virgin Mary does not have existence independent of the visionary, but is a construction of the visionary's culturally mediated mind. There is a deeply rooted ideological bias in such a perspective informing the scholarship. The problem with this approach is that the nonexistence of the Virgin Mary has not been proven; it is assumed from the outset because such an assumption fits into modernity's metaphysic of absence.

Orsi's emphasis on mediation touches on issues surrounding the debate between constructivists and perennialists. Classical perennialists believed that mystical experiences are not mediated but, rather, constitute direct encounters with the transcendent, thus believing in what Orsi would phrase as a worldview of presence: people do encounter supernatural presences. Constructivists, in line with their reading of Kant's epistemology of mediation, believe that everything, including mystical experiences, are mediated and possess degrees of cultural construction. This logic is in line with the philosophical assumptions of the linguistic turn, permeating academic culture with its influence.

> From this perspective, Bernadette's encounter with *aquero* [the French word for "that one," the term with which Bernadette first identified her Marian apparition] and other such meetings of the human and the gods really present to them are events fully constituted and anticipated within the discourses, technologies, and vicissitudes of power in the social worlds of modern France and global Catholicism. The key words here are "produce," "create," "structure," and "construct." These terms limn an epistemology in which causal explanations premised on some version of social construction, whether political, psychological, or demographic, are sufficient. This is modernity's ontological singular.[100]

Orsi's proposal for the methodological approach of abundant history hopes to consider the essence of the experience—as best as is possible, meaning the dynamism at the heart of the encounter between the human and the divine, which the aforementioned approach does not touch on. It is this essence of the experience that has made Lourdes what it is: a place of inspiration and hope that has attracted millions of people around the world. "Relationships were at the core of the Lourdes event," Orsi explains.[101] Thus, beyond everything else—beyond all the externals and secondary circumstances, accidents, and consequences; beyond the social and political dynamics between the church and the state surrounding Lourdes; beyond the medical culture that formed around investigating healing miracles; beyond the economics and consumerism arising around a pilgrimage shrine; beyond the psychological and anthropological analyzing of Bernadette and her local culture—first and foremost there was a relationship: the relationship between Bernadette and the woman in white who appeared to her and called herself the Immaculate Conception. It is from this encounter and relationship that everything else receives its meaning, and from which other relationships connected to Lourdes originate. "What these phenomena share—from the water in Lourdes to the cheapest trinket sold in a souvenir shop—is that they are instances of relationship between human beings going about the course of their days and the powerful supernatural figure of the Blessed Mother who is present to them. This is what draws people to pilgrimage: relationships and the promise of relationships."[102] Here, we step into the heart of the matter.

Orsi's point that we need to advance beyond the methodological limitations of an ontology of absence dictating the rules of the game, how history and religion are to be studied, and consider a more robust perspective in an ontology of presence is, therefore, important on a couple of levels. First, this allows historical and religious subjects to be studied in terms of their own self-understanding instead of having the preexistent views of individual scholars imposed on them. In advancing a third-way method, between religious and secular confessional history, Gregory puts it thus: "The key distinction to be made is not between purportedly neutral, sophisticated, critical secular views and biased, naïve, uncritical religious ones, but rather between our convictions and assumptions, *whatever they are*, and those of the people we want to understand. The first prerequisite is one of the most difficult: we must be willing to set aside our *own* beliefs—about the nature of reality, about human priorities, about morality—in order to try to understand *them*."[103] Orsi's call for an ontology of presence would open the door to such a methodological consideration, as the naturalistic metaphysic that dominates historical and religious studies would have to cut the path to the possibility of truth outside its own epistemological and ontological assumptions. This is not to say that naturalism cannot explain certain events; but it is to say that naturalism cannot extinguish all the possibilities of knowledge, all modes of knowing and understanding. Such a reductive framework, limiting the study of religion, history, and other disciplines to one ontology restricts human understanding and advancement in knowledge. Gregory rightly stresses that "it seems incumbent on scholars of religion to proceed as if the religious beliefs of their subjects might be true, a possibility that a metaphysically neutral methodology leaves open. On what basis could one justify the contrary, other than dogmatism?"[104] Gregory's emphasis here is on the *might*—"might be true"— meaning that this emphasis does not constitute an uncritical acceptance of religious views but, rather, an open-minded approach that does not, out of an inverse dogmatism, assume from the outset that they cannot be true.

Another reason Orsi's approach is significant is for the very reason that Orsi expressed: because people have not stopped having experiences of presence. Spirits, and experiences of them, have not been demonstrably proven to disappear. Even in the twentieth century and into the twenty-first, people have continued to report Marian apparitions, visionary accounts of Jesus, weeping statutes and icons, the reception of the stigmata, miraculous healings, near-death experiences of the afterlife, and Pentecostal and Charismatic encounters with the Holy Spirit, often expressed in what is believed to be supernatural charisms and manifestations like speaking in tongues, being "slain in the Spirit," experiencing physical healings, and so on. Furthermore, the Catholic Church has an entire office within the Roman curia, the Congregation for the Causes of Saints, dedicated to the medical and scientific investigation of healing miracles, employing some of the most eminent doctors and scientists in the world to undertake the study. Such miracles are performed in the name of God through the intercession of deceased persons who may be prospects for canonization. This refers to the Church's official process of canonizing a man or a woman as a saint: it must be shown, through extensive medical examination, that a healing took place that was instantaneous and permanent, and is scientifically unexplainable, and which can, spiritually and theologically, be connected to the miraculous intercession of the deceased person, whose intercession the suffering person on earth was praying for.[105] Hence, there is a reciprocal relationship in play here between the suffering person on earth who prays for the intercession of the deceased person in heaven, who in turn brings the intention before God, who in turn works a miracle for the suffering person on earth, bringing the process full circle. This is a process rooted in an ontology of presence rather than absence.

It would, therefore, be highly erroneous and problematic to assume that experiences of presence, and therefore a history of presence, have disappeared with the medieval and ancient past. In the modern and post-modern world, people around the globe claim to encounter and possess a reciprocal relationship with the spiritual world and with supernatural agents. This reality has not disappeared. Granted, a critical naturalistic perspective may claim that all these aforementioned phenomena—from miraculous healings to saintly intercession from heaven, and the presence of apparitions—must have natural explanations. But the issue is that such a perspective is assumed and cannot be demonstrated, as it is making an ontological claim. "It is an undemonstrable belief to hold that any religious claim that violates metaphysical naturalism must be false."[106] It is thus a metaphysical belief, not an empirical fact. But it is a metaphysical belief that has, falsely, assumed the status of a neutral and objective fact in its seemingly universal acceptance as a method informing a majority of scholarly approaches. Gregory explains the issue eloquently:

> But is dogmatic naturalism a metaphysical belief parallel to religious beliefs, rather than a demonstrated truth or a neutral description of reality? . . . Any conviction that precludes in principle the possibilities that transcendent, spiritual reality exists, that divine revelation is possible, that divinely worked miracles occur or have occurred, that there is an afterlife, and the like, cannot itself be demonstrated *a posteriori*, in our present or in any realistically foreseeable state of knowledge.[107]

A major problem, if such a trend continues among scholars in assuming one metaphysical approach over the other, is the disconnection that it may continue to further between the academic world and the lived reality of people's experiences, and thus promulgate a disservice toward knowledge and understanding of those experiences. If the presence of spirits is "an absolute limit that contemporary scholars of religion and history refuse to cross," Orsi explained, "then they will miss the empirical reality of religion in contemporary affairs and they will fail to understand much of human life."[108]

Components of a Different Method

One answer to such methodological dilemmas—an answer that is displayed well when considering the scientific studies on the Medjugorje
visionaries—is to take up a different method for approaching the subject
of religious experiences. This different method must possess at least two
vital components. First, the method must take up the important call of
interdisciplinary integration, thus avoiding the danger of allowing one system of thought to monopolize the study of religious experiences. Second,
the method must have an inductive approach, thus avoid the danger of
scholars' applying interdisciplinary integration simply to justify their own
epistemological and ontological assumptions about religious experiences.

Regarding the first component, interdisciplinary integration, and the
danger that it avoids of allowing one discipline to dominate the study of
religious experience, it is important to note that such a monopolizing tendency has been present in the work of both *sui generis* and reductionistic thinkers, influencing the scholarship of both sides of the discourse.
William Rogers calls such an approach "the reductionistic model," explaining how it has been applied by both sides of the debate. In the reductionistic model, he enunciates:

> One dominating perspective or discipline assumes that it can
> interpret within its purview literally any phenomena, although
> to do so often necessitates a blurring of the richness and particu-
> larity of experience or perhaps a negation of self-understandings
> and alternative explanations given the same experience. Often the
> interpretative scheme is built from reflection on one dimension of
> life—for instance, valuing and decision-making or psychopathology
> and therapy—but its categories are then applied as though exhaus-
> tively sufficient to explain other realms of life—for instance, reli-
> gious belief and practice. The example could, of course, be reversed.
> There are instances where religious and philosophical perspectives
> have been assumed to account for all experience, demanding a
> reductionism of other realms of both experience and interpretation
> to those philosophical categories.[109]

Therefore, Rogers aptly concludes by acknowledging that the "difficulty
here is twofold: Not only does such reductionism imply an imperialization
of one set of interpretations over all others, but it also diminishes rather

than enhances our depth of appreciation," also noting that the "arrogance of such reductionistic judgments" is hardly the way to expand interdisciplinary cooperation.[110]

The points here are noteworthy, for they speak to important realities. One is an irony of sorts if we consider the perspective of *sui generis* thinkers. Scholars who adhered to a traditional *sui generis* understanding of religious experience were very skeptical and hesitant of reductionist approaches. Inversely, as Rogers hints, there is another irony here, for by abiding by a solely theological or religious interpretation (a *sui generis* framework), the hermeneutical approach of such scholars *also* constitutes a form of methodological reductionism, as the object of study is being reduced to the interpretative categories of one system of thought. Thus, what is being "reduced" in this regard is not necessarily the integrity of the religious experience, as the object of study, but the methodological approach—therefore, the hermeneutical lens—with its epistemological restrictions that exclude interdisciplinary integration. By contrast, in the reductionism of Freud, for instance, we see a twofold reductionism, wherein both the religious experience, as the object of study, and the methodological approach, with its epistemological restrictions, are the victims of reductionism. Both sides, however—the *sui generis* and the constructivist/attributional scholars—fall into forms of reductionism, whether it is singular or twofold in its execution.

While the first component of the proper method for studying religious experiences is to take up the call for interdisciplinary integration, the second essential component is that the method cannot fall into the trap of applying interdisciplinary research solely to justify predetermined conclusions about religious experiences. Such a deductive hermeneutic should be avoided in the study of religious experiences, for it poses too much risk of setting up research to support a faulty premise or conclusion, thereby becoming detrimental to progress in religious studies by risking the possibility of advancing false ideas. The example of Michael Carroll's work speaks for itself in this regard, as the author based his research on the premise that all Marian apparitions must be hallucinations or illusions, presuming to understand the Medjugorje apparitions as daily and long-term hallucinations—a theory that has, essentially, been empirically disproven as false by the scientific studies on the seers. Rogers warned that a reductionistic hermeneutic can blur the richness and particularity of a phenomenon. This can be seen, however, not only when one system of thought is used to monopolize or, as Rogers would say, "imperialize" the interpretative framework by elevating one discipline over all others, but also when interdisciplinary research is used to support the structural presuppositions of a hermeneutic whose underlying premise supports one predetermined conclusion over all others.[111]

Observing these methodological weaknesses that should be avoided, let us now consider a hermeneutic that by contrast may provide a methodological solution to the matter of interpreting religious experiences.

An Inductive Constructive-Relational Approach

Rogers, in fact, proposes a hermeneutic whose methodological approach seems ideal to the study of religious experiences; however, not without one reservation that deserves to be addressed (in fact, revised) if we are to consider the hermeneutic as an approach to the study of extraordinary and mystical experiences. Let us first consider the hermeneutical method before addressing the single reservation.

Rogers calls his hermeneutical method toward interpreting religious experience the "constructive-relational" approach.[112] It is important to note that the term "constructive" in the context of this method is used differently from the manner in which constructivist (vs. perennialist) scholars have been identified in previous chapters. "Constructive," in the context of this method, is pointing to the fact that as divergent perspectives are brought together to study a phenomenon, one is able to "construct" a larger picture of the phenomenon, possibly revealing elements about it that were not previously seen. This approach fits well with the call for interdisciplinary integration in the study of religious experiences, as the focus of the constructive-relational approach is to use multiple disciplines of study to interpret the subject without reducing the discourse to one hermeneutical framework, and without treating any one discipline as more valuable than another. Therefore, the method strives for a more holistic understanding by establishing a multidisciplinary approach that engages various perspectives for greater comprehension. Rogers explains that it "is unlikely that the wisdom of any single theoretical genius will be sufficient to comprehend the whole," thus advocating the need for interdisciplinary integration.[113]

The single reservation about Rogers's method, specifically in relation to the study of *extraordinary* religious and *mystical* experiences,[114] can be seen if we compare the approach to other approaches that advocate interdisciplinary integration. Thus, considering the methodology of Proudfoot and Taves, both scholars apply a deductive-attributional approach, one that begins with the predetermined premise that religious experiences are not inherently religious or mystical but they simply receive those ascriptions. These scholars, therefore, use interdisciplinary research to support the theory that the object of study is not, in its essence, what it is believed to be but simply receives that "essence" through subsequent ascriptions.[115] Rogers's hermeneutic, on the other hand, can tend toward the other extreme of this understanding, its inversion. According to Rogers, the constructive-relational method "is one which attempts to remain faithful to the primary phenomena, while encouraging relational attention to multiple disciplines of interpretation—moving toward a more constructive and holistic understanding (that cannot be 'claimed' or reduced by any *one* of the various approaches)."[116] Thus, Rogers's method uses interdisciplinary research to study the various dimensions of a religious experience but, ultimately, remains faithful to the theological groundings of that experience.

Here, it is important to note that Rogers's method, as he presents it in his essay, is used as a hermeneutical approach to studying various issues in religious and moral development. In other words, when Rogers speaks of "religious experience," he is not necessarily concerned with *extraordinary* religious experiences, such as mystical experiences, but applies the terminology more eclectically to denote various forms of *ordinary* religious or moral experiences. This is important to highlight, for Rogers's method can be perfectly suited as it is, without reservations, to studying such ordinary forms of religious or moral experience. However, if our focus is on extraordinary and mystical experiences, then a revision is necessary before the constructive-relational method can be used properly.

When approaching the subject of extraordinary religious experiences, one is essentially forced to tackle the underlying question of *authenticity;*[117] in many ways, this is the central question. Therefore, it would be equally erroneous to apply a method that uses interdisciplinary integration to "remain faithful to the primary phenomena" (Rogers) as it would be to use interdisciplinary integration to support a predetermined conclusion against the authenticity of the primary phenomena. The tenets of the constructive-relational method—specifically, the equal application of various disciplines to reach a more holistic hermeneutic in understanding the subject wherein no one discipline is treated as more important than the other—are important. However, if the method is to be applied to the study of *extraordinary* religious and mystical experiences, where questions of discerning authentic from false experiences become essential, then

the method should not attempt to "remain faithful to the primary phenomena" (only in the form of describing it accurately) but, on the other
hand, *be open to the possibility* of the primary phenomena, as well as *be
open to the possibility of alternative explanations* for the primary phenomena. There must be a complete intellectual openness to the hermeneutic
for it to have perfect integrity and objectivity in regard to extraordinary
religious experiences. Such an openness does not exclude any possibility
as a viable option for the phenomena of study—whether that possibility is
to be supernatural, natural, or pathological—and such an openness, by its
methodological nature, is inductive and not deductive. Therefore, a phenomenological investigation using interdisciplinary means is conducted
to ascertain a conclusion about the object of study, and not the inversion
wherein interdisciplinary research is used to support a predetermined
theory about the object of study. The former constitutes an appropriate,
integral way to use interdisciplinary and hermeneutical methods to investigate reports of extraordinary religious experiences. The latter constitutes
not an investigation of extraordinary religious experiences but, rather, a
systematic reduction of such cases to fit the preconceived structures (present within the hermeneutical methodology) of a scholar's predetermined
biases. The latter approach does not do justice to the multidimensional
richness of the subject.

One of the issues that have been voiced in this regard, as invoked by
Fitzgerald, Curtis, Spickard, Gregory, Orsi, and the work of Milbank, is the
ideological positioning of scholars performing the research on religious
experiences as allowing their own metaphysical assumptions to influence
their hermeneutical approaches and, therefore, their conclusions. This can
be seen from both sides of the ideological divide, whether it is Proudfoot
accusing *sui generis* thinkers of "protective strategies" in their scholarship
on religious experiences and Taves likewise calling for the violation of *sui
generis* taboos, or Curtis speaking of a secular heroism that fuels the ideological motives of many cognitive approaches, akin to Milbank seeing
various sociological approaches toward religion as disguised forms of metaphysics that domesticate the sacred into the secular. An important remedy for the matter of ideological positioning that becomes embedded in
the hermeneutical approaches of scholars is to structure scholarly methods toward the study of extraordinary religious experiences as *inductive*,
rather than deductive, approaches. This simple but crucial methodological
decision can become the difference between a hermeneutic that ascertains
as much as can be known about a religious experience, on the one hand,

and a hermeneutic whose conclusions become a reflection of a scholar's predetermined assumptions about the religious experience, on the other hand. An example associated with Medjugorje can illuminate this point.

In the introduction of this work we observed the case of Dr. Marco Margnelli, the Italian neurophysiologist who was an expert on altered states of consciousness[118] and who, as an avowed atheist, admitted that he traveled to Medjugorje in the summer of 1988 looking for "any evidence that would contradict it or expose it as a fake."[119] However, despite his own preexistent views on the subject, Margnelli did not deductively posit a metaphysic that set the rules for explanation and then simply read the results back from the rules he had set. On the contrary, he decided to approach the matter inductively, from the bottom up. Thus, Margnelli traveled to Medjugorje, conducted an array of scientific tests on the visionaries, and reached his conclusions, which became different from his initial assumptions, only after empirically examining the totality of the events there.[120] This is in contrast to the method of Carroll, for example, who, as has been observed, deductively presumed that all such phenomena as Marian apparitions can be naturalistically explained and posited an explanation of hallucination for the experiences of the Medjugorje visionaries that fit the hermeneutical confines of his predetermined conclusion. The fact that subsequent scientific studies on the visionaries provided empirical evidence against any form of hallucination in their experiences points to erroneous conclusions in Carroll's approach. Margnelli, however, despite having his own prejudices against the experiences in Medjugorje (admitting that he came there hoping to disprove the experiences as false), reached polar opposite conclusions from his initial assumptions because he allowed the scientific studies (thus, the empirical data) and firsthand experiences of the phenomena that he, as an investigator, encountered to guide his conclusions, not the ideological biases of his predetermined views.

Recall how after conducting his examinations of the apparitions, Margnelli described the experiences of the visionaries as "a genuine state of ecstasy," declaring that the visionaries do enter into another state of consciousness; and, while admitting that as a scientist (therefore, an etic observer) he cannot make the judgment whether the apparitions are authentic or not, he did acknowledge that "we were certainly in the presence of an extraordinary phenomenon."[121] These conclusions were radically different from Margnelli's initial, *a priori* judgments about the phenomenon in Medjugorje, and they speak volumes to the importance of an *inductive* method in studying such experiences, especially when considering the contrast to the deductive approaches of other scholars, like Carroll with Marian apparitions or Freud with "oceanic feelings," whereby the conclusions are predetermined and one is only seeking results that can satisfy the hermeneutical *and ontological* confines of those conclusions.

The benefits of an inductive constructive-relational approach are many. Let us further examine how it can bring diverse, at times seemingly antithetical, hermeneutical approaches together by considering the matter of etic and emic perspectives in greater detail.

Etic and Emic Perspectives

As previously noted, Taves makes the distinction, in articulating the logic behind her approach, between emic and etic observers—the former referring to "insiders" in relation to the religious experiences that are being observed and the latter referring to "outsiders." Therefore, an emic observer (coming from an insider's perspective) is an individual who is associated with a certain tradition (such as Catholicism or Pentecostalism, for example) and can make judgments about the authenticity, or lack thereof, of religious experiences on the basis of the criteria for discernment and analysis that his or her tradition provides. Etic observers, on the other hand, "are those who do not consider the event in question as special (that is, as an OE [originary event]) and thus stand outside the composite broadly defined by the OE. If the originary event is understood as deeming Jesus as the Messiah, then Jews and Muslims (along with atheists, Buddhists, and many others) stand outside the composite defined by that OE."[122] Herein lies the basis for distinguishing between approaches that study the meaning and authenticity of a religious experience within the interpretive structures of a theological tradition while also incorporating other sciences, such as psychology or neuroscience, on the one hand; and approaches that study the processes by which meaning is ascribed to an experience as being religious, on the other hand. Taves explains: "Insiders typically turn to matters of authenticity—that is, to criteria for discerning the authenticity of the experience in light of the beliefs that they hold with respect to the OE—while scholars taking an etic stance typically try to explain what made the experience of the OE *seem real to the subject*."[123] Taves expounds:

> Only emic observers are capable of making determinations of authenticity. This is simply a matter of logic, not policy. Etic

observers, because they do not view the events in question as originary, simply have no criteria for judging whether a sensory perception authentically reproduces an originary event or not. Although
observers cannot argue for or against the authenticity of a re-creation
of an OE from an etic perspective, etic observers can and frequently
do argue that a claim is delusional—that is, an incorrect inference
about external reality—on the grounds that an event (taken specifically or generally) should not be deemed religious, and thus that no
practice is capable of re-creating it.[124]

Where there needs to be caution, however, is in considering how far interpreters take etic perspectives, especially when evident restrictions are recognized regarding how much the hermeneutic can say. For example, Taves
considers the question of how spontaneous experiences might seemingly
become real to subjects. She analyzes the matter by looking at research
that studies dreams and that "links dreams to play."[125] In this regard, she
considers the work of J. Allen Cheyne, who "theorizes that dreams allow
individuals to simulate threats and other unusual situations in which practice can improve the individual's ability to respond. Dreams thus may provide a safe space in which to test the limits of our ability to respond under
exaggerated and unusual conditions."[126] Taking into account Cheyne's theories about dreams, Taves goes back to Barnard's out-of-body experience
that he (the subject) understood as a mystical experience. She writes: "Our
test case—Barnard's sense of being lifted outside himself—was triggered
by the attempt to visualize (simulate) an extreme situation, specifically his
attempt to envision his self-awareness not existing after his death. Though
his experience was triggered by informal visualization and took place during the day, it would seem likely that it involved processes of this sort."[127]

One issue is that Taves does not consider that Barnard's ascription—
his understanding of the experience as *mystical*—may in itself possess
some validity, considering the profound and unique nature of the felt
experience.[128] Taves is associating Barnard's experience with processes
that have been theorized about in dreams, essentially associating the experience with a natural process, such as dreaming. But within such an association there is an implicit reductionism that does not take into account
various factors, perhaps most importantly the fruit of the experience: it
changed Barnard, his life and goals, drastically, inspiring him to pursue
studies in Eastern meditation and scriptures and become a practitioner of
spirituality. Most dreams usually do not have such life-altering results for

their subjects, implying that there is something radically different about the experience that does not fit perfectly into the same phenomenological association as the components underlying a dream state.

While caution must be expressed in terms of recognizing the interpretive limitations of etic perspectives, it is also important to note that such perspectives are essential, being incredibly useful toward helping scholars reach a greater understanding of religious subjects, particularly phenomena such as extraordinary religious experiences. This is especially the case when etic perspectives are used to purify religious experiences of false interpretations through the inclusion of empirical sciences whose contributions about the various elements of a phenomenon are able to ascertain a clearer, more holistic, understanding of the object of study. Let us consider and clarify this notion by turning to criteria of evaluation that have incorporated such ideas.

Criteria of Adequacy

Dermont A. Lane explains that a number of Christian theologians see the need to evaluate religious experiences on two different levels; one level he categorizes as "criteria of adequacy" and the other as "criteria of appropriateness."[129] The purpose of the criteria of adequacy is to evaluate whether "a religious interpretation of experience is at least consistent with a secular understanding of life."[130] Conversely, the criteria of appropriateness, as applied by Christian theologians, evaluate "at the same time that this religious interpretation of experience is faithful to the demands of a specifically Christian understanding of existence."[131] Thus, the latter applies theological, specifically Christological, criteria to the discernment of religious experiences. For our purposes, however, we will look here at the former—the criteria of adequacy.

Lane uses the work of the Catholic theologian David Tracy, who outlined three main criteria of adequacy in formulating an interpretative framework for analyzing religious experiences. Tracy suggested that criteria of adequacy should consider: (1) meaningfulness: that the religious interpretation should be rooted in common human experience, being associated with lived, universal, immediate human experience; (2) meaning: that the cognitive and conceptual claims of an understanding of religious experience be coherent with, and not contradict, the established claims of secular and scientific knowledge; (3) truth: that the religious experience reaffirms the worthwhileness of existence and the well-being of humanity, the necessary triumph of good over evil, seeing God as the source of existence and, therefore, the basis for safeguarding humanity's well-being.[132]

Lane explains that:

> The application of these "criteria of adequacy" should not be construed as a reduction of Christian theology to the norms of the secular world. What it does mean, however, is that the construction of theology for tomorrow, on the basis of these "criteria of adequacy," will be spared the embarrassment of having to apologise for religious ideas that are at variance with the established findings of the modern, scientific community. Christian theology, to remain credible, must be safeguarded against idolatry, naïve psychological projections, and the creation of a new "God of the gaps." In an address to the Pontifical Academy of Sciences Pope John Paul II points out that "the critical spirit (of science) purifies it (religion) of a magical conception of the world and of surviving superstitions and exacts a more and more personal and active adherence to the faith." The "criteria of adequacy" are designed to perform these tasks. Furthermore, the theologians who employ these "criteria of adequacy" note explicitly that these criteria alone are insufficient; they must be complemented by Christian "criteria of appropriateness."[133]

In the purpose of the criteria of adequacy, as criteria meant to purify the ideas and experiences underlying religion by testing whether religious ideas and experiences live up to the established facts of secular and scientific knowledge, we see a direct connection to etic perspectives.

Taves explained that etic observers study religious phenomena from the perspective of the outsider. Therefore, for etic observers who approach religious experiences from purely secular perspectives—meaning without the recognition of grace at work—they cannot comment on the authenticity of such experiences (as the incorporation of grace is necessary to do so), but they can comment on experiences being inauthentic (as their sciences can ascertain such conclusions in applicable cases). Thus, neuroscience and psychology can show that persons who believe to be experiencing religious visions are, in fact, suffering from cases of hallucination or epilepsy, among other possible pathologies—purifying, in the process, false ideas about "religious experiences." Conversely, as in the case of the Medjugorje seers, the opposite can happen: neuroscience and psychology (and other sciences) can show that persons who believe they are experiencing religious visions are not suffering from any form of pathology but that their experiences do, in fact, live up to the established tests of modern secular and scientific knowledge, satisfying the criteria of adequacy and purifying the experiences of false interpretations.

It is important to recognize, therefore, that etic approaches help us with the criteria of adequacy, and thus are especially useful. The problem is when etic perspectives are taken too far, beyond what they are able to show and into the realm of speculative reductionism, theorizing more than they can empirically demonstrate and reaching for natural explanations through metaphysical speculation instead of empirically ascertaining them. To be sure, it is fine, and should be considered appropriate, when an etic perspective is able to show that a purported religious experience is, in fact, something else, disproving its validity. Such an example is not a case of speculative reductionism but, rather, empirical clarification (as the topic is not being "reduced" to something that it is *not* but is being clarified to what it *is*); such an approach is helpful to both religion and science, as it uses the latter to purify the former of false ideas.

However, there can be a danger when etic observers prematurely dismiss the metaphysical assumptions of an ontology of presence, the dismissal itself being undergirded by a different (often, purely secular) metaphysical assumption of an ontology of absence. The danger is that such a dismissal can lead to a method that is never able to get to the heart of the experience because it does not consider *the possibility*[134] that the believer's ascription of his or her experience may in itself possess some validity, having to do with the essence of the experience. In such a case, one form of metaphysics (presence) is dismissed for another (absence), as Orsi and others would contend. There is in certain experiences—again, the example of Medjugorje speaks well to this reality—that something "more" which science, and therefore a completely etic perspective, cannot fully account for in terms of explanation. Essentially, what is necessary is to combine etic and emic approaches for a more holistic method and, consequently, understanding of such subjects. This leads to a constructive-relational approach. Such an approach does not exclude the possibility of grace (respecting the Jamesian "more" in religious experiences), therefore the possibility of a religious or spiritual explanation, while incorporating every perspective (thus both etic and emic), even seemingly antithetical ones,[135] that can help to ascertain a more complete and richer understanding of the subject of study.

The Constructive-Relational Approach in Medjugorje

It is important to recognize that the approach of the various scientific teams that investigated the Medjugorje visionaries did fit into the structural guidelines of the intellectually open, constructive-relational method proposed here. Consider Dr. Henri Joyeux's French team. Dr. Joyeux admitted, after reading René Laurentin's book on Medjugorje, that he and his colleagues were intrigued about the apparitions "but not convinced."[136] Yet, they decided to travel to Medjugorje and draw their conclusions *after* conducting their scientific examinations. Thus, from the very beginning, no predetermined presuppositions were made by the French doctors as to whether the experiences of the visionaries are authentic or not; the question was left open, displaying an intellectual integrity that did not, from the threshold, fall into ideological filters of preconceived interpretation or determinism. This intellectual openness was followed by an execution of constructive-relational methodology in the sense of bringing a number of disciplines, and therefore a diversity of doctors and scientists, together to investigate the various elements of the phenomenon in order to reach a more holistic and comprehensive understanding of the experiences of the visionaries.

The same constructive-relational methodology was used here in chapter 5 by examining the various interdisciplinary studies conducted on the visionaries by the different scientific teams, and by incorporating a cooperative interaction between the various disciplines whose integrated contributions can help to construct a fuller picture of the phenomenon of study. Such a method was especially evident in the way the EEG tests and the algometer testing on the Medjugorje visionaries were combined. The latter was able to show by itself that the visionaries are impervious to pain during their apparitions. The former was able to show, among other things, that the visionaries are in a state that is hyper-awake during their apparitions. However, by combining the algometer results with the EEG tests we reach an even deeper understanding of the phenomenon: as in a state of hyper-wakefulness, an individual would be very vulnerable to pain; the fact that the visionaries were hyper-awake and yet impervious to pain presented a paradox that is scientifically unexplainable. This scientifically inexplicable paradox points, first and foremost, to the uniqueness of the apparitional experience that the visionaries encounter, but it also points to the strength of the constructive-relational methodology in the way that integration of two disciplines allows deeper understanding of the phenomenon.

Therefore, the central components of the constructive-relational method are especially seen in the way the various studies from the diverse scientific teams were analyzed in chapter 5 in juxtaposition to one another. The constructive-relational methodology is perceivable in the approach the scientific teams took in studying every component regarding the visionaries' experiences using a multidisciplinary approach: the daily psychological stability of the visionaries; the neuroscientific component of measuring brain-wave activity during their apparitions; the ocular and visual functions to test the integrity of the altered state of consciousness; computerized polygraph examinations that were able to contrast the heart-beat activity and nervous systems of the visionaries during an apparition state and a state of hypnosis, distinguishing between the two; electrocardiograph (EKG) tests examining heart-rate activity; the algometer tests measuring the seers' sensitivity to pain before and during the apparition; and so on. A remarkable degree of multidisciplinary integration was applied in an inductive manner to reach a number of empirically observable, intelligent conclusions about the extraordinary religious experiences of the visionaries, eliminating a number of alternative natural and pathological explanations for the apparitions and, therefore, narrowing the choice of viable possibilities that can be used as explanations for the phenomenon in Medjugorje.

Conclusion

THIS WORK INVESTIGATED a number of issues about epistemological debates and hermeneutics concerning extraordinary religious experiences. The hermeneutical history of this work began with William James, a figure whose influence reappears throughout the book. James believed in using the human person as a "document" of study to understand religious experiences—the *documents humains*, he called the approach.[1] James, therefore, used first-person accounts of extraordinary religious experiences to form his method, placing an emphasis on individual experience as the underlying foundation of all religion. In the case of Medjugorje, we have an even more direct and immediate example of using the *documents humains* to study religious experiences—in this case, the emphasis is not on accounts of individual experiences but on the actual individuals while they undergo their experiences, empirically examining these experiences as they transpire.

James was no stranger to the cultures of medical reductionism, on the one hand, and the world of Marian apparitions and visions, on the other. Mark Micale explains that in the late nineteenth and early twentieth centuries, when major debates were arising between the worlds of science and religion, or even more specifically between the worldviews of psychology and Christian mysticism, France was a major setting for the discussion, as two important events were taking place in France that greatly influenced the discourse. Jean Martin Charcot was making his breakthrough contributions to the study of hysteria, while at the same time he was becoming one of the first to rediagnose the extraordinary religious experiences of the great Christian mystics and visionaries, like Francis of Assisi and Teresa of Avila, as forms of hysteria. At the same time, Bernadette Soubirous, the young peasant girl from the town of Lourdes reported experiencing appa-ritions of the Virgin Mary, which eventually led to Lourdes becoming a popular pilgrimage site and a healing shrine—a combination that resulted in the formation of the famous Medical Bureau of Lourdes, established to medically investigate alleged miraculous healings. Micale explains that as the great cultural debates were occurring in France between science and religious experience, a few years later, at the turn of the nineteenth century, "the most thoroughgoing critique of the practice of rediagnos-ing religious phenomena in neuropathological terms came from the pen of an American physician-philosopher who had observed both Charcot's lectures at the Salpêtrière and events at Lourdes."[2]

Micale was referring to the pen of William James, who wrote a chapter in his *Varieties of Religious Experience* titled "Religion and Neurology," offer-ing his critique of the "medical materialism" he had been exposed to in the worlds of psychology and medicine.[3] Evelyn Underhill was not blind to this reality either, particularly the great influence that Charcot and French psychology played in rediagnosing the religious experiences of mystics, visionaries, and saints into psychopathological categories. In chapter 3, we observed how Underhill referred to those whom James accused of "medi-cal materialism" as the "strangely named rationalists," who, she explained, were convinced they had settled the debate between religion and science, or that between religious experience and pathology. Underhill wrote that the "strangely named rationalists"

> feel that they have settled the matter once for all by calling atten-tion to the obvious parallels which exist between the bodily symp-toms of acute spiritual stress and the bodily symptoms of certain forms of disease. These considerations, reinforced by those com-fortable words "auto-suggestion," "psychosensorial hallucination" and "association neurosis"—which do but reintroduce mystery in another and less attractive form—enable them to pity rather than blame the peculiarities of the great contemplatives. French psychol-ogy, in particular, revels in this sort of thing: and would, if it had its way, fill the wards of the Salpêtrière with patients from the Roman Calendar.[4]

The great debate—what Underhill termed "that eternal battle-ground"[5]—which both she and James (and like-minded thinkers) partook in with challenges to the radical reductionism that reinterpreted all extraordinary religious experiences into pathological categories, continues to this day.[6]

We have noted that neurologists such as Andrew Newberg and Eugene D'Aquili have questioned the all-encompassing reductionism of scholars who attempt to explain away the extraordinary experiences of the great mystics through diagnoses of an epileptic seizure, theorizing instead that distinctions between such states (the mystical and the epileptic) exist—despite some similarities—and need to be recognized. We have also observed how skeptical thinkers such as Richard Dawkins and Michael P. Carroll reduced all forms of visionary and apparitional experience (for Carroll's project, specifically Marian experiences) to pathological or natural categories of interpretation such as hallucination, illusion, or lucid dreaming. This modern reductionism, seeing religious experiences as a product of the human mind (and not any transcendent source), has its roots in earlier Enlightenment and post-Enlightenment philosophy about God and religion, as promulgated through such thinkers as David Hume, Benedict Spinoza, and later Ludwig Feuerbach, and Friedrich Nietzsche—and eventually, through the psychoanalytical phenomenology of Sigmund Freud.

In chapter 4, we observed the developments of the hermeneutical and epistemological debates between scholars of religious experience, with particular attention given to the perennialist–constructivist debate, its philosophical foundations, and the deeper issues underlying the discourse. Traditional perennialism came under scrutiny and received a great challenge in the late twentieth century with the scholarship of Steven Katz and fellow constructivists. This constructivist scholarship questioned perennial notions that identified extraordinary religious experiences as unmediated, universal, and transcending sociohistorical categories of interpretation with an essentialism that is *sui generis* in nature—in a class of its own. The subsequent work of scholars like Wayne Proudfoot and Ann Taves added to the debate by incorporating ideas from attribution theory to the discourse, in many ways renewing constructivist conclusions through a combination of interdisciplinary integration and ascriptive phenomenology. Taves especially has made a contribution in expanding the grasp of constructivist conclusions on religious experiences by considering not only top-down (culture sensitive) but also bottom-up (culture insensitive) processes in analyzing these experiences, thus promulgating a method that takes the idea of unconscious processing more seriously than did traditional constructivism.

Classical perennialism, however, also witnessed an intellectual renewal in the latter twentieth century with the work of Robert Forman and fellow neo-perennialists. These scholars wrote of a pure conscious experience that, in refreshing perennial ideas of an unmediated, trans-historical and cross-cultural universalism, pointed to the presence of a *content-less*, mystical experience across religious traditions that purportedly transcends the epistemological framework of a constructivist hermeneutic. Neo-perennialist scholarship has even led to a reexamination of the philosophical foundations that constructivism is based on, by tackling the underlying issue of Kantian epistemology and the fundamental question of whether Kant's thinking has been misapplied in constructivist interpretations of extraordinary religious experiences.

Traditional models of thinking have been challenged in this debate, as a bigger issue—one whose consequences extend beyond religious studies—underlies the current constructivist and neo-perennialist debate. Within this discourse are the institutional frameworks of thinking that have greatly influenced academic culture. Specifically, by challenging constructivism, neo-perennialists have also challenged the dominant framework of thought that has permeated the humanities and social sciences after the linguistic turn—challenging, therefore, not just scholars of religion but also an entire established way of understanding scholarship in much of academia. Inversely and previously, by challenging traditional perennialism, constructivists were challenging the (previously) dominant *sui generis* model that was instrumental in posing resistance to interdisciplinary integration within religious studies by elevating religious experiences into a class of their own. The central caution that adherents of the *sui generis* model showed toward embracing interdisciplinary integration lies in the underlying issue of reductionism—the concern that other disciplines of study would be used not to explain but to *explain away* extraordinary types of religious experiences in light of natural or pathological categories of interpretation. The fear was not without merit, as various nineteenth- and twentieth-century scholars have applied theories from other disciplines to reductively reinterpret religious experiences into natural and/or pathological explanations.

As chapters 5 and 6 examined, the scientific studies on the Medjugorje visionaries are able to make important contributions to such debates about religious experience. Behavioral and psychological studies have consistently shown the visionaries to be mentally healthy individuals, thereby excluding such diagnoses as hysteria, neurosis, psychosis, or any indications of fraud on their part. The neuroscientific studies, starting with the EEG tests measuring their brain waves, have shown that the apparitional experiences are not the product of any lucid dream or sleep state, pathological hallucination, or epilepsy, eliminating these alternative explanations. Furthermore, computerized polygraphs, measuring different neurovegetative systems and heart-beat rates, were able to distinguish between the apparitional state that the visionaries enter and other states of consciousness—such as of hypnosis, of visualization of mental images, and of a normal wakeful state—showing that the apparitions are not self-induced through suggestion, visualization, or imagination, as it was not possible to "reproduce" the same apparitional state through natural efforts.

Ophthalmological studies on ocular and visual functions further corroborated the depth of the altered state of consciousness that the visionaries enter. Visual hallucination was excluded as an explanation, the ocular systems of the visionaries being shown to be anatomically and functionally normal. The blasting of 1,000-watt bulbs at the pupils of the visionaries did not produce a reaction, their eyes remaining unusually dilated and their blinking remaining minimal (and at times nonexistent), showing a significant disconnect from the external world. One doctor called it the most complete "suspension of consciousness of their relationship with the exterior world" she had ever witnessed in a subject.[7] Electro-oculogram tests showed that the eye balls of the visionaries become simultaneously immobile at the beginning of the apparitions—simultaneity to one-fifth of a second—and begin to simultaneously move again after the apparitions. One ophthalmologist on the French team said that such synchronism "was so far beyond the capacity of normal human functioning that no form of collusion or manipulation could account for it."[8]

Auditory and voice functions were also tested, and the results were able to exclude further alternative explanations for the apparitions. Auditory hallucination of an epileptic type was eliminated, as the various pathways to the brain from the ear were shown to be normal in the visionaries. While the auditory pathways were normal, interestingly the visionaries were shown to be impervious to external noise during their apparitions, a 90 decibel sound producing no reaction. It was further observed that the voices of the visionaries become silent during apparitions, the larynx (controlling the vocal cords) stopping completely, although their lips and facial muscles continue moving normally as if communicating. The normal movement of the facial muscles excludes the possibility of catalepsy, as in a cataleptic state the muscles would be immobile. The algometer results, showing the visionaries to be impervious to pain during apparitions, further showed the depth of their suspension from the external world when they have their visionary experiences, alongside the pupil tests (blasting lights into the eyes with no reactions) and the auditory tests (blasting a 90 decibel noise into the ears without a reaction). The results of these tests, combined with the EEGs that showed the visionaries to be hyper-awake during apparitions, presented a scientifically unexplainable paradox about the ecstasies that they enter as a state of hyper-wakefulness would make one very vulnerable to exterior pain and stimuli—yet the visionaries remain impervious.

A lot of recent scholarship has been dedicated to applying cognitive sciences like neuroscience to study various types of alleged religious experiences. Unfortunately, very little attention has been given in academia to the scientific studies of the phenomenon in Medjugorje, a subject that has been largely ignored by scholars of religion. This is notwithstanding the fact that the uniqueness of the Medjugorje apparitions as spontaneous and visionary phenomena—constituting not just religious experiences but, more distinctly, *extraordinary* religious experiences—gives scholars of religion the opportunity to study a much rarer, and perhaps more significant, form of experience than more common, cultivated, or self-induced "religious experiences."[9] A newly emerging field in recent years has been the area of study known as "neurotheology," wherein the interdisciplinary connections between neuroscience, spirituality, and theology have been formed to better understand the relationships between the brain and religious experiences, behaviors, and beliefs—or, as Newberg and D'Aquili have put it, to better "understand the link between brain function and *all* important aspects of religion."[10] Newberg emphasizes that originally studies in neurotheology "analyzed the relationship between electrical changes in the brain (measured by electroencephalography, EEG) and meditative states."[11] However, more "recent studies of religious and spiritual practices have utilized brain imaging techniques such as single photon emission computed tomography (SPECT), positron emission tomography (PET), and functional magnetic resonance imaging (fMRI)."[12] Scholars of neurotheology—sometimes called "neurotheologians"—have used EEGs to study meditative states, and therefore such states have been incorporated into their scholarship. However, visionary and apparitional experiences such as those of the Medjugorje visionaries, although tested by EEGs, and although providing a significant opportunity to study an exceptionally rare religious phenomenon, have yet to be incorporated into mainstream scholarship on neurotheology, again remaining largely ignored. The fact that more recent neuroimaging technologies (SPECTs, PETs, and fMRIs) have been utilized to study spiritual practices,[13] such as meditation or prayer, shows that the door is open for original research on that which has remained unstudied: the examination of extraordinary religious experiences with such neuroimaging techniques, as three of the Medjugorje visionaries still report experiencing daily apparitions.

Newberg warns of the limitations of such studies, however; or, more specifically, the limitations of techniques required to orchestrate such studies. He emphasizes that placing "a subject in a scanner with noise or in uncomfortable positions might adversely affect the ability to study accurately a particular practice."[14] With the experiences of the Medjugorje visionaries, however, such a "limitation" would not even be a factor, for the simple aforementioned reason that during their apparitions the visionaries experience such a profound disconnect from the exterior world that no provocation—visual, auditory, or physical (whether measuring their sensitivity to pain, blasting 90 decibel sounds in their ears, putting an opaque screen in front of them, or blasting their pupils with strong lights)—is able to disrupt their altered state of consciousness, their purported visionary experiences. Thus, this constitutes further reason as to why the experiences of the Medjugorje visionaries can be a fruitful subject of exploration for scholars of neurotheology to advance more original research in the field.

Significance of the Medjugorje Studies

The various scientific studies on the Medjugorje seers do allow us to make important judgments regarding major issues in discourses and debates about extraordinary religious experiences. René Laurentin has written about the scientific studies on the seers, and played an instrumental role in bringing the French team to Medjugorje to conduct the first major examinations on the visionaries. However, what Laurentin has not done, which this work has, is incorporate the results of the Medjugorje studies into major academic discourses on extraordinary religious and mystical experiences, particularly modern hermeneutical and epistemological discussions and debates.[15] This has been the first time that the scientific studies on the visionaries have been placed into conversation with major thinkers on religious experience, and the results have been illuminating. Medjugorje's contribution is fourfold to discourses on religious

experience: it is (1) epistemological, (2) hermeneutical, (3) beneficial to
strengthening the criteria of adequacy in discerning religious experiences,
and (4) ontological. Let us consider these individually.

Epistemological Contributions to Studying
Religious Experiences

The studies in Medjugorje show that it is erroneous to perceive all accounts
of extraordinary religious experiences through a reductive and absolutist
epistemology of "medical materialism," or an uncritical rationalism,[16] as
if every extraordinary religious phenomenon can be understood though
an *alternative* pathological or natural explanation in order to fit the pre-
ordained structures of an established system of thinking. There are elements within the Medjugorje studies that contradict and undermine such
reductive epistemologies, pointing to the "more" (to use James's phraseology) in the experiences of the visionaries.

It is important to recognize that when considering epistemologies
of radical reductionism, the arguments underlying such approaches are
trans-historical—*trans-historical* in the sense that such arguments challenge extraordinary religious experiences that have existed *throughout
history* and that have been subjected to various reductive epistemologies,
such as those proposing an epileptic-seizure or hysteria diagnosis to universally explain away the integrity of religious experiences. Here, thinkers
like Jean-Martin Charcot, Simone de Beauvoir, and Oliver Sacks come to
mind, each reducing the experiences of *medieval* mystics to psychopathological categories of interpretation. Yet the Medjugorje studies, by using
contemporary scientific technology and examination to investigate a contemporary phenomenon, present a more nuanced picture of the mystical phenomena, showing that these earlier interpreters who placed such
experiences into pathological categories may not have adequately grasped
the complexity and potential integrity of such cases. Here, it is important
to note that one contemporary case study cannot, of course, vindicate every
claim of extraordinary religious experience of the past—as natural and
psychopathological explanations are probable in various instances—but it
can challenge the universal applicability of such reductive interpretations
by providing a scientifically investigated exception to the rule that undermines the radical nature, even the trans-historical perennialism, of such
reductionist interpretations. As the Medjugorje studies show, one can no
longer claim that all such mystical phenomena can be totally understood

through natural or pathological explanations; this type of radical reductionism has been scientifically challenged and empirically undermined in the case of Medjugorje.

Hermeneutical Contributions to Studying Religious Experiences

The second major contribution that the Medjugorje studies make is hermeneutical. The studies show that a proper method for examining extraordinary religious experiences must have the two important components of being inductive and constructive-relational. Otherwise, there is a great risk of methodologically setting up one's research to support faulty premises and, therefore, advancing false conclusions about religious experiences. This was very evident in the work of Michael P. Carroll, who began with the premise that all Marian apparitions must be either illusions or hallucinations, and he developed a psychoanalytical phenomenology that could theoretically articulate an intelligent justification of that premise. Notwithstanding, Carroll's thesis, particularly in the case of the Medjugorje apparitions as daily hallucinations, has been proven to be false by the scientific studies of the visionaries.

Carroll's methodological approach was not entirely new or original, but it can, in fact, be traced back to the godfather of psychoanalysis, Sigmund Freud, who attempted to explain away the phenomenon of "oceanic feelings" through a hypothesis from psychoanalytical theory that could give such experiences a natural genesis with psychological origins. Freud's mistake, as observed, was twofold: (1) he allowed one discipline to monopolize the truth about religious experiences; and (2) his method began deductively with a general principle that constituted a predetermined conclusion about the object of study. Thus, not only did Freud's method avoid interdisciplinary integration, but it was also structured in such a way as to allow nothing but one conclusion to prevail—that of explanatory reductionism.

James warned of the epistemological tendency in academia of denigrating subjects that do not fit into the interpretive structures of an established intellectual system, seeing this propensity especially in regard to the treatment that mystical phenomena had received. William Harmless notes the ideological biases that James himself faced in delivering his Gifford Lectures with the intention of taking such phenomena, as extraordinary religious experiences, seriously:

James took religious experience seriously and knew that such an opinion went against the intellectual grain of many in his Edinburgh audience. Science and religion were then bitter antagonists. And so in his opening lecture, he took pains to justify his study of religious experience against scientific detractors, whom he labeled "medical materialists." He knew that many dismissed religious experiences as either undiagnosed medical pathology or psychosexual obsession.[17]

With scientists taking religious experiences seriously in Medjugorje, using a diverse array of medical and scientific examinations to study the case, the radical reductionism that medical materialism has historically advanced to explain away such phenomena begins to lose its prowess. Prominent rein-terpretations of religious experiences, such as Freud's dismissal of religion as a neurosis, are challenged.

As mentioned, Freud made the methodological decision of monopo-lizing the study of religious experience within the interpretive structures of one discipline. This is a mistake, however, that scholars from both perspectives—those critical of religious experiences and those support-ive of them—have made. Wayne Proudfoot accused perennial thinkers who apply a *sui generis* approach of hiding behind a "protective strategy," a protective strategy that defends religious sensibilities against modern scholarship and criticism by avoiding interdisciplinary integration. This is a valid critique, one articulated by Ann Taves as well, that speaks to an underlying ideological agenda within scholarship that shuns interdiscipli-nary integration.

However, as equally valid critics of Taves's interdisciplinary approach have noted, interdisciplinary integration does not by itself advance a more objective discourse on religious experiences, for the perspectives being integrated contain their own ideological positioning. Here, the work of John Milbank makes an insightful contribution, particularly in Milbank's contention that the social sciences possess their own ideological agendas when studying religion that tend to domesticate the sacred into the secu-lar, thus becoming a disguised form of metaphysics. Milbank's exposition of the "secular," as a historically constructed philosophy with its own *sui generis* assumptions undermining the popular understanding of the term as an autonomous vantage point of neutral discourse, is significant and reinforces the concerns of many scholars.

On the one hand, Proudfoot, Taves, and like-minded scholars make a noble call for interdisciplinary integration in studying the various facets of religious experiences, providing a valid critique of a classic perennial philosophy that created a false "sacred space" for religious experience through an ahistorical, *sui generis* essentialism that refused the contributions of other sciences. On the other hand, Milbank and other scholars are right to see that popular assumptions about the secular, as an autonomous neutral realm of objective discourse, contain their own *sui generis* pretensions, creating a false "sacred space" in the epistemological myth of secular neutrality. What such critics are saying is that, within many social and natural sciences there exists not only an epistemology but also an ontology at play. A hermeneutic that assumes secular neutrality does not allow for consideration of the metaphysical presuppositions embedded in that perspective.[18] Furthermore, as an exposition of Taves's approach has shown, one cannot make metaphysical claims about religious experiences while also claiming a naturalistic approach, as the underlying tenets of naturalism are in that case violated, the approach becoming a more subtle form of metaphysics.

Considering these various points, what is at issue are the numerous ideological commitments that scholars bring to their approaches to religious experiences. Consequently, multiple concerns arise. Of particular importance is the question of how we approach the study of religious experiences without applying the ideological filtering that various hermeneutics, whether perennial, neo-perennial, constructivist, attributionist, or any other, bring to their approaches. At the same time, the concerns evoked by scholars on each side of the debate about religious experience deserve further attention.

Interdisciplinary integration is by itself not enough to formulate an ideal approach to the study of religious experiences, owing to the ideological dimensions that scholars from various disciplines can bring to the subject. What is necessary is the incorporation of an *inductive* methodology alongside this interdisciplinary integration, such that being both inductive and interdisciplinary it can help mitigate the intrusion of ideological commitments in the study of religious experiences. In an approach that is both inductive and interdisciplinary, there is a healthy middle ground between perennialist and constructivist concerns. On the one hand, the interdisciplinary integration alleviates any constructivist fears of classical perennialism with *sui generis* pretensions that would exclude the value of other disciplines. On the other hand, fears that the study of religious experiences will become a wholly reductionistic enterprise are also diminished, alleviating perennialist concerns that interdisciplinary integration would be used simply to explain away such experiences, as the inductiveness of the approach would not allow for the preexistent assumptions of individual scholars (whether for or against religious experiences) to predetermine their conclusions.

The example of Dr. Marco Margnelli highlights the importance and advantage of approaching religious experiences through an inductive method. Although Margnelli admittedly came to Medjugorje with deeply held biases against the experiences of the visionaries, hoping to disprove them as false, as a scientist he was open to studying the events in Medjugorje inductively. Through a phenomenological process of investigation, this allowed him to reach different conclusions from his initial assumptions. He conducted an array of medical tests on the visionaries, had a lived experience with concurring phenomena around the apparitions, and allowed the scientific evidence and its conclusions to inductively speak for themselves. It was a process of open-ended, scholarly discovery, as opposed to applying presuppositions to deductively fashion the outcome. Margnelli's approach merits contrast with that of Michael Carroll. Instead of inductively investigating the various phenomena in Medjugorje, Carroll formulated a hypothesis from psychoanalytical theory that supported his predetermined conclusions against the authenticity of the apparitions. Thus, his approach was neither inductive nor interdisciplinary, applying the epistemological framework of one discipline to monopolize the interpretation of Marian apparitions. The fact that scientific studies on the visionaries would contain empirical evidence disproving Carroll's conclusions shows what a dangerous method a deductive approach can be in regard to examining such religious experiences. Margnelli's example, on the other hand, speaks to the contrary reality: presenting an inductive approach that remedied the potential predicament of a researcher's ideological commitments getting in the way of trustworthy scholarship.

This is why an inductive, constructive-relational method is best in studying extraordinary religious experiences. The approaches of the major scientific teams that studied the Medjugorje visionaries fit the structural guidelines of this inductive, constructive-relational method, which in its intellectual openness does not presume to know the nature of the subject but, through a phenomenological process of investigation and discovery, can reach intelligent conclusions after examining it. This result was achieved interactively, without regarding any one discipline as more valuable than the other; instead, multidisciplinary results were brought together to form a full picture of the visionary experiences.

Contributions to the Criteria of Adequacy

The third major contribution that the Medjugorje studies make pertains to the criteria of adequacy, particularly the criterion that seeks to measure religious experiences against the best scientific and secular knowledge available so as to better understand the veracity (or lack thereof) of such experiences. The component of the etic perspective is present here, wherein external scientific knowledge is used to determine as much as is possible about the phenomenon. Here, the input is connected to hermeneutics, as it is directly associated with the constructive-relational method. With its all-encompassing methodology, the constructive-relational approach incorporated neuroscience, psychology, and other sciences to flesh out the criteria of adequacy inherent in the Medjugorje experiences so as to measure whether those experiences meet the tests of modern secular and scientific knowledge. Indeed, this was the approach used by the teams who examined the visionaries.[19]

However, since the constructive-relational method is all-encompassing, application of such a method does not have to stop at the criteria of adequacy; it could, in fact, venture beyond it to consider spiritual or theological interpretations of the phenomenon, such as the 1985 Italian team did by combining the work of scientists, psychologists, and theologians to reach its twelve-point conclusion about the experiences of the visionaries. While, as was noted, the anthropologist Paolo Apolito was critical of this analysis—the combination of scientific empiricism with theological speculation (or, one could say, the combination of etic and emic perspectives)—there is a degree of validity to consider regarding this approach. That is, considering the constructive-relational approach of incorporating a theological framework along with every other discipline that may help in ascertaining a more holistic understanding of religious experiences (both the etic and the emic) is a way of keeping the door open to the Jamesian "more," instead of presumptuously closing off that cognitive consideration. With overly ascriptive/attributional approaches, interpreters may ascribe meaning to everything *except* the religious experience itself, too often dismissing the very possibility that there may be veracity in the purported content that the believer ascribes to the experience. The constructive-relational approach, however, keeps this possibility open by incorporating perspectives that can account for criteria of adequacy but also by considering perspectives that extend beyond it into the realm of ontology, spirituality, theology, and grace. It's a matter not of restricting knowledge but of keeping the epistemological considerations to the some-thing "more" accessible.

Ontological Contributions to Studying
Religious Experiences

The Medjugorje studies point to the Jamesian "more," as the visionar-ies are experiencing something during their apparitions that is scientif-ically unexplainable, identifying a "mysteriousness" to their experiences. A devoted naturalistic-materialist perspective might say that just because science cannot explain the apparitions now, that does not mean something natural is not happening—that science will eventually be able to explain it. But such a perspective remains metaphysical, claiming faith in a future that has not been demonstrably proven, that it is dogmatic worship given to the idol of scientism. Currently, what has been demonstrably proven and is supported by science is the fact that the Medjugorje visionaries are having an experience during their apparitions that is unique—that it is so profound that it transcends scientific and natural understanding. The Medjugorje studies thus further point to the epistemological poverty of assuming a metaphysical naturalism to explain all events and phenom-ena, as is currently the case dominating the study of religion and other disciplines.

Robert Orsi has written that "abundant events" like Marian appari-tions point to the limitations of an ontology of absence in studying his-tory and religion. Bruce Greyson has said that extraordinary encounters like near-death experiences show the limitations of a biological naturalism in fields like psychology, neuroscience, and philosophy of the mind. The Medjugorje studies support and complement such claims.

Orsi sees that a singular ontology has taken over the hermeneutical and epistemological assumptions underlying the work of historians and religious studies scholars. His claim that there is a need to expand our thinking to an ontology of presence is supported by the Medjugorje stud-ies: the visionaries are reporting an experience with a spiritual presence—an "abundant event," in Orsi's language—and no natural discipline, meaning no methodological explanation that would align with an ontol-ogy of absence, has been able to account for these experiences. Indeed, their experiences point to the possibility of an ontology of presence in their Marian encounters, a possibility that is supported by empirical evidence that has eliminated other natural and pathological explanations, thus also eliminating explanations that would fit into an ontology of absence, and thereby pointing to its limitations and to the need to consider other modes of thinking. If scholars refuse to open the door to other modes of thinking, then as Orsi has suggested, there remains a large disconnect between the world of scholarship, committed as it has been to the dogma of metaphysical naturalism, and the lived experiences of people who have reported encounters that transcend this naturalist understanding of reality.

The scientific studies have used psychological and neuroscientific examinations of the mystical experiences of these visionaries, signifying (just as scholars who have contributed to important works like *Irreducible Mind* have pointed to with other examples) that there are certain exceptional experiences that challenge dominant models of physicalism and materialistic reductionism that underscore the methodological assumptions of disciplines like psychology, neuroscience, and philosophy of the mind. The Medjugorje apparitions support this perspective with scientific evidence as to why the ontological "isms" that dominate modern scholarship—metaphysical naturalism, physicalism, uncritical rationalism, and reductive materialism—appear insufficient as explanatory models for such phenomena, thereby challenging their universal viability and dogmatic acceptance, and pointing to the need to pursue models that are open to other ontological possibilities.[20]

Reconciling Religion and Science

The Medjugorje studies bring clarity and much needed reconciliation to the dichotomous manner in which religion and science have in recent centuries been presented—as representing two divergent and contradictory worldviews. This has especially been the case since the 1800s in regard to the cultures of psychology and medical science, on the one hand, and Christian mysticism and supernatural religious beliefs, on the other. France provided a particularly important setting in highlighting this cultural divide between the influential medical reductionism of Charcot and the Neurology Clinic at La Salpêtrière Hospital in Paris, and the visionary experiences of Bernadette Soubirous and the alleged healing miracles associated with the events in Lourdes.[21] It is appropriate historically that a Marian apparition site was the center of debate in this cultural divide between science and religion. It is also appropriate, then, for the events at a modern Marian apparition site, in Medjugorje, to provide the much needed reconciliation of this debate.

What is significant about the experiences in Medjugorje is how the cultures of science and religion *have come together* to ascertain a comprehensive understanding of the nature of this phenomenon. An interdisciplinary integration transpired through a diversity of scientific studies on the Medjugorje visionaries and their religious experiences. This integration challenged the dichotomous ideology that pitted science and religion against each other, as two irreconcilable opposites that could not work together—two divergent worldviews that could not coexist.

Dr. Philippe Loron, who examined the Medjugorje visionaries in 1989, was (some irony is noteworthy) the former head of the Neurology Clinic at the Salpêtrière Hospital in Paris, an heir to that famous medical institute that at a certain point in history was renowned for rediagnosing mystical experiences into pathological categories and for dismissing mystics and visionaries as hysterics. About the experiences of the visionaries in Medjugorje, Dr. Loron would say: "This is the first time that medical science has been involved to such an extent in evaluating the phenomenon of ecstasy. And, in the process, what was confirmed in several ways was the moral and psychological integrity of the visionaries."[22] Unlike his famous predecessors at La Salpêtrière, this doctor was not able to diagnose a case of visionary experience as belonging to the condition of hysteria—or any other psychopathological category. Science would no longer allow it.

Notes

1. See Maureen Orth, "The World's Most Powerful Woman," *National Geographic* 228, no. 6 (December 2015): 30–59; Joan Wester Anderson, *Forever Young: The Life, Loves and Enduring Faith of a Hollywood Legend—the Authorized Biography of Loretta Young* (Allen, TX: Thomas More, 2000), 259–264; George P. Matysek Jr., "Justice Scalia Urges Christians to Have Courage," *Catholic Review*, October 25, 2010, www.catholicreview.org/article/work/justice-scalia-urges-christians-to-have-courage; Darko Zubrinic, "Jim Caviezel's Spiritual Journey from Medjugorje to Mel Gibson's Passion," *Crown: Croatia World Network*, April 19, 2010, www.croatia.org/crown/articles/9958/1/Jim-Caviezels-spiritual-journey-from-Medjugorje-to-Mel-Gibsons-Passion.html; Michael O'Loughlin, "Stephen Colbert's 'Catholic Throwdown' with Patricia Heaton," *Crux*, January 20, 2016, https://cruxnow.com/faith/2016/01/20/stephen-colberts-catholic-throwdown-with-patricia-heaton/; Martin Sheen portrayed Fr. Jozo Zovko in the 1995 drama film *Gospa*, directed by Jakov Sedlar and produced by Igor Prižmić.

2. See Daniel Klimek, "Pope John Paul II, 'Medjugorje – The Spiritual Heart of the World,'" *Medjugorje.org*, March 16, 2011, www.medjugorje.org/wordpress/archives/33; also, Slawomir Oder with Saverio Gaeta, *Why He Is a Saint: The Life and Faith of Pope John Paul II and the Case for Canonization* (New York: Rizzoli, 2010), 167–169; Oder dedicates a few pages of his book to observing the late pope's love for Medjugorje.

3. Quoted in Randall Sullivan, *The Miracle Detective: An Investigation of Holy Visions* (New York: Grove Press, 2004), 46.

4. Mary Craig, *Spark from Heaven: The Mystery of the Madonna of Medjugorje* (Notre Dame, IN: Ave Maria Press, 1988), 78.

5. Sullivan, *Miracle Detective*, 46.

6. Ibid., 47.

7. Ibid., 400, 48.
8. Ibid., 47.
9. Ibid., 48.
10. Ibid., 397–398.
11. Ibid., 400.
12. These included Italy's largest consumer protection group, Codacons, Giovanni Panunzio's Anti-Brainwashing Telephone Line, and the CICAP (the Committee for Investigation of the Paranormal), "whose cofounder Luigi Garlaschelli, the head of the organic chemistry department at the University of Pavia, was considered the leading scientific investigator of claimed miracles involving tears of blood," someone who took pride in exposing religious frauds; see Sullivan, *Miracle Detective*, 398, 47, 48.
13. Denis Nolan, *Medjugorje and the Church*, 4th ed. (Santa Barbara, CA: Queenship, 2007), 26.
14. "John Paul II and the Statue that Cried Blood," *RomeReports*, video uploaded May 17, 2011, www.youtube.com/watch?v=GHGH_b68MlY. See interview with Vatican journalist Andrea Tornielli within the video clip.
15. Nolan, *Medjugore and the Church*, 26.
16. Ibid., 165.
17. Pope Benedict XVI, originally quoted in the Italian newspaper *Ill Messagero* (June 1, 2005); cited here from Nolan, *Medjugorje and the Church*, 27.
18. Ibid.
19. This February 10, 2005 *Zenit*, report is cited in Nolan, *Medjugorje and the Church*, 26.
20. Ibid., 165.
21. Ibid., 27.
22. Quoted in Sullivan, *Miracle Detective*, 207.
23. See Marco Margnelli, *La droga perfetta: neurofisiologia dell'estasi* (Milan, Italy: Edizioni Riza, 1984). Michael O'Carroll explains that Margnelli "is a specialist in ecstasy and altered states of consciousness, author of a work *La Droga Perfetta*, in which he seeks to establish a parallel between changes in consciousness induced by chemical means and by religious experience." See Michael O'Carroll, *Medjugorje: Facts, Documents, Theology*, 4th ed. (Dublin: Veritas Publications, 1989), 70.
24. Sullivan, *Miracle Detective*, 207.
25. Ibid., 208.
26. Although such scholars do disagree on levels of constructivism—some being "complete constructivists" while others only believing in partial constructivism in a mystical experience. The nuances of these hermeneutical lenses will be examined in detail in chapter 4.
27. Chapter 4 will delve into the details of this debate.

28. Jensine Andresen and Robert K.C. Forman, "Methodological Pluralism in the Study of Religion: How the Study of Consciousness and Mapping Spiritual Experiences can Reshape Religious Methodology," in *Cognitive Models and Spiritual Maps: Interdisciplinary Explorations of Religious Experience*, ed. Robert K. C. Forman and Jensine Andresen (Bowling Green, OH: Academic Imprint, 2000), 8. Andresen and Forman's article first appeared in the *Journal of Consciousness Studies* 7, no. 11 (2000): 7–14.

29. Ibid., 10.

30. Chapter 3 tackles the nuances of these threefold visionary categories in depth.

CHAPTER 1

1. Sullivan, *Miracle Detective*, 72.

2. See Mark I. Miravalle, *The Message of Medjugorje: The Marian Message to the Modern World* (Lanham, MD: University Press of America, 1986), 1–6; Sullivan, *The Miracle Detective*, 67–107; Craig, *Spark from Heaven*, 11–20; Sandra Zimdars-Swartz, *Encountering Mary: From La Salette to Medjugorje* (Princeton, NJ: Princeton University Press, 1991), 233–240; Svetozar Kraljevic, *The Apparitions of Our Lady at Medjugorje, 1981–1983: A Historical Account with Interviews*, edited by Michael Scanlan, T.O.R. (Chicago: Franciscan Herald Press, 1984), 3–41, 121–150; Wayne Weible, *Medjugorje: The Message* (Brewster, MA: Paraclete Press, 1989), 6–25. The vast majority of literature on Medjugorje constitutes devotional and apologetic works from religious presses; however, a small number of academic and journalistic works have been published on the topic. Miravalle's book (constituting the author's doctoral dissertation) is the most comprehensive theological examination of the messages of Medjugorje, studying their veracity within the Catholic tradition through a hermeneutic of continuity that considers the Medjugorje messages in light of the teachings of the Church Fathers, the Second Vatican Council, and major—Church-approved—apparitions such as Lourdes and Fátima. Sullivan's book (a journalistic account) provides the most comprehensive and in-depth account of the history of the apparitions, as well as the varieties of scientific studies conducted on the visionaries throughout the decades. Craig's journalistic account provides an informative overview of the early years of the apparitions, covering historical, anthropological, and ecclesial elements regarding the apparitions, as well as the major scientific studies conducted on the visionaries during the 1980s. The book by Zimdars-Swartz is one of the first academic works dedicated specifically to the phenomena of Marian apparitions; her section on Medjugorje covers the subject of *secrets*, as the Medjugorje visionaries have reported receiving secrets from the Virgin that allegedly are to affect the world (similarly to claims made by other Marian visionaries, such as the children of Fátima). The work by Weible, a former journalist, is one of the

most popular devotional books on the subject, combining a firsthand journalistic account with a believer's devotion for the authenticity of the apparitions.
As Zimdars-Swartz points out, however, sources on Medjugorje do disagree on
certain facts; Weible is an example. His understanding of how the Medjugorje
visionaries are to transmit the secrets that they allegedly receive from the Virgin
is different from René Laurentin's understanding, as articulated in his work *The
Apparitions at Medjugorje Prolonged*, trans. J. Lohre Stiens (Milford, OH: Riehle
Foundation, 1987). See Zimdars-Swartz, *Encountering Mary*, 237. It is noteworthy that conflicting facts between Medjugorje authors have, most often, been
present in regard to secondary information (see, as another example, note 70 in
chapter 5). However, the primary details of the history of the apparitions have
been consistent in most works, although some works (like that of Sullivan and
Craig) are more informative in the detail they provide. Though showing evident favor for the apparitions, Weible's work is useful for scholarly, and specifically historical, purposes as it provides a firsthand account of some of the major
events and figures of the early years of the apparitions. Weible was present, for
example—and provides a lively account of the event—when the then-bishop of
Mostar Pavao Žanić gave a (now) notorious homily in the parish of Medjugorje
in July 1987, making his opposition public through a condemnation of the apparitions. It was that opposition that made Medjugorje an increasingly controversial subject in the Catholic Church. See Weible, *Medjugorje*, 274–282. The book
by Kraljevic, a Franciscan priest who was present during the beginning of the
apparitions, provides a valuable historical account, including original interviews
with the visionaries and with one of the earliest doctors to examine the seers
as their experiences were unfolding. The greatest area of difference between
authors is in interpretation of the authenticity of the apparitions. Miravalle and
Weible are proponents of the authenticity of the apparitions; Craig provides a
Jungian psychological theory in postulating a natural explanation for the apparitions; while Sullivan and Zimdars-Swartz leave the question open.

3. Mirjana Soldo with Sean Bloomfield and Miljenko Musa, *My Heart Will Triumph*
(Cocoa, FL: CatholicShop, 2016), 11.
4. Wayne Weible, *Letters from Medjugorje* (Brewster, MA: Paraclete Press, 1991), 2.
5. Kraljevic, *The Apparitions*, 142.
6. As quoted in Craig, *Spark from Heaven*, 14.
7. Soldo et al., *My Heart*, 12.
8. Ibid.
9. Ibid.
10. Ibid.
11. Craig, *Spark from Heaven*, 15.
12. Soldo et al., *My Heart*, 28–29.
13. Ibid., 47–48.
14. Ibid., 48.

15. Craig, *Spark from Heaven*, 16.
16. Kralijevic, *The Apparitions*, 9.
17. Quoted in Craig, *Spark from Heaven*, 17.
18. Ibid., 169, as reported by Craig.
19. Quoted in Joseph A. Pelletier, A.A., *The Queen of Peace Visits Medjugorje* (Worcester, MA: Assumption Publications, 1985), 15.
20. Soldo et al., *My Heart*, 28.
21. Quoted in Sullivan, *Miracle Detective*, 79.
22. Craig, *A Spark from Heaven*, 17.
23. Ibid., 16–17.
24. Ibid., 18.
25. Ibid., 18.
26. Kralijevic, *The Apparitions*, 16.
27. Cited in Christine Watkins, *Full of Grace: Miraculous Stories of Healing and Conversion through Mary's Intercession* (South Bend, IN: Ave Maria Press, 2010), 192.
28. Miravalle, *Message of Medjugorje*, 24.
29. Ibid., xiii, 110.
30. Soldo et al., *My Heart*, 83.
31. Ibid.,
32. Ibid., 120.
33. Miravalle, *Message of Medjugorje*, 46.
34. Ibid.
35. Ibid., 53.
36. Ibid., 55.
37. Ibid., 25.
38. Soldo et al., *My Heart*, 185.
39. Ibid.
40. Kralijevic, *The Apparitions*, 126.
41. Soldo et al., *My Heart*, 186.
42. Kralijevic, *The Apparitions*, 124.
43. Soldo et al., *My Heart*, 186.
44. Miravalle, *Message of Medjugorje*, 54.
45. See Todd Burpo with Lynn Vincent, *Heaven Is for Real: A Little Boy's Astounding Story of His Trip to Heaven and Back* (Nashville, TN: Thomas Nelson, 2010). For the film, see Randall Wallace and Christopher Parker, *Heaven Is for Real*, TriStar Pictures 2014.
46. Eben Alexander, *Proof of Heaven: A Neurosurgeon's Journey into the Afterlife* (New York: Simon and Schuster, 2012).
47. Sullivan, *Miracle Detective*, 155.
48. Soldo et al., *My Heart*, 151.
49. Ibid., 152.

50. Ibid., 151.
51. Sullivan, *Miracle Detective*, 156.
52. Soldo et al, *My Heart*, 152.
53. Sullivan, *Miracle Detective*, 155.
54. Soldo et al., *My Heart*, 150.
55. Sullivan, *Miracle Detective*, 155.
56. Heather Parsons, *Marija and the Mother of God* (Blanchardstown, Dublin: Robert Andrews Press, 1993), 123.
57. Soldo et al., *My Heart*, 150.
58. Ibid.
59. Sullivan, *Miracle Detective*, 156.
60. Ibid.; Soldo et al., *My Heart*, 150.
61. Miravalle, *Message of Medjugorje*, 54.
62. Parsons, *Marija and the Mother of God*, 123.
63. Ibid.
64. Ibid.
65. Ibid.
66. Kralijevic, *The Apparitions*, 121–122.
67. Sullivan, *Miracle Detective*, 156.
68. Ibid.
69. Parsons, *Marija and the Mother of God*, 124.
70. Sullivan, *Miracle Detective*, 156.
71. Soldo et al., *My Heart*, 152.
72. Kralijevic, *The Apparitions*, 122.
73. Soldo et al., *My Heart*, 151.
74. Kralijevic, *The Apparitions*, 121.
75. Soldo et al., *My Heart*, 150.
76. Kralijevic, *The Apparitions*, 122.
77. Soldo et al, *My Heart*, 150.
78. Parsons, *Marija and the Mother of God*, 124.
79. Ibid.
80. Craig R. Lundahl, "A Comparison of Other World Perceptions by Near-Death Experiencers and by the Marian Visionaries of Medjugorje," *Journal of Near-Death Studies* 19 (2000): 45–52.
81. A recent edition of Moody's classic with a foreword by Eben Alexander is Raymond Moody Jr., *Life After Life* (New York: HarperCollins, 2015).
82. A recent edition of the book, with a foreword by Ira Byock, is Elisabeth Kübler-Ross, *On Death and Dying: What the Dying have to Teach Doctors, Nurses, Clergy & Their Own Family* (New York: Scribner, 2014).
83. Dean Mobbs and Caroline Watt, "There Is Nothing Paranormal about Near-Death Experiences: How Neuroscience can Explain Seeing Bright Lights,

Meeting the Dead, or Being Convinced You are One of Them," *Trends in Cognitive Sciences* 15, no. 10 (2011): 447–449.

84. Bruce Greyson, Janice Miner Holden, and Pim van Lommel, " 'There Is Nothing Paranormal about Near-Death Experiences' Revisited: Comment on Mobbs and Watt," *Trends in Cognitive Sciences* 16, no. 9 (September 2012): 445.

85. Mobbs and Watt, "Nothing Paranormal," 447–449.

86. Greyson et al., "Nothing Paranormal Revisited," 445.

87. Ibid.

88. Ibid.

89. Ibid.

90. Cf. Bruce Greyson, "Implications of Near-Death Experiences for a Postmaterialist Psychology," *Psychology of Religion and Spirituality* 2, no. 1 (2010): 37–45, esp. 41–43.

91. "However, scholars need to respond to all relevant data, not just data supporting the *a priori* assumption that NDEs must be reducible to known neurophysiology"; Greyson et al., "Nothing Paranormal Revisited," 445.

92. Greyson, "Implications of Near-Death Experiences," 38.

93. Dean Mobbs, "Response to Greyson *et al.*: There is Nothing Paranormal about Near-Death Experiences," *Trends in Cognitive Sciences* 16, no. 9 (2012): 446.

94. "The particular challenge of NDEs to materialist reductionism lies in one central feature that makes this phenomenon uniquely important in any consideration of the mind—brain problem: specifically, the occurrence of vivid and complex mentation, sensation, and memory formation under conditions in which the materialist models of the mind deem impossible." See Greyson, "Implications of Near-Death Experiences," 38.

95. Michael Grosso, *The Man Who Could Fly: St. Joseph of Copertino and the Mystery of Levitation* (Lanham, MD: Rowman and Littlefield, 2016), 10.

96. Enrico Facco, Christian Agrillo, and Bruce Greyson, "Epistemological Implications of Near-Death Experiences and Other Non-Ordinary Mental Expressions: Moving Beyond the Concept of Altered States of Consciousness," *Medical Hypotheses* 85, no. 1 (2015): 85–93.

97. Important works that have been published on this topic include the book by Edward F. Kelly, Emily Williams Kelly, Adam Crabtree, Alan Gauld, Michael Grosso, and Bruce Greyson, *Irreducible Mind: Toward a Psychology for the 21st Century* (Lanham, MD: Rowman & Littlefield, 2007); and a later book by Edward F. Kelly, Adam Crabtree, and Paul Marshall, eds., *Beyond Physicalism: Toward Reconciliation of Science and Spirituality* (Lanham, MD: Rowman & Littlefield, 2015).

98. Cf. Facco et al., "Epistemological Implications," 85–93.

99. Lundahl, "Comparison of Other World Perceptions," 46.

100. Ibid.

101. Ibid.

102. Ibid., 46–47.
103. Ibid., 47.
104. Ibid.
105. See Howard Storm, *My Descent into Death: A Second Chance at Life*, foreword by Anne Rice (New York: Doubleday, 2005).
106. Lundahl, "Comparison of Other World Perceptions," 50–52.
107. Craig R. Lundahl and H. A. Widdison, *The Eternal Journey: How Near-Death Experiences Illuminate Our Earthly Lives* (New York: Warner Books, 1997).
108. Lundahl, "Comparison of Other World Perceptions," 49.
109. See the comparative table in Lundahl, "Comparison of Other World Perceptions," 51.
110. Ibid., 50.
111. Ibid., 51.
112. Ibid., 50.
113. Ibid., 50–51.
114. Ibid., 51–52.
115. Ibid., 52.
116. The other distressing types the authors categorize as "inverse" and "void." See Nancy Evans Bush and Bruce Greyson, "Distressing Near-Death Experiences," *Missouri Medicine* 111, no. 5 (2014): 372.
117. Ibid., 375.
118. Ibid., 372–373.
119. Ibid., 373.
120. Parsons, *Marija and the Mother of God*, 124.
121. Quoted in Bush and Greyson, "Distressing Near-Death Experiences," 373.
122. Ibid., 373.
123. Quoted in James Paul Pandarakalam, "Marian Apparitions and Discarnate Existence." Royal College of Psychiatrists, 2013, p. 15, http://www.rcpsych.ac.uk/pdf/James%20Pandarakalam%20Marian%20Apparitions%20and%20Discarnate%20Existence.x.pdf.
124. Sullivan, *Miracle Detective*, 121.
125. Ibid.
126. Kralijevic, *The Apparitions*, 149.
127. Ibid.
128. Miravalle, *Message of Medjugorje*, 55.
129. Sullivan, *Miracle Detective*, 210.
130. Miravalle, *Message of Medjugorje*, 55.
131. Ibid.
132. Kralijevic, *The Apparitions*, 95.
133. As quoted in Miravalle, *Message of Medjugorje*, 55.
134. Sullivan, *Miracle Detective*, 210.

135. For a good discussion on the secrets of Medjugorje, see Zimdars-Swartz, *Encountering Mary*, 233–240, and Soldo et al., *My Heart*, 120–121, 140–142.
136. Mirjana, quoted in Sullivan, *Miracle Detective,* 189.
137. Ibid.
138. Zimdars-Swartz, *Encountering Mary*, 238–239.
139. Soldo et al., *My Heart*, 146.
140. Ibid., 120.
141. Ibid.
142. Ibid., 121.
143. Ibid.
144. Zimdars-Swartz, *Encountering Mary*, 234.
145. Kralijevic, *The Apparitions*, 127.
146. Soldo et al., *My Heart*, 120.
147. Ibid., 142.

CHAPTER 2

1. Paragraph 10 of *Dei Verbum*, the dogmatic constitution on divine revelation promulgated at the Second Vatican Council, explains: "It is clear, therefore, that, in the supremely wise arrangement of God, sacred tradition, sacred scripture, and the magisterium of the church are so connected and associated that one of them cannot stand without the other. Working together, each in its own way under the action of the one holy Spirit, they all contribute effectively to the salvation of souls." See Austin Flannery, ed., *Vatican Council II: The Basic Sixteen Documents—Constitutions, Decrees, Declarations* (Northport, NY: Costello Publishing, 1996), 103–104.
2. Mark Miravalle, *Private Revelation: Discerning with the Church* (Santa Barbara, CA: Queenship, 2007), 4; Zimdar-Swartz, *Encountering Mary*, 9.
3. Benedict XIV, *Heroic Virtue: A Portion of the Treatise of Benedict XIV on the Beatification and Canonization of the Servants of God*, vol. III, trans. the English Fathers of the Oratory (London: Thomas Richardson and Son, 1850), 395.
4. Ibid.
5. Benedict cites the authority of Augustine and Thomas Aquinas, as well as the Italian cardinal, philosopher, and theologian Thomas Cajetan (1469–1534) to make the point. See ibid., 396.
6. As cited in Miravalle, *Private Revelation*, 8–9. For the original source, see John XXIII, Papal Radio Message at the Close of the Celebration of the Centenary of the Apparitions of the Immaculate at Lourdes, *L'Osservatore Romano*, February 18, 1959, daily edition, 1.
7. Popularly known as "Saint Faustina," her full religious name was Sister Maria Faustina Kowalska, born as Helena Kowalska in the village of Glogowiec, Turek County, Lodz Province, Poland, on August 25, 1905.

8. Steven Fanning, *Mystics of the Christian Tradition* (London and New York: Routledge, 2001), 204–205.

9. George Weigel, *Witness to Hope: The Biography of Pope John Paul II* (New York: HarperCollins, 1999), 386.

10. Maria Faustina Kowalska, *Diary of Saint Maria Faustina Kowalska: Divine Mercy in My Soul*, 3rd ed., with revisions, 8th printing (Stockbridge, MA: Marian Press, 2011), 320. In Faustina's diary the voice of God, which includes Jesus, is high-lighted in boldface type throughout the work, while the voice of the Virgin Mary, who Faustina also claimed spoke to her, is highlighted in italics. Here and in the following citation I have, for the sake of simplicity, replaced the boldface with quotation marks.

11. Ibid., 24.

12. Ibid.

13. John Allen Jr., "A Saint Despite Vatican Reservations," *National Catholic Reporter*, August 30, 2002, http://natcath.org/NCR_Online/archives2/2002c/083002/083002f.htm.

14. Information gathered from Mark Miravalle, *Meet Mary: Getting to Know the Mother of God* (Manchester, NH: Sophia Institute Press, 2007), 79; Catherine M. Odell, *Those Who Saw Her: Apparitions of Mary*, rev. ed. (Huntington, IN: Our Sunday Visitor, 2010), 71–73; Miravalle, *Private Revelation*, 56–58.

15. Miravalle, *Private Revelation* 60.

16. Miravalle rightly notes two unhealthy extremes regarding private revela-tions: wholesale rejection of them or undiscerning acceptance. He further notes that a number of important studies on private revelation, including the work of Augustin Poulain and Benedict Groeschel, which we will observe later in the chapter, do not reflect a healthy balance of caution and openness toward private revelations but are inclined toward a cautionary negativity. See ibid., 3–4, 38n74.

17. Francis Cardinal Šeper, "Norms Regarding the Manner of Proceeding in the Discernment of Presumed Apparitions or Revelations," *Sacred Congregation for the Doctrine of the Faith*, document issued February 24, 1978, www.vatican.va/roman_curia/congregations/cfaith/documents/rc_con_cfaith_doc_19780225_norme-apparizioni_en.html.

18. Gianni Cardinale, "Tempi e criteri per 'giudicare' le apparizioni," *Eroici Furori*, September 17, 2008.

19. Miravelle, *Private Revelation*, 47.

20. Ibid.

21. Ibid.

22. Ibid., 48.

23. Šeper, "Discernment of Presumed Apparitions or Revelations."

24. Ibid.

25. Ibid.

26. Ibid.

27. Ibid.
28. See Louis J. Puhl, S.J., ed., *The Spiritual Exercises of St. Ignatius* (Chicago: Loyola University, 1951), 149–150.
29. The edition cited here will be Augustin Poulain, S.J., *The Graces of Interior Prayer* (London: Routledge and Kegan Paul, 1950).
30. Benedict J. Groeschel, C.F.R., *A Still, Small Voice: A Practical Guide on Reported Revelations* (San Francisco: Ignatius Press, 1993).
31. Ibid., 51.
32. See Daniel Klimek, "The Gospels According to Christ? Combining the Study of the Historical Jesus with Modern Mysticism," *Glossolalia* 1 (2009): 1–18; my article uses the research of David J. Webster, "Cities, Villages and Natural Geographical Sites in Palestine Mentioned in the Poem," www.saveourchurch.org/descriptionspoem.pdf. See also Stephen Austin, *A Summa and Encyclopedia to Maria Valtorta's Extraordinary Work* (e-book, February 2017 edition), www.bardstown.com/~brchrys/Summa.pdf; and for a study of the various personalities in Valtorta's revelations in light of the Gospels, see René Laurentin, François-Michel Debroise, and Jean-Francois Lavere, *Dictionnaire des personnages de l'évangile selon Maria Valtorta* (Paris: Salvator, 2012).
33. Groeschel, *A Still, Small Voice*, 57.
34. Sullivan, *Miracle Detective*, 107.
35. Ibid.
36. Groeschel, *A Still, Small Voice*, 64.
37. Poulain, *Graces of Interior Prayer*, 338.
38. Groeschel, *A Still, Small Voice*, 67.
39. Poulain, *Graces of Interior Prayer*, 339.
40. Ibid.
41. Miravalle, *Private Revelation*, 42.
42. Ibid., 42–43.
43. Ibid., 42.
44. Šeper, "Discernment of Presumed Apparitions or Revelations."
45. Ibid.
46. Elizabeth Ficocelli, *The Fruits of Medjugorje: Stories of True and Lasting Conversion* (Mahwah, NJ: Paulist Press, 2006), 1.
47. Robert A. Orsi, *History and Presence* (Cambridge, MA: Belknap Press, 2016).
48. See John Paul II, "List dla Pana Marka Skwarnicki i Pani Zofia Skwarnicka," December 8, 1992, in *Medjugorje and the Church*, ed. Denis Nolan, 4th ed. (Santa Barbara, CA: Queenship Publishing, 2007); John Paul II, "List dla Mana Marka Skwarnicki," Watykan, May 28, 1992; John Paul II, "List dla Pana Marka Skwarnicki i Pani Zofia Skwarnicka," Watykan, February 25, 1994; John Paul II, "List dla Pana Marka Skwarnicki I Pani Zofia Skwarnicka," Castel Gandolfo, September 3, 1994. All available in Nolan, *Medjugorje and the Church*, 152, 154, 156, 159.

49. "Teraz chyba lepiej rozumie sie Medjugorie. To jakies 'naleganie' Matki rozumie sie dzis lepiej" ["Now, however, we have a better understanding of Medjugorje. This type of 'call' from our Mother is better understood today], translation mine, from John Paul II, "List dla Pana Marka Skwarnicki i Pani Zofia Skwarnicka."

50. Oder dedicates a few pages of his book to documenting John Pau II's support of Medjugorje. See Oder and Gaeta, *Why He Is a Saint*, 167–169.

51. See Klimek, "Pope John Paul II, 'Medjugorje'; Denis Nolan, "John Paul II Believed in Medjugorje," *Mother of All Peoples Marian E-zine*, June 26, 2010, http://www. motherofallpeoples.com/2010/06/john-paul-ii-believed-in-medjugorje/; Oder and Gaeta, *Why He Is a Saint*, 168; Soldo et al., *My Heart Will Triumph*, 197–198.

52. As quoted in Nolan, *Medjugorje and the Church*, 24.

53. Sullivan, *Miracle Detective*, 43.

54. There are two main theories as to why the bishop retracted his positive opinion of the apparitions: (1) that the bishop succumbed to pressures, which included the threat of arrest and imprisonment by the communist government, and (2) because of a political dispute between the bishop's diocese and the local Franciscans (the Franciscans were in charge of the parish of Medjugorje). Regarding the first theory, the communist government reacted strongly to claims of the apparitions. They arrested, imprisoned, and tortured the pastor of the Medjugorje parish, Fr. Jozo Zovko. Correspondingly, the day that Fr. Jozo was arrested, "the bishop went silent on the subject of Medjugorje for the next five months," despite previously having been a wholehearted and vocal supporter of the apparitions (Sullivan, *Miracle Detective*, 122). Shortly thereafter the bishop changed his position, disavowing the apparitions. Regarding the second theory, it is an unfortunate reality that there has been a long history, in the Bosnia-Herzegovina region, of rivalry between the secular clergy and the Franciscans, the petty politics of which have infiltrated discourses about the apparitions in Medjugorje. According to Craig and others, Žanić developed a notorious reputation for making incendiary and often unsubstantiated remarks against the apparitions, the visionaries, and the Franciscans of the Medjugorje parish, even after being ordered by the Yugoslav bishops to maintain silence on the subject until a full investigation is completed. In October 1984, Žanić issued a report to episcopal conferences around the world, which quickly spread throughout the Catholic press, labeling the experiences of the visionaries as a case of "collective hallucination." This statement made Medjugorje an increasingly controversial subject within the Church. Following the report, René Laurentin, who was a part of the 1984 French team that scientifically studied the apparitions of the visionaries, "conveyed his astonishment" at Žanić's proclamation of "collective hallucination," noting that this claim completely contradicted the medical and scientific tests performed on the visionaries that ruled out any forms of hallucination during their apparitions. French and Italian doctors from separate investigative teams, Laurentin noted, came to the same conclusions, ruling out such pathological states. See Craig, *Spark from Heaven*, 145, 172; Sullivan, *Miracle Detective*,

122, 205; O'Carroll, *Medjugorje*, 149–153; Weible, *Medjugorje*, 277. Notably, Craig titles her chapter (143–156), recording Žanić's false statement against the experiences of the visionaries, "A Campaign of Disinformation."

55. Cited in O'Carroll, *Medjugorje*, 152. For full letter see 149–153.

56. Weible, *Medjugorje*, 277; Craig, *Spark from Heaven*, 172.

57. Sullivan, *Miracle Detective*, 206; see also Sr. Emmanuel Maillard and Denis Nolan. *Medjugorje: What Does the Church Say?* (Santa Barbara, CA: Queenship, 1998), 1–2. For a brief overview of some of Cardinal Ratzinger's/Pope Benedict's involvements with Medjugorje, see James Mulligan, *Medjugorje: What's Happening?* (Brewster, MA: Paraclete Press, 2011), 244–245; also see Nolan, *Medjugorje and the Church*, 3: "But Cardinal Ratzinger (presently Pope Benedict XVI) rejected these negative conclusions [of Bishop Žanić's commission]. And—an event without precedent in the history of apparitions—the local bishop (Bishop Žanić) was relieved of the dossier. The fact was not widely reported. Rome dissolved Bishop Žanić's commission and then put the matter into the hands of the Yugoslavian Episcopal Conference. A new commission was subsequently appointed under the presidency of Bishop Komarica (of Banja Luka, Bosnia-Hercegovina)."

58. Weible, *Medjugorje*, 277.

59. Copy of full declaration available in Nolan, *Medjugorje and the Church*, 175.

60. Ibid., 6; emphasis Nolan's.

61. As quoted in Nolan, *Medjugorje and the Church*, 175.

62. Full copy of letter, dated May 26, 1998, available in Nolan, *Medjugorje and the Church*, 19; emphasis Nolan's.

63. "Vatican Forms Medjugorje Study Commission," *ZENIT*, March 17, 2010, www.zenit.org/en/articles/vatican-forms-medjugorje-study-commission.

64. Archbishop Allessandro D'Errico, "Statement of Apostolic Nuncio to Bosnia and Herzegovina About International Commission for Medjugorje," March 20, 2010, http://medjugorje.hr/en/news/statement-of-apostolic-nuncio-to-bosnia-and-herzegovina-about-international-commission-for-medjugorje,2922.html, Archbishop D'Errico initially made this statement on March 18, 2010, at the end of the 48th Bishop's Conference of Bosnia and Herzegovina.

65. "Pope Francis' Opinion on the Medjugorje Apparitions," *Rome Reports*, May 15, 2017, www.romereports.com/2017/05/15/pope-francis-opinion-on-the-medjugorje-apparitions.

66. Andrea Tornielli, "Medjugorje; the Findings of the Ruini Report," *Vatican Insider: La Stampa*, May 16, 2017, www.lastampa.it/2017/05/16/vaticaninsider/eng/the-vatican/medjugorje-the-findings-of-the-ruini-report-hvBaZ3ssAeDicjdmEcS3UN/pagina.html.

CHAPTER 3

1. William James, *The Varieties of Religious Experience: A Study in Human Nature* (New York: Library of America Paperback Classic, 2010), xii.

2. Harvey D. Egan, S.J., *What Are They Saying about Mysticism?* (New York: Paulist Press, 1982), 6.

3. G. William Barnard. *Exploring Unseen Worlds: William James and the Philosophy of Mysticism* (Albany: State University of New York Press, 1992), 1.

4. Ibid., 1.

5. Louise Nelstrop, Kevin Magill, and Bradley B. Onishi, *Christian Mysticism: An Introduction to Contemporary Theoretical Approaches* (Burlington, VT: Ashgate, 2009), 3.

6. William Harmless, S.J., *Mystics* (New York: Oxford University Press, 2008), 14.

7. James, *Varieties of Religious Experience*, 12.

8. Ann Taves, *Religious Experience Reconsidered: A Building-Block Approach to the Study of Religion and Other Special Things* (Princeton, NJ: Princeton University Press, 2009), 5.

9. See Louis Bouyer, "Mysticism: An Essay on the History of the Word," in *Understanding Mysticism* ed. Richard Woods (New York: Image Books, 1980), 42–55. See Amy Hollywood, *Sensible Ecstasy: Mysticism, Sexual Difference, and the Demands of History* (Chicago: University of Chicago Press, 2002), 146–147. Also Richard Kieckhefer, while applying it himself to describe the experiences of rapture and revelation in his work on medieval mystics, agrees that the "term 'mysticism,' more familiar in modern scholarly parlance than it would have been to the [medieval] mystics themselves, can mean various things." See Kieckhefer, *Unquiet Souls: Fourteenth-Century Saints and Their Religious Milieu* (Chicago: University of Chicago Press, 1984); esp. useful is Kieckhefer's discussion on the numerous forms of mystical experiences on pages 150–179.

10. James, *Varieties of Religious Experience*, 342–343.

11. Ibid., 342.

12. Ibid., 343.

13. Ibid.

14. Ibid.

15. Ibid.

16. Ibid.

17. Ibid.

18. Ibid., 343–344.

19. Ibid., 344.

20. Ibid.

21. Ibid.

22. Ibid.

23. Ibid., 373.

24. These included lectures XI, XII, XIII, titled "Saintliness," and lectures XIV and XV titled "The Value of Saintliness." See James, *Varieties of Religious Experience*, 239–298, 299–341.

25. Egan, *What Are They Saying*, 9.

26. James, *Varieties of Religious Experience*, 373.

27. Ibid.

28. Evelyn Underhill, *Mysticism: A Study in Nature and Development of Spiritual Consciousness* (London: Aziloth Books, 2011[1911]), 138.

29. Harmless, *Mystics*, 67.

30. Egan, *What Are They Saying*, 6.

31. Taves, *Religious Experience Reconsidered*, 5.

32. Egan, *What Are They Saying*, 6.

33. James, *Varieties of Religious Experience*, 381, 385–386.

34. Nelstrop et al., *Christian Mysticism*, 4.

35. Barnard, *Exploring Unseen Worlds*, 116.

36. Nelstrop et al., *Christian Mysticism*, 4.

37. Ibid., 4.

38. Ibid., 4.

39. The Greek term *ekstasis*, formed of *ek*, meaning "outside" or "beyond," and *stasis*, meaning "standing" or "stature," connotes a standing outside or beyond the self.

40. Egan, *What Are They Saying*, 9.

41. Ibid., 8.

42. James, *Varieties of Religious Experience*, 378.

43. The best representations of modern perennialism, or "neo-perennialism," reviving the classic interpretation, are two works edited by Robert K. C. Forman: *The Problem of Pure Consciousness: Mysticism and Philosophy* (New York: Oxford University Press, 1990), and *The Innate Capacity: Mysticism, Psychology, and Philosophy* (New York: Oxford University Press, 1998). In addition to these books, which include essays from various contemporary neo-perennialist scholars, Forman has personally authored a book on these issues, particularly the perennialist-constructivist debate, called *Mysticism, Mind, Consciousness* (Albany: State University of New York Press, 1999).

44. Steven T. Katz is the main proponent of the constructivist view in regard to the study of mysticism. He has edited two of the earliest influential books on the subject, *Mysticism and Philosophical Analysis* (New York: Oxford University Press, 1978), and *Mysticism and Religious Traditions* (New York: Oxford University Press, 1983).

45. Robert Forman, for example, identifies at least two forms of constructivism— "complete constructivism" and "incomplete constructivism"—while William Parsons sees three "subtypes" or "models" of perennialism: the "perennial invariant" model, the "perennial variant" model, and the "typological variant" model. See Forman, *Problem of Pure Consciousness*, 13; see William Parsons, *The Enigma of the Oceanic Feeling: Revisioning the Psychoanalytic Theory of Mysticism* (New York: Oxford University Press, 1999), 113.

46. Egan, *What Are They Saying*, 8.

47. James, *Varieties of Religious Experience*, 381.

48. Ibid., 381.
49. Ibid., 381.
50. Barnard, *Exploring Unseen Worlds*, 75.
51. Underhill's wide erudition is evident in the eclectic mastery of the diverse subject matter present in her publications. Steven Fanning notes that "Underhill's literary production is staggering, for 'in thirty-nine years she produced forty books, editions, and collections, and more than three hundred and fifty articles, essays, and reviews.' Equally amazing is her list of 'firsts': [S]he was the first woman to lecture in theology at Oxford college, the first woman to lecture Anglican clergy, and one of the first women to be included in Church of England commissions. These accomplishments, along with her work as a retreat leader, made Evelyn Underhill a prominent figure in her day." See Fanning, *Mystics of the Christian Tradition*, 209–211.
52. Ibid., 209.
53. Bernard McGinn, *The Essential Writings of Christian Mysticism* (New York: Modern Library, 2006), 558. Underhill's other publications on the subject include *The Mystic Way* (1913), *Practical Mysticism* (1914), *The Essentials of Mysticism* (1920), and *The Mystics of the Church* (1964).
54. As quoted in Fanning, *Mystics of the Christian Tradition*, 2.
55. As cited in Fanning, *Mystics of the Christian Tradition*, 221n11. For the original source, see Denise Lardner Carmody and John Tully Carmody, *Mysticism: Holiness East and West* (New York: Oxford University Press, 1996), 10.
56. As cited in Fanning, *Mystics of the Christian Tradition*. For the original source, see F. C. Happold, *Mysticism: A Study and an Anthology*, rev. ed. (New York: Penguin Books, 1973), 19.
57. Fanning, *Mystics of the Christian Tradition*, 2.
58. Avery Dulles, S.J., *Models of Revelation*, rev. ed. (New York: Orbis Books, 1992), 69.
59. Ibid., 76, 69.
60. Taves, *Religious Experience Reconsidered*, 20.
61. Andresen and Forman, "Methodological Pluralism," 12.
62. See James, *Varieties of Religious Experience*, 207–210.
63. Ibid., 208.
64. Quoted in ibid., 208–209.
65. Ibid., 209.
66. An "intellectual vision," constituting the reception of new knowledge—thus, illumination—is one of the three categories of visionary phenomena, alongside imaginative and corporal visions. All three are discussed in detail in the following section.
67. Quoted in James, *Varieties of Religious Experience*, 209–210.
68. Evelyn Underhill, *Mysticism: A Study in the Nature and Development of Man's Spiritual Consciousness* (Santa Cruz, CA: Evinity Publishing, 2009), 158; Kindle edition by Digireads, 2009, is from the Evinity edition.

69. Underhill, *Mysticism* (Evinity ed.), 51.

70. Ibid., 51.

71. Ibid., 52.

72. Ibid., 52.

73. Ibid., 53.

74. Ibid., 53.

75. Ibid., 53.

76. Egan, *What Are They Saying*, 41.

77. Underhill, *Mysticism* (Evinity ed.), 55.

78. Ibid., 55.

79. Ibid., 54.

80. Ibid., 57.

81. Ibid., 57.

82. Egan, *What Are They Saying?* 41.

83. Underhill, *Mysticism* (Evinity ed.), 58.

84. Egan, *What Are They Saying?* 42.

85. "We now come to that eternal battle-ground, the detailed discussion of those abnormal psychic phenomena which appear so persistently in the history of the mystics" (Underhill, *Mysticism* [Evinity ed.], 156).

86. Underhill, *Mysticism* (Evinity ed.), 156.

87. Ibid., 157.

88. Underhill, *Mysticism* (Aziloth ed.), 213.

89. Ibid.

90. Ibid.

91. Ibid., 220.

92. Niels Christian Hvidt, *Christian Prophecy: The Post-Biblical Tradition* (New York: Oxford University Press, 2007), 135. Veerle Fraeters, "*Visio*/Vision," in *The Cambridge Companion to Christian Mysticism*, ed. Amy Hollywood and Patricia Beckman (New York: Cambridge University Press, 2012), 178–179.

93. Hvidt., *Christian Prophecy*, 136.

94. Veerle Fraeters explains that Augustine's classification of visions "deals not so much with seeing as knowing. He is interested in the epistemological question of how a human being can know and correctly understand the meaning of God's Word. In line with Neo-Platonic philosophers, he uses the metaphor of vision in order to consider, in an intelligible way, the invisible process of cognition." Fraeters, "*Visio*/Vision," 178.

95. Hvidt, *Christian Prophecy*, 136.

96. Ibid., 136.

97. Ibid., 136–137.

98. Ibid., 137.

99. Ibid., 136; Miravalle, *Private Revelation*, 24–25.

100. Poulain, *Graces of Interior Prayer*, 301.

101. Miravalle, *Private Revelation*, 24; Hvidt, *Christian Prophecy*, 136; Fraeters, "Visio/ Vision," 178. Fraeters explains that Augustine perceived the corporal vision as the "lowest form" of visionary experience: "The lowest form is seeing by means of the eye, the external organ of vision (*visio corporalis*). This material seeing is inadequate to perceive God's eternal truth; the viewer's position in time and in space necessarily limits his perspective. When one turns away from outer seeing to inner seeing—a turning away Augustine calls rapture (*raptus*)—a higher, spiritual form of vision is accessed (*visio spiritualis*)."

102. Poulain, *Graces of Interior Prayer*, 301.

103. Miravalle, *Private Revelation*, 25.

104. Hvidt, *Christian Prophecy*, 137.

105. Miravalle, *Private Revelation*, 25.

106. Poulain, *Graces of Interior Prayer*, 301.

107. Teresa explains: "When the soul is in this suspension [a rapture], the Lord likes to show it some secrets, things about heaven, and imaginative visions. It is able to tell of them afterward, for these remain so impressed on the memory that they are never forgotten. But when the visions are intellectual, the soul doesn't know how to speak of them. For there must be some visions during these moments that are so sublime that it's not fitting for those who live on this earth to have further understanding necessary to explain them. However, when the soul is again in possession of its senses, it can say many things about these intellectual visions." See Teresa of Avila, "Interior Castle," in *The Collected Works of St. Teresa of Avila*, vol. 2, trans. Kieran Kavanaugh, O.C.D., and Otilio Rodriguez, O.C.D. (Washington, DC: ICS Publications, 1980), 380.

108. Hvidt, *Christian Prophecy*, 137.

109. Kowalska, *Diary of Saint Maria Faustina Kowalska*, 64–65. The notion that the intellectual vision is more reliable than the imaginative (which relies on inner sense perception) or the corporal (which relies on external sense perception) is prominent among Christian mystics and writers of mysticism. The idea that sense perception filters and can distort knowledge, however, is an issue that is not exclusive to religious or mystical experiences but is, at its core, an epistemological matter that can be traced back as far as ancient Greek philosophy. In his dialogue *Phaedo*, Plato has Socrates explain that truth and wisdom are only attainable by "pure thought alone"—in other words by thinking that transcends sense perception. This constituted part of Plato's soul–body dichotomy; he associated pure thinking as knowledge that is attainable only by the soul when it is untouched by the senses while, conversely, he associated the senses with the body, whose passions, desires, and filters distort pure knowledge and, therefore, pose an obstacle to the attainment and pursuit of truth and wisdom. A person who attains pure knowledge will do this most perfectly, according to Plato, when approaching "the object with thought alone, without associating

any sight with thought, or dragging in any sense perception with his reasoning, but who, using pure thought alone, tries to track down each reality pure and by itself, freeing himself as far as possible from eyes and ears, and in a word, from the whole body, because the body confuses the soul and does not allow it to acquire truth and wisdom whenever it is associated with it." See Plato, *Phaedo*, in *Introductory Readings in Ancient Greek and Roman Philosophy* ed. C. D. C. Reeve and Patrick Lee Miller (Indianapolis/Cambridge: Hackett, 2006), 111.

110. Underhill, *Mysticism* (Aziloth ed.), , 223.
111. Ibid., 226.
112. Ibid., 223.
113. Ibid.
114. Ibid., 223.
115. Ibid., 224.
116. Ibid.
117. Ibid., 225.
118. Ibid.
119. Ibid., 226.
120. Ibid.
121. Ibid.
122. Ibid., 227.
123. Ibid., 226.
124. Ibid., 227.
125. Ibid.
126. Ibid.
127. Ibid.
128. Interview with Groeschel in Sullivan, *Miracle Detective*, 419.
129. Underhill, *Mysticism* (Aziloth ed.), , 227.
130. Ibid.
131. Ibid., 227–228.
132. Ibid., 214, 220.
133. Poulain, *Graces of Interior Prayer*, 299.
134. Underhill, *Mysticism* (Aziloth ed.), 214.
135. Ibid., 215.
136. Ibid., 216.
137. Ibid.
138. Ibid., 216–217.
139. See Michael H. Crosby, O.F.M., Cap., "A Response to 'Saint Francis as Mystic: The Multifarious Mysticism of Francis of Assisi,'" *Franciscan Connections: The Cord—A Spiritual Review* 66, no.1 (March 2016): 6–7. For my original articles, to which Crosby is replying, see Daniel Maria Klimek, T.O.R., "Saint Francis as Mystic: The Multifarious Mysticism of Francis of Assisi," Part I, *Franciscan*

Connections: The Cord—A Spiritual Review 65, no. 3 (September 2015): 32–37; and Part II, *Franciscan Connections* 65, no. 4 (December 2015): 29–33.

140. Crosby, "A Response," 6.

141. Teresa of Avila, "Interior Castle," 430.

142. Ibid.

143. I am highlighting that this is the case for Teresa, as in my own interpretation I do acknowledge, as mentioned earlier, that "complex experiences," which Jensine Andresen and Robert Forman have pointed to, do exist wherein both dualistic and non-dualistic qualities of religious experiences are combined. The mentioned example of Alphonse Ratisbonne's Marian apparition, being a unitive experience while possessing a degree of dualism, speaks to this reality, that certain corporal visions do have the qualities of mystical experiences.

144. Bernard McGinn, *The Flowering of Mysticism: Men and Women in the New Mysticism—1200-1350* (New York: Crossroad, 1998), 27.

145. Ibid., 26.

146. Ibid.

147. Cf. Ewert Cousins, "Francis of Assisi: Christian Mysticism at the Crossroads," in *Mysticism and Religious Traditions*, ed. Steven T. Katz (New York: Oxford University Press, 1983), 163–190.

148. Underhill writes: "What then do we really mean by mysticism? A word which is impartially applied to the performances of mediums and the ecstasies of the saints, to 'menticulture' and sorcery, dreamy poetry and medieval art, to prayer and palmistry, the doctrinal excesses of Gnosticism, and the tepid speculations of the Cambridge Platonists—even, according to William James, to the higher branches of intoxication—soon ceases to have any useful meaning. Its employment merely confuses the inexperienced student, who ends with the vague idea that every kind of supersensual theory and practice is somehow 'mystical.'" See Underhill, *Mysticism* (Aziloth ed.), 61.

149. See James, *Varieties of Religious Experience*, 348–354.

150. Egan, *What Are They Saying*, 11.

151. James, *Varieties of Religious Experience*, 349.

152. Ibid., 348–349.

153. Ibid., 349.

154. Egan, *What Are They Saying*, 11.

155. McGinn, *Essential Writings of Christian Mysticism*, 559. See also Egan, *What Are They Saying*, 32.

156. Zaehner wrote: "In *The Doors of Perception* Mr. Huxley seemed to assume that preternatural experiences, conveniently described by the all-embracing term 'mysticism,' must all be the same in essence, no matter whether they be the result of intensive ascetic training, of a prolonged course of Yoga techniques, or simply of the taking of drugs." Zaehner ironically articulated how drug-induced states have more in common with pathological states and, therefore,

by abiding by his perennial notion that mystical states are universal, and that intoxicants also produce such states, Huxley was unwittingly flirting with the idea of reducing all seemingly mystical experiences to a paradigm of artificial and pathological states of consciousness. See R. C. Zaehner, "*Mysticism Sacred and Profane*," in *Understanding Mysticism*, ed. Richard Woods (New York: Image Books, 1980), 56–57; also see Egan, *What are They Saying*, 32.

157. Ibid., 57.

158. Ibid.

159. Underhill, *Mysticism* (Aziloth ed.), 220.

160. Ibid., 220.

161. Ibid., 210.

162. James, *Varieties of Religious Experience*, 20–21.

163. Ibid., 20–21.

164. Underhill, *Mysticism* (Aziloth ed.), 212.

165. Ibid.

166. A short biography of Valtorta's experiences is recorded by Emilio Pisani in the preface to Maria Valtorta, *The Poem of the Man-God*, vol. 1, trans. Nicandro Picozzi and Patrick McLaughlin (Isola del Liri, Italy: Centro Editoriale Valtortiano, 1986), iv. Also see Maria Valtorta, *Autobiography*, trans. David G. Murray (Isola del Liri, Italy: Centro Editoriale Valtortiano, 1991).

167. It is noteworthy that the publisher of Valtorta's work (Centro Editoriale Valtortiano) has recently retitled the English edition to *The Gospel as It Was Revealed to Me*. This title seems more apt than *The Poem of the Man God*, as Valtorta's revelations depict extensive and vivid accounts of the life of Jesus, working with prose not poetry to form a detailed narrative; albeit the beauty of the prose can be compared to poetry.

168. See Laurentin et al., *Dictionnaire des personnages de l'évangile selon Maria Valtorta;* Klimek, "The Gospels According to Christ?"; Austin, *Summa and Encyclopedia to Maria Valtorta's Extraordinary Work*.

169. For an overview of Neumann's fasting and inedia, including the clinical examination of her status, see Josef Teodorowicz, *Mystical Phenomena in the Life of Theresa Neumann*, trans. Rudolph Kraus (St. Louis, MO: B. Herder, 1940), 324–356. See also the work of Hilda C. Graef, *The Case of Therese Neumann* (Westminster, MD: Newman Press, 1951).

170. Teodorowicz, *Mystical Phenomena*, 469–503. This chapter (XIX) is titled "Phenomena of Speech." Specifically pages 473–477 record Neumann's Aramaic during her ecstasies, documenting investigations made by linguists and clergy that were present at her side during the phenomenon. The American stigmatic Rhoda Wise (1888–1948) was reported to experience similar phenomena as identified in Neumann's case, including the identifiable uttering of Aramaic phrases during her ecstasies. See Karen Sigler, *Her Name Means Rose: The Rhoda Wise Story* (Birmingham: EWTN Catholic Publishing, 2000).

My appreciation to Fr. Sean Sullivan, T.O.R., for pointing me to information on Therese Neumann, and to Br. Gabriel Mary Amato, T.O.R., for pointing me to the case of Rhoda Wise.

171. Underhill, *Mysticism* (Aziloth ed.), 212.

172. As cited in Fanning, *Mystics of the Christian Tradition*, 211. For von Hügel's most eminent work on mysticism, see Friedrich von Hügel, *The Mystical Element of Religion: As Studied in Saint Catherine of Genoa and Her Friends* (New York: Herder & Herder, 1999[1908/1923]).

173. Both Bernadette Soubirous (1844–1879) of Lourdes and Lucia dos Santos (1907–2005), the main visionary of Fátima, would become cloistered nuns, their apparitional experiences having a deep religious influence on their lives. The other two visionaries of Fátima, siblings Jacinta (1910–1920) and Francisco Marto (1908–1919), died at a young age due to the 1918 influenza epidemic that killed millions. For accounts of both the Lourdes and Fátima apparitions, see Zimdar-Swartz, *Encountering Mary*, esp. 43–56, 77–91, 190–219.

174. See Šeper, "Discernment of Presumed Apparitions or Revelations."

175. Underhill, *Mysticism* (Aziloth ed.), 212.

176. Ibid., 232n572.

177. Ibid.

178. Egan, *Anthology of Christian Mysticism*, 525.

179. Ibid.

180. Ibid., 521.

181. Ibid., 522.

182. The examples of twenty-first-century Christians reporting encounters with the devil have not been absent. As observed, one of the Medjugorje visionaries, Mirjana, is someone who has reported an apparitional encounter with—thus, a corporal vision of—the devil. Similarly, Catholic exorcists have reported various paranormal phenomena in their work which they connect with the devil or the demonic. Additionally, mystics, visionaries, and near-death experiencers (as chapter 1 observed) have reported encounters with the afterlife, which have included indications of the realm of hell and manifestations of the demonic. For a description of her experience, see interview with Mirjana Dragičević in Kralijevic, *The Apparitions*, 125–126. For an insightful study of demonic possession and exorcism within the historical context of early modern Catholicism, see Moshe Sluhovsky, *Believe Not Every Spirit: Possession, Mysticism, and Discernment in Early Modern Catholicism* (Chicago: University of Chicago Press, 2007). Especially insightful is Sluhovsky's hermeneutical discourse on the various interpretations of possession that modern scholars apply, including psychological, anthropological, sociological, and spiritual frameworks, found on pages 1–10. For a brief but informative study of demonology and the ministry of exorcism by a Vatican-approved exorcist, see José Antonio Fortea, *Interview with an Exorcist: An Insider's Look at the Devil, Demonic Possession, and the Path*

to Deliverance (West Chester, PA: Ascension Press, 2006). Fortea is an internationally known Spanish exorcist who has done scholarly work, primarily in Spanish, on the topic of exorcism and demonology.

183. Harvey Egan, *An Anthology of Christian Mysticism* (Collegeville, MN: Pueblo Books, 1996), 524.

184. Ibid., 525.

185. Ibid.

CHAPTER 4

1. In addition to the already mentioned works of James and Underhill, see Aldous Huxley, *The Perennial Philosophy* (New York: Harper and Row, 1944); Rudolf Otto, *The Idea of the Holy*, trans. John W. Harvey (New York: Oxford University Press, 1923), and *Mysticism East and West*, trans. Bertha Bracey and Richenda C. Payne (New York: Macmillan, 1932); Joseph Maréchal, S.J., *The Psychology of the Mystics*, trans. Algar Thorold (Mineola, NY: Dover, 2004), originally published in English from the French in 1927 by Burns Oates & Washbourne; W. T. Stace, *The Teachings of the Mystics* (New York: New American Library, 1960), and *Mysticism and Philosophy* (London: Macmillian, 1960); Huston Smith, *Forgotten Truth: The Primordial Tradition* (New York: Harper and Row, 1976).

2. See R. C. Zaehner, *Mysticism Sacred and Profane* (New York: Schocken Books, 1961), and *Hindu and Muslim Mysticism* (New York: Schocken Books, 1969); Bruce Garside, "Language and the Interpretation of Mystical Experiences," *International Journal for Philosophy of Religion*, 3 (Summer 1972): 91–94. An especially influential essay leading the constructivist critique of the perennial philosophy has been Steven Katz's "Language, Epistemology, and Mysticism," 22–74 and Robert Gimello, "Mysticism and Meditation," 170–199, both in *Mysticism and Philosophical Analysis*, ed. Steven T. Katz (New York: Oxford University Press, 1978). See also Gimello's "Mysticism in its Contexts," 61–88, and Hans H. Penner, "The Mystical Illusion," 89–116, both in *Mysticism and Religious Traditions*, ed. Steven T. Katz (New York: Oxford University Press, 1983). The other works edited by Katz, in his four-volume corpus on mysticism, include *Mysticism and Language* (New York: Oxford University Press, 1992) and *Mysticism and Sacred Scripture* (New York: Oxford University Press, 2000). For the earlier work of Inge and Jones, see William Ralph Inge, *Studies of English Mystics* (London: John Murray, 1906), and *Christian Mysticism* (London: Methuen, 1899); and Rufus M. Jones, *Studies in Mystical Religion* (Eugene, OR: Wipf and Stock, 2004[1909]).

3. See R. L. Franklin's essay "Postconstructivist Approaches to Mysticism," in Robert K. C. Forman, *The Innate Capacity: Mysticism, Psychology, and Philosophy* (New York: Oxford University Press, 1990). 231–243, For more on the perennial perspective, also see Forman, *Mysticism, Mind, Consciousness*, 31–32.

4. Franklin, "Postconstructivist Approaches," 231.

5. Forman, *Mysticism, Mind, Consciousness*, 31.

6. Ibid., 32.

7. Ibid.

8. Parsons, *Enigma of the Oceanic Feeling*, 112–113.

9. Ibid., 113.

10. Ibid.

11. Ibid.

12. Ibid.

13. Forman, *Problem of Pure Consciousness*, 12.

14. It has been suggested that constructivist scholars should be called "contextualists"—and not "constructivists"—as their major project is to contextualize the experiences of mystics; however, the usage of the label "constructivists" is preferred in this writing, as neo-perennialists and many traditional perennialists also believe in the contextualization of mystical experiences; thus contextualism by itself would not constitute the major hermeneutical difference between the two and, therefore, would not properly constitute a distinguishing marker in identifying one side over the other. The central issue does not pertain to contextualism but to the proper placing of contextualism within the phenomenology of a mystical experience, whether it is placed in the content or the form of the experience; if it is placed entirely in the beginning, in the shaping of content itself, then the experience is *constructed* and that becomes the central epistemological issue of debate; it's not that one side contextualizes and the other does not—as both sides, to some extent, do—but that one side argues for an experience *constructed* by the self while the other for an experience *received* from Another—essentially becoming a debate between constructivism and receptivity. For discussion, see Nelstrop et al., *Christian Mysticism*, 11n21. The authors here use "contextualists" to refer to constructivist scholars and argue for such usage. However, for the aforementioned reasons, I believe that "constructivists" is the more suitable label.

15. Forman, *Problem of Pure Consciousness*, 10–11.

16. See Michael Bentley, *Modern Historiography: An Introduction* (London and New York: Routledge, 1999), 20–21.

17. Forman, *Mysticism, Mind, Consciousness*, 34.

18. Steven Katz, "Mystical Speech and Mystical Meaning," in *Mysticism and Language*, 5.

19. Forman, *Problem of Pure Consciousness*, 13.

20. Ibid., 13–14.

21. As quoted in Forman, *Problem of Pure Consciousness*, 13. For Gimello's text, see Gimello, "Mysticism in its Contexts," 85.

22. Forman, *Problem of Pure Consciousness*, 13.

23. Ibid., 13.

24. Ibid.
25. Ibid.
26. Ibid.
27. Ibid., 13–14.
28. Ibid., 14.
29. Katz, "Language, Epistemology, and Mysticism," 62.
30. Ibid.
31. Ibid.
32. Ibid.
33. Forman, *Mysticism, Mind, Consciousness*, 52–54.
34. See note 43 of chapter 3.
35. Robert K. C. Forman, "Eckhart, *Gezucken*, and the Ground of the Soul," in *The Problem of Pure Consciousness: Mysticism and Philosophy*, ed. Robert K. C. Forman (New York and Oxford: Oxford University Press, 1990), 98–120. Forman's introduction to the work frames the main issues underlying the modern constructivist and neo-perennialist debate; see Forman, "Introduction: Mysticism, Constructivism, and Forgetting," in his *Problem of Pure Consciousness*, 3–52.
36. See note 43 of chapter 3.
37. Andrew B. Newberg, *Principles of Neurotheology* (Burlington, VT: Ashgate, 2010), 189.
38. Barnard, *Exploring Unseen Worlds*, 136.
39. Stephen Bernhardt, "Are Pure Conscious Events Unmediated," in *The Problem of Pure Consciousness: Mysticism and Philosophy*, ed. Robert K. C. Forman (New York and Oxford: Oxford University Press, 1990), 232.
40. Forman explains that if a "mystic's 'set' provides his or her content, the different 'sets' from the various traditions should provide sharply different experiences. But, as is demonstrated in Part I [of *The Problem of Pure Consciousness*], there are experiences from many traditions and ages which are not sharply different. How could experiences with identical definitions (wakeful objectless consciousness) arise from such divergent sources if different contents are provided?" Part I, as Forman refers to the text, includes essays on pure consciousness and Indian Buddhism, Christian mysticism, and Jewish mysticism, pointing to the cross-cultural presence of the contentless and unitive pure consciousness experience in various religious traditions. See Forman, "Introduction: Mysticism, Constructivism, and Forgetting," 24. Also in *The Problem of Pure Consciousness*, see the following essays: Paul J. Griffiths, "Pure Consciousness and Indian Buddhism," 71–97; Forman, "Eckhart, Gezucken, and the Ground of the Soul," 98–120; Daniel C. Matt, "Ayin: The Concept of Nothingness in Jewish Mysticism," 99–121.
41. As quoted in Forman, *Mysticism, Mind, Consciousness*, 17. Original quotation from Steven T. Katz, "The 'Conservative' Character of Mystical Experience," in *Mysticism and Religious Traditions*, ed. Steven T. Katz (New York: Oxford University Press, 1983), 5.

42. Forman, *Mysticism, Mind, Consciousness*, 18.

43. John Horgan, *Rational Mysticism: Dispatches from the Border between Science and Spirituality* (Boston and New York: Houghton Mifflin, 2003), 36.

44. Forman's *Mysticism, Mind, Consciousness* applies the very technique. See pages 21–30 for Forman's conducted interviews with practitioners of different spiritualities.

45. Quoted in Forman, *Mysticism, Mind, Consciousness*, 52; Gimello's original essay found in Katz, *Mysticism and Philosophical Analysis*.

46. Forman, *Mysticism, Mind, Consciousness*, 52.

47. Katz, "Language, Epistemology, and Mysticism," 38.

48. Forman, *Mysticism, Mind, Consciousness*, 47.

49. Anthony N. Perovich Jr., "Does the Philosophy of Mysticism Rest on a Mistake?" in *The Problem of Pure Consciousness: Mysticism and Philosophy*, ed. Robert K. C. Forman (New York and Oxford: Oxford University Press, 1990), 238.

50. See Katz, "Language, Epistemology, and Mysticism," 22–74; Peter Moore, "Mystical Experience, Mystical Doctrine, Mystical Technique," in *Mysticism and Philosophical Analysis*, ed. Steven T. Katz (New York: Oxford University Press, 1978), 101–131; and Gimello, "Mysticism and Meditation," 170–199. See also Katz, "Conservative Character of Mystical Experience," 3–60; Gimello, "Mysticism in Its Contexts," 61–88; and H. P. Owen, "Experience and Dogma in the English Mystics," 148–162, and John E. Smith, "William James's Account of Mysticism: A Critical Appraisal," 247–279, both in *Mysticism and Religious Traditions*, ed. Steven T. Katz (New York: Oxford University Press, 1983).

51. Forman, *Mysticism, Mind, Consciousness*, 56.

52. Perovich explains: "In this essay I seek to distinguish between ideas that are Kantian, that is, held by Kant himself, from those that are Kantian, that is, inspired by, or comparable to, views held by Kant though not, in fact, actually adhered to by him." The attributions "Kantian" and "neo-Kantian" are often used interchangeably to refer to the latter definition. Another term similarly used to refer to ideas that go beyond Kant himself, though they are inspired by his thought, is "hyper-Kantianism," introduced by William Forgie. See Perovich, "Philosophy of Mysticism," 251n.10; and William Forgie, "Hyper-Kantianism in Recent Discussions of Mystical Experience," *Religious Studies* 21 (1985): 205–218.

53. Perovich, "Philosophy of Mysticism," 237–253.

54. Ibid., 239–240.

55. Ibid., 240.

56. For example, Forman, as referenced earlier, challenging Katz's idea that the Buddhist experience of *nirvana* is different from what the Jew experiences as *devekuth*, argues that such logic is fallacious for it "implicitly denies the possibility that there may be two terms with different senses which have the same referent." Forman identifies Katz as a "neo-Kantian" thinker earlier in the

text, associating Katz's epistemological paradigm with Kant's philosophy. See Forman, *Mysticism, Mind, Consciousness*, 34, 47.

57. Perovich, "Philosophy of Mysticism," 240.

58. Ibid., 241–242.

59. Ibid., 242.

60. Ibid., 241.

61. Ibid.

62. Ibid., 242.

63. Ibid., 242–243.

64. Ibid., 243.

65. Ibid., 242.

66. Ibid., 243.

67. Ibid.

68. As quoted in Perovich, "Philosophy of Mysticism," 244; taken from Immanuel Kant, *Religion Within the Limits of Reason Alone*, trans. with an introduction and notes by Theodore M. Greene and Hoyt H. Hudson, with an essay by John R. Silber (New York: Harper & Row, 1960), 163.

69. Perovich, "Philosophy of Mysticism," 244.

70. Ibid.

71. Ibid., 248.

72. Ibid., 247, italics in original.

73. Ibid., 249.

74. Ibid., 250.

75. Ibid.

76. Taves, *Religious Experience Reconsidered*, 3.

77. Ibid., 3n1.

78. Ibid., 3. See also Eric Leigh Schmidt, "The Making of 'Mysticism' in the Anglo-American World: From Henry Coventry to William James," *Wiley-Blackwell Companion to Christian Mysticism*, ed. Julia A. Lamm (Oxford: Blackwell, 2013), 452.

79. Wayne Proudfoot, *Religious Experience* (Berkeley: University of California Press, 1985), 1.

80. Ibid., 2.

81. Ibid.

82. Ibid.

83. Ibid.

84. Schmidt, "Making of 'Mysticism,'" 452.

85. Taves, *Religious Experience Reconsidered*, 3–4.

86. Ibid., 4.

87. Schmidt, "Making of 'Mysticism,'" 452.

88. Ibid., 452; also, for the original source, see Penner, "Mystical Illusion," 89.

89. Schmidt, "Making of 'Mysticism,'" 453.

90. The "linguistic turn" is a prominent, postmodern movement of the twentieth century within academic and intellectual culture that reexamines epistemological assumptions in the humanities and social sciences. Scholars who have applied this postmodern critique argue that all knowledge is mediated and stress, therefore, the way that language shapes knowledge and the way that specific discourses shape social reality, undermining the perennial notion that there is a "pure" or unmediated way to know. The linguistic turn has had an effect on how historians, philosophers, theologians, anthropologists, and other academicians within the humanities and social sciences focus their scholarship. See Richard M. Rorty, ed., *The Linguistic Turn: Essays in Philosophical Method* (Chicago: University of Chicago Press, 1992); and Elizabeth A. Clark, *History, Theory, Text: Historians and the Linguistic Turn* (Cambridge, MA: Harvard University Press, 2004). Taves explains that the linguistic turn has been more embraced in the humanities than the social sciences. See Taves, *Religious Experience Rexamined*, 5n4.

91. Ibid., 5.

92. Ibid.

93. Forman, "Introduction: Mysticism, Constructivism, and Forgetting," 4.

94. Ibid.

95. Ibid., 4–5.

96. Taves, *Religious Experience Reconsidered*, 88.

97. Forman, "Introduction: Mysticism, Constructivism, and Forgetting," 5.

98. Schmidt, "Making of 'Mysticism,'" 452; Proudfoot, *Religious Experience*, xix, 199–208.

99. Ibid. Proudfoot writes of a major purpose for his project: "Some recent attempts to deny the appropriateness of explanation of religious phenomena are examined and shown to conceal protective strategies not unlike those of the tradition of Schleiermacher" (xix). For Proudfoot's section on "protective strategies," see 199–208.

100. Barnard, *Exploring Unseen Worlds*, 103.

101. James, *Varieties of Religious Experience*, 20–21.

102. Proudfoot, *Religious Experience*, xix; for his discussion of descriptive and explanatory reductionism, see 196–198; see also Taves, *Religious Experience Reconsidered*, 89.

103. Proudfoot, *Religious Experience*, 196.

104. Taves, *Religious Experience Reconsidered*, 89.

105. Proudfoot, *Religious Experience*, 196–197.

106. Ibid., 197.

107. Ibid.

108. Ibid., 190.

109. Ibid., 198.

110. In the following section of this chapter, called "Religious Experience and Reductionism," the issue of explanatory reductionism is taken up in detail.

111. See Taves, *Religious Experience Reconsidered*, 100; see also 88–119 to get Taves's overview of her usage of attribution theory and analysis in the discourse between religious experience and representation.
112. Ibid., 17.
113. Ibid.
114. Taves explains that in the early 1980s after psychologists "recognized that attribution theories provided a theoretical bridge between cognitive theory and social psychology," the subfield of social cognition was formed (90). Subsequently, attribution theory was advanced by European social psychologists with the identification of various layers, or levels, through which attributions are made, incorporating both cognitive and societal aspects; and in recent years, neuroscience has come into the picture as "psychologists linked the subfield of social cognition with the neurosciences to form the subfield of social neuroscience"; see 90–91.
115. See Wayne Proudfoot and Phillip Shaver, "Attribution Theory and the Psychology of Religion," *Journal for the Scientific Study of Religion* 14, no. 4 (1975): 317–330.
116. Taves, *Religious Experience Reconsidered*, 92.
117. Ibid., 93.
118. Barnard, *Exploring Unseen Worlds*, 127–129.
119. Ibid., 129.
120. Ibid., 127–128.
121. Ibid., 128.
122. Ibid.
123. Ibid.
124. Ibid.
125. Ibid., 128–129.
126. Taves, *Religious Experience Reconsidered*, 98.
127. Ibid., 97–98.
128. Ibid., 93.
129. In this regard, Taves offers a note of criticism toward the way that Proudfoot's usage of attribution theory conveyed the erroneous impression that the attribution process must be a conscious one (this is a major reason as to why constructivism and attribution theory have been overidentified, according to Taves). Taves explains, however, that the process of attribution can be based on "intended behavior" or "unintended behavior" (101)—in other words, conscious or unconscious factors. She notes that "Proudfoot's use of the conversion account of Stephen Bradley—a nineteenth-century American evangelical Protestant who experienced heart palpitations after a religious revival and attributed them to the Holy Spirit—to illustrate the attribution process heightened the constructivist slant of his theory by giving the impression that the attributional process is a conscious one" (93). For his interpretative usage of

Stephen Bradley's conversion account, see Proudfoot, *Religious Experience*, 102–105, 193–195. Proudfoot takes Bradley's account from William James, who used it in his Gifford Lectures (Lecture IX, James's lecture on conversion). For his usage of Bradley's account, see James, *Varieties of Religious Experience*, 177–181.

130. Taves, *Religious Experience Reconsidered*, 109.

131. Ibid.

132. Ibid.

133. Ibid., 110.

134. Ibid.

135. Ibid.

136. Ibid., 110, italics in original.

137. Taves writes: "I am hypothesizing that the mental paradox involved in the visualization triggered the dissolution of self-other boundaries [the altered state of consciousness]" (ibid., 110).

138. She cites: S. Arzy, G. Thut, C. Mohr, C. M. Michael, and O. Blanke, "Neural Basis of Embodiment: Distinct Contributions of Temporoparietal Junction and Extrastriate Body Area," *Journal of Neuroscience* 26, no. 31 (2006): 8074–8081; Olaf Blanke, T. Landis, L. Spinelli, and M. Seeck, "Out-of-Body Experience and Autoscopy of Neurological Origin," *Brain: A Journal of Neurology* 127, no. 2 (2004): 243–258; Olaf Blanke and Christine Mohr, "Out-of-Body Experience, Heautoscopy, and Autoscopic Hallucination of Neurological Origin: Implications for Neurocognitive Mechanisms of Corporal Awareness and Self-Consciousness," *Brain Research Reviews* 50, no. 1 (2005): 184–199; Olaf Blanke, C. Mohr, C.M. Michel, A. Pascual-Leone, P. Brugger, M. Seeck, T. Landis, and G. Thut, "Linking Out-of-Body Experience and Self-Processing to Mental Own-Body Imagery at the Temporoparietal Junction," *Journal of Neuroscience* 25, no. 3 (2005): 550–557.

139. Taves, *Religious Experience Reconsidered*, 111.

140. Ibid.

141. Ibid., 110.

142. Ibid.

143. Taves references, for example, an article that reports on studies of the role of visions in shamanism; see Richard Noll Jr., "Mental Imagery Cultivation as a Cultural Phenomenon: The Role of Visions in Shamanism," *Current Anthropology* 16, no. 4 (1985): 443–461.

144. Ibid.

145. See Tanya M. Luhrmann, "Yearning for God: Trance as a Culturally Specific Practice and its Implications for Understanding Dissociative Disorders," *Journal of Trauma and Dissociation*. Special Issue: *Dissociation in Culture* 5, no. 2 (2004): 101–129, and "The Art of Hearing God: Absorption, Dissociation, and Contemporary American Spirituality," *Spiritus* 5, no. 2 (2005): 133–157.

146. Callahan explains that dissociative disorder has become a prominent patholog-
     ical category with which many scholars reduce claims of demonic possession:
     "claims for the existence of demons and demonic possession are dismissed.
     Once it is known that an impaired or intoxicated or highly suggestible mind
     can create horrible hallucinations of persecuting voices or induce voluntary
     tics or spasms or create alternative identities in dissociated states, it is no
     longer necessary to see Satan or demons as the cause. Dissociated identity dis-
     orders, or what used to be called multiple personality disorders, can produce
     weird conditions in which different persona with different voices and behav-
     iors are manifested within one individual." See Sidney Callahan, *Women Who
     Hear Voices: The Challenge of Religious Experience*, 2003 Madeleva Lecture in
     Spirituality (New York and Mahway, NJ: Paulist Press, 2007), 14–15.
147. Taves, *Religious Experience Reconsidered*, 118–119.
148. Ibid., 19.
149. Taves writes that her attributional approach is an extension of Proudfoot's epis-
     temological work, explaining her goals: "While Proudfoot's argument fueled
     the constructivist fires of the 1990s and contributed to the growing critique
     of the sui generis model within religious studies, few scholars of religion fol-
     lowed him into psychology in order to further develop the attributive model for
     use in religious studies. Now, as the cognitive revolution is sweeping through
     psychology and is even gaining a foothold in religious studies, it is time to
     recover and extend Proudfoot's efforts in light of more recent work in psychol-
     ogy" (ibid., 94).
150. Finbarr Curtis makes a similar argument, contending that the call for advanc-
     ing scholarship by violating *sui generis* taboos (or "protective strategies") in the
     work of Taves and like-minded scholars conveys an intellectual heroism that,
     at its core, is underlined by an ideological agenda rather than the objective
     boundaries of cognitive research that such scholars purport to promote. See
     Finbarr Curtis, "Ann Taves's *Religious Experience Reconsidered* is a Sign of a
     Global Apocalypse that Will Kill Us All," *Religion* 40 (2010): 288–289.
151. David Hume, *Dialogues and Natural History of Religion*, edited by J. C. A. Gaskin
     (New York: Oxford University Press, 1993), 127. It is important to note that the
     secularization thesis—the notion that a major secularization of Western culture
     emerged during the Enlightenment period—has, in recent years, been chal-
     lenged by historians. However, even those who challenge the thesis recognize
     the eminent contribution of skeptical philosophers to the intellectual debates
     on religious experience present in Enlightenment Europe. See, for instance,
     the work of Jane Shaw, *Miracles in Enlightenment England* (New Haven, CT: Yale
     University Press, 2006). While Shaw acknowledges the diversity of religious
     practices present in Enlightenment Christianity, she does not deny the impor-
     tant impact that skeptics like David Hume or deists like John Toland had on
     Western intellectual thought. See, esp., 144–173. For a work that supports the

secularization thesis, see Owen Chadwick, *The Secularization of the European Mind in the Nineteenth Century* (Cambridge: Cambridge University Press, 1990). Chadwick's point, though ironic, is noteworthy: "Enlightenment was of the few. Secularization is of the many" (9).

152. Hume, *Dialogues and Natural History*, 184.

153. Brad S. Gregory, "The Other Confessional History: On Secular Bias in the Study of Religion," *History and Theory* 45, no. 4 (December 2006): 137.

154. See Ludwig Feuerbach, *The Essence of Christianity*, trans. George Eliot (Amherst, NY: Prometheus Books 1989). For Feuerbach's critiques of mysticism, see esp., 87–100.

155. Ibid., 88–89.

156. Feuerbach writes: "indeed, it is precisely our task to show that theology is nothing else than an unconscious, esoteric pathology, anthropology, and psychology, and that therefore real anthropology, real pathology, and real psychology have far more claim to the name of theology than has theology itself, because this is nothing more than an imaginary psychology and anthropology" (ibid., 88–89).

157. Among the most prominent thinkers that have been influenced by Feuerbach's views on religion are Karl Marx (1818–1883) and Sigmund Freud (1856–1939). Hans Küng explains: "Like Marx's opium theory at an earlier stage, Freud's illusion theory is grounded in Feuerbach's projection theory." See Hans Küng, *Freud and the Problem of God*, trans. Edward Quinn (New Haven, CT and London: Yale University Press, 1990), 75. See also W. W. Meissner, S.J., *Psychoanalysis and Religious Experience* (New Haven, CT: Yale University Press, 1986), 88.

158. Cited from Nelstrop et al., *Christian Mysticism*, 233. For Nietzsche's original discourse on the "death of God," see Friedrich Nietzsche, *The Gay Science*, trans. J. Nauckhoff and A. Del Caro (Cambridge: Cambridge University Press, 2001), 119–120.

159. Callahan, *Women Who Hear Voices*, 1.

160. Hollywood, *Sensible Ecstasy*, 243.

161. Ibid., 243. Hollywood notes that Charcot also attempted to pathologically explain demonic possession as a form of hysteria. See ibid., 347n22. For the original work, see Jean-Martin Charcot and Paul Richer, *Les demoniaques dans l 'art suive de "La foi qui guerit"* (Paris: Macula, 1984).

162. Ann Taves, *Fits, Trances, and Visions: Experiencing Religion and Explaining Experience from Wesley to James* (Princeton, NJ: Princeton University Press, 1999), 248.

163. Ibid.

164. Beauvoir, quoted in Hollywood, *Sensible Ecstasy*, 243.

165. Ibid.

166. Callahan, *Women Who Hear Voices*, 11.

167. As quoted in ibid., 10. For original source, see Oliver Sacks, "The Visions of Hildegard," in *The Man Who Mistook His Wife for a Hat and Other Clinical Tales* (New York: Harper & Row, 1987), 168.

168. See Harmless, *Mystics*, 67.

169. Callahan, *Women Who Hear Voices*, 10.

170. Sluhovsky, *Believe Not Every Spirit*, 2–3.

171. See Callahan, *Women Who Hear Voices*, 14–15.

172. Sluhovsky, *Believe Not Every Spirit*, 2–3.

173. Ibid., 2–3.

174. Callahan, *Women Who Hear Voices*, 16.

175. Ibid., 17.

176. Meissner, *Psychoanalysis and Religious Experience*, 88.

177. Küng, *Freud and the Problem of God*, 75.

178. Ibid., 76.

179. "Oceanic feeling" was a phrase first used in a correspondence between Romain Rolland and Freud in regard to religion and extraordinary experiences. In a letter dated December 5, 1927, Rolland had written to Freud about the "oceanic feeling," shortly after Freud's publication of *The Future of an Illusion*, one of Freud's major works on religion which Rolland was replying to. Freud subsequently wrote in *Civilization and Its Discontents* that the "views expressed by the friend whom I so much honour [Rolland], and who himself once praised the magic of illusion in a poem, caused me no small difficulty. I cannot discover this 'oceanic' feeling in myself." Interestingly, Freud's admission is not dissimilar from that of William James who, in an essay on mysticism, wrote: "Much interest in the subject of religious mysticism has been shown in philosophical circles of late years. Most of the writings I have seen have treated the subject from the outside, for I know of no one who has spoken as having the direct authority of experience in favor of his views. I also am an outsider." However, G. William Barnard argues that to say that James was an outsider to experience is far from true. "While it is obvious that James is by no means a 'professional mystic,' at the same time, it is also apparent that he has had many, often quite dramatic, and typically unasked for, experiences that struck *him* as being 'quasi-mystical.' After all, as James himself admits in this essay ["A Suggestion about Mysticism"], it was several of these recent personal experiences that prompted him to propose once again a theory that could account for these sudden and powerful alterations of consciousness." See Sigmund Freud, *Civilization and Its Discontents*, trans. and ed. James Strachey (New York/London: W.W. Norton, 1961), 11, n. 2; William James, "A Suggestion about Mysticism" *Journal of Philosophy, Psychology and Scientific Methods* 7, no. 4 (February 17, 1910): 85; James's essay is also available in Richard Woods, *Understanding Mysticism* (New York: Image Books, 1980), 215–222; and G. William Barnard, *Exploring Unseen Worlds*, 61.

180. Callahan, *Women Who Hear Voices*, 17.

181. Modern scholars, Amy Hollywood explains, make a distinction between "female mysticism" and "male mysticism," identifying the former as very bodily, affective, experiential, visionary and even sensual and erotic, the kind of mysticism associated with Angela of Foligno, Mechthild of Magdeburg, and Teresa of Avila, among others. The latter type of mysticism, associated with males, is identified as intellectual and apophatic, the kind of mysticism seen in figures like Pseudo-Dionysius. Hollywood argues convincingly, however, that the distinction "does not quite fit the evidence," seeing prominent exceptions to this gender-specific categorizing: "The twelfth-century Cistercian Bernard of Clairvaux, the greatest of the male monastic commentators on the Song of Songs, both initiated and provided the vocabulary and images for erotic mysticism of the thirteenth and fourteenth centuries. The thirteenth century beguine, Marguerite Porete, on the other hand, eschewed visionary experience and erotic ecstasies in favor of an absolute union of the annihilated soul with the divine"; Hollywood, *Sensible Ecstasy*, 8. For an examination of the Songs of Songs as the text inspiring an erotic mysticism in medieval writing and spirituality, see Denys Turner, *Eros and Allegory: Medieval Exegesis of the Song of Songs* (Kalamazoo, MI: Cistercian Publications, 1995). Also see Constance M. Furey, "Sexuality," in *The Cambridge Companion to Christian Mysticism*, ed. Amy Hollywood and Patricia Beckman (New York: Cambridge University Press, 2012), 328–340.

182. Callahan, *Women Who Hear Voices*, 18.

183. Meissner, *Psychoanalysis and Religious Experience*, vii.

184. See Sigmund Freud, "Obsessive Actions and Religious Practices" (1907), *The Freud Reader*, ed. Peter Gay (New York: W.W. Norton, 1995[1989]), 429. Freud's other major works on religion are *Totem and Taboo* (1912), *The Future of an Illusion* (1927), *Civilization and its Discontents* (1930), and *Moses and Monotheism* (1939).

185. Meissner, *Psychoanalysis and Religious Experience*, 58.

186. William R. Rogers, "Interdisciplinary Approaches to Moral and Religious Development: A Critical Overview," in *Toward Moral and Religious Maturity: The First International Conference on Moral and Religious Development*, ed. James Fowler and Antoine Vergote (Morristown, NJ: Silver Burdett, 1980), 31.

187. Ibid., 31.

188. Callahan, *Women Who Hear Voices*, 25.

189. Callahan, *Women Who Hear Voices*, 12.

190. Quoted in John Horgan, *Rational Mysticism*, 75.

191. Newberg, *Principles of Neurotheology*, 186.

CHAPTER 5

1. Henri Joyeux and René Laurentin, *Etudes scientifiques et médicales sur les apparitions de Medjugorje* (Paris: O.E.I.L., 1985), 21.

2. Craig, *Spark from Heaven*, 135.
3. Ibid., 140.
4. Sullivan, *Miracle Detective*, 386.
5. Ibid., 206.
6. Quoted in ibid.
7. Ibid., 206–207. Similarly, Andrew Newberg and his colleagues explain important distinctions between mystics and psychotics, writing that the two "tend to have very different interpretations of the meaning of their experiences. Psychotics in delusional states often have feelings of religious grandiosity and inflated egotistical importance—they may see themselves, for example, as special emissaries from God, blessed with an important message for the world, or with the spiritual power to heal. Mystical states, on the other hand, usually involve a loss of pride and ego, a quieting of the mind, and an emptying of the self—all of which is required before the mystic can become a suitable vessel for God." See Andrew Newberg and Eugene D'Aquili with Vince Rause, *Why God Won't Go Away: Brain Science and the Biology of Belief* (New York: Ballantine Books, 2001), 110.
8. Quoted in Sullivan, *Miracle Detective*, 206–207.
9. Joyeux and Laurentin, *Etudes scientifiques et médicales*, 67.
10. René Laurentin and Henry Joyeux, *Scientific and Medical Studies on the Apparitions at Medjugorje*, trans. Luke Griffin (Dublin: Veritas, 1987), 46. Curiously, the French edition of this work (Joyeux and Laurentin, *Etudes scientifiques et médicales*) provides a transcription of this paragraph—describing the visionaries— that omits the sentence about the visionaries' dress with an ellipsis; the English translation provides a more complete description. (From the French edition: "Ce sont des jeunes de la champagne qui paraissent ne pasavoir besoin ni de psychologue, ni de pschiatre. . . . Ils ne donnent pas plus l'impression d'etre bigots, mais semblent avoir chacun leur personnalite; avec chacun d'eux, on se sent tres a l'aise: ni genies, ni simplets, ni manipules mais libres, rayonnant d' une santé solide, et sains de corps et d'espirit," 66–67.) It is noteworthy that in the English edition, Laurentin is identified as the first author while in the French edition it is Joyeux; therefore, the order of the authors will be cited here accordingly in relation to which edition is being referenced, with the corresponding shortened title.
11. Sullivan, *Miracle Detective*, 152.
12. Quoted in Kraljevic, *The Apparitions*, 198; emphasis in original. For Dr. Stopar's full report, see pages 197–199.
13. Quoted in Laurentin and Joyeux, *Scientific and Medical Studies*, 17.
14. Sullivan, *Miracle Detective*, 162.
15. Quoted in Laurentin and Joyeux, *Scientific and Medical Studies*, 17.
16. Sullivan, *Miracle Detective*, 162.
17. Laurentin and Joyeux, *Scientific and Medical Studies*, 16.
18. Ibid., 17.

19. Sullivan, *Miracle Detective*, 242.

20. Ibid.

21. Andreas Resch et al., "Commissions and Teams: Research on the Visionaries," *Medugorje*, http://www.medjugorje.hr/en/medjugorje-phenomenon/church/scientific-researches/commissions/.

22. Sullivan, *Miracle Detective*, 386.

23. Paolo Apolito, *The Internet and the Madonna: Religious Visionary Experience on the Web*, trans. Antony Shugaar (Chicago: University of Chicago Press, 2005), 136.

24. Michael Mayr and Andreas Resch, *The Visionaries from Medjugorje: On Trial by Science*, documentary film. FilmGruppeMunchen, 2004.

25. Ibid.

26. Ibid.

27. Mirjana, who as a teenager used to visit the village of Medjugorje in the summers, was raised in the urban environment of Sarajevo and attended the University of Sarajevo. Owing to personal persecution that she received from the Yugoslav communist authorities, which involved harassment from her professors, Mirjana decided not to continue and finish her studies, but remains the only visionary to have attended college.

28. Mayr, *Visionaries from Medjugorje*

29. Ibid.

30. For Dr. Sanguinetti's report see, again, Sullivan, *Miracle Detective*, 206.

31. Ibid., 160.

32. Quoted in ibid., 161.

33. Ibid., 162.

34. Laurentin and Joyeux, *Scientific and Medical Studies*, 54.

35. Ibid., 20.

36. Sullivan, *Miracle Detective*, 203.

37. Ibid.

38. Laurentin and Joyeux, *Scientific and Medical Studies*, 55.

39. Ibid., 20.

40. Ibid., 64.

41. Sullivan, *Miracle Detective*, 386.

42. Resch et al., "Commissions and Teams."

43. Sullivan, *Miracle Detective*, 387.

44. Ibid.

45. Mayr, *Visionaries from Medjugorje*.

46. Ibid. Quotation provided by documentary narrator (unnamed).

47. Resch et al., "Commissions and Teams."

48. Quoted in Mayr, *Visionaries from Medjugorje*.

49. Apolito, *Internet and the Madonna*, 136.

50. Quoted in Mayr, *Visionaries from Medjugorje*.

51. Philippot's studies recorded in Laurentin and Joyeux, *Scientific and Medical Studies*, 64–66.

52. Ibid., 64.

53. Ibid., 65.

54. Ibid., 64.

55. Craig, *Spark from Heaven*, 138.

56. Ibid., 140.

57. Laurentin and Joyeux, *Scientific and Medical Studies*, 64. Both Ivan Dragičević c and Vicka Ivanković, ages 19 and 20 during the experiments, experienced no eyelid movements during their apparitions. Dragičević's experience was recorded on October 7, 1984, while Ivanković's was recorded a day earlier on October 6, 1984.

58. In distinction from the 1985 Italian team, who conducted more in-depth studies.

59. Sullivan, *Miracle Detective*, 163.

60. Ibid.

61. Laurentin and Joyeux, *Scientific and Medical Studies*, 65.

62. Ibid., 65.

63. Ibid., 66, emphasis added.

64. Sullivan, *Miracle Detective*, 202–203.

65. Laurentin and Joyeux, *Scientific and Medical Studies*, 35.

66. Ibid.

67. Rouquerol's studies recorded in ibid., 70.

68. Craig, *Spark from Heaven*, 138.

69. Laurentin and Joyeux, *Scientific and Medical Studies*, 27.

70. There is some ambiguity as to what the name is of the doctor who performed this test, given (slightly) contradictory reports from sources. Craig identifies him simply as "Professor Santini" while Sullivan identifies him as "Dr. Michael Sabatini"; Nolan, as Craig, reports "Professor Santini" while James Paul Pandarakalam identifies him as "Dott Santini." Sullivan writes of "Dr. Michael Sabatini" as "a psychopharmocologist fresh from the faculty of Columbia University, where he had spent years studying the 'problem of pain.'" Nolan's report corroborates this content, though differing in the provided name, listing "Professor Santini" as a "neuro-psycho-pharmacologist, who for many years has studied the problem of pain at the Columbia University of New York." See Craig, *Spark from Heaven*, 140; Sullivan, *Miracle Detective*, 204; Denis Nolan, *Medjugorje: A Time for Truth, a Time for Action* (Santa Barbara, CA: Queenship, 1993), 143; James Paul Pandarakalam, "Are the Apparitions of Medjugorje Real?" *Journal of Scientific Exploration* 15, no. 2 (2001): 231.

71. Craig, *Spark from Heaven*, 140.

72. Pandarakalam, "Apparitions of Medjugorje," 232.

73. Craig, *Spark from Heaven*, 140.

74. Sullivan, *Miracle Detective*, 204.

75. Quoted in ibid., 204.

76. Laurentin and Joyeux, *Scientific and Medical Studies*, 70.

77. Pandarakalam, "Apparitions of Medjugorje," 234.

78. Laurentin and Joyeux, *Scientific and Medical Studies*, 71, 75.

79. Ibid., 26.

80. Pandarakalam, "Apparitions of Medjugorje," 235.

81. Craig, *Spark from Heaven*, 134.

82. See Pandarakalam, "Apparitions of Medjugorje," 232–233; Joyeux and Laurentin, *Etudes scientifiques et médicales*, 47; Craig, *Spark from Heaven*, 139.

83. Pandarakalam, "Apparitions," 232.

84. Ibid.

85. Ibid.

86. Laurentin and Joyeux, *Scientific and Medical Studies*, 72.

87. Ibid.

88. My appreciation to Fr. Philip Simo, O.S.B., for clarification on this topic. Cf., Evelyn Underhill writes, "For the time of his ecstasy the mystic is, for all practical purposes, as truly living in the supersensual world as the normal human animal is living in the sensual world. He is experiencing the highest and most joyous of those temporary and unstable states—those 'passive unions'—in which his consciousness escapes the limitations of the senses, rises to freedom, and is united for an instant with the 'great life of the All.'" Underhill, *Mysticism* (Aziloth ed.), 287.

89. Laurentin and Joyeux, *Scientific and Medical Studies*, 74–75.

90. Ibid., 75.

91. Resch et al., "Commissions and Teams."

92. Apolito, *Internet and the Madonna*, 137.

93. Ibid., 137. For a more in-depth account of the theological grounding that the Italian team incorporated in its results, see Marco Margnelli and Gorgio Gagliardi, *Le apparizioni della Madonna: da Lourdes a Medjugorje* (Milan, Italy: Edizioni Riza, 1987).

94. Apolito, *Internet and the Madonna*, 137.

95. Resch et al., "Commissions and Teams."

96. Ibid.

97. Ibid.

98. Sullivan, *Miracle Detective*, 387.

99. Resch et al., "Commissions and Teams."

100. Cited in Nolan, *Medjugorje and the Church*, 4.

CHAPTER 6

1. Mario Beauregard and Vincent Paquette "EEG Activity in Carmelite Nuns during a Mystical Experience," *Neuroscience Letters* 444 (2008): 1.

2. We will see the same reality later in the work of Michael P. Carroll and Richard Dawkins.

3. Beauregard and Paquette reference various studies on neuroscience and religious experiences in their sources without any mention of the studies in Medjugorje, indicating a lack of knowledge of the Medjugorje studies. A major reason for this—as it is not an isolated incident of scholarly ignorance toward the Medjugorje studies—may be that when René Laurentin published the initial findings of the scientific studies on the visionaries, he did so with a Catholic publisher, thus using a religious press as opposed to an academic press, which scholars would be more likely to read.

4. Callahan, *Women Who Hear Voices*, 12

5. Beauregard and Paquette, "EEG Activity in Carmelite Nuns," 2.

6. Ibid.

7. Ibid.

8. It is noteworthy that in a future article the authors apply *identical* methodology when, again, using the Carmelite nuns as subjects. See Beauregard and Paquette, "Neural Correlates of a Mystical Experience in Carmelite Nuns," *Neuroscience Letters* 405 (2006): 186–190. In this article the authors write, repeating their methodology verbatim from their previous work: "In the Mystical condition, subjects were asked to remember and relive (eyes closed) the most intense mystical experience ever felt in their lives as a member of the Carmelite Order. This strategy was adopted given that the nuns told us before the onset of the study that 'God can't be summoned at will'" (187).

9. Nina P. Azari et al., "Neural Correlates of Religious Experience," *European Journal of Neuroscience* 13, no. 8 (2001): 1649–1652.

10. Ann Taves writes of Azari's scholarly work as constituting "pioneering use of brain-imaging techniques to identify neural correlates of religious experience" and emphasizes that Azari "provides the most sophisticated attempt so far to come to terms with the issues surrounding the neuroscientific study of religious experiences." See Taves, *Religious Experience Reconsidered*, 11.

11. Proudfoot's influence is strongly evident in the article "Neural Correlates of Religious Experience," two of his most prominent works being used to form the basis for a cognitive attributional theory as an explanation for religious experience. See Azari et al., "Neural Correlates," 1649.

12. Ibid., 1649.

13. Ibid.

14. Ibid., 1650.

15. Ibid.

16. Ibid., 1652.

17. Newberg and D'Aquili, *Why God Won't Go Away*, 1–10; Andrew Newberg and Mark Robert Waldman, *How God Changes Your Brain: Breakthrough Findings from a Leading Neuroscientist* (New York: Ballantine Books, 2010), 41–56.

18. Newberg and D'Aquili, *Why God Won't Go Away*, 3.

19. As one example of how neuroscience can discern such factors like compassion or social awareness through areas of the brain, Newberg and Waldman explain that many forms of meditation stimulate an important part of the brain known as the anterior cingulate cortex. "The anterior cingulate cortex is situated between the frontal lobe and the limbic system, acting as a mediator between our feelings and our thoughts. It is involved in social awareness and intuition, and is larger in women than in men. This may explain why women generally are more empathic, socially skilled, and more reactive to fear-inducing stimuli." The fact that spiritual practices like meditation can stimulate the anterior cingulate cortex shows how spirituality can affect the brain and, essentially, influence the shape of characteristics that define a person. See Newberg and Waldman, *How God Changes Your Brain*, 52–53.

20. Edward F. Kelly and Michael Grosso, "Mystical Experience," in Kelly et al., *Irreducible Mind*, 567.

21. As was the case, recounted in chapter 2, when the visionaries initially believed that their apparitions would end on July 3, 1981, after reading a book on the apparitions in Lourdes and presuming that they would experience the same number of daily apparitions as Bernadette Soubirous did in 1858. On July 4 the visionaries no longer met in church in front of a crowd with the expectation of receiving another apparition but went their separate ways that evening, believing their experiences have ended, and still each visionary unexpectedly experienced an apparition in their individual circumstances.

22. Quoted in Horgan, *Rational Mysticism*, 75.

23. Newberg and D'Aquili, *Why God Won't Go Away*, 111.

24. Ibid. I accentuate in the italics that it is an opinion here, for Newberg and his colleagues, in order to emphasize the contribution that the Medjugorje studies are able to make by taking such an important opinion and turning it into a demonstrable fact through empirical findings.

25. Ibid., 111–113.

26. Laurentin and Joyeux, *Scientific and Medical Studies*, 74–75.

27. Ibid., 70.

28. See Newberg and D'Aquili, *Why God Won't Go Away*, 112.

29. Laurentin and Joyeux, *Scientific and Medical Studies*, 17.

30. Mark S. Micale, *Approaching Hysteria: Disease and Its Interpretations* (Princeton, NJ: Princeton University Press, 1995), 261.

31. In fact, Charcot had an influence on a young Sigmund Freud. Hans Küng explains that as a young doctor Freud obtained "a travel scholarship to go to the 'Mecca of neurology,' the Paris nerve clinic [to work] under the great Jean Martin Charcot. Here he began to take an interest in hysteria . . . and in hypnosis (as a healing method), the first beginnings of his *investigation of the soul,* the turning from neurology to psychopathology" (Küng, *Freud and the Problem of God*, 17; emphasis in original). Stephen A. Mitchell and Margaret J. Black

further explain that "Freud started out as a researcher in neurophysiology, and when he switched from research to clinical practice, he treated patients suffering from what were understood to be neurological conditions, victims of damaged or weakened nerves. The dramatic demonstrations of the renowned neurologists Jean-Martin Charcot and Hippolyte Bernheim he witnessed during a stay in France sparked his interest in unconscious ideas, fatefully shifting his focus from brain to mind." Thus not only was Feud influenced by Charcot and the Salpêtrière School but also by Charcot's major rival Bernheim and the Nancy School. Such influences led to breakthrough work for Freud, particularly with patients suffering from hysteria. Mitchell and Black continue: "Before Freud, hysterics—patients who suffered from physical disabilities but evidenced no obvious actual physical impairment—were regarded as malingerers, morally suspect fakers, or victims of a generally weakened nervous system that produced random, meaningless disturbances in functioning. Freud, following Charcot, Bernheim, and other practitioners of medical hypnotism, demonstrated that hysterics suffered a disease not of brain but of mind. It was ideas, not nerves, that were the source of trouble." See Stephen A. Mitchell and Margaret J. Black, *Freud and Beyond: A History of Modern Psychoanalytical Thought* (New York: Basic Books, 1995), 2–3.

32. The term was introduced by Émile Littré in 1869. Robert Kugelmann explains: "For Littre, demonic possession, miracles such as happened at Lourdes, and mystical experiences were all hysterical in nature. Charcot affirmed Littre's retrospective diagnoses, using his categories of the stages of hysteria." See Robert Kugelmann, *Psychology and Catholicism: Contested Boundaries* (Cambridge: Cambridge University Press, 2011), 150–151; also Micale, *Approaching Hysteria*, 263.

33. Sofie Lachapelle explains: "Physicians have been included in the proceedings of canonization since the Middle Ages, but the role of medicine in religious enquiries became more important during the nineteenth century. The intrusion of the scientific into the religious has been discussed mostly in regard to Lourdes." Sofie Lachapelle, "Between Miracle and Sickness: Louise Lateau and the Experience of Stigmata and Ecstasy," *Configurations* 12, no. 1 (Winter 2004): 88n20. For a great discussion of the role that Lourdes played in debates on science and religion, especially in the medical culture of nineteenth-century France, see Micale, *Approaching Hysteria*, 262–277. Kugelmann makes a connection between the miraculous culture of Lourdes and the culture of nineteenth-century Spiritualism, as these topics related to the development of psychology; see Kugelmann, *Psychology and Catholicism*, 144–151. For more comprehensive treatments of Lourdes, see Ruth Harris, *Lourdes: Body and Spirit in the Secular Age* (New York: Viking Press, 2009); and Suzanne Kaufman, *Consuming Visions: Mass Culture and the Lourdes Shrine* (Ithaca, NY: Cornell University Press, 2005).

34. Lachapelle, "Between Miracle and Sickness," 104.

35. Ibid., 103.

36. Ibid., 102.
37. Micale, *Approaching Hysteria*, 261. Lachapelle explains that the work dealt not only with "new contributions to the pathologization of mystical phenomena" but also with "classics of the witchcraft and demonic traditions" (Lachapelle, "Between Miracle and Sickness," 102).
38. Micale, *Approaching Hysteria*, 264.
39. Ibid.
40. Micale explains that "Bernheim and his colleagues contributed to the transition to twentieth-century psychological medicine by revealing the errors and excesses of the school of Salpêtrière." Ibid., 26.
41. Ibid., 264.
42. Ibid.
43. Hollywood, *Sensible Ecstasy*, 2–3.
44. Lachapelle, "Between Miracle and Sickness," 101.
45. Thomas Acklin, O.S.B. "Religious Symbolic Transformations of Desire: A Psychoanalytical and Theological Perspective on Desire in Religion," Ph.D. diss., Katholieke Universiteit te Leuven, 1982, 373. Noteworthy here is the parallelism between Janet and Freud, both connecting ecstasy or, in Freud's case, the "oceanic feeling," to a regressive and infantile state, or at least an analogous thought pattern resembling such a state.
46. Hollywood, *Sensible Ecstasy*, 2.
47. It is important to note, as Hollywood explains, that while partaking in the reinterpretation of Madeleine's experiences into pathological categories, Janet, however, "was much more sensitive to Madeleine's religious beliefs and practices than many of his contemporaries, most notably his teacher and collaborator Jean-Martin Charcot, who used retrospective diagnosis as a way of dismissing the religious claims of mystics (as well as demoniacs). Janet allowed a religious advisor to administer to Madeleine while she was in the hospital. He also noted her creativity, delicacy of mind, and intelligence. . . . After her discharge in 1904, Madeleine stayed in close touch with Janet until her death in 1918" (Ibid., 2–3). Similarly, noting how much sincerity Janet saw in Madeleine, notwithstanding his pathological diagnosis of her experiences, Lachapelle explains that "Janet never even considered the possibility of fraud in the case of Madeleine." Lachapelle, "Between Miracle and Sickness," 104.
48. Lachapelle, 104.
49. Ibid.
50. Cited in Kugelmann, *Psychology and Catholicism*, 150; original reference from Jan Goldstein, "The Hysteria Diagnosis and the Politics of Anticlericalism in Late Nineteenth-Century France," *Journal of Modern History* 54, no. 2 (June 1982): 209–239.
51. Micale, *Approaching Hysteria*, 261. Betraying the ideological ambitions of an evident scientism, Janet wrote on the subject of miraculous healings: "we must study the science of miracles so that we may be able to reproduce them at will.

Day by day . . . the domain of the supernatural is being restricted, thanks to the extension of the domain of science. One of the most notable among scientific victories over the mysteries of the universe will be achieved when we have tamed, have domesticated, the therapeutic miracle." Cited in Kugelmann, *Psychology and Catholicism*, 154–155; original reference from Pierre Janet, *Psychological Healing: A Historical and Clinical Study*, trans. E. Paul and C. Paul (New York: Arno, 1972); first published 1925.

52. Sofie Lachapelle, *Investigating the Supernatural: From Spiritism and Occultism to Psychical Research and Metapsychics in France, 1853-1931* (Baltimore, MD: Johns Hopkins University Press, 2011), 60.

53. As quoted in Callahan, *Women Who Hear Voices*, 10. For original source, see Sacks, "The Visions of Hildegard," 168.

54. Laurentin and Joyeux, *Scientific and Medical Studies*, 54.

55. Richard Dawkins, *The God Delusion* (New York: Houghton Mifflin, 2006), 91.

56. Michael P. Carroll, *The Cult of the Virgin Mary: Psychological Origins* (Princeton, NJ: Princeton University Press, 1986). For reviews of Carroll's book, see Daniel Bornstein, *Church History* 57, no. 4 (December 1988): 581–583; Jeffrey Burton Russell, *Journal of the American Academy of Religion* 55, no. 3 (Autumn 1987): 593–597; John H. Gagnon, *Contemporary Sociology* 17, no. 3 (May 1988): 376–377.

57. Zimdars-Swartz, *Encountering Mary*, 278.

58. Carroll, *Cult of the Virgin Mary*, 56.

59. Ibid., 59.

60. In fact, Carroll's hermeneutical methods in reaching these conclusions have been highly criticized by reviewers. Daniel Bornstein has alleged that Carroll displays limited knowledge of the vast literature on Marian apparitions and claims that Carroll "often distorts the studies that he does cite." Of particular concern to Bornstein is Carroll's elevation of psychoanalysis as the one and only framework of thought through which to understand the subject of apparitions, seeing an unhealthy dogmatism in the approach. "For Carroll, the psychoanalytic method constitutes an autonomous belief system, a sort of religion with its own sacred texts (the words of Freud, to which Carroll turns for guidance in any moment of uncertainty), its own revealed truth (the sexual origin of all activity), and its own fundamentalist insistence on the superiority of that revealed truth over mere sensory perception or human reason." Bornstein uses strong language in criticizing Carroll's book, arguing that scholars "interested in a sophisticated application of psychological theory to religious history will find this book an embarrassment," and concludes his review with an incendiary note regarding Carroll's publisher: "Princeton University Press should be ashamed of itself." While using less incendiary language, other reviews of Carroll's methodology have been equally negative. Jeffrey Burton Russell has written that while "claiming to describe the origins of the cult [of the Virgin Mary], Carroll shows virtually no understanding of modern historical scholarship" and "ignores contemporary studies of sexuality and religion in the early and medieval church—for example,

the work of Peter Brown, Caroline Bynum, and Charles Wood." Russell argues that Carroll's book "is a very model of reductionism." Akin to Bornstein, Russell is highly critical of how Carroll applies a single intellectual system—one branch of psychology in Freudian psychoanalysis—to account for the entire truth regarding the complexity of religious apparitions. Coming from a sociological perspective, John H. Gagnon likewise finds Carroll's reductionist approach unimpressive, explaining: "Perhaps the fundamental problem is using the tools of modern positivist social science to *explain away* religious experience, rather than attempting to interpret and understand acts of devotion and adoration" (emphasis in original). See Bornstein, *Church History*, 582–583; Russell, *Journal of the American Academy of Religion*, 594; Gagnon, *Contemporary Sociology*, 377; all three reviews as cited in note 56 of this chapter.

61. Carroll, *Cult of the Virgin Mary*, 117.
62. Ibid., 123.
63. Ibid.
64. Ibid., 124.
65. Ibid.
66. Ibid., 117, emphasis in the original.
67. Ibid., 123.
68. Quoted in Sullivan, *Miracle Detective*, 204.
69. Taves, *Religious Experience Reconsidered*, 110.
70. In addition to studies by neuroscientists who "have recently identified the regions of the brain that govern the sense of embodiment . . . and are now able to experimentally induce rudimentary out-of-body experiences . . . though there are as yet no studies that link practices [such as visualization, fasting, prayer] with the manipulation of those brain areas." In other words, while Taves additionally uses the work of neuroscientists who have identified regions of the brain associated with embodiment to support her argument, she concedes that such regions have not been linked with practices such as visualization; thus identifying an evident gap in the argument. See Ibid., 111.
71. Küng, *Freud and the Problem of God*, 36.
72. Volney P. Gay, *Freud on Ritual: Reconstruction and Critique* (Missoula, MT: Scholars Press, 1979), 2.
73. Gay qualifies this by explaining that: "Of course the trust and hope which the pious place upon their ritual acts may be quite misbased in fact and have their origins in dynamically unconscious notions of grandiosity, the omnipotence of thoughts, and other fantasies typical of the neurotic. However, it is not a man's fantasies which make him a neurotic, it is his ego's response to those fantasies, namely repression, which determines the extent of the symptoms generated by internal conflict. If we assume with Freud that the pious person's ego does not repress, but only suppresses, it follows that his worries and behavior cannot rightly be called neurotic." Ibid., 8.

74. Ibid., 28.

75. Ibid., 6–7.

76. It is clear that Freud equates these terms as he, in fact, uses them in the same sentence to denote the same function. Gay notes Freud's words in articulating that religious formation "seems to be based on the suppression, the renunciation of, certain instinctual impulses." Ibid., 6–7.

77. Ibid., 6.

78. Ibid., 7.

79. Gay contrasts the usage of terminology in Freud's essay, noting the significance in the distinctions as referring to diametrically different processes. "The primary fact which lies at the bottom of obsessional neurosis is always *'the repression of an instinctual impulse* . . . ['Verdrangung einer Triebregung'],"* Freud explains, while further explaining that the "formation of religion . . . seems to be based on the suppression, the renunciation of, certain instinctual impulses ['. . . der Religionsbildung scheint die Unterdruckung, der Verzicht auf gewisse Triebregungen zugrunde zu liegen.']." Ibid., 6.

80. Ibid., emphasis mine.

81. Ibid., 7.

82. Ibid., 9.

83. Ibid., 15.

84. Laurentin and Joyeux, *Scientific and Medical Studies*, 54.

85. Bernard McGinn, *The Foundations of Mysticism: Origins to Fifth Century* (New York: Crossroad, 1991), 332.

86. Freud, *Civilization and Its Discontents*, 11.

87. McGinn, *Foundations of Mysticism*, 332.

88. Ibid.

89. Ibid.

90. Ibid.

91. For an excellent usage of Freudian psychoanalysis to understanding the psychological dynamics of an alleged case of possession, see Antoine Vergote, *Guilt and Desire: Religious Attitudes and Their Pathological Derivatives*, trans. M. H. Wood (New Haven, CT: Yale University Press, 1988), 214–221.

92. In claiming that Gay's thesis is developed and advanced by the Medjugorje studies, I am referring to the fact that if there is not a technical connection made between neurosis and religion in the original psychoanalytic literature, as Gay claims, the absence of that connection (between neurosis and religion) is further promulgated by the Medjugorje studies, even if no direct reference is made to Freud or psychoanalysis.

CHAPTER 7

1. William James, "The Hidden Self," *Scribner's Magazine* 7, no. 3 (March 1890): 361.

2. Ibid., 361–362.

3. Ibid., 361.

4. Ibid.

5. Freud, *Civilization and Its Discontents*, 12.

6. James, "Hidden Self," 362, emphasis in original.

7. Taves, *Religious Experience Reconsidered*, 17.

8. "In the sui generis model, it is assumed that religious things exist and have inherently special properties. In the ascription model, it is assumed on the contrary that people ascribe religious characteristics to things which they then attribute religious causality." Ibid., 20.

9. James V. Spickard, "Does Taves Reconsider Experience Enough? A Critical Commentary on *Religious Experience Reconsidered*," *Religion* 40 (2010): 312. The reference to Rudolf Otto's work pertains to terminology found in Otto's book *The Idea of the Holy* (1923).

10. Ibid., 311.

11. Ibid., 312.

12. This is the essential component of Taves's hermeneutic that sets it apart from traditional constructivism and from Proudfoot's culturally conditioned attributional approach, as we noted earlier.

13. Taves's analysis of Stephen Bradley's and William Barnard's purported mystical experiences constitutes the key example of this approach in her book. See Taves, *Religious Experience Reconsidered*, 107–119.

14. Spickard, "Does Taves Reconsider Experience," 312. For the work that he is referencing, see James V. Spickard, "Spiritual Healing among the American Followers of a Japanese New Religion: Experience as a Factor in Religious Motivation," *Research in the Social Scientific Study of Religion* 3 (1991): 135–156; and "Body, Nature, and Culture in Spiritual Healing," in *Studies of Alternative Therapy 2: Bodies and Nature*, ed. H. Johannessen, 65–81 (INRAT/Odense: University Press, Copenhagen, 1995).

15. Furthermore, in response to Spickard, Taves conveys her belief that explaining religious experiences naturalistically does not necessarily explain them away by pointing to two anecdotal facts: that she once taught at an institution where many students identified themselves as religious but not believers in the supernatural, and that she once belonged to a denomination that promoted a naturalistic understanding of religion. Such personal and anecdotal details, however valid to Taves's own experiences or that of her former students, ignore the important subjectivity of the perspectives of the individuals that Taves's approach is analyzing. Taves, in other words, is not analyzing her own experiences or those of her former students who have a naturalistic understanding of religion but, rather, the experiences of individuals who have a supernatural understanding, wherein the reduction of that understanding, its "naturalization," can, in fact, explain away the integrity of the experiences. This is the case with Taves's naturalistic

analysis of Bradley's and Barnard's experiences. See Ann Taves, "Experience as Site of Contested Meaning and Value: The Attributional Dog and its Special Tail," *Religion* 40 (2010): 321–322; Taves, *Religious Experience Reconsidered*, 107–119.

16. Taves, "Experience as Site of Contested Meaning," 322.
17. Ibid.
18. Ibid., 322n2.
19. See the documentary *Mystery Files: Joan of Arc*, written and directed by Kate Haddock, narrated by Struan Rodger (Smithsonian Channel, 2010); for Taves's unconscious processing of Bradley's and Barnard's experiences, see Taves, *Religious Experience Reconsidered*, 104–111. Joan of Arc is a figure whose visionary and auditory experiences have often been the victim of reductive interpretations that denigrate the integrity of her encounters through pathological diagnosis, notwithstanding the incredible results that came from Joan's experiences. Sydney Callahan explains: "But even Joan the heroic maid, despite her extraordinary meteoric achievements and down-to-earth common sense, has been diagnosed as neurotic or psychotic by secular thinkers. At the end of the nineteenth century the famous French novelist [Émile] Zola could dub Joan a 'hysterical peasant girl whose dreamy-eyed interpreters were ignoring the scientific truth.'" Callahan, *Women Who Hear Voices*, 7–8.
20. Curtis, "Ann Taves's *Religious Experience Reconsidered*," 288.
21. Ibid., 289; Taves, *Religious Experience Reconsidered*, 34–35.
22. Curtis, "Ann Taves's *Religious Experience Reconsidered*," 289.
23. More on this will be observed in the following section with a brief overview of the work of John Milbank, who identifies the notion of secular neutrality as a mythos of modern thought. Proudfoot's very critique of *sui generis* thinkers as operating under a "protective strategy," and the goal of challenging such a framework, would in Curtis's logic constitute an ideological motive on Proudfoot's part, as he sees in Taves the advocacy to violate *sui generis* taboos. For his section on "protective strategies" see Proudfoot, *Religious Experience*, 199–208.
24. Timothy Fitzgerald, "'Experiences Deemed Religious': Radical Critique or Temporary Fix? Strategic Ambiguity in Ann Taves' Religious Experience Reconsidered," *Religion* 40 (2010): 297.
25. Ibid., 298.
26. Taves, "Experience as Site of Contested Meaning," 321.
27. Ibid.
28. Fitzgerald, "'Experiences Deemed Religious,'" 299.
29. Ibid.
30. Fitzgerald explains that the very concept "experience" is problematic in speaking of Barnard's out-of-body experience, as in "ordinary English an experience implies a subject and an object of experience, yet his testimony strains against the boundaries"; ibid., 299. While a valid point in terms of identifying the often apophatic nature of such experiences like Barnard's, as transcending adequate

linguistic conceptualization, perhaps Fitzgerald is overplaying this point. As was highlighted in chapter 3, mystical experiences have generally been designated into two (sometimes three) general locations: either as being unitive to the point that self-other boundaries are completely annihilated or being unitive while still maintaining degrees of a self-other distinction, as is often the case in visionary and apparitional experiences (the experiencing subject being distinct from the object of the vision/apparition). Barnard's altered state of consciousness seems aptly located within the former category of a unitive *experience* that transcended self-other boundaries.

31. Ibid., 299.
32. Ibid., 299; Taves, *Religious Experience Reconsidered*, 94.
33. Fitzgerald, "'Experiences Deemed Religious,'" 299.
34. Ibid.
35. Herein is the basis for Taves's discourse on the important distinction between etic and emic perspectives—which we will consider in greater detail below—in studying religious experiences, and how much each perspective can say. Taves, *Religious Experience Examined*, 158.
36. Ibid., 104–106.
37. Especially revealing in this regard is a table located in chapter 3 of Taves's book presenting different levels of explanation in analyzing Bradley's and Barnard's purported mystical experiences within intrapersonal, interpersonal, intragroup, and intergroup dynamics. Taves distinguishes three levels of analysis in observing their experiences within these categories: (1) What Explained [the] Event/Experience; (2) How Explained by Attributor; and (3) How Experience might be Explained by Researchers. The second level of analysis gives Bradley's and Barnard's explanations for their experiences, the former seeing his as an experience of the Holy Spirit and the latter seeing his as a mystical experience. However, the first level of analysis—"What Explained [the] Event/Experience"—gives Taves's explanation of these experiences, reinterpreting the ontological foundations through a naturalistic interpretation of each event which, under the third category—"How Experience might be Explained by Researchers"—articulates a way for scholars to naturalistically understand and interpret, through unconscious processing, both the process and the origins of these experiences. What this table implies, particularly the contradistinction between the first level of analysis [What Explained (the) Event/Experience] and second level of analysis [How Explained by Attributor] is exactly the critique that Spickard pointed to: that the explanations of the subjects (or the attributors) of their own experiences are wrong compared to the "real" explanations (meaning, Taves's reinterpretation) of these experiences. See ibid., 113; also the discussion accompanying the table, ibid., 104–119.
38. Taves, "Experience as Site of Contested Meaning," 322.

39. Curtis, "Ann Taves's *Religious Experience Reconsidered*," 289; emphasis mine.
40. Ibid.
41. Spickard, "Does Taves Reconsider Experience," 312.
42. There are, to be sure, things to be gained from understanding the human dynamics of extraordinary religious experiences that illuminate the psychological processes of such experiences, constituting a healthy, benign reductionism, without claiming to explain the totality of a phenomenon through complete reductionism.
43. Spickard acknowledges that Taves's reduction is not all-encompassing while, at the same time, stressing that her reduction does lean toward an all-encompassing proclivity. He explains that there are three perspectives present in Taves's book—experiences "can be religious in themselves, they can be deemed religious, or they can be mistakenly identified as religious"—while also stating that "Taves too often equates these last two. Though she claims to focus on 'deeming' experiences, in fact she focuses on explaining them naturalistically—and as something other than what they appear to be." Ibid., 312.
44. Taves's analysis of Bradley's and Barnard's purported mystical experiences does constitute the key examples of this approach. See Taves, *Religious Experience Reconsidered*, 104–119.
45. Again, Taves's ascriptive approach claims that "religious or mystical or spiritual or sacred 'things' are created when religious significance is assigned to them." In other words, experiences are not understood, through this hermeneutic, as innately religious or mystical but simply "receive" that identity once such an ascription is given to them. Taves contrasts this approach with the *sui generis* model, which "assumes implicitly or explicitly" that there "are uniquely religious (or mystical or spiritual) experiences, emotions, acts, or objects." See ibid., 17.
46. Spickard's point comparing the metaphysical tendencies of Taves's hermeneutic with Otto's could easily be applied here, with the substitution of Freud for Otto: "Each posits a metaphysic that sets the rules for explanation, then reads the results back from the rules it has set." Spickard, "Does Taves Reconsider Experience," 312.
47. Taves, *Religious Experience Reconsidered*, 158.
48. It is noteworthy to recall that both James and Freud admitted studying religious experiences from an outsider's perspective, thus an etic angle, although with very different approaches, James notably respecting the possibility that something more is happening in mystical experiences than science can fully grasp while Freud restricting explanations of such experiences to the naturalistic, interpretive parameters of psychoanalysis. As previously noted, Freud wrote in relation to mystical experiences, "I cannot discover this 'oceanic' feeling in myself" while James, similarly, wrote, "Much interest in the subject of religious mysticism has been shown in philosophical circles of late years. Most of the writings I have seen have treated the subject from the outside, for I know of no one

who has spoken as having the direct authority of experience in favor of his views. I also am an outsider" (see chapter 4, note 179).

49. James's hermeneutic of the "more" is deeply indebted to his understanding of the subconscious, an understanding that was inspired by the work of Frederic Myers. Taves explains: "Indeed, for James the real beauty of Myers's (as opposed to [Pierre] Janet's) understanding of the subconscious was that it ultimately said very little about origins. In adopting Myers's conception, James left open the question of where the subconscious ended, whether in the personal self or beyond it, and thus placed *ultimate* questions about origins outside the purview of the science of religions." See Ann Taves, "Religious Experience and the Divisible Self: William James (and Frederic Myers) as Theorist(s) of Religion," *Journal of the American Academy of Religion* 71, no. 2 (June 2003): 319; also, for an expanded version of this article, see Taves, *Fits, Trances, Visions*, 250–260.

50. It is noteworthy that James considered the subconscious to be the place where the "more," meaning the encounter between the human and the divine—James called the subconscious "the mediating term" (*Varieties of Religious Experience*, 457)—can take place. Taves explains that James's understanding of the subconscious in relation to religious experiences and his open-ended hermeneutic of the "more" were greatly influenced by Myers. Myers, like James and other early fathers of psychology, examined spiritualist phenomena, and Myers used his examinations of the activities of such subjects as spiritualist mediums to formulate his theories on the workings of the subconscious. Unlike Pierre Janet and his mentor Jean-Martin Charcot, thus the Salpêtrière School in Paris, Myers did not interpret the presence of a secondary self within a person—a dissociative model of consciousness that pointed to a subliminal subconscious as a second personality—as something that must be associated with pathology, specifically as being symptomatic of hysteria (Janet's interpretation). Taves explains that Myers and James, "like Charcot's rivals at Nancy, believed that secondary centers of consciousness could exist in healthy persons." Thus, by "placing the pathological, the normal, and the potentially supranormal within a common frame of reference, Myers created a theoretical space (the subliminal) through which influences beyond the individual, should they exist, might be expected to manifest themselves. In explaining spirit possession as a 'shifting of the psychical centre of energy *within the personality of the automatist*' without ruling out 'the possibility that *some influence external* to the [automatist] may at times be operative,' Myers modeled the open-ended approach to explanation that James later adopted in the *Varieties*." What is also noteworthy here, particularly by contrast between contemporary and traditional interpretations, is the development of the ontological understandings of the subconscious—specifically, the fact that a number of the forefathers of psychological research, like Myers and James, were open to the possibility of an ontological participation of the divine or a spiritual reality (articulated in the pluralistic formulation of the "more") in the workings

of the subconscious, while many contemporary scholars have (de)ontologically reinterpreted the workings of the unconscious in a purely secular fashion, at times even as a substitute for the divine. See James, *Varieties of Religious Experience*, 456–457; Taves, "Religious Experience and the Divisible Self," 311, 317; for a historical account of the relationships between early psychology, spiritualism, and Catholic mysticism, see Kugelmann, *Psychology and Catholicism*, 165–202.

51. Quoted in Parsons, *Enigma of the Oceanic Feeling*, 65.

52. Spickard: "Though she claims to focus on 'deeming' experiences, in fact she focuses on explaining them naturalistically—and as something other than what they appear to be." The critiques that both Spickard and Fitzgerald invoke of Taves's treatment of Barnard's out-of-body experience speak well to this reality in highlighting that she is making metaphysical claims about the experience that transcend that which can be empirically known. Taves's explanation of the ascriptive approach to interpreting religious experiences that she uses underlies such a metaphysical commitment within the hermeneutic by deductively beginning with the conclusion that experiences are not inherently religious or mystical. See Spickard, "Does Taves Reconsider Experience," 312; Fitzgerald, "'Experiences Deemed Religious,'" 299; Taves, *Religious Experience Reconsidered*, 17.

53. See Dermot A. Lane, *The Experience of God: An Invitation to Do Theology*, rev. ed. (New York/Mahwah, NJ: Paulist Press, 2003), 37–38.

54. Spickard, "Does Taves Reconsider Experience," 313.

55. Again, the distinction should be stressed between, on the one hand, unconscious processing, which Taves is naturalistically able to do—for example, analyzing unintentional behavior and thought-patterns associated with Bradley's and Barnard's purported religious experiences (see Taves, *Religious Experience Reconsidered*, 104–106)—and on the other hand, ontologically locating the source of the purported religious experiences in the unconscious, which a naturalistic perspective is unable to do, violating its own hermeneutical parameters.

56. Alexandra Klaushofer, "Faith Beyond Nihilism: The Retrieval of Theism in Milbank and Taylor," *Heythrop Journal* 40 (1999): 136. The cited words are Klaushofer's paraphrase of Milbank's ideas. Milbank contends that Wittgenstein put it well: "in so far as people think they can see 'the limits of human understanding,' they believe of course that they can see beyond these." Milbank continues: "The 'critique of metaphysics' which sociology, as [Peter] Berger says, claims to carry forwards, thus turns out to be a new metaphysics." John Milbank, *Theology and Social Theory: Beyond Secular Reason*, 2nd ed. (Oxford: Blackwell, 2006), 106. For critical perspectives of Milbank's ideas, see Nico Vorster, "The Secular and the Sacred in the Thinking of John Milbank," *Journal for the Study of Religions and Ideologies* 11, no. 32 (Summer 2012): 109–131; Richard Roberts, "Transcendental Sociology? A Critique of John Milbank's *Theology and Social Theory: Beyond Secular Reason*," *Scottish Journal of Theology* 46 (1993): 527–535;

Debra Dean Murphy, "Power, Politics and Difference: A Feminist Response to John Milbank," *Modern Theology* 10 (1994): 131–142.

57. Milbank, *Theology and Social Theory*, 9.

58. Ibid., emphasis in original.

59. It is important to note, however, that the totality of Milbank's thesis extends beyond what Fitzgerald and Curtis are saying. It is true that these thinkers identify the "secular," and the positioning of social and natural scientists, as not belonging to a domain of objective discourse but, rather, one that contains its own ideological components. However, Milbank, as a thinker with a theological project (something that neither Fitzgerald nor Curtis is invested in), takes his argument in a different direction from Fitzgerald's or Curtis's; as Frank Burch Brown explains, "Indeed, Milbank argues that secular reason always turns incoherent and, in the end, nihilistic—entailing or inventing, despite itself, some kind of inadequate meta-narrative and quasi-religious metaphysic. Focusing on modern social science in particular, Milbank claims that such a science, far from evincing rational integrity and independence, turns out to be either a kind of Christian heresy or an insidious form of neo-paganism." Milbank thus reaches conclusions in his theological project which Fitzgerald and Curtis (who are not theologians) may not agree with. See Frank Burch Brown, "Radical Orthodoxy and the Religion of Others," *Encounter* 63 (2002): 47; Vorster, "Secular and the Sacred," 110.

60. Gregory, "Other Confessional History," 137.

61. Cited in ibid., 139.

62. Vorster explains that Milbank considers "the date of 1300 as the turning point in modern human thought. Around this date the traditional centrality of the doctrine of metaphysical participation and the unity between Scripture, tradition and reason in theology was abruptly challenged." Milbank sees this shift in intellectual thought as the beginnings of secular thought. He, therefore, understands the "secular" not in a *sui generis* fashion, as a transhistorical and elevated sphere of autonomous discourse, but through a constructivist lens: reading the "secular" as a historically located construct of late-medieval thought. See Vorster, "Secular and the Sacred," 110–111.

63. Milbank's ideas have inspired the Cambridge theological movement Radical Orthodoxy, whose theologians prominently locate the construction of the "secular" in the theology of the late medieval Franciscan thinker John Duns Scotus, particularly Scotus's theory on the univocity of being as replacing an ontology of participation, which according to Radical Orthodoxy thinkers would lead to a significant shift in intellectual history undermining the predominance of metaphysical participation for a newly formed, deontological philosophy of autonomous reason, constituting the early construct of the "secular." As James K. A. Smith explains, "Ushered in as a process, modernity generated the invention of the secular by rejecting the participatory ontology that preceded it"; James K. A.

Smith, *Introducing Radical Orthodoxy: Mapping a Post-Secular Theology* (Grand Rapids, MI: Baker Academic, 2004), 88. Although few would dispute Radical Orthodoxy's claim that a major shift transpired in intellectual history from ontological participation to an autonomous understanding of reason, Radical Orthodoxy's historical narrative of locating the beginning of that shift in the late medieval period through Scotus has been debated. See Smith, *Introducing Radical Orthodoxy*, 88–89, 96–105; Daniel M. Klimek, T.O.R., "Franciscan Radical Orthodoxy: Reconciling Cambridge with Assisi," *Franciscan Connections: The Cord—A Spiritual Review* 66, no. 2 (2016): 35–43; Richard Cross, "'Where Angels Fear to Tread': Dun Scotus and Radical Orthodoxy," *Antonianum* 76 (2001): 7–41; Luke D. Zerra, "Duns Scotus: The Boogieman of Modernity? A Response to John Milbank on the Univocity of Being," *The Cord* 63, no. 4 (2013): 374–384. The most comprehensive response by a Radical Orthodoxy theologian to critics on this issue has been Catherine Pickstock, "Duns Scotus: His Historical and Contemporary Significance," *Modern Theology* 21, no. 4 (October 2005): 545–573. For the most comprehensive critique of Radical Orthodoxy's interpretation of Scotus, see Daniel P. Horan, *Postmodernity and Univocity: A Critical Account of Radical Orthodoxy and John Duns Scotus* (Minneapolis, MN: Fortress Press, 2014).

64. Spickard, "Does Taves Reconsider Experience," 312.

65. Ibid., 312. Spickard's claim that Taves speaks of religion "as a faces-in-the-clouds phenomenon . . . in which the (postulated) human tendency to find patterns in random events imagines supernatural agents to be active in the world" and that she makes metaphysical claims about the origins of religious experiences is best seen in Taves's reductionistic treatment—Taves would not deny the explanatory reductionism that encapsulates her approach—of Bradley's purported experience of the Holy Spirit and Barnard's purported mystical experience. Of Bradley's encounter, Taves writes: "The process was composed of conscious and tacit thoughts that triggered both physiological sensations and feelings that were explained in terms of cultural scripts. The explanation cued a cultural role that triggered a physiological response, a vision, an explanation, and a resultant thought. The narrative of the experience was intended for an audience and included explanations of the attribution of the experience to the Holy Spirit in order to make it as convincing as possible." In other words, what Bradley believed to be an experience of the Holy Spirit Taves reinterprets as a process of conscious and tacit thoughts that triggered physiological sensations in Bradley's body and received the attribution as coming from the Holy Spirit by Bradley in order to appeal to an audience whose spiritual beliefs placed a great emphasis on experience with the Holy Spirit. Of Barnard's experience, Taves writes: "It [Barnard's experience] is precipitated by the unsuccessful attempt to visualize a widespread secular cultural script (the idea that the soul/self is extinguished with the death of the body). The idea of trying to visualize the self not existing

after death apparently emerged spontaneously. I am hypothesizing that the mental paradox involved in the visualization triggered the dissolution of self-other boundaries, that the dissolution of self-other boundaries triggered feelings of ecstasy and exhilaration, and that the novelty, intensity, and suddenness of this experience triggered the need for explanation." Here, it is the mental paradox of trying to imagine oneself as not existing that Taves hypothesizes is the root of Barnard's experience, leading to the dissolution of self-other boundaries and the triggering of feelings of ecstasy and exhilaration. Since, as Spickard emphasizes, this explanation—a mental paradox leading to the dissolution of self-other boundaries—cannot be empirically ascertained but, as Taves admits, is hypothesized, Taves is making metaphysical claims to reach her conclusion. What is noteworthy—and evokes Milbank's critique of academic theories that, under the guise of objective discourse, become forms of metaphysics that domesticate the sacred into the secular—is how Taves's reinterpretation of these experiences changes their ontological origins from a sacred into a secular genesis. Again, what Bradley believed to be a sacred experience of the Holy Spirit Taves reinterprets as a secular experience of conscious and tacit thinking triggering physiological sensations leading to a cultural attribution. What Barnard believed to be a mystical experience Taves reinterprets as a mental paradox in thinking that triggered an altered state of consciousness and led to euphoric feelings. See Taves, *Religious Experience Reconsidered*, 109–110.

66. Gregory, "Other Confessional History," 136.

67. Ibid., 137.

68. It is, of course, appropriate to use such a metaphysical approach within discourses of theology and philosophy; however, such is not the case with naturalistic discourses of religious studies, for if this approach is defined as a metaphysically free, naturalistic perspective, then it becomes a misnomer, as such a designation does not account for the metaphysical means by which the hermeneutic reaches empirically unexaminable conclusions.

69. Robert A. Orsi, "Abundant History: Marian Apparitions as Alternative Modernity," *Historically Speaking* 9, no. 7 (September/December 2008): 12–16.

70. Amy Hollywood, *Acute Melancholia and Other Essays: Mysticism, History, and the Study of Religion* (New York: Columbia University Press, 2016), 4–5.

71. Ibid., 6; Hollywood paraphrasing Mahmood.

72. Ibid., 119.

73. Ibid., 124.

74. Orsi, "Abundant History," 13.

75. Gregory, "Other Confessional History," 136.

76. Ibid., 136.

77. Ibid., 137; emphasis Gregory's.

78. Orsi, *History and Presence*, 58.

79. Greyson, "Implications of Near-Death Experiences," 40.

80. Ibid.

81. Edward F. Kelly, "A View from the Mainstream: Contemporary Cognitive Neuroscience and the Consciousness Debates," in Kelly et al., *Irreducible Mind*, 30.

82. See Emily Williams Kelly, Bruce Greyson, and Edward F. Kelly, "Unusual Experiences Near Death and Related Phenomena," in Kelly et al., *Irreducible Mind*, 367–421; Greyson, "Implications of Near-Death Experiences," 37–43; Facco et al., "Epistemological Implications," 85–93; Lauren E. Moore and Bruce Greyson, "Characteristics of Memories for Near Death Experiences," *Consciousness and Cognition* 51 (2017): 116–124; Bruce Greyson, "Western Scientific Approaches to Near Death Experiences," *Humanities* 4, no. 4 (2015): 775–796.

83. Kelly, "View from the Mainstream," 25–46.

84. Greyson, "Implications of Near-Death Experiences," 37–38.

85. Kelly, "View from the Mainstream," 42.

86. Ibid., 45.

87. Orsi, "Abundant History," 14.

88. Harris, *Lourdes*, 12–13.

89. Orsi, "Abundant History, 14.

90. Ibid.

91. Hollywood, *Acute Melancholia*, 120.

92. Orsi, "Abundant History," 14.

93. Robert A. Orsi, "A Response to the Commentary on 'Abundant History,'" *Historically Speaking* 9, no. 7 (2008): 25–26.

94. Orsi, "Abundant History," 13.

95. Ibid.

96. Orsi, *History and Presence*, 58–59.

97. Orsi, "A Response," 26.

98. Orsi, *History and Presence*, 64.

99. Ibid., 58–59.

100. Ibid., 58–59.

101. Orsi, "Abundant History," 14.

102. Ibid.

103. Gregory, "Other Confessional History," 147.

104. Ibid.

105. The classic work on this topic is from the journalist Kenneth Woodward, *Making Saints: How the Catholic Church Determines Who Becomes a Saint, Who Doesn't, and Why* (New York: Simon and Schuster, 1990).

106. Gregory, "Other Confessional History," 138.

107. Ibid., 137.

108. Orsi, *History and Presence*, 252.

109. Rogers, "Interdisciplinary Approaches," 15.

110. Ibid.

111. In this sense, Rogers has called for the importance of "observational authenticity" in formulating a hermeneutical method toward studying religion and religious experiences. He explained "observational authenticity" as "attention

to given features in object description, and a quest for implicit order and process relationships rather than the imposition of order in the interests of theoretical coherence—that is, looking honestly and anew at events, for instance, the early life of the child in response to religious images, without predetermination of structures or interpretations. Interpretive issues may guide one's questions, and may be a second step in the analysis. But in between we must observe accurately and authentically the lived phenomena." The critique of predetermined structures and interpretations is monumental as it exposes many unexamined presuppositions about the shortcomings of various hermeneutical approaches toward the study of religious experiences, similarly to Rogers' observations here on religious and moral development. Ibid., 44.

112. Ibid., 16–17.

113. Ibid., 45.

114. It is important to note that this reservation about the constructive-relational method may not be present in relation to the study of other, more *ordinary*, religious experiences, to which the constructive-relational method may be *perfectly* suited; however, in light of *extraordinary* and *mystical* experiences, for whom the question of discerning true from false experiences becomes essential, the reservation must be invoked in order to avoid the familiar methodological fallacy of basing one's research on predetermined premises.

115. Barnard provides an astute description of this approach in Proudfoot's work: "According to Proudfoot, the noetic quality of a mystical experience is merely the cerebral judgment made by the mystic that a certain experience is not solely his or her subjective creation. This judgment that an experience is 'religious' is not made because the experience possesses certain identifiable, directly felt, intrinsic religious qualities, but instead, an experience is understood to be religious because the person who has the experience superimposes a ready-made label of 'religious' onto any unexplained shift in his or her physical or psychological equilibrium." See Barnard, *Exploring Unseen Worlds*, 103; Taves, *Religious Experience Reconsidered*, 17, 20.

116. Rogers, "Interdisciplinary Approaches," 16–17.

117. This is the case even if one is approaching the subject from an etic perspective that cannot directly comment *for* the authenticity of an experience but can naturalistically ascertain conclusions that either strengthen or weaken the integrity of an experience.

118. See Margnelli, *La droga perfetta*.

119. As quoted in Sullivan, *Miracle Detective*, 207; for Margnelli's account, see also O'Carroll, *Medjugorje*, 70–71; and Nolan, *Medjugorje: A Time for Truth*, 141–142.

120. Sullivan, *Miracle Detective*, 207–208; O'Carroll, *Medjugorje*, 70–71; Nolan, *Medjugorje: A Time for Truth*, 141–142.

121. As quoted in Sullivan, *Miracle Detective*, 207–208.

122. Taves, *Religious Experience Reconsidered*, 157.

123. Ibid., 159; emphasis in original.
124. Ibid., 158.
125. Ibid., 160.
126. Ibid.
127. Ibid.
128. Andresen and Forman similarly have critiqued a methodological approach that focuses on how components like society, ritual, sociological behavior patterns, and interpersonal behavior patterns study religion and religious experiences. "Too often, historians and sociologists of religion focus primarily on this approach to the exclusion of all others, as if to reduce the understanding of religion to anthropology and socio-political dynamics. This approach generally leaves out the 'felt experience' of the religious practitioner, which is similar to a deaf person's studying music through the analysis of written musical notes, or a reviewer of written recipes never tasting the cuisine. It tends to devalue the religious lives of others and the idiosyncracies of religious experience itself." Andresen and Forman, "Methodological Pluralism," 11.
129. Lane, *Experience of God*, 37–38.
130. Ibid., 37.
131. Ibid., 37–38.
132. Ibid., 38–39.
133. Ibid., 39–40.
134. I highlight these words to emphasize the distinction between etic observers who would be open to emic possibilities and those who would dismiss emic interpretations as untenable, stressing here the hermeneutical dangers of the latter perspective, as already seen in the completely reductive methodologies conveyed by various scholars referenced in this book—as opposed to a healthier, benign reductionism that identifies psychological and human dynamics in religious phenomena while leaving the door open to the possibility of spiritual and theological components.
135. This is not to say that etic and emic perspectives are, or have to be, antithetical, but is simply commenting on the holistic nature of the constructive-relational method as an approach that can bring historically antithetical disciplines together to form a better understanding of the phenomena of study.
136. Joyeux and Laurentin, *Etudes scientifiques et médicales*, 67.

CONCLUSION

1. James, *Varieties of Religious Experience*, 12.
2. Micale, *Approaching Hysteria*, 272.
3. See James, *Varieties of Religious Experience*, 11–31.
4. Underhill, *Mysticism* (Aziloth ed.), 210.
5. Ibid., 156.

6. And, as mentioned, the challenge for Underhill was double-sided: the absolutism that she criticized belonging not only to "the strangely named rationalists" and their reductionism of religious experiences but also to the "supernaturalists" who tried to depict religious experiences as objective in nature. Underhill argued for that middle-ground approach that challenged the hermeneutical absolutism of each side by allowing the interpretation of extraordinary religious experiences as both subjective and authentic.

7. Words of Dr. M. Frederica Magatti, who was a member of the early 1984 group of Italian doctors that examined the visionaries; quoted in Sullivan, *Miracle Detective*, 163.

8. Dr. Jacques Philippot, member of the 1984 French team; cited in Sullivan, *Miracle Detective*, 202–203.

9. The matter of whether all such self-induced experiences warrant the label "religious experience" remains highly questionable, as the example of Beauregard's and Paquette's study on Carmelite nuns shows. Since the Carmelites were asked to re-create the most profound mystical experiences of their lives in their minds, the exercise constituted less of a "religious experience" and more an exercise in imagination, memory, and suggestion.

10. Newberg and D'Aquili, *Why God Won't Go Away*, 175.

11. Newberg, *Principles of Neurotheology*, 168.

12. Ibid.

13. Newberg explains that these "studies have helped to determine which parts of the brain are responsible for a variety of neurocognitive processes. . . . Activation studies with the functional neuroimaging techniques have been employed to determine the areas in the brain that are involved in the production and understanding of language, visual processing, and pain reception and sensation." Ibid., 169. Seeing which areas of the brain would be affected in the visionaries by their apparitional experiences, were the seers open to be subjected to further neuroscientific study (beyond electroencephalography), through such methods as SPECT, PET, or fMRI testing, presents a significant and rare research opportunity for the field of neurotheology.

14. Ibid., 169.

15. Laurentin has noted that phenomena like the Medjugorje apparitions challenge the hypercritical trends in academic thought like rationalism and *a priori* reductionism, but beyond noting this reality, Laurentin has not examined the topic in detail by placing the scientific studies within the context of major hermeneutical and epistemological debates considering extraordinary religious and mystical experiences, as this work has. In addition to Laurentin's work with Henri Joyeux (*Scientific and Medical Studies*), see René Laurentin and Ljudevit Rupcic, *Is the Virgin Mary Appearing at Medjugorje? An Urgent Message for the World Given in a Marxist Country*, trans. Francis Martin (Washington, DC: The Word Among Us Press, 1984), esp. 11–12.

16. Newberg and D'Aquili provide a great explanation of what is meant here by an "uncritical rationalism," going back to a number of thinkers who have been referenced in this work:

> When philosopher Friedrich Nietzsche, in 1885, made his famous proclamation that God was dead, he was saying, of course, that God had never really lived at all. Like other great rationalistic thinkers of the nineteenth and early-twentieth centuries—Marx, Freud, James Frazer, Ludwig Feuerbach, and Bertrand Russell, to name a few—Nietzsche regarded God as just another vestige of an unscientific past that humanity would soon outgrow. It was the great expectation of many in that world-changing generation of realistic explanations for the mysteries of existence, the irrational appeal of religion would simply fade, and God, in all his incarnations, would simply go away.
>
> God, however, has not obliged, and as we enter the new millennium—an age of unprecedented scientific and technological enlightenment—religion and spirituality continue to thrive. If Nietzsche and his contemporaries were alive to see it, they would most likely regard God's survival as a triumph of ignorance over reason. Convinced that religious belief is based on superstition and fearful self-delusion, they would have no choice but to conclude—as many modern rationalists have done—that humans cling to God because they lack the strength and courage to face the world without Him.
>
> This cynical interpretation is so firmly entrenched in the thinking of rational materialism that few rationalistic thinkers would even bother to question it, but an open-minded inquiry shows that this idea may not be as intellectually sound as it seems. . . . Evidence suggests that the deepest origins of religion are based in mystical experience, and that religions persist because the wiring of the human brain continues to provide believers with unitary experiences that are often interpreted as assurances that God exists. (Newberg and D'Aquili, *Why God Won't Go Away*, 129)

17. Harmless, *Mystics*, 11.

18. An interesting history to consider in this regard is that of psychology. Kugelmann traces how Catholic neoscholastic psychology came under criticism by the "new psychology" emerging at the turn of the twentieth century, which hoped to abandon religious categories such as "the soul" from its domain. It is noteworthy that many of the founding fathers of psychology, such as William James and Carl Jung, considered religious questions important pursuits for psychology while later trends in the field abandoned such matters. "As the new psychology at the turn of the twentieth century sought to distance itself from notions of the soul, it ran head-on into Neoscholastic conclusions about the soul as a first cause of human life. For the Neoscholastics, psychology's abandonment of the soul was a failure of intellectual nerve at best or misguided materialism at worst" (Kugelmann, *Psychology and Catholicism*, 69). Proponents of the new psychology, which became the dominant psychology, hoped to abandon the influence of

religious and metaphysical thinking for a purely empirical and objective science. The question of neutrality, however, through the removal of religious categories from the discipline, remains highly debated. Paul Vitz sees a secular human-ism underlying many modern psychologies that possesses its own ideological assumptions. Similarly, Don Browning has analyzed the various hermeneutical assumptions that major modern psychologies hold. See Kugelmann, *Psychology and Catholicism*, esp. 32–118; Paul C. Vitz, *Psychology as Religion: The Cult of Self-Worship*, 2nd ed. (Grand Rapids, MI: Eerdmans, 1994); Don S. Browning, *Religious Thought and the Modern Psychologies* (Philadelphia: Fortress, 1987).

19. This is an observation about the nature of the methodological approach—which was constructive-relational—of the teams that studied the visionaries, and not a claim that they conscientiously or formally used Rogers's constructive-relational approach as published in his paper.

20. As William James pointed out, mystic states challenge an ideological rationalism and open the possibility to "other orders of truth." James, *Varieties of Religious Experience*, 381.

21. Micale writes:

> To the best of my knowledge, the appearance of the miraculous in the final quarter of the nineteenth century, during the years that are supposed to have represented the heyday of atheistic scientism, has not yet been adequately explained by historians. It is probably not coincidental that Lourdes was founded and flourished during the highpoint of what William James called "medical materialism." The late nineteenth century was a period of asser-tive positivist ideology . . . in which science was believed by many people to provide self-sufficient explanations for all natural as well as social phenom-ena. In this light, Lourdes, to many members of the scientific intelligentsia, represented an affront to the spirit of the age, a perverse throwback to a superstitious prescientific past. (Micale, *Approaching Hysteria*, 263)

> Similarly, Lachapelle explains:

> While church attendance dropped and atheism, positivism, and scientism were dominant trends of the time, the nineteenth century, particularly its second half, was also a vibrant period for Catholicism. . . . At the popular level, spiritual beliefs were made tangible through physical evidence of the supernatural. Stigmatics, ecstatics, visionaries, miraculously cured persons were an important part of the spiritual landscape of the period. The rich, mystical character of the second half of the nineteenth century is now well established. (Lachapelle, "Between Miracle and Sickness," 79)

22. Quoted in Sullivan, *Miracle Detective*, 240–241.

Bibliography

Acklin, Thomas, O.S.B. "Religious Symbolic Transformations of Desire: A Psychoanalytical and Theological Perspective on Desire in Religion." Ph.D. dissertation, Katholieke Universiteit te Leuven, Faculty of Theology, 1982.

Alexander, Eben. *Proof of Heaven: A Neurosurgeon's Journey into the Afterlife.* New York: Simon and Schuster, 2012.

Allen, John Jr., "A Saint Despite Vatican Reservations." *National Catholic Reporter,* August 30, 2002. http://natcath.org/NCR_Online/archives2/2002c/083002/083002f.htm.

Anderson, Joan Wester. *Forever Young: The Life, Loves and Enduring Faith of a Hollywood Legend—the Authorized Biography of Loretta Young.* Allen, TX: Thomas More, 2000.

Andresen, Jensine, and Robert K. C. Forman. "Methodological Pluralism in the Study of Religion: How the Study of Consciousness and Mapping Spiritual Experiences can Reshape Religious Methodology." In *Cognitive Models and Spiritual Maps: Interdisciplinary Explorations of Religious Experience,* edited by Jensine Andresen and Robert K. C. Forman, 7–14. Bowling Green, OH: Academic Imprint, 2000.

Apolito, Paolo. *The Internet and the Madonna: Religious Visionary Experience on the Web,* translated by Antony Shugaar. Chicago: University of Chicago Press, 2005.

Arzy, Shahar, Gregor Thut, Christine Mohr, Christoph M. Michel, and Olaf Blanke. "Neural Basis of Embodiment: Distinct Contributions of Temporoparietal Junction and Extrastriate Body Area." *Journal of Neuroscience* 26 (2006): 8074–8081.

Austin, Stephen. *A Summa and Encyclopedia to Maria Valtorta's Extraordinary Work.* E-book, February 2017 edition. www.bardstown.com/~brchrys/Summa.pdf.

Azari, Nina P., Janpeter Nickel, Gilbert Wunderlich, Michael Niedeggen, Harald Hefter, Lutz Tallmann, Hans Herzog, Petra Stoerg, Dieter Birnbacher, and Rudiger J Seitz. "Neural Correlates of Religious Experience." *European Journal of Neuroscience* 13 (2005): 1649–1652.

Azari, Nina P., John Missimer, and Rudiger J. Seitz. "Religious Experience and Emotion: Evidence for Distinctive Cognitive Neural Patterns." *International Journal for the Psychology of Religion* 15, no. 4 (2005): 263–281.

Barnard, G. William. *Exploring Unseen Worlds: William James and the Philosophy of Mysticism*. Albany: State University of New York Press, 1997.

Beauregard, Mario, and Vincent Paquette. "Neural Correlates of a Mystical Experience in Carmelite Nuns." *Neuroscience Letters* 405 (2006): 186–190.

Beauregard, Mario, and Vincent Paquette. "EEG Activity in Carmelite Nuns during a Mystical Experience." *Neuroscience Letters* 444 (2008): 1–4.

Benedict XIV. *Heroic Virtue: A Portion of the Treatise of Benedict XIV on the Beatification and Canonization of the Servants of God*, vol. III, translated by the English Fathers of the Oratory. London: Thomas Richardson and Son, 1850.

Bentley, Michael. *Modern Historiography: An Introduction*. London and New York: Routledge, 1999.

Bernhardt, Stephen. "Are Pure Conscious Events Unmediated?" In *The Problem of Pure Consciousness: Mysticism and Philosophy*, edited by Robert K.C. Forman, 220–236. New York and Oxford: Oxford University Press, 1990.

Blanke, Olaf, Theodor Landis, Laurent Spinelli, and Margitta Seeck. "Out-of-Body Experience and Autoscopy of Neurological Origin." *Brain: A Journal of Neurology* 127 (2004): 243–258.

Blanke, Olaf, and Christine Mohr. "Out-of-Body Experience, Heautoscopy, and Autoscopic Hallucination of Neurological Origin: Implications for Neurocognitive Mechanisms of Corporal Awareness and Self-Consciousness." *Brain Research Reviews* 50 (2005): 184–199.

Blanke, Olaf, Christine Mohr, Christopher M. Michel, Alvaro Pascual-Leone, Peter Brugger, Margitta Seeck, Theodor Landis, and Gregor Thut. "Linking Out-of-Body Experience and Self-Processing to Mental Own-Body Imagery at the Temporoparietal Junction." *Journal of Neuroscience* 25 (2005): 550–557.

Bouyer, Louis. "Mysticism: An Essay on the History of the Word." In *Understanding Mysticism*, edited by Richard Woods, 42–55. New York: Image Books, 1980.

Brown, Frank Burch. "Radical Orthodoxy and the Religion of Others." *Encounter* 63 (2002): 45–53.

Browning, Don S. *Religious Thought and the Modern Psychologies*. Philadelphia: Fortress, 1987.

Burpo, Todd, with Lynn Vincent. *Heaven Is for Real: A Little Boy's Astounding Story of His Trip to Heaven and Back*. Nashville, TN: Thomas Nelson, 2010.

Bush, Nancy Evans, and Bruce Greyson. "Distressing Near-Death Experiences." *Missouri Medicine* 111, no. 5 (2014): 372–376.

Callahan, Sidney. *Women Who Hear Voices: The Challenge of Religious Experience*. 2003 Madeleva Lecture in Spirituality at St. Mary's College, Notre Dame, Indiana. New York/Mahwah, NJ: Paulist Press, 2007.

Cardinale, Gianni. "Tempi e criteri per 'giudicare' le apparizioni." *Eroici Furori*, September 17, 2008. https://web.archive.org/web/20120308204442/http://www.eroicifurori.com/modules.php?name=News&file=article&sid=3780.

Carmody, Denise Lardner, and John Tully Carmody. *Mysticism: Holiness East and West*. New York: Oxford University Press, 1996.

Carroll, Michael P. *The Cult of the Virgin Mary: Psychological Origins*. Princeton, NJ: Princeton University Press, 1986. Also, reviews of this book in Daniel Bornstein, *Church History* 57, no. 4 (December 1988): 581–583; Jeffrey Burton Russell, *Journal of the American Academy of Religion* 55, no. 3 (Autumn 1987): 593–597; John H. Gagnon, *Contemporary Sociology* 17, no. 3 (May 1988): 376–377.

Chadwick, Owen. *The Secularization of the European Mind in the Nineteenth Century*. Cambridge: Cambridge University Press, 1990.

Charcot, Jean-Martin, and Paul Richer. *Les demoniaques dans l 'art suive de "La foi qui guerit"* Paris: Macula, 1984.

Clark, Elizabeth A. *History, Theory, Text: Historians and the Linguistic Turn*. Cambridge, MA: Harvard University Press, 2004.

Cousins, Ewert. "Francis of Assisi: Christian Mysticism at the Crossroads." In *Mysticism and Religious Traditions*, edited by Steven T. Katz, 163–190. New York: Oxford University Press, 1983.

Craig, Mary. *Spark from Heaven: The Mystery of the Madonna of Medjugorje*. Notre Dame, IN: Ave Maria Press, 1988.

Crosby, Michael H. "A Response to 'Saint Francis as Mystic: The Multifarious Mysticism of Francis of Assisi.'" *Franciscan Connections: The Cord—A Spiritual Review* 66, no. 1 (2016): 6–7.

Cross, Richard. "'Where Angels Fear to Tread': Dun Scotus and Radical Orthodoxy." *Antonianum* 76 (2001): 7–41.

Curtis, Finbarr. "Ann Taves's *Religious Experience Reconsidered* Is a Sign of a Global Apocalypse that Will Kill Us All." *Religion* 40 (2010): 288–292.

Dawkins, Richard. *The God Delusion*. New York: Houghton Mifflin, 2006.

D'Errico, Allessandro. "Statement of Apostolic Nuncio to Bosnia and Herzegovina about International Commission for Medjugorje," March 20, 2010. http://med-jugorje.hr/en/news/statement-of-apostolic-nuncio-to-bosnia-and-herzegovina-about-international-commission-for-medjugorje,2922.html.

Dulles, Avery, S.J. *Models of Revelation*, rev. ed. New York: Orbis Books, 1992.

Egan, Harvey. *What Are They Saying about Mysticism?* New York: Paulist Press, 1982.

Egan, Harvey. *An Anthology of Christian Mysticism*. Collegeville, MN: Pueblo Books, 1996.

Facco, Enrico, Christian Agrillo, and Bruce Greyson. "Epistemological Implications of Near- Death Experiences and Other Non-Ordinary Mental Expressions: Moving beyond the Concept of Altered States of Consciousness." *Medical Hypotheses* 85, no. 1 (2015): 85–93.

Fanning, Steven. *Mystics of the Christian Tradition*. London and New York: Routledge, 2001.

Feuerbach, Ludwig. *The Essence of Christianity*, translated by George Eliot. Amherst, NY: Prometheus Books, 1989.

Ficocelli, Elizabeth. *The Fruits of Medjugorje: Stories of True and Lasting Conversion.* Mahwah, NJ: Paulist Press, 2006.

Fitzgerald, Timothy. "'Experiences Deemed Religious': Radical Critique or Temporary Fix? Strategic Ambiguity in Ann Taves' Religious Experience Reconsidered." *Religion* 40 (2010): 296–299.

Flannery, Austin, ed. *Vatican Council II: The Basic Sixteen Documents—Constitutions, Decrees, Declarations.* Northport, NY: Costello Publishing, 1996.

Forgie, William. "Hyper-Kantianism in Recent Discussions of Mystical Experience." *Religious Studies* 21 (1985): 205–218.

Forman, Robert K. C. "Eckhart, Gezucken, and the Ground of the Soul." In *The Problem of Pure Consciousness: Mysticism and Philosophy*, edited by Robert K. C. Forman, 98–120. New York and Oxford: Oxford University Press, 1990.

Forman, Robert K. C. "Introduction: Mysticism, Constructivism, and Forgetting." In *The Problem of Pure Consciousness: Mysticism and Philosophy*, edited by Robert K. C. Forman, 3–52. New York and Oxford: Oxford University Press, 1990.

Forman, Robert K. C., ed. *The Problem of Pure Consciousness: Mysticism and Philosophy.* New York and Oxford: Oxford University Press, 1990.

Forman, Robert K. C., ed. *The Innate Capacity: Mysticism, Psychology, and Philosophy.* New York: Oxford University Press, 1998.

Forman, Robert K. C. *Mysticism, Mind, Consciousness.* Albany: State University of New York Press, 1999.

Fortea, José Antonio. *Interview with an Exorcist: An Insider's Look at the Devil, Demonic Possession, and the Path to Deliverance.* West Chester, PA: Ascension Press, 2006.

Fraeters, Veerle. "*Visio*/Vision." In *The Cambridge Companion to Christian Mysticism*, edited by Amy Hollywood and Patricia Beckman, 178–188. New York: Cambridge University Press, 2012.

Franklin, R. L. "Postconstructivist Approaches to Mysticism." In *The Innate Capacity: Mysticism, Psychology, and Philosophy*, edited by Robert K. C. Forman, 231–243. New York: Oxford University Press, 1998.

Freud, Sigmund. *Civilization and Its Discontents*, translated and edited by James Strachey. New York and London: W.W. Norton, 1961.

Freud, Sigmund. "Obsessive Actions and Religious Practices." In *The Freud Reader*, edited by Peter Gay, 429–435. New York: W.W. Norton, 1995. [Reprint of 1989 edition.]

Furey, Constance M. "Sexuality." In *The Cambridge Companion to Christian Mysticism*, edited by Amy Hollywood and Patricia Beckman, 328–340. New York: Cambridge University Press, 2012.

Garside, Bruce. "Language and the Interpretation of Mystical Experiences." *International Journal for Philosophy of Religion* 3 (1972): 91–94.

Gay, Volney P. *Freud on Ritual: Reconstruction and Critique.* Missoula, MT: Scholars Press, 1979.

Gimello, Robert. "Mysticism and Meditation." In *Mysticism and Philosophical Analysis*, edited by Steven T. Katz, 170–199. New York: Oxford University Press, 1978.

Gimello, Robert. "Mysticism in Its Contexts." In *Mysticism and Religious Traditions*, edited by Steven T. Katz, 61–88. New York: Oxford University Press, 1983.

Goldstein, Jan. "The Hysteria Diagnosis and the Politics of Anticlericalism in Late Nineteenth- Century France." *Journal of Modern History* 54, no. 2 (June 1982): 209–239.

Graef, Hilda C. *The Case of Therese Neumann.* Westminster, MD: Newman Press, 1951.

Gregory, Brad S. "The Other Confessional History: On Secular Bias in the Study of Religion." *History and Theory* 45, no. 4 (December 2006): 132–149.

Greyson, Bruce. "Western Scientific Approaches to Near Death Experiences." *Humanities* 4, no. 4 (2015): 775–796.

Greyson, Bruce. "Implications of Near-Death Experiences for a Postmaterialist Psychology." *Psychology of Religion and Spirituality* 2, no. 1 (2010): 37–45.

Greyson, Bruce, Janice Miner Holden, and Pim van Lommel. "'There Is Nothing Paranormal About Near-Death Experiences' Revisited: Comment on Mobbs and Watt." *Trends in Cognitive Sciences* 16, no. 9 (September 2012): 445.

Griffiths, Paul J. "Pure Consciousness and Indian Buddhism." In *The Problem of Pure Consciousness: Mysticism and Philosophy*, edited by Robert K. C. Forman, 71–97. New York and Oxford: Oxford University Press, 1990.

Groeschel, Benedict J. *A Still, Small Voice: A Practical Guide on Reported Revelations.* San Francisco: Ignatius Press, 1993.

Grosso, Michael. *The Man Who Could Fly: St. Joseph of Copertino and the Mystery of Levitation.* Lanham, MD: Rowman and Littlefield, 2016.

Haddock, Kate. *Mystery Files: Joan of Arc.* Documentary film, directed and produced by Kate Haddock. Smithsonian Channel, 2010.

Happold, F. C. *Mysticism: A Study and an Anthology*, rev. ed. New York: Penguin Books, 1973.

Harmless, William. *Mystics.* New York: Oxford University Press, 2008.

Harris, Ruth. *Lourdes: Body and Spirit in the Secular Age.* New York: Viking Press, 2009.

Hollywood, Amy. *Sensible Ecstasy: Mysticism, Sexual Difference, and the Demands of History.* Chicago: University of Chicago Press, 2002.

Hollywood, Amy. *Acute Melancholia and Other Essays: Mysticism, History, and the Study of Religion.* New York: Columbia University Press, 2016.

Horan, Daniel P. *Postmodernity and Univocity: A Critical Account of Radical Orthodoxy and John Duns Scotus.* Minneapolis, MN: Fortress Press, 2014.

Horgan, John. *Rational Mysticism: Dispatches from the Border between Science and Spirituality.* Boston: Houghton Mifflin, 2003.

Hume, David. *Dialogues and Natural History of Religion*, edited by J. C. A. Gaskin. New York: Oxford University Press, 1993.

Huxley, Aldous. *The Perennial Philosophy.* New York: Harper and Row, 1944. [Reprinted 1945, 1970.]

Hvidt, Niels Christian. *Christian Prophecy: The Post-Biblical Tradition.* New York: Oxford University Press, 2007.

Inge, W. R. *Christian Mysticism*. London: Methuen, 1899.

Inge, W. R. *Studies of English Mystics*. London: John Murray, 1906.

Janet, Pierre. *Psychological Healing: A Historical and Clinical Study*, translated by E. Paul and C. Paul. New York: Arno, 1972 [reprint of 1925 edition].

James, William. "The Hidden Self." *Scribner's Magazine* 7, no. 3 (March 1890): 361–373.

James, William. "A Suggestion about Mysticism." *Journal of Philosophy, Psychology and Scientific Methods* 7 (1910): 85–92. [Also available in *Understanding Mysticism*, edited by Richard Woods, 215–222. New York: Image Books, 1980.]

James, William. *The Varieties of Religious Experience: A Study in Human Nature*. New York: Library of America Paperback Classic, 2010. [Originally produced as the Gifford Lectures in 1902.]

John Paul II. "List dla Pana Marka Skwarnicki." *Watykan*. May 28, 1992, 154.

John Paul II. "List dla Pana Marka Skwarnicki i Pani Zofia Skwarnicka." *Watykan*, February 25, 1994, 156.

John Paul II. "List dla Pana Marka Skwarnicki I Pani Zofia Skwarnicka." *Castel Gandolfo*, September 3, 1994, 159.

John Paul II. "List dla Pana Marka Skwarnicki i Pani Zofia Skwarnicka." December 8, 1992, in *Medjugorje and the Church*, edited by Denis Nolan, 4th ed., 152. Santa Barbara, CA: Queenship, 2007.

"John Paul II and the Statue that Cried Blood." *Rome Reports*. Video posted May 17, 2011. www.youtube.com/watch?v=GHGH_b68MlY.

Jones, Rufus M. *Studies in Mystical Religion*. Eugene, OR: Wipf and Stock, 2004. [Originally published by Macmillan in 1909.]

Joyeux, Henry, and René Laurentin. *Etudes scientifiques et médicales sur les apparitions de Medjugorje*. Paris: O.E.I.L., 1985.

Kant, Immanuel. *Religion Within the Limits of Reason Alone*, translated by Theodore M. Greene and Hoyt H. Hudson, essay by John R. Silber. New York: Harper & Row, 1960.

Katz, Steven T. "Language, Epistemology, and Mysticism." In *Mysticism and Philosophical Analysis*, edited by Steven T. Katz, 22–74. New York: Oxford University Press, 1978.

Katz, Steven T., ed. *Mysticism and Philosophical Analysis*. New York: Oxford University Press, 1978.

Katz, Steven T. "The Conservative Character of Mystical Experience." In *Mysticism and Religious Traditions*, edited by Steven T. Katz, 3–60. New York: Oxford University Press, 1983.

Katz, Steven T., ed., *Mysticism and Religious Traditions*. New York: Oxford University Press, 1983.

Katz, Steven T. "Mystical Speech and Mystical Meaning." In *Mysticism and Language*, edited by Steven T. Katz, 3–41. New York: Oxford University Press, 1992.

Katz, Steven T., ed., *Mysticism and Language*. New York: Oxford University Press, 1992.

Katz, Steven T., ed., *Mysticism and Sacred Scripture*. New York: Oxford University Press, 2000.

Kaufman, Suzanne. *Consuming Visions: Mass Culture and the Lourdes Shrine*. Ithaca, NY: Cornell University Press, 2005.

Kelly, Edward F., Adam Crabtree, and Paul Marshall, eds., *Beyond Physicalism: Toward Reconciliation of Science and Spirituality*. Lanham, MD: Rowman & Littlefield, 2015.

Kelly, Edward F., Emily Williams Kelly, Adam Crabtree, Alan Gauld, Michael Grosso, and Bruce Greyson. *Irreducible Mind: Toward a Psychology for the 21st Century*. Lanham, MD: Rowman & Littlefield, 2007.

Kieckhefer, Richard. *Unquiet Souls: Fourteenth-Century Saints and Their Religious Milieu*. Chicago: University of Chicago Press, 1984.

Klaushofer, Alexandra. "Faith Beyond Nihilism: The Retrieval of Theism in Milbank and Taylor." *Heythrop Journal* 40 (1999): 135–149.

Klimek, Daniel M. "The Gospels According to Christ? Combining the Study of the Historical Jesus with Modern Mysticism." *Glossolalia* 1 (2009): 1–18.

Klimek, Daniel M. "Pope John Paul II, 'Medjugorje – The Spiritual Heart of the World.'" *Medjugorje.org*, posted March 16, 2011. www.medjugorje.org/word-press/archives/33.

Klimek, Daniel M. "Saint Francis as Mystic: The Multifarious Mysticism of Francis of Assisi." Part I. *Franciscan Connections: The Cord—A Spiritual Review* 65, no. 3 (2015): 32–37.

Klimek, Daniel M. "Saint Francis as Mystic: The Multifarious Mysticism of Francis of Assisi." Part II. *Franciscan Connections: The Cord—A Spiritual Review* 65, no. 4 (2015): 29–33.

Klimek, Daniel M. "Franciscan Radical Orthodoxy: Reconciling Cambridge with Assisi." *Franciscan Connections: The Cord—A Spiritual Review* 66, no. 2 (2016): 35–43.

Kowalska, Maria Faustina. *Diary of Saint Maria Faustina Kowalska: Divine Mercy in My Soul*, 3rd ed. with rev. Stockbridge, MA: Marian Press, 2011.

Kralijevic, Svetozar, O.F.M., *The Apparitions of Our Lady at Medjugorje, 1981-1983: A Historical Account with Interviews*, edited by Michael Scanlan, T.O.R. Chicago: Franciscan Herald Press, 1984.

Kübler-Ross, Elisabeth. *On Death and Dying: What the Dying have to Teach Doctors, Nurses, Clergy & Their Own Family*, foreword by Ira Byock. New York: Scribner's, 2014.

Kugelmann, Robert. *Psychology and Catholicism: Contested Boundaries*. Cambridge: Cambridge University Press, 2011.

Küng, Hans. *Freud and the Problem of God*, translated by Edward Quinn. New Haven, CT: Yale University Press, 1990.

Lachapelle, Sofie. "Between Miracle and Sickness: Louise Lateau and the Experience of Stigmata and Ecstasy." *Configurations* 12 (2004): 77–105.

Lachapelle, Sofie. *Investigating the Supernatural: From Spiritism and Occultism to Psychical Research and Metapsychics in France, 1853-1931*. Baltimore: Johns Hopkins University Press, 2011.

Lane, Dermot A. *The Experience of God: An Invitation to Do Theology*, rev. ed. New York and Mahwah, NJ: Paulist Press, 2003.

Laurentin, René. *Dernieres Nouvelles de Medjugorje: Vers la fin des apparitions*. Paris: O.E.I.L., 1985.

Laurentin, René. *The Apparitions at Medjugorje Prolonged*, translated by J. Lohre Stiens. Milford, OH: Riehle Foundation, 1987.

Laurentin, René, François-Michel Debroise, and Jean-François Lavere. *Dictionnaire des personnages de l'évangile selon Maria Valtorta*. Paris: Salvator, 2012.

Laurentin, René, and Henry Joyeux, *Scientific and Medical Studies on the Apparitions at Medjugorje*, translated by Luke Griffin. Dublin: Veritas, 1987.

Laurentin, René, and Rupcic, Ljudevit. *Is the Virgin Mary Appearing at Medjugorje? An Urgent Message for the World Given in a Marxist Country*, translated by Francis Martin. Washington, DC: The Word Among Us Press, 1984.

Louis J. Puhl, S.J., ed. *The Spiritual Exercises of St. Ignatius*. Chicago, IL: Loyola University, 1951, 149–150.

Luhrmann, Tanya M. "Yearning for God: Trance as a Culturally Specific Practice and its Implications for Understanding Dissociative Disorders." *Journal of Trauma and Dissociation, Special Issue: Dissociation in Culture* 5 (2004): 101–129.

Luhrmann, Tanya M. "The Art of Hearing God: Absorption, Dissociation, and Contemporary American Spirituality." *Spiritus* 5 (2005): 133–157.

Lundahl, Craig R. "A Comparison of Other World Perceptions by Near-Death Experiencers and by the Marian Visionaries of Medjugorje." *Journal of Near-Death Studies* 19 (2000): 45–52.

Lundahl, Craig R., and H. A. Widdison. *The Eternal Journey: How Near-Death Experiences Illuminate Our Earthly Lives*. New York: Warner Books, 1997.

Maillard, Emmanuel, and Denis Nolan. *Medjugorje: What Does the Church Say?* Santa Barbara, CA: Queenship, 1998.

Maréchal, Joseph, S.J. *The Psychology of the Mystics*, translated by Algar Thorold. Mineola, NY: Dover, 2004. [Originally published in English from the French by Burns Oates & Washbourne in 1927.]

Margnelli, Marco. *La droga perfetta: neurofisiologia dell'estasi*. Milan, Italy: Edizioni Riza, 1984.

Margnelli, Marco, and Giorgio Gagliardi. *Le apparizioni della Madonna: da Lourdes a Medjugorje*. Milan, Italy: Edizioni Riza, 1987.

Matt, Daniel C. "Ayin: The Concept of Nothingness in Jewish Mysticism." In *The Problem of Pure Consciousness: Mysticism and Philosophy*, edited by Robert K. C. Forman, 99–121. New York and Oxford: Oxford University Press, 1990.

Matysek Jr., George P. "Justice Scalia Urges Christians to have Courage," *Catholic Review*, October 25, 2010. www.catholicreview.org/article/work/justice-scalia-urges-christians-to-have-courage.

Mayr, Michael, and Andreas Resch. *The Visionaries from Medjugorje: On Trial by Science*. Documentary film. Munich: FilmGruppeMünchen, 2004.

McGinn, Bernard. *The Foundations of Mysticism: Origins to the Fifth Century.* New York: Crossroad, 1991.

McGinn, Bernard. *The Flowering of Mysticism: Men and Women in the New Mysticism—1200-1350.* New York: Crossroad, 1998.

McGinn, Bernard, ed. *The Essential Writings of Christian Mysticism.* New York: Modern Library, 2006.

Meissner, W. W., S.J. *Psychoanalysis and Religious Experience.* New Haven, CT: Yale University Press, 1986.

Micale, Mark S. *Approaching Hysteria: Disease and Its Interpretations.* Princeton, NJ: Princeton University Press, 1995.

Milbank, John. *Theology and Social Theory: Beyond Secular Reason*, 2nd ed. Oxford: Blackwell, 2006.

Miravalle, Mark. *The Message of Medjugorje: The Marian Message to the Modern World.* Lanham, MD: University Press of America, 1986.

Miravalle, Mark. *Meet Mary: Getting to Know the Mother of God.* Manchester, NH: Sophia Institute Press, 2007.

Miravalle, Mark. *Private Revelation: Discerning with the Church.* Santa Barbara, CA: Queenship, 2007.

Mitchell, Stephen A., and Margaret J. Black. *Freud and Beyond: A History of Modern Psychoanalytical Thought.* New York: Basic Books, 1995.

Mobbs, Dean. "Response to Greyson et al.: There Is Nothing Paranormal about Near-Death Experiences." *Trends in Cognitive Sciences* 16, no. 9 (2012): 446.

Mobbs, Dean, and Caroline Watt. "There Is Nothing Paranormal About Near-Death Experiences: How Neuroscience can Explain Seeing Bright Lights, Meeting the Dead, or Being Convinced You are One of Them." *Trends in Cognitive Sciences* 15, no. 10 (2011): 447–449.

Moody Jr., Raymond. *Life After Life*, foreword by Eben Alexander. New York: HarperCollins, 2015.

Moore, Lauren E., and Bruce Greyson, "Characteristics of Memories for Near Death Experiences." *Consciousness and Cognition* 51 (2017): 116–124.

Moore, Peter. "Mystical Experience, Mystical Doctrine, Mystical Technique." In *Mysticism and Philosophical Analysis*, edited by Steven T. Katz, 101–131. New York: Oxford University Press, 1978.

Mulligan, James. *Medjugorje: What's Happening?* Brewster, MA: Paraclete Press, 2011.

Murphy, Debra Dean. "Power, Politics and Difference: A Feminist Response to John Milbank." *Modern Theology* 10 (1994): 131–142

Nelstrop, Louise, Kevin Magill, and Bradley B. Onishi. *Christian Mysticism: An Introduction to Contemporary Theoretical Approaches.* Burlington, VT: Ashgate, 2009.

Newberg, Andrew B. *Principles of Neurotheology.* Burlington, VT: Ashgate, 2010.

Newberg, Andrew, and Eugene D'Aquili, with Vince Rause. *Why God Won't Go Away: Brain Science and the Biology of Belief.* New York: Ballantine Books, 2001.

Newberg, Andrew, and Mark Robert Waldman. *How God Changes Your Brain: Breakthrough Findings from a Leading Neuroscientist*. New York: Ballantine Books, 2010.

Nietzsche, Friedrich. *The Gay Science*, translated by J. Nauckhoff and A. Del Caro. Cambridge: Cambridge University Press, 2001.

Nolan, Denis. *Medjugorje: A Time for Truth, a Time for Action*. Santa Barbara, CA: Queenship, 1993.

Nolan, Denis. "John Paul II Believed in Medjugorje." *Mother of All Peoples Marian E-zine*, June 26, 2010. http://www.motherofallpeoples.com/2010/06/john-paul-ii-believed-in-medjugorje/.

Nolan, Denis. *Medjugorje and the Church*, 4th ed. Santa Barbara, CA: Queenship, 2007.

Noll, Richard, Jr. "Mental Imagery Cultivation as a Cultural Phenomenon: The Role of Visions in Shamanism." *Current Anthropology* 16 (1985): 443–461.

O'Carroll, Michael. *Medjugorje: Facts, Documents, Theology*, 4th ed. Dublin: Veritas, 1986.

Odell, Catherine M. *Those Who Saw Her: Apparitions of Mary*, rev. ed. Huntington, IN: Our Sunday Visitor, 2010.

Oder, Slawomir, and Saverio Gaeta. *Why He Is a Saint: The Life and Faith of Pope John Paul II and the Case for Canonization*. New York: Rizzoli, 2010.

O'Loughlin, Michael. "Stephen Colbert's 'Catholic Throwdown' with Patricia Heaton." *Crux*, January 20, 2016. https://cruxnow.com/faith/2016/01/20/stephen-colberts-catholic-throwdown-with- patricia-heaton/.

Orsi, Robert A. "Abundant History: Marian Apparitions as Alternative Modernity." *Historically Speaking* 9, no. 7 (2008): 12–16.

Orsi, Robert A. "A Response to the Commentary on 'Abundant History.'" *Historically Speaking* 9, no. 7 (2008): 25–26.

Orsi, Robert A. *History and Presence*. Cambridge, MA: Belknap Press, 2016.

Orth, Maureen. "The World's Most Powerful Woman." *National Geographic* 228, no. 6 (December 2015): 30–59.

Otto, Rudolf. *The Idea of the Holy*, translated by John W. Harvey. London and New York: Oxford University Press, 1923. [Reprinted 1950, 1958.]

Otto, Rudolf. *Mysticism East and West*, translated by Bertha Bracey and Richenda C. Payne. New York: Macmillan, 1932.

Owen, H. P. "Experience and Dogma in the English Mystics." In *Mysticism and Religious Traditions*, edited by Steven T. Katz, 148–162. New York: Oxford University Press, 1983.

Pandarakalam, James Paul. "Are the Apparitions of Medjugorje Real?" *Journal of Scientific Exploration* 15 (2001): 229–239.

Pandarakalam, James Paul. "Marian Apparitions and Discarnate Existence." *Royal College of Psychiatrists* (2013): 1–18. www.rcpsych.ac.uk/pdf/James%20Pandarakalam%20Marian%20Apparitions%20and%20Discarnate%20Existence.x.pdf.

Pangle, Teresa Marie. "Medjugorje's Effects: A History of Local, State, and Church Response to the Medjugorje Phenomenon." M.A. thesis, Bowling Green State University, 2011.

Parsons, Heather. *Marija and the Mother of God*. Blanchardstown, Dublin: Robert Andrews Press, 1993.

Parsons, William. *The Enigma of the Oceanic Feeling: Revisioning the Psychoanalytic Theory of Mysticism*. New York: Oxford University Press, 1999.

Pelletier, Joseph A. *The Queen of Peace Visits Medjugorje*. Worcester, MA: Assumption, 1985.

Penner, Hans H. "The Mystical Illusion." In *Mysticism and Religious Traditions*, edited by Steven T. Katz, 89–116. New York: Oxford University Press, 1983.

Perovich Jr., Anthony N. "Does the Philosophy of Mysticism Rest on a Mistake?" In *The Problem of Pure Consciousness: Mysticism and Philosophy*, edited by Robert K. C. Forman, 237–253. New York and Oxford: Oxford University Press, 1990.

Pickstock, Catherine. "Duns Scotus: His Historical and Contemporary Significance." *Modern Theology* 21 (2005): 545–573.

Plato. *Phaedo*. In *Introductory Readings in Ancient Greek and Roman Philosophy*, edited by C. D. C. Reeve and Patrick Lee Miller, 107–137. Indianapolis and Cambridge: Hackett, 2006.

"Pope Appoints Special Envoy to Medjugorje." *Vatican Radio*, February 11, 2017. www.news.va/en/news/pope-appoints-special-envoy-to-medjugorje.

"Pope Francis' Opinion on the Medjugorje Apparitions." *Rome Reports*, May 15, 2017. www.romereports.com/2017/05/15/pope-francis-opinion-on-the-medjugorje-apparitions.

Poulain, Augustin, S.J. *The Graces of Interior Prayer*. London: Routledge and Kegan Paul, 1950.

Proudfoot, Wayne. *Religious Experience*. Berkeley: University of California Press, 1985.

Proudfoot, Wayne, and Phillip Shaver. "Attribution Theory and the Psychology of Religion." *Journal for the Scientific Study of Religion* 14 (December 1975): 317–330.

Resch, Andreas, Giorgio Gagliardi, Marco Margnelli, Marianna Bolko, and Gabriella Raffaelli. "Commissions and Teams: Research on the Visionaries." *Medugorje*, December 12, 1998, www.medjugorje.hr/en/medjugorje-phenomenon/church/scientific-researches/commissions/.

Roberts, Richard. "Transcendental Sociology? A Critique of John Milbank's Theology and Social Theory: Beyond Secular Reason." *Scottish Journal of Theology* 46 (1993): 527–535.

Rogers, William R. "Interdisciplinary Approaches to Moral and Religious Development: A Critical Overview." In *Toward Moral and Religious Maturity: The First International Conference on Moral and Religious Development*, edited by James Fowler and Antoine Vergote, 11–50. Morristown, NJ: Silver Burdett, 1980.

Rorty, Richard M., ed. *The Linguistic Turn: Essays in Philosophical Method*. Chicago: University of Chicago, 1992.

Rupcic, Ljudevit, and Viktor Nuic, *Once Again the Truth About Medjugorje*. Zagreb: K. Kresimir, 2002.

Sacks, Oliver. "The Visions of Hildegard." In *The Man Who Mistook His Wife for a Hat And Other Clinical Tales*, 166–172. New York: Harper & Row, 1987.

Schmidt, Eric Leigh. "The Making of 'Mysticism' in the Anglo-American World: From Henry Coventry to William James." In *The Wiley-Blackwell Companion to Christian Mysticism,* edited by Julia A. Lamm, 452–472. Oxford: Blackwell, 2013.

Šeper, Francis. "Norms Regarding the Manner of Proceeding in the Discernment of Presumed Apparitions or Revelations." *Sacred Congregation for the Doctrine of the Faith.* Document issued February 24, 1978. www.vatican.va/roman_ curia/congregations/cfaith/documents/rc_con_cfaith_doc_19780225_norme-apparizioni_en.html.

Shaw, Jane. *Miracles in Enlightenment England.* New Haven, CT: Yale University Press, 2006.

Sigler, Karen. *Her Name Means Rose: The Rhoda Wise Story.* Birmingham, AL: EWTN Catholic Publishing, 2000.

Sluhovsky, Moshe. *Believe Not Every Spirit: Possession, Mysticism, and Discernment in Early Modern Catholicism.* Chicago: University of Chicago Press, 2007.

Smith, Huston. *Forgotten Truth: The Primordial Tradition.* New York: Harper and Row, 1976.

Smith, James K. A. *Introducing Radical Orthodoxy: Mapping a Post-Secular Theology.* Grand Rapids, MI: Baker Academic, 2004.

Smith, John E. "William James's Account of Mysticism: A Critical Appraisal." In *Mysticism and Religious Traditions,* edited by Steven T. Katz, 247–279. New York: Oxford University Press, 1983.

Soldo, Mirjana, with Sean Bloomfield, and Miljenko Musa. *My Heart Will Triumph.* Cocoa, FL: CatholicShop Publishing, 2016.

Spickard, James V. "Spiritual Healing among the American Followers of a Japanese New Religion: Experience as a Factor in Religious Motivation." *Research in the Social Scientific Study of Religion* 3 (1991): 135–156.

Spickard, James V. "Body, Nature, and Culture in Spiritual Healing." *Studies of Alternative Therapy 2: Bodies and Nature,* edited by H. Johannessen, 65–81. INRAT/Odense: University Press, Copenhagen, 1995.

Spickard, James V. "Does Taves Reconsider Experience Enough? A Critical Commentary on Religious Experience Reconsidered." *Religion* 40 (2010): 311–313.

Stace, W. T. *The Teachings of the Mystics.* New York: New American Library, 1960.

Stace, W. T. *Mysticism and Philosophy.* London: Macmillian, 1960.

Storm, Howard. *My Descent into Death: A Second Chance at Life,* foreword by Anne Rice. New York: Double Day, 2005.

Sullivan, Randall. *The Miracle Detective: An Investigation of Holy Visions.* New York: Grove Press, 2004.

Taves, Ann. *Fits, Trances, and Visions: Experiencing Religion and Explaining Experience from Wesley to James.* Princeton, NJ: Princeton University Press, 1999.

Taves, Ann. "Religious Experience and the Divisible Self: William James (and Frederic Myers) as Theorist(s) of Religion." *Journal of the American Academy of Religion* 71 (2003): 303–326.

Taves, Ann. *Religious Experience Reconsidered: A Building-Block Approach to the Study of Religion and Other Special Things.* Princeton, NJ: Princeton University Press, 2009.

Taves, Ann. "Experience as Site of Contested Meaning and Value: The Attributional Dog and its Special Tail." *Religion* 40 (2010): 321–322.

Teodorowicz, Josef. *Mystical Phenomena in the Life of Theresa Neumann,* translated by Rudolph Kraus. St. Louis, MO: B. Herder Book, 1940.

Teresa of Avila, "Interior Castle." *The Collected Works of St. Teresa of Avila,* vol. 2, translated by Kieran Kavanaugh, O. C. D., and Otilio Rodriguez, O. C. D. Washington, DC: ICS Publications, 1980.

Tornielli, Andrea. "Medjugorje; the Findings of the Ruini Report." *Vatican Insider: La Stampa,* May 16, 2017. www.lastampa.it/2017/05/16/vaticaninsider/eng/the-vatican/medjugorje-the-findings-of-the-ruini-reporthvBaZ3ssAeDicjdmEcS3UN/pagina.html.

Turner, Denys. *Eros and Allegory: Medieval Exegesis of the Song of Songs.* Kalamazoo, MI: Cistercian Publications, 1995.

Underhill, Evelyn. *Mysticism: A Study in the Nature and Development of Man's Spiritual Consciousness.* Santa Cruz, CA: Evinity, 2009.Underhill, Evelyn. *Mysticism: A Study in the Nature and Development of Man's Spiritual Consciousness,* 12th ed. London: Aziloth Books, 2011. [First published by Methuen & Co in 1911.]

Valtorta, Maria. *The Poem of the Man-God,* vol. 1, translated by Nicandro Picozzi and Patrick McLaughlin. Isola del Liri, Italy: Centro Editoriale Valtortiano, 1986.

Valtorta, Maria. *Autobiography,* translated by David G. Murray. Isola del Liri, Italy: Centro Editoriale Valtortiano, 1991.

"Vatican Forms Medjugorje Study Commission." *ZENIT,* March 17, 2010. www.zenit.org/en/articles/vatican-forms-medjugorje-study-commission.

Vergote, Antoine. *Guilt and Desire: Religious Attitudes and Their Pathological Derivatives,* translated by M. H. Wood. New Haven, CT: Yale University Press, 1988.

Vitz, Paul C. *Psychology as Religion: The Cult of Self-Worship,* 2nd ed., Grand Rapids, MI: Eerdmans, 1994.

von Hügel, Friedrich. *The Mystical Element of Religion: As Studied in Saint Catherine of Genoa and Her Friends.* New York: Herder & Herder, 1999. [Originally published in 1908 and revised in 1923.]

Vorster, Nico. "The Secular and the Sacred in the Thinking of John Milbank." *Journal for the Study of Religions and Ideologies* 11 (2012): 109–131.

Wallace, Randall, and Christopher Parker. *Heaven Is for Real.* Dramatic film, directed by Randall Wallace and produced by Joe Roth and T. D. Jakes. United States: TriStar Pictures, 2014.

Watkins, Christine. *Full of Grace: Miraculous Stories of Healing and Conversion through Mary's Intercession.* South Bend, ID: Ave Maria Press, 2010.

Weible, Wayne. *Medjugorje: The Message.* Brewster, MA: Paraclete Press, 1989.

Weible, Wayne. *Letters from Medjugorje.* Brewster, MA: Paraclete Press, 1991.

Weigel, George. *Witness to Hope: The Biography of Pope John Paul II*. New York: HarperCollins, 1999.

Woodward, Kenneth. *Making Saints: How the Catholic Church Determines Who Becomes a Saint, Who Doesn't, and Why*. New York: Simon & Schuster, 1990.

Zaehner, R. C. *Mysticism Sacred and Profane*. New York: Schocken Books, 1961.

Zaehner, R. C. *Hindu and Muslim Mysticism*. New York: Schocken Books, 1969.

Zaehner, R. C. "Mysticism Sacred and Profane." In *Understanding Mysticism*, edited by Richard Woods, 56–77. New York: Image Books, 1980.

Zerra, Luke D. "Duns Scotus: The Boogieman of Modernity? A Response to John Milbank on the Univocity of Being." *The Cord* 63 (2013): 374–384.

Zimdar-Swartz, Sandra L. *Encountering Mary: From La Salette to Medjugorje*. Princeton, NJ: Princeton University Press, 1991.

Zubrinic, Darko. "Jim Caviezel's Spiritual Journey from Medjugorje to Mel Gibson's Passion." *Crown: Croatia World Network*, April 19, 2010. www.croatia.org/crown/articles/9958/1/Jim-Caviezels-spiritual-journey-from-Medjugorje-to-Mel-Gibsons-Passion.html.

Index

on "oceanic feeling" and regression
to infantile experience, 164–66,
216, 219–21, 231–32, 258, 273,
313n179, 329–30n48
Oedipal complex and, 166, 207
primitive peoples' religious attitudes
studied by, 212
on religion as wish
fulfillment, 164–65
religious rituals viewed as neurosis
by, 165–66, 201, 212–14, 216–17
repression and suppression in the
work of, 213–14, 325n79
*Freud on Ritual: Reconstruction and
Critique* (Gay), 213
Frigerio, Luigi, 175, 184, 209
functional magnetic resonance imaging
(fMRI), 270
The Future of an Illusion (Freud),
201, 216

Gabrici, Enzo, 175, 200
Gagliardi, Giorgio, 176, 180
Galgani, Gemma, 118–19
Garrigou-LaGrange, Reginald, 95
Garside, Bruce, 122
Gatian de Clérambault, Gaëtan, 161
Gauld, Alan, 241
Gay, Volney P., 213–15, 217, 324n73,
325n79, 325n92
Genesi ad litteram (Augustine of
Hippo), 94
Gimello, Robert, 122, 127–28, 133, 135
The God Delusion (Dawkins), 206
Godfernaux, Andre, 112
Goldstein, Jan, 204
The Graces of Interior Prayer
(Poulain), 56–57
Gregori, Fabio, 3–5
Gregory, Brad S.
on metaphysically neutral
methodologies, 250

on metaphysical naturalism, 218,
240–41, 251
on religion's metaphysical
commitments, 237
on religious confessional history
versus secular confessional
history, 240, 249
on social sciences' metaphysical
commitments, 236–37, 241, 256
Gregory the Great (pope), 94
Greyson, Bruce
on distressing near-death
experiences, 37–38
materialistic reductionism criticized
by, 241
on near-death experiences and
REM-intrusion, 30–31
on near-death experiences' defiance
of materialistic-physicalist
explanations, 242–43, 278
on near-death experiences'
neurophysiological correlates,
32, 287n94
on near-death experiences *versus*
hallucinations, 31
Grillo, Gerolmo, 3–6
Groeschel, Benedict, 56–60, 100
Grosso, Michael, 32–33, 197–98, 241

hallucination
Medjugorje Marian apparitions
considered as, 174–75, 178–79,
181, 184, 189–90, 200, 210, 269
mysticism equated with, 127–28, 134,
206–8, 210–11
visionary experiences and, 111–13, 117
Happold, F. C., 83
Harmless, William, 72, 78, 162, 273
Harris, Ruth, 244
Heaton, Patricia, 2
heaven
active imaginary visions and, 98

messages from, 1, 9, 17, 19–23, 26–27, 40

near-death experiences reported during, 9, 23–29, 33–39

neuroscience studies of visionaries of, 7–9, 62, 170–71, 178–79, 194–96, 198, 205–6, 209, 257, 261–62, 264, 269–71, 319n3

ontological contributions to studying, 278–79

pain sensitivity studies among visionaries of, 183–84, 209, 263–64, 270

pathologies ruled out among visionaries of, 173–75, 177–79, 181, 189–93, 200, 205–7, 215, 230, 261–62, 268–69, 273

physical descriptions of, 13–16

polygraph tests of visionaries of, 180, 264, 269

pontifical shrine recommendation regarding, 70

preconceptions among visionaries of, 58–59

Queen of Peace title and, 20

question of subjective or objective experience regarding, 186–89

reductive theories of mysticism challenged by, 11, 198, 210–11, 215, 217, 230, 272–74, 279

Satan and, 22–23, 302n182

secrets and, 41–44

studies on auditory functions among visionaries of, 183–84, 187, 200, 206, 208, 269–71

studies on ocular and visual functions among visionaries of, 181–83, 187, 206, 208, 264, 269–71

studies on voice functions among visionaries of, 184–86, 269

supernatural sign promises and, 42–44

Vatican team study (1989) of visionaries of, 175–76

Virgin of Civitavecchia statute and, 3–6

Zadar Declaration and, 66, 68

Meissner, W. W., 164–65

mescaline, 109

metaphysical naturalism
ascendancy in academia of, 243, 247–48
Durkheim and, 236–37
Gregory on secular academia and, 218, 240–41
metaphysical commitments embedded in, 222–23, 225, 235–36, 240–41, 275
metaphysically neutral methodology contrasted with, 250
the supernatural rejected in, 238–39, 251, 278–79
Taves and, 222–35, 275, 326–27n15

Micale, Mark S., 201, 203–4, 265–66, 340n21

Milbank, John
on secularism's historical origins, 237, 274, 332nn62–63
on social sciences' metaphysical commitments, 235–37, 241, 256, 274–75, 331n56, 332n59

Milka. *See* Pavlović, Milka

Miraculous Medal devotion, 50–51

Miravalle, Mark, 21, 23, 40, 53, 61, 95, 283–84n2

Mirjana. *See* Dragičević-Soldo, Mirjana

Mobbs, Dean, 30–32

Models of Revelation (Dulles), 84

Mohammed (prophet of Islam), 199

Moody, Raymond, 29–30

Moore, Peter, 135

Moses and Monotheism (Freud), 201

Mother Teresa, 64

on constructivist scholars and Kant, 135–36, 215

critiques of, 141–43

on fundamental tenet of Kant's epistemology, 134

on Kant's views of mysticism, 139–41, 188

Neoplatonism and, 136

Philippot, Jacques, 181–82

Pius IX (pope), 51

Plato, 12, 24, 298–99n109

Plotinus, 136–37

Podbrdo. *See* Apparition Hill

The Poem of the Man God (Valtorta), 113–14

Porphyry, 94

positron emission tomography (PET), 270–71

Poulain, Augustin, 56–57, 60, 95–96, 101

Pratt, James, 117

Prince of Peace (Kramarik), 23

private revelations

Catholic Church's means of evaluating, 52–63, 109–10, 116

De Servorum Dei Beatificatione et de Beatorum Canonizatione and, 46

development of doctrine and, 48–52

human faith *(fides humana)* and, 46–47

Kowalska and, 48

Marian apparitions classified as, 45–46

visionary experiences classified as, 46

The Problem of Pure Consciousness (Forman), 131

Proof of Heaven: A Neurosurgeon's Journey into the Afterlife (Alexander), 24

Proudfoot, Wayne

attribution theory and, 148, 151, 157, 196, 267, 309–10n129, 311n149

deductive-attributional approach of, 254–55

descriptive reductionism and, 148–50, 157, 167, 224

explanatory reductionism and, 148–50, 156–58, 167, 224

Hollywood's critique of, 245

on inadequacy of supernatural explanations, 239

James critiqued by, 148

medical materialism and, 148

psychological aspects of mysticism and, 148

on Schleiermacher, 144–45

sui generis model of religious epistemology critiqued by, 144, 147–48, 158, 167, 227, 256, 274

Psalm 23, 197

public revelation, 45–47, 60

pure conscious experience (PCE), 131–32, 136–37, 268

purgatory

active imaginary visions and, 98

Medjugorje Marian apparition visions and messages about, 24–27, 35–37

"Realm of Bewildered Spirits" and, 35–36

souls and, 25–26

Quelen, Hyacinthe-Louis de, 51

Ratisbonne, Alphonse, 71, 85–87

Ratzinger, Joseph, 45, 66–67. *See also* Benedict XVI

Rause, Vince, 197

Religious Experience (Proudfoot), 147, 151

Religious Experience Reconsidered (Taves), 222

Resch, Andreas, 176–77

Milton Keynes UK
Ingram Content Group UK Ltd.
UKHW022140090924
448107UK00003B/65